Public Opinion

Public Opinion

Carroll J. Glynn
Ohio State University

Susan Herbst
Northwestern University

Garrett J. O'Keefe
University of Wisconsin at Madison

Robert Y. Shapiro
Columbia University

Westview Press
A Member of the Perseus Books Group

Copyright © 1999 by Westview Press, A Member of the Perseus Books Group

Published in 1999 in the United States of America by Westview Press, 5500 Central Avenue, Boulder, Colorado 80301-2877, and in the United Kingdom by Westview Press, 12 Hid's Copse Road, Cumnor Hill, Oxford OX2 9JJ

Library of Congress Cataloging-in-Publication Data
Public opinion / Carroll
    J. Glynn . . . [et al.].
        p.   cm.
    Includes bibliographical references and index.
    ISBN 0-8133-2916-7 (hc) — ISBN 0-8133-2917-5 (pbk.)
    1. Public opinion—United States.   2. Public opinion—Political
aspects—United States.   I. Glynn, Carroll J.
HN90.P8P84 1999
303.3'8'0973—dc21   98-27824
                                                                          CIP

The paper used in this publication meets the requirements of the American National Standard for Permanence of Paper for Printed Library Materials Z39.48-1984.

10   9   8   7   6

Contents

PART TWO
THEORIES OF PUBLIC OPINION

PART THREE
PUBLIC OPINION IN CONTEXT

Illustrations

Tables

Figures

Boxes

Preface

This book began many years ago as a collaborative project among several scholars, all interested in the essential nature of public opinion. We all believe that public opinion is a vital component in the democratic process, and so we were drawn to the topic long ago as students ourselves. Now, as researchers and teachers, we still think that students of politics and communication need to understand how people form opinions, how public opinion is measured, and how the data of public opinion are used in American policymaking and journalism. Without public opinion, we do not have much of a democracy at all, so the way public sentiments are expressed and evaluated is crucial for scholars, students, and citizens alike.

The authors of this volume come from the diverse fields of political science, communications, and journalism, and we therefore bring with us a large arsenal of ideas and perspectives. We take an open, interdisciplinary approach to the topic, unlike that seen in most public opinion textbooks. We look at public opinion from the macrohistorical level, the institutional level, the level of small group interaction, and the micropsychological level. We are interested in how Americans come to have opinions in the first place, how the media enable or prevent the formation of certain attitudes, and how our leaders acknowledge or fail to acknowledge the public mood with regard to various policies. There are a great many moments when public opinion matters, thus we study public opinion dynamics during campaigns and between them. It is the case that public opinion is most obvious during election campaigns or national crises, but here we try hard to study day-to-day attitude formation with regard to issues on the contemporary scene: affirmative action, unemployment, defense spending, and the like. You will find, in the course of reading through this comprehensive book, that Americans' attitudes are sometimes stable and at other times malleable, sometimes liberal and at other times conservative. We hope that you will enjoy reading about yourselves as members of the large and diverse American public, but we also hope that you will realize the challenges and complexities of public opinion.

This book was an enormous, although also very gratifying, undertaking. We have many people to thank, although a few stand out for their relentless and good-natured support. It is safe to say that this book would still be a disorganized collection of smaller manuscripts and interesting ideas had it not been for Jill Edy. We are grateful for her terrific administrative skills as well as her sense of humor. Mark Lindeman is coauthor of Chapter 8, but we must also thank him for his extensive and thoughtful comments on several chapters in this book. We were fortunate enough to receive suggestions from a variety of other scholars in the field of public opinion, and their comments are reflected in the much-revised pages that follow: Thanks go to Barbara Bardes, Jack Citrin, Rosalee Clausson, Sharon Dunwoody, Ted Jelen, Silvo Lenert, Franco Mattei, Maxwell McCombs, and Michael Traugott. A variety of students at Cornell University and Northwestern University read parts of this manuscript, and we are indebted to them for their reactions to the text. For their excellent research and administrative assistance, we thank Martha Kayler, Nancy Jacobs, Carol Adomiak, Greg Shaw, David Park, and Noah Kaplan. We are also grateful to our editor, Leo Wiegman, and to Jennifer Knerr (formerly of Westview), both of whom were loyal cheerleaders for this project.

Our families were vital in sustaining us during this multiyear project and generally enriched our lives. Many thanks to our significant others: Dan McDonald, Doug Hughes, Mary Lucy DeFlorio, Jane Viste, Lucy Miller, and Julie Schumacher. And to all of our children, whom we hope will be active and engaged democratic citizens someday: Patric, Ryan, Daniel, Rebecca, Margaret, Harriet, Emma, and Isabella.

Carroll J. Glynn
Susan Herbst
Garrett J. O'Keefe
Robert Y. Shapiro

Public Opinion

Part One

Introducing Public Opinion

Chapter One

The Meanings of Public Opinion

Were they alive today, our nation's founders might not be surprised that public opinion is still an important force in American politics. Yet they would be astonished to learn just how pervasive discussions of public opinion have become. The president, members of Congress, candidates for public office, interest group leaders, journalists, and corporate executives, as well as ordinary citizens, constantly ask the same question: "What does the public think?" Our leaders need to know what sorts of policies and initiatives voters support, but a variety of other groups and individuals also need to have a working knowledge of public opinion at any given time. Interest group leaders must decide which battles to wage and how strongly their efforts will be supported by their constituents. Journalists, who are key players in the measurement and communication of public opinion, need to know what their readers and viewers want to hear about, but they also survey the political landscape for those of us who are curious about the attitudes of our fellow citizens. Even corporate executives who do not hold political office must keep their "ears to the ground" in order to understand trends in American culture—what consumers think about, what they purchase, and, generally, how they choose to live.

Since so many parties need to understand the state of American public opinion, there are a variety of sources that interested groups and individuals can turn to for such information. One of the most obvious indicators of public opinion is the sample survey or opinion poll. These quantitative data can often give us a sense of how Americans feel about policy issues, social practices, or lifestyle issues. Another source of information about public opinion is vote tallies after elections or referenda. These reports often reveal citizens' preferences in very dramatic ways. Yet students of American politics must go beyond these obvious techniques for assessing public opinion and think about all of the "places" that citizens' opinions can be found—in the scripts of television programming; at political rallies, town meetings, or city council hearings; in the rhetoric of journalism; in the dialogue among friends who frequent a coffeehouse or neighborhood bar; and even in the political discussions one hears on talk radio or sees on the Internet. This book focuses on all the ways that public opinion is measured and expressed, taking a broad view of what the phrase "public opinion" really means. If one thinks of public opinion only as the result of opinion polls, one will not achieve a sophisticated understanding of our political culture.

There are three key terms that summarize the concerns of this text: politics, communication, and social process. What do we mean by these words? *Politics*, in the context of this book, refers to the ways we govern ourselves and divide national resources. Many of the chapters include discussions of how public opinion is translated into policy and how it shapes our institutions. Public opinion is certainly important during political campaigns, and journalists do—for better or worse—keep us abreast of the "horse race" as it unfolds. Yet public opinion plays an extremely important role in public and private policy debates—on both domestic and foreign affairs—among our legislators. A good example is President George Bush's decision to enter the conflict in the Persian Gulf in the spring of 1991. On the basis of opinion polling, media reports, and other sources, Bush believed that Americans supported military action, so he pursued an aggressive foreign policy. It is doubtful that he would have engaged the Iraqi army had it not been for the supportive nature of public opinion. Bush, like most late-twentieth-century American presidents, was extraordinarily dependent on public opinion—a fact that did not escape political cartoonists (see Figure 1.1).

The notion that public opinion and politics are connected is obvious, but *communication* issues have received far less scholarly attention than they deserve. How is public opinion expressed in America? Do the media influence the ways opinions are communicated, as well as the actual substance of those opinions? In the late twentieth century, we have come to assume that we are in an "information age," but what does that really mean with regard to public opinion? This book explores how both mass media and interpersonal forms of communication shape public sentiment. In the realm of interpersonal communication, for example, we draw upon social psychology in order to understand how a tendency toward conformity among citizens often guides the ways they behave and how they vote. And since the diffusion of film in the early years of this century, communication researchers have studied how mass media can construct the political world by reflecting our preferences and often dictating those preferences. In recent years, for example, talk radio has become an important forum for political discussion and has often had an immediate effect on politics. In one analysis, researchers have argued that talk radio almost single-handedly forced Zoë Baird, a nominee for U.S. attorney general, to withdraw from the confirmation process in 1992. This is a particularly interesting case of the

FIGURE 1.1   Presidents are very much attuned to their poll standings, as this cartoon about former President George Bush notes. SOURCE: Jim Borgman © 1992. Reprinted with permission of King Features Syndicate.

importance of talk radio, as newspaper and broadcast journalists believed that Baird would be easily confirmed. Although national journalists predicted that Baird's nomination would receive a "rubber stamp" from the Senate, talk radio program hosts were inundated with calls from a public outraged by Baird's violation of the social security laws. In this case, as in many others, talk radio joined the conventional communication outlets (newspapers, nightly news broadcasts, and news magazines) as a powerful force in American politics.[1]

Finally, public opinion is the result of *social processes*, and social processes affect the nature of American attitudes. By this, we mean that public opinion is intertwined with a variety of societal forces and institutions, such as the changing American demographic profile, the problems of inner cities, and the state of family life. For example, in Chapter 5 we spend some time discussing fads in fashion and language that reflect changing public attitudes, but we also consider how changes in material or linguistic culture might also affect the ways we view our government, our leaders, and each other. The point is that public opinion is embedded in culture: It is not an entity that can be easily disentangled from social life, so we must always be aware of the conditions surrounding the communication of opinions and beliefs.

Why Study Public Opinion?

Public opinion research is a very broad field, because scholars in many disciplines need to understand how attitudes about public affairs are formed, communicated, and measured. As we will see in Chapter 2, public opinion study is as old as democracy itself: The ancient Greek philosophers knew that the analysis of popular sentiments was crucial to the design of government by the people. There are, however, some very specific reasons that so many scholars and public officials study and care about the state of public opinion:

1. Policy, in democratic states, should rest on public opinion.

Although democratic theorists have disagreed about how much of a role the public should play in the design of public policy, almost all believe that people should have some say in how they are governed. The role of public opinion in discussions of democracy takes two forms.

First, there are people's global opinions about institutions. For example, how much do members of the public trust their leaders? Do they believe that Congress is responsive to their needs? Do Americans think that political campaigns are instructive and efficient or simply "horse races" orchestrated by highly paid political consultants? The answers to these questions are complex and will be discussed in subsequent chapters of this book, but the point is that public opinion about the *general* state of politics is important and worthy of our attention. If trust in government is low or if a large segment of the population does not believe that their congressional representatives are responsive to their needs, a democratic state may deteriorate: Voting rates may decline dramatically, and demagogues might emerge with rather undemocratic ways of "fixing" the system. Over the last few decades, Americans have grown far more cynical about their institutions, but we have yet to witness the sort of severe decay in institutional loyalty that destroys many budding democracies.

Second, beyond the general attitudes people hold about political institutions and leadership are the opinions they have about specific policy matters. Chapter 9 explores the links between public opinion and public policy in depth, and that linkage is among the most important reasons we study popular attitudes. Presidents, members of Congress, state legislators, and even local city council members must always be aware of public opinion as they design the sorts of regulations and programs that affect our daily lives. Sometimes, leaders promote a policy and the public quickly supports their ideas, as in the early days of a military conflict (the "rally round the flag" effect). Under other conditions, there is a groundswell of opinion, and leaders respond to expressions of public sentiment with legislative action (see Figure 1.2). In the vast majority of cases, however, the interaction between public opinion and the formation of public policy is far more complex because communication among involved parties is so imperfect. Journalists,

FIGURE 1.2   Public opinion was often expressed through rallies and demonstrations during the Vietnam War years. (Photo courtesy of the Library of Congress)

for example, can often, either knowingly or unknowingly, distort public opinion through their reports, so policymakers find it difficult to figure out whose voices they are listening to—those of media professionals or average citizens. Alternately, journalists can misrepresent or fail to cover aspects of a policy debate, and that can affect the ways that the public responds to legislative endeavors.

2. Respect for public opinion is a safeguard against demagoguery.

In all nations, and in all eras, there is a risk that a single demagogue or group of dictators may grab the reins of power. We have witnessed many such occurrences over the course of the twentieth century. Understanding and respecting public opinion is not an absolute safeguard against the rise of a dictator, yet public opinion is one of the few potentially effective checks on leadership available in a democracy.

In less dramatic cases, for instance, where leaders show bad judgment or are incompetent or corrupt, public opinion can force public officials out of office, either directly or indirectly. In the summer and fall of 1995, for example, U.S. Senator Bob Packwood (R–Oregon) was pressured to resign from the Senate over allegations of sexual misconduct and financial improprieties. At the start of Packwood's troubles years earlier, his colleagues had mixed reactions to the charges, with some calling for his resignation and others arguing that the case against him was overblown. Yet public opinion, both in Oregon and around the nation, gradually turned against

Packwood, and the Senate was forced to acknowledge popular sentiment. This acknowledgment most certainly played a role in the way the Senate Ethics Committee investigated the Packwood matter and in its eventual findings.

There are a variety of ways that public opinion serves as a check on leadership. In many instances, such as the Packwood case, a group or groups of citizens are upset about the actions of a public official and other leaders share those sentiments. Under these circumstances, there is an interaction between public officials and the electorate, with both reinforcing the other's opinions. In other cases, there is truly a "bottom-up" display of public annoyance or outrage with the actions of a leader, and government reacts or fails to react to that display. Finally, in some instances, political actors attempt to block the actions of other elites and try to persuade the public to join them in such maneuvering. In all three cases, public opinion serves as a powerful force that can direct the actions of our elected and appointed leaders.

3. Public opinion provides clues about culture.

Understanding public opinion on policy and social issues is crucial to students of American culture, because understanding popular sentiment toward specific issues gives us insight into larger currents in American life. Since it is difficult for social scientists to "measure" and report on the many dimensions of American culture, we need to make inferences about that larger culture from narrower studies of public attitudes.

An example of this approach—trying to understand cultural values and trends by studying particular issue attitudes—is research on public feeling toward welfare programs. Since the creation of a set of antipoverty programs in the 1960s, public opinion researchers have asked citizens how they feel about such initiatives. Although such questions present a variety of difficulties to survey researchers, as the way such programs are described can elicit very different answers from respondents, results of these studies tell us a lot about American norms and values. If survey researchers, over the course of several years, ask about whether welfare benefits should be tied to work on the part of aid recipients and respondents increasingly support this idea, we learn something about changing values: The trend may indicate a growing impatience with the poor, a renewal of the work ethic, or a general resurgence of conservative political ideology. All of these hypotheses need more rigorous study, but social scientists are often "tipped off" about larger cultural trends by survey results.

Although we will take up this issue in Chapter 3 in our discussion of methodologies for understanding public opinion, one might argue that public opinion and culture are so intertwined as to be inseparable. In addition to being the source of aesthetic "products" (e.g., art, music, dance, and the like), culture is a sum of people's norms, values, and sentiments (see Box 1.1). Relatedly, the best public opinion research usually reveals norms,

Box 1.1   Culture, Art, and Public Opinion

History often provides excellent examples of how culture and public opinion are interwoven. Let us take one interesting historical case of this relationship—the popularity of Shakespearean drama in nineteenth-century America—to illustrate that nexus. Our example comes from a book by historian Lawrence Levine, entitled *Highbrow, Lowbrow: The Emergence of Cultural Hierarchy in America.*

Levine argues that Shakespeare was incredibly popular in the nineteenth century, far more than today and across class lines, because his drama appealed to some basic beliefs among Americans at the time. In particular, Shakespearean drama emphasized the struggle of the individual: "His plays had meaning to a nation that placed the individual at the center of the universe and personalized the large questions of the day."[1] Levine gives an example of how popular political feeling of the period manifested itself in May 1849, when two leading Shakespearean actors (the American Edwin Forrest and the British star William Charles Macready) were giving competing performances in two different New York theaters:

> Forrest's vigorous acting style, his militant love of his country, his outspoken belief in its citizenry, and his frequent articulation of the possibilities of self-improvement and social mobility endeared him to the American people, while Macready's cerebral acting style, his aristocratic demeanor, and his identification with the wealthy gentry made him appear Forrest's diametric opposite. On May 7, Macready and Forrest appeared against one another in separate productions of *Macbeth*. Forrest's performance, at the Broadway Theater, was a triumph both dramatically and politically. When Forrest spoke Macbeth's lines, "What rhubarb, senna or what purgative drug will scour these English hence?" the entire audience, according to the actor Lester Wallack, "rose and cheered for many minutes." Macready's performance, at the Astor Place Opera House, was never heard—he was silenced by a storm of boos and cries of "Three groans for the codfish aristocracy," which drowned out appeals for order from those in the boxes, and by an avalanche of eggs, apples, potatoes, lemons, and ultimately, chairs hurled from the gallery, which forced him to leave the stage in the third act.[2]

The next evening, 1,800 people gathered at the Opera House to shout Macready down. A riot ensued, and when it was over, twenty-two people were dead and over 150 injured.

For our purposes, this colorful yet tragic incident in American theatrical history has a variety of implications. To begin with, it demonstrates how the performing arts rest upon ideology: Americans of the mid-nineteenth century, as well as those living in the late twentieth century, have often been hostile

(continues)

Box 1.1   *(continued)*

toward art and artists who somehow reflect unpopular beliefs. This example also underscores the fact that public opinion and culture are inextricably intertwined: Americans have never drawn a sharp dividing line between politics and art. Finally, the riot illustrates how political expression (violent expression, in this instance) manifests itself in a variety of forms. In this case, a dramatic performance served as a trigger for public discourse and action, but often speeches, telecasts, and actions of our leaders serve as catalysts for the display of pent-up ideological feeling.

_____

1. Lawrence W. Levine, *Highbrow, Lowbrow: The Emergence of Cultural Hierarchy in America* (Cambridge: Harvard University Press, 1988), p. 63.
2. Ibid.

---

values, and sentiments. In this text, we try to take a broad approach to understanding public opinion, and although we do not use the phrase "public opinion" and the word "culture" interchangeably, we often draw parallels between the two concepts.

4. Public opinion must, at times, be mobilized.

During national emergencies, and at times of war, presidents must urge citizens to act in prescribed ways. The most obvious circumstance is wartime, when Americans must make compromises—by sending sons and daughters off to war, by conserving scarce resources, and volunteering where needed. During World War II, this sort of mobilization was not particularly difficult. That war was, to use Studs Terkel's phrase, a "good war," one in which our goals seemed just and there was consensus that we were engaged in a struggle for freedom. Other mobilizations for war have been more difficult or more complicated. A vocal and intelligent antiwar sentiment existed in the days before our entry into World War I, for example, as a variety of writers and artists attempted to persuade Americans that the United States should stay out of European affairs (see Figure 1.3). And much more recently, in the 1960s, President Lyndon B. Johnson attempted to convince an increasingly resistant public that U.S. military action in Vietnam was proper and morally sound.

Regardless of one's feelings about U.S. involvement in the two world wars or in Vietnam, it is clear that a president who needs to mobilize public opinion must first understand the nature of public opinion. The same holds true for students of politics, who try to make sense of government-inspired collective action. Under what circumstances do people support the president with patriotic fervor, and why? How should military leaders present the nature of a conflict to the public in order to make the cause a popular one? An understanding of public attitudes, beliefs, and values is important

Having Their Fling

FIGURE 1.3 "Having Their Fling." This cartoon, drawn by the artist Art Young in 1917, depicts a variety of parties who supported U.S. participation in World War I, which Young opposed. The drawing was eventually used in a landmark sedition case against Young and several other writers and artists who produced the antiwar, So-cialist magazine called the *Masses*. A jury found the group not guilty, although the *Masses* eventually folded due to a variety of other financial and political problems. Reprinted from the *Masses*, July, 1917 issue.

if leaders are to persuade us with their rhetoric, but they must also have a good grasp of public opinion dynamics—the interaction of media and public opinion, the notion that different channels of communication have different effects on audiences, and the like.

5. Public opinion dictates the bounds of U.S. foreign policy.

The relationship between foreign policy and public opinion is a complex one and will be discussed in greater detail in Chapter 9. Yet this connection is so important that it should be mentioned here as one of the reasons that students of American politics need to be concerned with the nature of public opinion.

In general, making foreign policy is the domain of our leaders, who usually have both more expertise and more information than the average citizen. However, this does not mean that public officials design foreign policy without attention to popular sentiment: The president, Congress, and the State Department typically make foreign policy within ideological boundaries determined by American values and priorities. In other words, public opinion determines the broad framework within which foreign affairs are debated. How do our leaders discern this framework so they can act? Policymakers have a variety of tools for doing this. They can rely on opinion polls, which ask both general and specific questions about foreign affairs. A general question might concern citizens' notions about the purposes of foreign aid or whether the United States should tie trade agreements to human rights standards. Specific questions typically focus on contemporary events that demand some sort of response from American leadership.

Beyond polling, though, presidents and other policymakers can use history as a guide when trying to discern what policies or interventions Americans will accept or reject. Thus, for example, when the possibility of intervention in a foreign conflict arises, presidents and members of Congress often look for previous cases on which to base policy. In cases like the civil war in the former Yugoslavia, for instance, policymakers debated the suitability of intervention—particularly in the early days of the conflict. Many drew parallels between Nazi atrocities committed during World War II and the reports of torture inflicted upon Bosnian civilians by the Serbs. Many argued that the United States might have saved a large number of Jews had it intervened in the internal politics of Nazi Germany (e.g., bombing train lines to concentration camps) instead of just concerning itself with the threats to American interests and American soldiers. Whether such humanitarian actions were really possible or not, the analogy between Nazi Germany and the situation in Bosnia gave policymakers a framework for thinking about what sorts of foreign policy maneuvers Americans will or will not tolerate. Another example is the national debate over aid to the Nicaraguan contras in the 1980s (see Box 1.2). Many decisionmakers, both those who agreed with President Reagan's pleas for increased aid and those who disagreed, did

Box 1.2   Did the Public Play a Role in the Contra Aid Debate?

In 1979, Socialist rebels took over the government in the Central American nation of Nicaragua. They replaced a dictator, Anastasio Somoza, who had headed a largely corrupt government known for a horrific number of human rights abuses. President Reagan feared the changes a Socialist government might make in Nicaragua and also argued that this left-wing regime would threaten U.S. interests in Latin America more generally. In 1982, a group of rebels who came to be known as the "contras" staged their first attack against the new Sandinista government in order to challenge its rule. Throughout the 1980s, Reagan asked Congress for funds to help the contras overthrow the Sandinista government. Much aid was approved. Fighting and bloodshed escalated until 1989, when President Ortega, representing the Sandinistas, agreed to hold open elections. In 1990, the UNO Party—a political faction supported by the Bush administration—won the popular vote and the contras officially disbanded.

The case of U.S. military and nonmilitary aid to the Nicaraguan contras, who, as noted above, were rebels fighting to undermine the Socialist Sandinista government, is an ironic one from the viewpoint of democratic theory. In this instance, the majority of Americans were solidly opposed to aiding the contras, even though President Reagan argued strongly for helping these rebels overthrow their government. Most surveys indicated that somewhere between 53 percent and 63 percent of Americans polled during 1986 and 1987 thought that we should not aid the contras.[1] Yet Congress regularly approved aid packages, despite the wishes of the public as discerned through opinion polls. Why such a mismatch? Does this case demonstrate that democratic theory is flawed—that leaders do not listen to the public when making foreign policy? William LeoGrande, a professor of political science and former staff member of the House Democratic Caucus on Central America, is in a good position to explain. He asks:

> Did the public matter? Not in the way that theories of democratic representation would normally prescribe. Public opinion was consistently opposed to the Reagan administration's policy of aiding the Nicaraguan contras, yet the administration pursued it doggedly throughout the decade and the Congress supported it to one degree or another from 1982 to 1984 and again from 1985 to 1987. Both Congress and the executive could afford to be unresponsive to public opinion because the issue never achieved a high enough level of salience for the mass public to focus on it. When their opinions were elicited by pollsters, people expressed dissatisfaction with the direction in which the Reagan administration was headed, *but they had only the vaguest idea of what was going on in the region.* . . . Even though opposition to Reagan's Nicaragua

(continues)

Box 1.2   *(continued)*

policy remained uniformly high for almost a decade, Democrats never quite believed the polls. They worried that a crisis in the region would allow Reagan to act decisively, the public would "rally 'round the flag," and the Democrats would be politically vulnerable. Thus the Democrats felt compelled to support some policy other than simply abandoning the contras, lest Nicaragua develop into "another Cuba." . . . The ghost of Joe McCarthy and the hysteria over "Who lost China?" stalked the Democrats throughout the contra aid debates. (our emphasis)[2]

LeoGrande's remarks, which are the concluding section of his study, demonstrate just how complex the relationship between public opinion and foreign policy can be. In the case of Nicaragua, Reagan was not able to achieve his central goal—the immediate overthrow of the Sandinista government. But he was able to get aid to the contra rebels because it seemed less distasteful to Democratic congressmen than sending in U.S. troops and because public attitudes about Nicaragua were so vague and ill-formed. Thus, here is a case of a mismatch between public opinion and policy that was the result of weak expression of public opinion and also, one might argue, weak leadership skills on the part of Democratic congressional leaders. Conceivably, those leaders might have solidified public opinion further, in opposition to aid, and might have mobilized voters. But they did not.

Also interesting in LeoGrande's comments are the multiple references to history. We noted above how important collective memory is when it comes to making foreign policy. In the case of Nicaragua, policymakers had a variety of memories to contend with in their attempts to avoid upsetting Americans. Because Republicans feared "another Vietnam," they were cautious in their rhetoric about our involvement in the Central American nation, but Democrats were concerned that the traditional American fear of communism might persuade the public that Reagan's policy was the right one.

---

1. Richard Sobel, ed., *Public Opinion in U.S. Foreign Policy: The Controversy over Contra Aid* (Lanham, MD: Rowman and Littlefield, 1993).

2. William M. LeoGrande, "Did the Public Matter? The Impact of Opinion on Congressional Support for Ronald Reagan's Nicaragua Policy," in Sobel, *Public Opinion in U.S. Foreign Policy*, pp. 185–186.

---

worry about repeating American mistakes in Vietnam. Our policy toward Vietnam was a catalyst for a tremendous public outcry, although it took many years for this rebuff of administration policy to emerge.

The Meaning of Public Opinion

Although "public opinion" is an essential concept in democratic theory, it has been very difficult to define. Given the importance of public opinion, it may seem odd that scholars do not agree on a definition. The reason for this lack of consensus is rooted in the fact that so many researchers and theorists from so many different disciplines have contributed to the field but have come to the study of public opinion with different assumptions and methodologies. Yet this is not the only reason that public opinion is hard to define. Some of the ambiguity in the term simply reflects the problematic nature of the concept, which is inherently vague and nebulous. In addition, the meaning of public opinion is also tied to historical circumstance—the sort of political culture that exists, the nature of communication technology, and the importance of public participation in the everyday workings of government.

A good place to begin our discussion of how to define "public opinion" is to consider what constitutes a "public." The concept of a public grew out of Enlightenment democratic ideals and the many important social transformations that took place in the late nineteenth and early twentieth centuries. A working definition of a public grew from its contrasts to other kinds of social formations, most prominently *crowds* and *masses*.

The Crowd

In the early twentieth century, the new science of "crowd psychology" (a forerunner of social psychology) developed to explain how individuals could be caught up in mass behavior and transformed. How was it that people were collectively enticed to do things they would never dream of doing alone? For example, how can cheerleaders at a football game get people in the stands to jump, shout, yell, and dance, behaviors in which these people would not normally engage? During the early twentieth century, societies were becoming more urban and the labor and Socialist movements were beginning to assert themselves. There were strikes, riots, and other instances of collective behavior that many elites feared signaled future disaster.

The most prominent of the crowd psychology scholars was Gustave Le Bon, who wrote about public opinion in the early decades of the twentieth century. He believed that crowd behavior resulted from (1) the anonymity of crowd members resulting in a perception of "invincibility" and lack of personal responsibility, (2) the contagion of ideas and feelings in the crowd producing rapid shifts in behavior, and (3) the suggestibility of the crowd, enabling people to hold ideas and behave in ways they would not normally behave.[2] In fact, William Trotter likened crowds to animal herds—with the actions of the "lead" individuals transmitting to the others by "suggestion."[3]

The crowd is essentially defined by its "unity of emotional experience."[4] According to contemporary opinion researcher Vincent Price, "The crowd develops in response to shared emotions."[5] However, the study of crowds has expanded to consider fads, crazes, and social movements, and some scholars believe that crowdlike phenomena could be central to the early formation and expression of public opinion.[6]

The Mass

Crowds are defined by their shared emotional experiences, but masses are defined by their interpersonal isolation. Sociologist Herbert Blumer notes that a mass is composed of anonymous individuals who engage in very little interaction or communication,[7] and Price notes that a mass is extremely heterogeneous, including people from all strata of society and all walks of life.[8] A mass "merely consists of an aggregation of individuals who are separate, detached, anonymous," reacting in response to their own needs, Blumer argues.[9]

This concept of mass also grew out of the social transformations occurring at the turn of the century. People became more mobile. They moved to the cities and became disconnected from their roots in family and village life. They worked long hours and returned home to anonymous neighborhoods. This kind of disconnection was troubling, because it removed the checks on antisocial behavior that are possible in families and villages where everyone knows everyone else. Blumer suggests that what binds a mass together is a common focus of interest or attention. Examples of a mass mentioned by Blumer include individuals "who are excited by some national event, those who share in a land boom, those who are interested in a murder trial which is reported in the press, or those who participate in some large migration."[10] People who are members of a mass share an experience or an idea in common, but they may be unaware of this fact because they are unaware of each other. Despite this lack of awareness, mass behavior can have social consequences, for example, when the individual buying decisions of millions of people turn an unknown recording artist into a star. Similarly, individual voting decisions can elect a new and largely unknown political candidate to office.

The Public

A public can be positively contrasted to a crowd and a mass. The crowd develops in response to shared emotions; the public organizes in response to an issue. Entering the crowd requires only "the ability to feel and empathize," whereas joining the public requires also "the ability to think and reason with others." The behavior of the public could be guided at least partially by a shared emotional drive, but "when the public ceases to be critical, it dissolves or is transformed into a crowd."[11]

Unlike a mass, a public is self-aware. Blumer defines a public as "a group of people (a) who are confronted by an issue, (b) who are divided in the ideas as to how to meet the issue, and (c) who engage in discussion over the issue."[12] Thus, the essence of a public's activity is discourse over a controversy. This process of discourse, according to Blumer, means that public opinion is always rational, though it is not always intelligent. When a public becomes a crowd, it creates "public sentiment" rather than public opinion.

Another important difference between a public and a mass was emphasized by the sociologist C. Wright Mills in the 1950s. In a public, individuals should be as capable of expressing opinions as they are of receiving them. Debate continues over whether a "true" public so defined actually exists in twentieth-century America. Some, like Mills, argue that American citizens are more like a mass of isolated individuals who receive opinions via the media. Others take a more positive view of public discourse, citing interpersonal discussions and phenomena like talk radio.

Despite a chronic definitional problem, public opinion research is still a field with boundaries. Not all studies of American culture are studies of public opinion, because the study of public opinion does concern the *formation, communication, and measurement of citizens' attitudes toward public affairs.* We believe that there are five reasonable definitions of public opinion that are distinct but that also overlap to some extent. It is best not to treat these categories as mutually exclusive, since the lines between them are not as clear as we might like.

Category 1: Public opinion is an aggregation of individual opinions.

Many researchers, journalists, policymakers, and citizens think of public opinion as the simple sum of many individual opinions. This is the most common definition of public opinion in contemporary American politics, and it serves as the justification for using surveys and polls to measure public opinion. By using the process of random selection, opinion polls enable an efficient aggregation of individual opinions. The fact that all professionally conducted polls randomly select individuals—across social groups—to be interviewed means that one can take the results of those interviews and make general claims about the entire population.

This definition is widely shared in public life today for several reasons. First, it gives one straightforward direction about how to measure the public mood: If public opinion is the aggregation of individual opinions, it is clear that we must interview individuals and add their opinions together to ascertain public opinion. Relatedly, the methodology of polling has become routinized over the last decade, so that any trained researcher with resources and computers can conduct a competent survey of the public. Second, this definition of public opinion resonates with the structure of the popular election, which serves as the basis for democratic process. Surveys are like elections in the way they tally "votes" (opinions), so they seem to fit our particular system of governance. Third, this sort of quantitative approach to understanding public opinion enables researchers, journalists, and others to engage in complex causal analyses of public opinion. If an analyst polls a sample of American citizens about welfare reform, for example, that makes it possible to test hypotheses about the relationship between support for reform and one's race, class, gender, political affiliation, or religion. Furthermore, the researcher can analyze how political attitudes and values are connected: Do those citizens who trust government officials tend to support reform? Or do those who have immense trust in government fear welfare reform proposals that reduce government's role in managing entitlement programs?

Polling is used by legislators, presidents, and journalists to get a sense of how people feel about various policy issues, but surveys also give us some insight into more general attitudes about social life. The mass media offer up an enormous number of surveys each day that describe public attitudes on race relations, gender roles, religious values, and the like. Sometimes these polls shed light on policy debates, but more often they are interesting notes on culture, in and of themselves.

Category 2: Public opinion is a reflection of majority beliefs.

Several theorists argue that we need to think of public opinion as the equivalent of social norms—that the values and beliefs of the majority of citizens are the true basis of public opinion. Another way of saying this is that the only public opinion that really matters, when it comes to policy-making, is what most Americans think. Theorists who use this definition are not making a judgment about the majority being right or wrong on a particular subject: They are simply reporting that people do pay close attention to the opinions of friends, coworkers, and neighbors and tend to conform to majority opinion among their significant others.

One researcher who supports this definition of public opinion is Elisabeth Noelle-Neumann, whose work we discuss in subsequent chapters. She argues that public opinion is best defined as the "opinions on controversial issues that one *can* express in public without isolating oneself."[13] Noelle-Neumann believes that citizens do a surveillance of their environment, try to get a sense of what majority opinion is like on a particular topic, and then either express themselves or keep quiet on the subject. She calls this theory the "spiral of silence" because she thinks that people remain silent when they realize that they hold a minority opinion and, as a result, minority opinion appears to be even less pervasive than it really is. Noelle-Neumann bases her theory on the tracts of great philosophers (e.g., John Locke and Jean-Jacques Rousseau), as well as on the large number of conformity experiments in the field of social psychology.

There is considerable debate about Noelle-Neumann's hypothesis. First, there have been a variety of assaults on her methodology, that is, how she studies the problem of conformity in public opinion. Second, one wonders whether people really feel the need to conform to majority opinion on all policy and social issues. Finally, there is a bit of confusion about citizens' sources of information—where we learn about majority opinion. Do we learn about majority opinion from media reports and polls? Or are our significant others a more important source of information (and persuasion) than the mass media? These questions are complex, and Chapter 11 explores them in greater depth.

If one believes that public opinion is simply the aggregation of individual opinions (the first definition above), it is easy to measure it through polls and surveys. Yet if someone believes that the opinions we express are not always honest, polling becomes much more problematic. When people say one thing to a pollster but in their hearts believe just the opposite, researchers need to develop much more sophisticated methods for understanding public opinions (those we are willing to articulate aloud) and private opinions (those opinions we keep to ourselves).

Category 3: Public opinion is found in the clash of group interests.

Some scholars believe that public opinion is not so much a function of what individuals think as a reflection of how their opinions are cultivated, crystallized, and eventually communicated by interest groups. These may be political parties, trade organizations, corporations, or activist groups like the Sierra Club or the Christian Coalition (see Figure 1.4). The strength of this definition is that it underscores power dynamics: In political reality, organized groups are the ones that lobby for legislation, have spokespeople who influence journalists, and mobilize votes during election campaigns. Under this definition, then, public opinion is the result of public debate among groups.

This definition of public opinion assumes that conflict is pervasive in social and political life, that groups are constantly engaged in a struggle to define social problems and provide solutions to them. People who ascribe to this definition do not discount the opinions and attitudes of individuals but are most interested in how those opinions are translated into interest group opinion, since interest groups act in a more powerful fashion than do individuals. Citizens can accomplish more when they join forces, because policymakers and journalists are more likely to be interested in group opinion than in single opinions.

One theorist advocating this definition of public opinion is Herbert Blumer, mentioned earlier in our discussion of masses and publics. In 1948, Blumer presented a now famous attack on survey research, in which he argued that polls are an artificial means for describing public opinion, since they do not tell us much about who the respondents are and which interest groups they support (see Box 1.3). Opinion polls purposefully treat all individual respondents equally: Each opinion is given the same weight, and all opinions are seen as equally important. Blumer believes that this is an unrealistic approach to understanding society, since all citizens are not equal.

FIGURE 1.4   Abortion Rights March, Boston. Abortion has been and continues to
be one of the most contested social issues in contemporary American life. Public
opinion on the subject has remained fairly stable because it is one issue about which
people have intense and highly emotional attitudes. In the debate over abortion, interest groups have been crucial. They organize demonstrations, lobby Congress and
state legislatures, and try to influence media coverage of reproductive issues. (Photo
courtesy of Michael A. Dwyer)

Pollsters can find out the gender and race of respondents and whether they
are wealthy and educated or poor and without much formal schooling. But
it is much harder to discern whether respondents are influential in their
social circle or whether they are active citizens who effectively lobby local
public officials and journalists, give money to particular causes, and the
like. Sophisticated survey research can, in theory, probe many aspects of respondents' behavior, but this is both expensive and time-consuming for
those respondents. Survey response rates have been declining in the 1980s
and 1990s, and pollsters have been working to make participation in polls
a positive (and brief) experience.

   Category 4: Public opinion is media and elite opinion.

   Twentieth-century students of politics have wondered whether public
opinion is a reflection of citizens' opinions or simply the projection of what
journalists, politicians, pollsters, and other "elites" believe. This notion—
that public opinion is a creation of social leaders—may sound cynical, but
it has a large number of adherents. The most famous is probably Walter

---

Box 1.3   Do Groups Matter More Than Individuals, When It Comes to Public Opinion?

In his 1948 essay on opinion polling, sociologist Herbert Blumer tried to take the perspective of a legislator or executive. What kind of public opinion data is important to them: the results of surveys or the opinions communicated by interest groups?[1] He argued:

[The administrator] has to view society in terms of groups of divergent influence; in terms of organizations with different degrees of power; in terms of individuals with followings; in terms of indifferent people—all, in other words, in terms of what and who counts in his part of the social world. This type of assessment which is called for in the instance of an organized society in operation is well-nigh impossible to make in the case of the findings of public opinion polls. We are unable to answer such questions as the following: how much power and influence is possessed by those who have the favorable opinion or the unfavorable opinion; who are these people who have the opinion; whom do they represent; how well organized are they; what groups do they belong to that are stirring around on the scene and that are likely to continue to do so; are those people who have the given opinion very much concerned about their opinion; are they going to get busy and do something about it; are they going to get vociferous, militant, and troublesome; are they in the position to influence powerful groups and individuals *who are known*; does the opinion represent a studied policy of significant organizations which will persist and who are likely to remember; is the opinion an ephemeral or momentary view which people will quickly forget? These sample questions show how markedly difficult it is to assess the results of opinion polling from the standpoint of the things that have to be taken into account in working in an organized society. (emphasis in original)

SOURCE: "Public Opinion and Public Opinion Polling," *American Sociological Review* 13 (1948):542–554, quoted passage at p. 547.

---

1. On interest groups as public opinion, see also Susan Herbst, *Reading Public Opinion: How Political Actors View the Democratic Process* (Chicago: University of Chicago Press, 1998).

Lippmann, a journalist and political philosopher who also served as a consultant to a variety of American legislators and presidents from World War I through the early years of the Vietnam War. He argued that the common citizen could not possibly stay informed on all affairs of state and, given this impossibility, could hardly be relied upon to produce intelligent opinions on all public affairs. As a result, "public opinion" is best conceptualized as a symbolic phrase used by orators to make their own arguments and fight their own battles with each other. Lippmann was not arguing that people are stupid or that they need to be guided by benevolent dictators. Yet he did believe that people lacked the time and the energy to focus on political matters in the ways called upon by high democratic theory.

One can find a large number of policy matters about which the American public knows very little (see Box 1.4). Our earlier discussion of the contra aid debate in Box 1.2 serves as a good example of Lippmann's point. Very few citizens even knew where Nicaragua was located! The public's confusion about the issue undoubtedly enabled the Reagan administration to construct public opinion in a manner most supportive of their policies. In general, the public knows far less about foreign affairs than it should if citizens are to form thoughtful opinions about America's overseas activities. Lippmann understood this, and as a result, he advocated that American government should be advised by bureaus of experts instead of by the average citizen. As his biographer Ronald Steele notes, Lippmann was so disillusioned with mass democracy that he could only turn to a government of "specialists" as a solution to the problem of an ignorant public.[14] Lippmann wrote in 1925:

> My sympathies are with [the private citizen], for I believe that he has been saddled with an impossible task and that he is asked to practice an unattainable ideal. I find it so myself for, although public business is my main interest and I give most of my time to watching it, I cannot find time to do what is expected of me in the theory of democracy, that is, to know what is going on and to have an opinion worth expressing on every question which confronts a self-governing community. And I have not happened to meet anybody, from a President of the United States to a professor of political science, who came anywhere near to embodying the accepted ideal of the sovereign and omnicompetent citizen.[15]

Thus, not only did Lippmann realize the problematic nature of an informed citizenry as described in democratic theory but he also took issue with the possibility of public opinion being a useful entity and advocated that citizens be listened to less often in the construction of social policy.

Category 5: Public opinion is a fiction.

Whereas Lippmann and other scholars see public opinion as the expression of elite opinion, some theorists have gone even further in an attempt to question the meaning of the phrase "public opinion." They argue that public opinion is a phantom—a rhetorical construction used so freely in our newspapers and on television as to be meaningless. They posit, for example, that journalists and congressional representatives often talk about the state of public opinion on a particular issue when they have no evidence at all to back up such assertions about popular feeling. Critics in this category ask difficult questions. For example, if people use the phrase so indiscrimi-

---

Box 1.4   An Ignorant Public?

Civic knowledge levels among Americans, as measured by surveys, have always been lower than political scientists would like. Two researchers who have probed citizens about what they know are Michael X. Delli Carpini and Scott Keeter. In 1989, they conducted a study in order to measure knowledge about basic constitutional issues and contemporary events and people. Some of their results are recorded below. Do you think Americans should be able to answer these questions correctly?

Question	Percentage of Respondents Giving the Correct Answer
For how many years is a president of the United States elected—that is, how many years are there in one term of office?	96
Can you tell me the name of the current governor of your state?	74
Will you tell me who the vice president of the United States is?	74
What are the first ten amendments to the Constitution called?	46
Can you remember offhand the name of the U.S. congressman from your district?	29
Do you happen to know the names of the two U.S. senators from your state?	25

SOURCE: Michael X. Delli Carpini and Scott Keeter, *What Americans Know About Politics and Why It Matters* (New Haven: Yale University Press, 1996), questionnaire results throughout appendix, pp. 307–328.

---

nately, without qualitative or quantitative evidence to support their versions of how the public feels, does the phrase have any value at all? Even if a president or member of Congress has an opinion survey demonstrating support for the position he or she is taking, how solid are the opinions measured? Are they informed opinions? And equally important, would people *act* on those opinions? Scholars who believe that public opinion is equivalent to media and elite opinion (category 4 above) may think that public officials and journalists construct images of public opinion to fit their own needs, but these elites are normally basing their arguments on some sort of empirical reality. Theorists in the present category are far more critical, believing that public opinion—in any form—really does not exist: It has no basis in the actual public sphere.

Scholars in this category write at great length about rhetoric—about the fact that anyone can manufacture a public (and its opinions). For example, polls can be used, with questions asked in such a way that the results will be those desired. This sort of biasing of questions is often done unintentionally, but it might be done deliberately as well. Besides crafting quantitative data to support their claims, legislators or interest group spokespersons might simply use inclusive terminology when talking about a social problem, beginning their public statements with, "As Americans, we believe . . . ." Public opinion can also be manufactured through sophisticated public relations efforts and the use of visual imagery, to make it seem as though there is majority opinion on a topic.

In addition to arguing that public opinion can be manufactured through rhetoric, critics in this category have other strong arguments based on linguistics and cognitive psychology. For example, scholars have noted that citizens think about politics using different terminology than do pollsters and policymakers. Some wonder whether average citizens and political elites (legislators, journalists, and pollsters, for example) even recognize the same problems as *political* in nature. Pierre Bourdieu, a French sociologist, put his objections to polling and the notion of public opinion this way:

> Journalists who want things to be simple, further simplify the already simplified [polling] data which they have been given, and when it reaches the public, it is likely to read as follows: "50 percent of the French are for the discontinuation of the railroads." A rigorous interpretation of the opinion polls would require an epistemological examination of each of the questions asked, plus, concerning the system of the questions, an analysis of the whole system of answers, which together would be the *only way to know what were the questions the people really thought they were answering.* (our emphasis)[16]

Bourdieu does believe that academics, with great care, can occasionally conduct useful surveys, but he does not think that these surveys necessarily measure a concrete entity called "public opinion." He and his colleagues have conducted surveys in which they ask questions like this one: "For you, is it political or not to go on strike, wear long hair, participate in a rock festival, etc." Yet even when such scholars try to figure out what it is people believe to be political activity or what they believe are political issues, they are troubled by the complexity of the results.

In order to further clarify how critics in this last category view public opinion, Table 1.1 takes up an example of an issue and discusses how each category of theorist might approach it. The restructuring of the health care system in America, an issue that will come up in subsequent chapters, is a good case for such an exercise.

TABLE 1.1   Thinking About and Measuring Public Opinion: American
Health Care

Definition of Public Opinion	In the Context of Health Care Reform
Category 1 (aggregation)	Researchers would argue that public opinion about health care delivery is the product of what most private citizens would say when questioned on the subject. These scholars would use sophisticated survey methods to probe American men and women about their visions of health care reform. Also, such researchers would question survey respondents about the various plans that have been introduced to reform the system, in order to get their opinions on the different plans. Focus groups might be used, also, in order to collect more data in a more conversational forum.
Category 2 (majoritarian)	Scholars would propose that public opinion is the most popular opinion—what people tend to say in public. Thus, if it is socially most acceptable to argue for a national system that guarantees low-cost coverage for all, that would be the "public opinion" worth paying attention to. Researchers in this category might use polls and surveys to discern this majority opinion, or they might conduct a content analysis of the mass media to get a sense of which opinion receives the most (and most favorable) news coverage.
Category 3 (clash of groups)	This approach would focus most rigorously on the "interests" and coalitions in the debate—the insurance industry, the American Association of Retired People (AARP), the administration, and a variety of other consumer and lobby groups. How do the leaders of these groups characterize the opinions of their constituents? Researchers taking this approach to understanding public opinion would study the public statements made by such groups but would also conduct interviews with group leaders and members. Most important, though, scholars in this category would attempt to understand the way groups clash—trying to discern points of contention, areas of common ground, and the evolution of groups' strategies and approaches.
Category 4 (elite/media opinion)	Using the definition of public opinion, one would recognize that a variety of powerful

(continues)

TABLE 1.1   (continued)

Definition of Public Opinion	In the Context of Health Care Reform
	players claim support among the public. All of them, however, may be exaggerating just how widely certain views are held. For example, the insurance industry representatives argued repeatedly in the 1993 debate about health care that choice among doctors was of utmost importance to the public. And there were some polls that indicated this was the case. Yet other polls indicated that people might be more flexible on the choice issue. The fact that the issue was complicated—in that citizens might trade off choice for some other benefits—was not part of industry rhetoric, however. One might argue that the insurance industry had a perspective, and set of interests, that drove it to construct public opinion in a way that suited its own agenda.
Category 5 (public opinion as fiction)	Scholars in this category would argue that people may have some feelings about health care reform and the kind of health care services they value but that the expression of these opinions is entirely constructed by interest groups, public officials, and media. These parties are exaggerating actual opinion at times, but often they are constructing "public opinion" out of nothing at all. The most worrisome aspect of this rhetorical construction of public opinion is that actual opinion—complex though it might be—gets overlooked.

All students of public opinion need to understand that the opinion expression and measurement process contains many dimensions. These dimensions are often evaluated using survey research instruments and give public opinion scholars an understanding of the nature of public opinion on various issues.

First, the *direction* of public opinion is important. That is, one must determine where people stand on issues. Often, direction is thought of as a simple "pro" or "con" answer for an issue, but more complex patterns are possible as well. For example, an individual may be in favor of a woman's right to decide whether to have an abortion but may be opposed to abortion after the first trimester of pregnancy or under certain conditions.

Second, the *intensity* of opinion can be critical. How strongly do people feel about an issue? Where an issue has intense advocates on either side, as the abortion issue does, the result can indicate deep social divisions. If an intense minority confronts a relatively apathetic majority, majority public opinion may be ignored by policymakers seeking to appease the vocal minority.

One of the unresolved problems of democracy is balancing majority and minority opinion. When a minority of people feels strongly on an issue, should its opinion outweigh that of the more apathetic majority? If neither majority nor minority are particularly intense, policymakers may view the public opinion environment as permissive and enact the policies they themselves favor. This situation occurred in the contra aid debate discussed earlier. Alternatively, if an issue draws an intense majority, policymakers may feel compelled to respond to the demands of public opinion.

Third, the *stability* of public opinion can affect scholars' and leaders' evaluation of the issue. Stability refers to the consistency of people's opinions over time. If public opinion on an issue is stable, leaders may be more likely to pay attention to it. If public opinion on an issue changes frequently, it is more likely to be dismissed. This tendency occurs because stable public opinion is believed to reflect true public desires, whereas unstable public opinion is perceived as capricious and uninformed. However, just because public opinion changes over time does not mean that those changes are not heeded by leaders. Political scientist Michael Corbett points out that "in 1953, 68 percent of Americans favored capital punishment for convicted murderers; then the proportion favoring capital punishment declined until it reached 42 percent in 1966; but then the proportion rose again until it reached 72 percent in 1985."[17] In this span of time, the death penalty was abolished, then reinstated.

The stability of public opinion can be affected by many things. One factor is intensity, which we have already discussed. But stability is also affected by the informational content of the opinion. *Information content* is the fourth quality of public opinion scholars frequently explore. There is much evidence to suggest that people do not know very much about public issues. Some of this evidence you have already seen in Box 1.4, and a more complete discussion appears in Chapter 8. For now, it may be enough to say that scholars are unsure about exactly how much information the public needs in order to form "rational" opinions about public issues. However, it seems unlikely that uninformed public opinion will have as much impact on political leaders as informed public opinion will.

You should also note that these dimensions of public opinion will interact with each other. That is, direction, intensity, stability, and informational content are interdependent aspects of public opinion. Often, these dimensions can be seen when we graph or plot the distribution of opinion on an issue. For example, in Figure 1.5, hypothetical results for the question "Should students be required to live in dorms?" is presented, showing various possible outcomes depending on whether freshmen, sophomores, juniors, or seniors are asked the question.

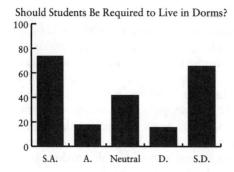

Should Students Be Required to Live in Dorms?

Question asked of freshmen:
A "W" distribution.

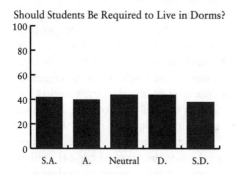

Should Students Be Required to Live in Dorms?

Question asked of sophomores:
A "flat" distribution.

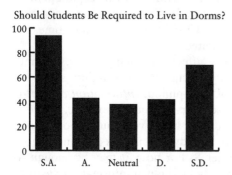

Should Students Be Required to Live in Dorms?

Question asked of juniors:
A "bimodal" or "U" distribution.

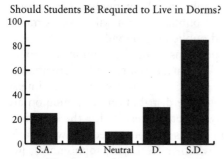

Should Students Be Required to Live in Dorms?

Question asked of seniors:
A "J" distribution.

FIGURE 1.5   Hypothetical Examples of Opinion Distributions

Which Meaning of Public Opinion Is Best?

Which definition of public opinion is the correct one? That is difficult to say. In contemporary American life, all of the definitions are used, depending upon the circumstances in which the public mood is being discussed. Scholars certainly use all five categories in their work, as do journalists and public officials. Some might argue that because of the popularity of polling, the first category (public opinion as aggregation of individual opinions) is most common, but journalists and our leaders often gain knowledge of public opinion by speaking with interest group leaders. And almost all reporters and policymakers have, either knowingly or unknowingly, manufactured notions of public opinion through their spoken and written rhetoric.

The definition one chooses depends upon several factors, including the following:

1. The type of research one is conducting. For example, if one is exploring the ways that American women of the late nineteenth century viewed suffrage (the right to vote), they might look for evidence of public opinion in the letters of suffragettes or in the documents of women's rights organizations. This research assumes that public opinion is the product of interaction between individuals and organized interest groups. Since the question is a historical one, a researcher cannot define public opinion as the opinions of an aggregation of individuals. That would demand a survey, and in this case, the respondents died long ago!

2. Historical conditions often dictate the kind of definition of public opinion one uses. We will see in the next chapter, for example, how form of government can influence the ways leaders and citizens think about the public. In a dictatorship, public opinion is often used rhetorically (category 5) in order to manipulate the populace and make people think that leaders are acting in the interest of the citizenry. In a situation like this, public opinion really is a phantom, manufactured to make people feel as though they are listened to (even if that is not the case).

3. The kind of technology that exists in a particular society at a certain point in time may determine which meaning of public opinion is used. Take opinion polling as an example of technology. These days, computers are used extensively in the interviewing process and in analysis of survey data. Although opinion polling was developed in order to aggregate individual opinions (category 1), the technology for conducting a scientific poll has become so easy to use that people employ the aggregation approach because they can do surveys so

quickly. This is not to say that the availability of technology always determines how we see the political and social world, but it is the case that we are attracted to techniques that enable us to understand the world in what seems an efficient manner.

As students of public opinion and political processes, we must live with ambiguity when it comes to defining public opinion. The fact that we cannot define the term with precision does not mean that the field has no boundaries, as we will see in subsequent chapters. The sorts of intellectual debates, political phenomena, and theories that are described in this book will give you a firm understanding of what the field of public opinion research is about—what is included under the general heading of "public opinion studies" and what is not.

Notes

1. See Benjamin I. Page and Jason Tannenbaum, "Populistic Deliberation: The Zoe Baird Uprising," paper presented at the Annual Meeting of the American Political Science Association, 1995, Chicago.

2. Gustave Le Bon, *The Crowd: A Study of the Popular Mind* (London: Unwin, 1948), pp. 27–38.

3. William Trotter, *Instincts of the Herd in Peace and War* (London: Oxford University Press, 1919).

4. Vincent Price, *Public Opinion* (Newbury Park, CA: Sage Publications, 1992).

5. Ibid., p. 26.

6. Nelson N. Foote and Clyde W. Hart, "Public Opinion and Collective Behavior," in Muzafir Sherif and Milbourne O. Wilson, eds., *Group Relations at the Crossroads* (New York: Harper and Bros., 1953), pp. 308–331.

7. Herbert Blumer, *Collective Behavior* (New York: Barnes and Noble, 1946).

8. Price, *Public Opinion.*

9. Blumer, *Collective Behavior.*

10. Ibid., p. 185.

11. Price, *Public Opinion*, p. 26; quotes from Robert E. Park, *The Crowd and the Public and Other Essays* (Chicago: University of Chicago Press, 1904), p. 80.

12. Blumer, *Collective Behavior*, p. 189.

13. Elisabeth Noelle-Neumann, *The Spiral of Silence: Public Opinion—Our Social Skin* (Chicago: University of Chicago Press, 1984).

14. Ronald Steele, *Walter Lippmann and the American Century* (New York: Vintage, 1980).

15. Walter Lippmann, *The Phantom Public* (New York: Harcourt, Brace and Company, 1925).

16. Pierre Bourdieu, "Public Opinion Does Not Exist," in Armand Mattelart and Seth Siegelaub, eds., *Communication and Class Struggle* (New York: International General, 1979), pp. 124–130.

17. Michael Corbett, *American Public Opinion Trends* (New York: Longman, 1991), p. 24.

Chapter Two

The History of Public Opinion

In the previous chapter, we discussed the various possible routes to understanding and measuring public opinion in the context of contemporary life, but we only made brief reference to the historical development of public opinion. This chapter is devoted to exploring the history of public opinion—the ways that intellectuals, citizens, and leaders have thought about that concept through the ages and the ways that these same individuals communicated and evaluated the popular sentiment.

There are two approaches to investigating the history of public opinion. One can examine the *intellectual* history of the concept itself in an attempt to follow the theoretical debates about the nature of public opinion. Intellectual history concentrates on how philosophers and theorists have thought about public opinion in different epochs. Alternately, one can pursue study of the *sociocultural* history of public opinion, paying close attention to the techniques people have used to communicate their opinions and the ways leaders have tried to assess those expressed beliefs. Neither approach is "better." On the contrary, these two forms of historical analysis complement each other. In this chapter, we explore both sorts of history so that you will understand the philosophical development of public opinion and the "nuts and bolts" of how public opinion has been expressed and measured in different communities at different points in history. We will begin with the intellectual history of the concept of public opinion and then move to social history.

Before we discuss philosophy, however, a few prefatory notes are in order. First, since the history of public opinion—intellectual and social—is so lengthy, we cannot explore all topics, debates, events, or theories in great depth. We will, however, give you enough of an introduction to the history of public opinion so that you have a skeletal map of this narrative. Second, this chapter focuses on the ways that public opinion has been discussed, expressed, and assessed in the West—primarily in the United States, the United Kingdom, and European nations. This geographical exclusiveness is

Box 2.1   One Philosopher's View

Jürgen Habermas is one of the most important and prolific philosophers of the twentieth century. Fortunately for us, he has focused his immense talents on the history and meaning of public opinion in a variety of books and journal articles. This chapter owes much to Habermas, a German scholar whose work has been enormously influential in almost all academic disciplines—political science, communications, sociology, philosophy, literature, anthropology, and history, among them. Habermas believes that the meaning of public opinion shifts in each era and that this meaning is always tied to the nature of the broader political and social arena that he calls the "public sphere."

The public sphere is the forum for discussion of politics outside of our homes but also outside of governmental circles. In other words, talk about family matters or discussion of politics within a household is not part of public sphere discourse, nor is talk among congressmen or between the president and his advisers. Public sphere talk is what one hears in a neighborhood bar or on talk radio. One can also find public sphere discussions in the editorial pages of newspapers, both regional and national, or in the large number of American current affairs magazines.

For Habermas, the meaning of public opinion and the ways we express it are always changing because the nature of public life itself is always shifting. In mid-nineteenth-century America, for example, women were typically not part of the public sphere. Middle-class women ruled the *domestic* sphere—caring for children and for their homes—but played only social roles in public (e.g., as hostesses, entertainers, or supporting players to husbands and fathers). Since women were largely absent from the *public sphere* in any serious sense, their voices were not considered part of *public opinion*. As a result, they could not vote and tended not to write letters to editors or vigorously campaign for political candidates. "Public opinion" in mid-nineteenth-century America meant the opinions of certain classes of men.

Habermas summarizes the connection between public opinion and public life in this way: "A concept of public opinion that is historically meaningful, that normatively meets the requirements of the constitution of a social-welfare state [such as our own], and that is theoretically clear and empirically identifiable can be grounded only in the structural transformation of the public sphere itself and in the dimension of its development."

SOURCES: Jürgen Habermas, *The Structural Transformation of the Public Sphere: An Inquiry into a Category of Bourgeois Society,* trans. Thomas Burger (Cambridge, MA: MIT Press, 1989), quoted passage at p. 244. An application of Habermas's ideas to the analysis of women in the nineteenth century is given in Mary Ryan's *Women in Public* (Baltimore, MD: Johns Hopkins University Press, 1990).

unfortunate, but contemporary notions of public opinion in America draw most heavily upon Western intellectual traditions. Through the ages, individuals in many South American, African, and Asian cultures have undoubtedly thought about the idea of public opinion, but not much of this thinking has been integrated into American political culture and institutions. Finally, just as different parties in contemporary American politics disagree on the meaning of public opinion, philosophers and citizens in different eras understood the phrase (or similar phrases) differently, depending on the political, technological, and cultural circumstances of the day (see Box 2.1). As a result, it may feel as though meaning of the term is always shifting. This is exactly the point of the current chapter as well as this entire text: The meaning of public opinion is always in flux, depending upon the context in which the term is used.

Why Does History Matter?

There are a great many important issues in the study of current public opinion: how Americans feel about U.S. intervention in foreign conflicts, whether we trust our president, differences in opinion among various social groups, among others. Given all the focus on contemporary attitudes, why should we be concerned about past notions of public opinion or the ways people expressed themselves centuries ago?

History matters for two major reasons. First, and most obvious, an understanding of history enables us to understand the present—how it is things got the way they are. Here is an analogy from social life: Suppose we want to understand a friend's behavior. If we are really interested in getting a full picture of why this friend acts the way she does, we need information about her life experiences—her family background, the region where she grew up, the sorts of schools she attended, and so on. Similarly, if we are to understand the political culture of contemporary America, we need to know about the past: how political parties evolved, how the Constitution has been amended, which social movements changed the practice of politics, and the like. In the narrower area of public opinion, we need to understand how opinions were communicated in the past in order to properly analyze the present. For example, one reason opinion polling became so popular in America is because George Gallup and others were so concerned with the way dictators—like Adolf Hitler—attempted to speak for the people instead of letting them express their own opinions. In the mid-twentieth century, after two bloody world wars and the rise of multiple totalitarian regimes, polling seemed like a very democratic way to communicate public opinion. The rise of surveys was, in part, a reaction to the menace of dictatorship.

Second, history gives us a sense of possibility. In the area of public opinion, we have become accustomed to polls and the statements of interest groups as indicators of public opinion, but history provides examples of the many innovative ways people have expressed themselves in the past. When we recognize, through our historical analyses, just how many options exist for communicating our beliefs, we can become more creative in expressing and evaluating public opinion. For example, later in this chapter we discuss the creative rituals of eighteenth-century Europeans and how those rituals expressed public sentiment about particular institutions. If we think about rituals *in general* as means for expressing of public opinion, we begin to recognize that some of our own twentieth-century rituals are also expressions of public opinion. Rituals like Memorial Day parades or commemorations of the Hiroshima and Nagasaki bombings at the end of World War II enable citizens to express both love of country and critical attitudes toward government.

Let us begin our exploration of the intellectual history of public opinion. Much of the early theorizing of the concept is tied to broader inquiries philosophers have made about governance, representation, political participation, and even human nature. We begin our journey in ancient Greece, the setting for early experiments in democracy.

Pre-Enlightenment Philosophies of Public Opinion

The particular phrase "public opinion" was not used widely before the nineteenth century, but many of the great political philosophers of the ancient period used similar phrases to speak about the popular sentiment. Plato, a Greek philosopher of the fourth century B.C., was very much interested in public opinion. He was respectful of its powers and believed that the public will should be heeded, though he was somewhat skeptical of the common person's wisdom. An early twentieth-century scholar named Ernest Barker has noted that Plato and many of his contemporaries thought that members of the public needed to be educated in order to understand and appreciate their government and the laws they lived under. This view is contrary to the modern one that puts the public first: Public opinion should be the basis of all law, and laws should be altered as the public mood shifts. Barker puts it this way: "The Greeks believed in the need of education to tune and harmonise social opinion to the spirit and tone of a fixed and fundamental sovereign law. The modern belief is in the need of representation to adjust and harmonise a fluid and subordinate law to the movement of a sovereign public opinion or general will."[1]

Plato generally distrusted the masses: He was not sure that people could realize their own best interests or strive toward the creation of a morally sound state. As a result, he argued that the democratic state should be ruled by philosopher kings. Above all, Plato valued reason and rationality as paths to the best sort of moral community. The people know what they want as far as immediate comforts (food, love, recreation) go, but they do not have the cognitive capacity to rule themselves in the most just and effective ways possible.

Plato represented an important strand of thought in ancient philosophy, but others writing in the same period disagreed sharply with his negative assessment of the public's capabilities. In particular, Aristotle argued most eloquently for the voice of the public, defending the wisdom of the common citizen. As scholar Robert Minar puts it, Aristotle believed in the power of community: "Aristotelian political theory seems to suggest that public opinion may be regarded as the vehicle of the spirit and continuity of the life of the organic community. It carries the enduring wisdom of the social organism and reflects that wisdom on the particular, immediate actions of government."[2]

Aristotle did not see public opinion as the sentiments people held toward particular issues of the day, although he saw those attitudes as important and worth articulating. Instead, he argued that public opinion is equivalent to the values, norms, and tastes of a civilization. This "climate of opinion," to borrow a phrase from sociologist Robert Merton, is then funneled through institutions (courts and schools, for example) that serve as moderating influences. In other words, institutions take "raw" opinion from communities, organize it, eliminate irrationalities, and make it coherent. Aristotle was undoubtedly more optimistic about the role and nature of public opinion than were many of his predecessors who advocated for democracy but still did not really trust the people (see Box 2.2).

The next set of philosophers to consider public opinion was the Romans, who like Plato, was skeptical of the common people and their desires. Cicero, the great statesman and orator, claimed, "*Sic est vulgus: ex veritate pauce, ex opinione multa aestimat*," which can be translated as "This is the common crowd: Judging few matters according to truth, many according to opinion." It was not the case that Romans dismissed public opinion completely. They simply believed that public opinion mattered most in the case of leadership. Were statesmen honored by the people? Were they popular? Much discussion of public opinion in Roman times was oriented around this narrow dimension of politics.[3]

Although it seems odd to leap across centuries, no further significant theorizing about public opinion occurred until Niccolo Machiavelli, the Italian statesman and writer, began to write at the start of the sixteenth century (see Figure 2.1). He is best known for his book on political strategy, written as an advisory tract for potential rulers. In *The Prince*, which is undoubtedly one of the most eloquent and persuasive manuals on political maneuvering ever written, Machiavelli illuminates the various dilemmas of the prince, discussing how a prince should act in public ("bear himself"), whether he needs to build fortresses, and whether it is better to be feared or

Box 2.2 Aristotle Versus Plato:
The Value of Public Opinion

Since Plato and Aristotle wrote about public opinion in the fourth century B.C., thousands of scholars of political theory have debated and reinterpreted their ideas. Even today, because those ancient texts were so immensely thoughtful and complex, a large number of thinkers scrutinize them, looking for cues about how democracy might work. Perhaps the best way to evaluate the argumentation of Plato and Aristotle is to turn to their original statements. These quotes are removed from their original contexts, but they will give you some idea of how these philosophers conceptualized the public will.

In *The Republic*, Plato explicates his famous analogy of "the cave" and writes on a variety of other topics from mathematics to child rearing. He argues that democracy produces a sort of chaos that makes its citizens lose sight of right and wrong, of beauty, and of all that is "good." Not all men have good character:

> In a democracy you must have seen how men condemned to death or exile stay on and go about in public, and no one takes any more notice than he would of a spirit that walked invisible. There is so much tolerance and superiority to petty considerations; such a contempt for all those fine principles we laid down in founding our commonwealth, as when we said that only a very exceptional nature could turn out a good man, if he had not played as a child among things of beauty and given himself only to creditable pursuits. A democracy tramples all such notions under foot; with a magnificent indifference to the sort of life a man has led before he enters politics, it will promote to honour anyone who merely calls himself the people's friend. . . . These then, and such as these, are the features of democracy, an agreeable form of anarchy with plenty of variety and an equality of a peculiar kind for equals and unequals alike.

Thus, Plato is concerned about the "side effects" of democracy: neglect of social values, lack of enforcement of societal norms, and an undeserved sort of equality. Citizens are far from equal in their intelligence, education, aesthetic sense, or integrity. Democracy, Plato argues, demands more from the public than it is capable of.

In contrast, Aristotle sees wisdom in the ideas and expressions of citizens acting in public. He glories in the diversity and the very inequalities underscored by Plato. He notes in *The Politics*:

> It is possible that the many, no one of whom taken singly is a good man, may yet taken all together be better than the few, not individually but collectively, in the same way that a feast to which all contribute is better than one given at one man's expense. For where there are many people, each has some share of goodness and intelligence, and when these are brought together, they become as it were one multiple man with many

pairs of feet and hands and many minds. So too in regard to character and the powers of perception. That is why the general public is a better judge of works of music and poetry; some judge some parts, some others, but their joint pronouncement is a verdict upon the whole. And it is this assembling in one what was before separate that gives the good man his superiority over any individual many from the masses.

Interestingly, the arguments between Plato and Aristotle about the value of public opinion continue today, although in a somewhat different form. One need only think about the arena of foreign affairs, where policymakers wonder whether the public knows enough to be consulted on complex issues— whether the United States should commit to an international peacekeeping effort or whether it should tie its foreign aid to human rights considerations.

SOURCES: Plato, *The Republic*, ed. and trans. Francis MacDonald Cornford (New York: Oxford University Press, 1956), quoted passage at p. 283; Aristotle, *The Politics*, ed. and trans. T. A. Sinclair (Baltimore, MD: Penguin Books, 1962), quoted passage at p. 132.)

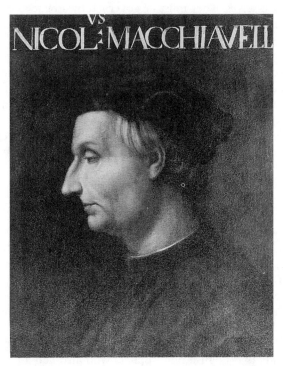

FIGURE 2.1   Niccolo Machiavelli, Political Adviser and Author of *The Prince*. (Courtesy of the Library of Congress)

loved by the people. One issue he discusses at great length is the nature of the people and what occupies them:

> For of men it may generally be affirmed that they are thankless, fickle, false, studious to avoid danger, greedy of gain, devoted to you while you are able to confer benefits upon them, and ready, as I said before, while danger is distant, to shed their blood, and sacrifice their property, their lives, and their children for you; but in the hour of need they turn against you. . . . Men are so simple, and governed so absolutely by their present needs, that he who wishes to deceive will never fail in finding willing dupes.[4]

Here we see how closely early theorizing about public opinion and governance was tied to observations about human nature. Before the twentieth century, it was conventional for philosophers to speculate about the essence of human nature so that they could provide a holistic picture of man as political animal: If one understands the inherent desires of people, their behavior in politics can be explored more fully. Machiavelli believed that humans are so obsessed with their immediate desires and comforts that they cannot rule themselves: They must be governed by a benevolent dictator.

Machiavelli was respectful of public opinion but only because it was a political force that could bring harm to the prince and to the state, not because public opinion has inherent value. He was not an advocate for the wisdom of public opinion as Aristotle had been centuries before. Unlike Aristotle, Machiavelli was not concerned with the harmony of the community or the moral state of the polity. It might seem tangential to bring Machiavelli up at all, since he is not considered a democratic theorist. Yet many of his insights reflect contemporary thoughts about the citizenry that are held by journalists, policymakers, and citizens alike—whether they choose to make negative remarks aloud or not.

Machiavelli is best described as a conflict theorist, one who believes that underlying even the most peaceful society are conflicting values, unfulfilled needs, and animosities. For Machiavelli, there was a fundamental conflict in society between ruler and ruled. These two parties are always suspicious of each other, although the prince always has the upper hand. Machiavelli warns leaders to underscore this fact to the public, yet appear to be acting with kindness and grace in the best interest of the people. To summarize: For Machiavelli, public opinion was volatile, irrational, and potentially explosive. Leaders must be vigilant by keeping a cautious eye on the public, making sure the people hold their statesmen in high regard.

Following Machiavelli in the seventeenth century were Thomas Hobbes and John Locke, two English philosophers who also had a great interest in the relationship between the people and the state. Hobbes, like Machiavelli, also had a negative view of human nature, believing that people live in constant competition as they vie for property, reputation, and personal safety.

And it was Hobbes who wrote in his book *The Leviathan* that life is "solitary, poor, nasty, brutish, and short." Hobbes's works are interesting from our perspective because he is an early "contract theorist," believing that public opinion is crucial to the formation of the state. Machiavelli does not discuss the public's role in the creation of government because statesmen design society in his philosophical world. Yet for Hobbes, people do participate in politics in that they devise the fundamental rules that establish government. After the state is established, Hobbes sees very little need for political participation by citizens and supports the notion of a benevolent dictator. Yet he does make it clear that the structure of the state is created through a "contract" between the public and its leadership. If the state were to crumble—due to internal or external pressure—it would be the citizenry that again creates a new governmental system.

John Locke, a contemporary of Hobbes, shared his belief in the contract—the agreement among people and leaders about how their community is to be governed. Yet Locke is far more optimistic about human nature and about the possibilities for genuine and regular participation in politics by citizens. His theory of government was so eloquent and democratic that it greatly influenced our own Founding Fathers, who drew upon Lockean political theory in their plans for uniting the American colonies. Locke spent considerable energy arguing for his theory of inalienable natural rights that should be protected by the state. He was, like many philosophers of his day, somewhat skeptical of popular opinion, though he believed fiercely in the articulation of public opinion as a critical part of politics.

It is strange that the idea of public opinion was valued by Aristotle but not picked up again until Locke wrote in the 1600s. Yet democracy itself, as we understand it, has had a fairly short history, given the length of human existence. Even the ancient Greeks, who are said to have "invented" the idea of democracy, were not quite democrats in the contemporary sense: In ancient Greece, women, foreigners, and slaves had no voice in politics whatsoever.

Public Opinion in the Age of Revolution

The eighteenth century was a time of immense change: It is the century of the French and American revolutions, and both were grounded in political philosophy. The most important discussions of democracy and public opinion occurred in Europe, although it is important to note that American statesmen like Thomas Jefferson and Benjamin Franklin spent considerable time in France and Great Britain, often participating in the great debates about politics of the age. Many contemporary scholars believe that modern American politics really owes a debt to the thinkers of the eighteenth century—particularly the French *philosophes*. This loose network of French philosophers produced some of the most original and compelling tracts on public opinion of all time during the eve of the French Revolution. This is a period often referred to as the Enlightenment, since there was so much emphasis on the development of the human mind and spirit through science, the arts, and participation in political discourse.

Perhaps the most important work on public opinion was produced by Jean-Jacques Rousseau, a brilliant and unruly Enlightenment thinker who challenged a variety of social norms and existing theoretical paradigms. The young Rousseau, who appeared on the Parisian philosophical scene from a rather humble background, developed an elegant theory of the state with public opinion occupying a central role. Again, like philosophers before him, he was somewhat suspicious of the commoner. But more than any thinker to date, Rousseau saw the necessity of placing a fair amount of power in the hands of the public.

Like John Locke, Rousseau was very concerned with the rights of individuals. Yet he also placed an enormous value on community and the need for people to respect and listen to each other. The state, Rousseau believed, was based on the *general will*—what citizens want when they think about *the whole of the community*. In other words, the general will is our most empathetic set of attitudes, or what we believe is the best course of action to promote the general welfare of the populace. Although Rousseau's discussion of the general will is somewhat complex and even confusing at times, he makes the argument that public opinion is both an aggregation of individual opinions *and* a more organic force rooted in shared values and attitudes. For Rousseau, then, citizens think about themselves and their needs but are also capable of thinking about the general good of society (see Box 2.3).

We should not leave the era of the French Revolution without mentioning the finance minister to Louis XVI, a man named Jacques Necker, believed by many to have popularized the phrase "public opinion." Necker recognized that political discourse and the nature of politics had shifted quite dramatically in the eighteenth century. For the first time, a bourgeoisie had emerged to gather and discuss politics through interpersonal dialogue and through the press. At the time, public opinion meant the opinion of the middle classes. Even in a monarchy, Necker recognized just how much of the institutional structure of the state rested on the benevolence of public opinion. He noted that most foreigners "have difficulty in forming a just idea of the authority exercised in France by public opinion; they have difficulty in understanding the nature of an invisible power which, without treasures, without a bodyguard, and without an army gives laws to the city, to the court, and even to the palaces of kings."[5]

In the nineteenth century, a variety of political philosophers tackled the difficult questions surrounding the nature of public opinion. Among that

Box 2.3 Rousseau on the General Will

Jean-Jacques Rousseau. (Courtesy of the Library of Congress)

In his book *The Social Contract*, Jean-Jacques Rousseau explicated the notion of a "general will," a broad form of public opinion. He believed, unlike so many philosophers before him, that people were difficult to manipulate. People, Rousseau argued, are basically honest and expect honesty from others—including their leaders. In the passage transcribed below, he discusses

(continues)

Box 2.3   *(continued)*

human nature and its relationship to the general will in a chapter entitled
"That the General Will Is Indestructible":

> So long as a number of men in combination are considered as a single
> body, they have but one will, which relates to the common preservation
> and to the general well-being. In such a case all the forces of the State are
> vigorous and simple, and its principles are clear and luminous; it has no
> confused and conflicting interests; the common good is everywhere
> plainly manifest and only good sense is required to perceive it. Peace,
> union, and equality are foes to political subtleties. Upright and simple-
> minded men are hard to deceive because of their simplicity; allurements
> and refined pretexts do not impose upon them; they are not even cunning
> enough to be dupes. When, in the happiest nation in the world, we see
> troops of peasants regulating the affairs of the State under an oak and al-
> ways acting wisely, can we refrain from despising the refinements of
> other nations, who make themselves illustrious and wretched with so
> much art and mystery?

Perhaps the most difficult line for us to understand is the one about how easy
it is to discern the common good. Even with all of our modern techniques for
measuring public attitudes, it is still tremendously difficult to state the public
interest in any definitive fashion.

SOURCE: Jean-Jacques Rousseau, *The Social Contract and the Discourse on the Ori-
gin of Inequality,* ed. Lester G. Croker (New York: Washington Square Press, 1967),
quoted passage at p. 109.)

---

group were the English scholars known as the Utilitarians. Jeremy Bentham
was the first of the Utilitarians to write extensively about public opinion,
and he was most interested in how public opinion acts as a *sanction*. In
other words, he believed that public opinion is a force that keeps society at
equilibrium by preventing people from engaging in nonnormative behavior.
People are afraid of public opinion, so they dare not step outside the
bounds of what is "acceptable" to most people. This may seem a dim view
of human society, but Bentham and other Utilitarians were most concerned
about maximizing happiness among the populace through the maintenance
of social harmony. Bentham and John Stuart Mill, another in this British
philosophical circle, were believers in democracy but emphasized the importance of majority opinion. In fact, they thought that laws are only
needed where the "law of opinion" is not working effectively.

Similar views of public opinion as a force of social control were held by
Alexis de Tocqueville, the French observer of nineteenth-century American

politics. In his landmark study *Democracy in America*, still cited as one of the most important books in political theory, Tocqueville had this to say about the way that public opinion affects writers and artists:

> In America the majority has enclosed throughout within a formidable fence. A writer is free inside that area, but woe to the man who goes beyond it. Not that he stands in fear of an *auto-da-fé* [style of public sentencing from the Inquisition], but he must face all kinds of unpleasantness and everyday persecution. A career in politics is closed to him, for he has offended the only power that holds the keys. He is denied everything, including renown. Before he goes into print, he believes he has supporters; but he feels that he has them no more once he stands revealed to all, for those who condemn him express their views loudly, while those who think as he does, but without his courage, retreat into silence as if ashamed of having told the truth.[6]

It was also in *Democracy in America* that Tocqueville made his famous argument about political equality and its relationship to mass opinion. He noted that in societies where there is much inequality—in an aristocracy, for example—public opinion is not viewed as particularly important. This is because people of impoverished circumstances recognize that others are better educated and more worldly than they are and therefore have more informed opinions. Yet as citizens achieve greater and greater equality, they see that they are just as capable as their friends, coworkers, and neighbors. In these settings, people become interested in numbers:

> The nearer men are to a common level of uniformity, the less they are inclined to believe blindly in any man or any class. But they are readier to trust the mass, and public opinion becomes more and more mistress of the world. . . . In times of equality men, being so like each other, have no confidence in others, but this same likeness leads them to place almost unlimited confidence in the judgment of the public. For they think it not unreasonable that, all having the same means of knowledge, truth will be found on the side of the majority.[7]

This insight is particularly relevant in an age of mass communication where it is possible for all people to gather large amounts of information about the public affairs upon which they may base their opinions. Although not all Americans are equal in terms of education and income, it is the case that most have televisions and can watch the nightly network news. We have a sense that our opinions are just as valuable as anyone else's, so we have a tendency to value majorities.

It is interesting that while Tocqueville was writing about American politics, Karl Marx was also thinking and writing about political and social life from an entirely different standpoint (see Figure 2.2). In Tocqueville, on the one hand, we see a celebration of some aspects of democracy and deep concerns about others. In Marx, on the other hand, we see a man who was

FIGURE 2.2   Karl Marx's Identity Card. Marx wrote about public opinion, although he used the language of class oppression to discuss formation of public attitudes. (Courtesy of the Library of Congress)

completely dissatisfied with the status quo and believed that democracy (like other forms of government) was subject to corruption by the forces of capitalism. This opinion is still very much alive in academic writing among scholars who note that democracy and capitalism are intricately intertwined but that democratic ideals have been crushed by consumer culture. The argument is complex, but simple examples of this conflation between democracy and capitalism abound. Neo-Marxists of the contemporary period cite examples of how Americans (and citizens of new Eastern European democracies) tend to think of freedom as consumer choice—the right to choose among a variety of products and lifestyles. Yet when it comes to serious engagement in freedom of speech—public debate about controversial issues—citizens are less concerned. The fact that in 1995 Congress seriously debated a constitutional amendment to ban flag burning (a quintessential free speech right), without much public participation in this debate, might be used as an example of how little Americans value free speech.

This is not the proper place for a discussion of Marxian thought about politics, but it is important to mention at least one of Marx's basic insights about public opinion. Marx did not often use the phrase "public opinion," in part because the phrase was not commonly used in German philosophical thought until later in the century. Yet he and Friedrich Engels, his collaborator and patron, did argue strongly that organic, grassroots public opinion is hard to come by. In *The German Ideology*, for example, Marx and Engels noted that common citizens tend to mimic the opinions of those in the ruling class—people with great wealth and power. In fact, these philosophers believed that people accept as common wisdom the attitudes and values of the ruling elite—even though these attitudes are often not in their best self-interest. As a result, Marx and Engels argue, the working class does not wield much political power: It is unable to realize its interests because its members have come to believe that the ruling class knows what is best. This process, in which the ideas of an elite class become widely held, is often called *hegemony* in the academic literature. Marx and Engels made the initial statement about this phenomenon, although since 1846 much more has been written on the subject:

> The ideas of the ruling class are in every epoch the ruling ideas, i.e. the class which is the ruling *material* force in society, is at the same time its ruling *intellectual* force. . . . For each new class which puts itself in the place of one ruling before it, is compelled, merely in order to carry through its aim, to represent its interest as the common interest of all the members of society, that is, expressed in ideal form: it has to give its ideas the form of universality, and represent them as the only rational, universally valid ones.[8]

Theory About Public Opinion: The Late Nineteenth and Early Twentieth Centuries

Late in the nineteenth century a British statesman named James Bryce visited the United States, traveling widely and observing the political scene. Bryce devoted large chapters in his two-volume masterwork *The American Commonwealth* to examining public opinion, in an attempt to understand how the concept fit into the constellation of American institutions. Bryce was interested in how the expression and measurement of public opinion were related to party activity, to legislatures, and to the mass media (newspapers, during this period). He is often cited as the first "modern" theorist of public opinion because his work was so sociological and empirical: Instead of speculating on the grand nature of public opinion, he looked for its manifestations in political culture. In fact, a criticism of Bryce is that he was far too empirical and that he might have spent more time developing a philosophical or social psychological basis for his observations.

Regardless of the academic debate about Bryce's emphasis, one thing is clear: Bryce understood—as no one before him really did—the very critical role of newspapers in the communication of public opinion. Tocqueville certainly recognized the value of newspapers, but Bryce explicated their role in far more detail. Bryce believed that the mass media were incredibly powerful in fin de siècle America and should hold a place among our other institutions (Congress, the courts) as a molder of public opinion. He noted in 1891, during an age when newspapers were far more obviously partisan than they are today: "It is chiefly in its . . . capacity as an index and mirror of public opinion that the press is looked to. This is the function it chiefly aims at discharging; and public men feel that in showing deference to it they are propitiating, and inviting the commands of, public opinion itself. In worshiping the deity you learn to conciliate the priest."[9]

For Bryce, newspapers both reflect *and* direct public opinion, so the place of this medium in the political process is crucial. Bryce's work has a contemporary ring to it in that his belief in the importance of mass media is so commonplace these days. The fact that journalists now value objectivity as a goal far more than they did in the late nineteenth century means that the role of newspapers as advocates has changed slightly, but they are still powerful movers of public opinion. Newspapers endorse candidates at election time and, more important, value investigative reporting that can greatly change the course of public policy.[10]

Bryce also recognized that the American newspaper contained multiple forms of public opinion, not only news stories and editorials but letters from citizens as well. Letters to the editor had long been overlooked by theorists as a source of public opinion data, but Bryce underscored their role in the communication of popular sentiment. Near the end of his discussion of newspapers, however, Bryce makes it clear that no one—politicians included—can depend entirely on newspapers to gain a comprehensive view of public opinion. As he noted:

> Every prudent man keeps a circle of [four or five discerning friends of different types of thought] . . . by whom he can test and correct his own impressions better than by the almost official utterances of the party journals [newspapers]. So in America there is much to be learnt—even a stranger can perceive it— from conversation with judicious observers outside politics and typical representatives of political sections and social classes, which the most diligent study of the press will not give.[11]

One theorist of public affairs who had even more to say on the relationship between newspapers and interpersonal discussion was a French sociologist named Gabriel Tarde, who wrote about public opinion in the early decades of the twentieth century. He noted in his essay "Opinion and Conversation" that "conversation at all times, and the press, which at present is the principal source of conversation, are the major factors in opinion."[12] In fact, Tarde presented a unidirectional model of opinion formation that can be depicted graphically (see Box 2.4).

Box 2.4   Gabriel Tarde's Model of Public Opinion

Media –> Conversation –> Opinion –> Action

This is one model to use when thinking about the relationship of newspapers to political action. Gabriel Tarde firmly believed that newspapers are a national springboard for political discussion. Conversation about politics, in turn, enables people to clarify their opinions about various political and social policies so that they can act accordingly by voting, volunteering for a campaign, attending a demonstration, and the like.

One might take issue with both the order of elements in this illustration and the linear nature of the model. For example, is it possible that conversation and discussion cause journalists to write particular articles? If that is the case, we need to put some sort of conversational variable in this equation *before* the element "media." And in terms of directionality, we might question whether exposure to the media commonly leads to political action. Some researchers have argued that media are more likely to debilitate or dissuade us from political action than they are to prompt us toward political participation.[1]

---

1. There is growing interest in Tarde, thanks in large part to Elihu Katz. See Elihu Katz, "Press-Conversation-Opinion-Action: Gabriel Tarde's Public Sphere," Annenberg School for Communication at the University of Pennsylvania, 1997. On the question of whether media dissuade or encourage political activity, the classic discussion can be found in Paul Lazarsfeld and Robert Merton's "Mass Communication, Popular Taste and Organized Social Action," in Lyman Bryson, ed., *The Communication of Ideas* (New York: Harper and Brothers, 1948).

After Tarde wrote, a variety of other political theorists tackled the fundamental questions about public opinion—what its meaning is, how it operates, and what its relationship to political institutions and culture is. Two of these scholars—Walter Lippmann and John Dewey—will be discussed in the context of democratic theory (the subject of Chapter 7). And more recent twentieth-century discussions of public opinion, particularly those based on empirical research, are covered in some of the other chapters to come. Yet it might be instructive to end this particular section on public opinion theory with discussion of an important (although largely overlooked) scholarly event that took place in 1924.

As you can see from the vast historical territory covered in this chapter, by 1924 a number of intellectuals had focused on the nature of public opinion. In fact, there were so many diverse perspectives on the nature and content of public opinion that political scientists became overwhelmed by the larger philosophical issues. Therefore, in 1924, a group of prominent scholars met at their yearly convention to conduct a roundtable discussion on the measurement of public opinion. After much argument, the researcher who wrote up the results of the roundtable noted:

> After some discussion of these points [about the nature of public opinion], it was agreed that an exact definition of public opinion might not be needed until after the technical problem of measuring the opinions of the individual members of the public had been disposed of. It was decided therefore that the round table might well proceed to consider the problem of measuring opinion, especially that related to political matters, and *avoid the use of the term public opinion if possible.* (our emphasis)[13]

In this book, we take just the opposite approach to understanding public opinion: By bringing together the most fundamental insights about public opinion from our greatest philosophers and illuminating the complexity of the topic, we hope to underscore that public opinion is a contested concept but still a rich and valuable one. Students need not avoid the term "public opinion" but instead can use it as a gateway for understanding the challenges of democratic theory and practice.

The Social History of Public Opinion: Expression and Measurement

Intellectual histories of public opinion such as the brief one provided above are crucial if you are to understand the philosophical development of the concept in political theory. Yet the social history of public opinion—how popular sentiment has been communicated and measured over time—is equally important and interesting. When we explore how public opinion has been expressed and assessed in previous eras, we gain much insight into the advantages and disadvantages of our own techniques for communicating popular attitudes.

In this section, we often refer to methods of public opinion communication as *technologies* of public opinion. By this, we mean that citizens and leaders alike use a variety of tools to both express opinions and evaluate them. In contemporary American politics, the public opinion poll or survey is one of the premier technologies for opinion expression and measurement. And one could argue that the newspaper is still an important organ for the communication of popular sentiment, just as it was during the years when Alexis de Tocqueville and Lord Bryce traveled America in hopes of understanding the nature of democracy.

Interestingly, the tools that we use to *express* public opinion can also be considered tools for *measuring* public opinion. Let us take demonstrations as an example. When thousands of people gather in Washington, D.C., to protest a government policy or to demonstrate that a large number of Americans share a particular cause, identity, or political agenda, the marchers are expressing their opinions. At the same time, however, others are measuring those opinions. Journalists and policymakers alike can assess the size of the crowd as well as the rhetoric of the speeches and the intensity of feeling among rally attendants. Thus, the political demonstration, as a technology of public opinion, enables both the expression and the evaluation of public feeling.

Here we discuss some of the more important technologies that humans throughout the centuries have employed to communicate their attitudes about public affairs. Before we take up this list of techniques, however, it might be instructive to underscore the grand trends in technological innovation over time. There are three forces that have altered the nature of public opinion technologies through the ages:

1. An increasing emphasis on order and routinization.
2. Movement toward private and anonymous means for communication opinion.
3. A shift from local to national and even global opinion expression and assessment.

We shall see as we advance through periods in the history of public expression that our techniques for communicating attitudes have become increasingly standardized and routinized. In other words, we have developed more rigorous schemes for quantifying and aggregating public opinion so that it can be more easily understood. Furthermore, in capitalist societies, public opinion data are a valuable commodity, so it is important to develop standard methods of opinion measurement that are valued by consumers, be they citizens, legislators, or newspapers. Random sampling techniques that enable a researcher to poll a small number of citizens and then generalize to all Americans are a relatively new set of tools developed in the mid-twentieth century. The representative public opinion poll uses a much more standardized methodology than other technologies (such as counting the crowd members at a demonstration). This is not to say that opinion polls are somehow better than other nonquantitative techniques of the past or present. All methods of communicating public opinion have their positive and negative aspects, as we shall see during this discussion.

That opinion expression has become increasingly private is closely connected with the development of two opinion technologies in the nineteenth and twentieth centuries. These periods saw the emergence of secret balloting during elections and the rise of the straw poll (which evolved into the sample survey of today). Before the widespread diffusion of the secret ballot and the confidential poll—methods where one's identity remains anonymous—technologies of public opinion demanded that citizens either sign their name or show their faces: One had to sign a petition, for example, or appear at a political demonstration. There is no protection of a citizen's identity in these cases.[14]

Another important trend in the history of techniques people have used to express and measure public opinion is the increasing emphasis on national—as opposed to local—opinion. The scholar to write most eloquently about this shift is historian Charles Tilly, who argues that expressions of opinion were largely local before the mid-nineteenth century. He notes:

> Broadly speaking, the repertoire [of opinion techniques] of the seventeenth to nineteenth centuries held to a *parochial* scope: It addressed local actors or the local representatives of national actors. It also relied heavily on *patronage*— appealing to immediately available power holders to convey grievances or settle disputes. . . . The repertoire that crystallized in the nineteenth century and prevails today is, in general, more *national* in scope: Although available for local issues and enemies, it lends itself easily to coordination among many localities. As compared with the older repertoire, its actions are relatively *autonomous*: instead of staying in the shadow of existing power holders and adapting routines sanctioned by those power holders, users of the new repertoire tend to initiate their own statements of grievances and demands. Strikes, demonstrations, electoral rallies, and similar actions build, in general, on much more deliberately constructed organization than used to be the case. (emphasis in original)[15]

This shift from local expression of opinion to national expression of opinion was made possible, in part, by the development of mass media— the newspaper in particular. Yet other factors played a role as well: the accelerated importance of the nation-state as global actor, improvements in transportation infrastructure (roads, trains, and so on), and the expansion of the size of the federal government.

Pre-Nineteenth-Century Opinion Communication Techniques

The number and variety of methods people have used to communicate and assess public opinion over time is extraordinarily large. Here we discuss some of the major techniques, those that scholars of public opinion history have focused on most closely. It is best to divide up the technologies into two periods, those used before the nineteenth century and those employed beginning in the early 1800s. The reason is that the nineteenth century is something of a turning point in the history of public opinion: Before the nineteenth century, technologies were less systematic, more public, and more local. After 1800, strategies for communicating public opinion became far more routinized, tended to focus on private expression of opinion, and were much more national in scope.

One of the earliest techniques for opinion communication was *rhetoric,* the art of public speaking and persuasion. Oratory and rhetoric were employed by a variety of citizens and leaders of the ancient Greek city-states of the fifth century B.C. in order to argue for policy in those young democracies. As Wilhelm Bauer, the great German historian of public opinion, put it, citizens assembled in the marketplaces of ancient Greece, where "oratory rapidly developed as the technique best suited to the manipulation of public opinion and continued throughout later Greek and Roman times as the most powerful instrument of political propaganda and agitation."[16] Obviously, rhetoric is still used extensively today, as presidents, members of Congress, interest group leaders, and ordinary citizens try to persuade each other about policy in a variety of areas—in health care, labor relations, education, and economics, among others. The ancient Greek philosophers, Aristotle and Plato included, spent an enormous amount of time thinking about the art of oratory, since democracy revolves around political communication and the expression of ideas and values. Citizens of ancient Greece and Rome were sophisticated consumers of oratory, as so many scholars have noted. Kathleen Hall Jamieson, a contemporary scholar of rhetoric, writes:

> Ancient oratory was considered a fine art, an art regarded by its cultivators, and by the public, as analogous to sculpture, to poetry, to painting, to music and to acting. This character is common to Greek and Roman oratory. So, for example, Isocrates [a Greek orator] notes that listeners broke into loud applause when antitheses, symmetrical clauses, or other striking rhetorical figures were skillfully presented. ... When the world of entertainment, persuasion and politics was in the main an oral one, listeners were drawn together in large numbers to experience a piece of communication.[17]

In ancient times, rhetoric occurred in unmediated forums. Speakers addressed crowds in arenas and marketplaces, at festivals and public meetings of all sorts. Such direct address still occurs today, as when legislators speak from the floor or when political candidates give speeches to gathered supporters. Yet these days, much of the public speaking in political life is mediated by television, and that technology has changed the nature of rhetoric itself (see Box 2.5).

Rhetoric is by far the oldest of all public opinion communication technologies, and there is quite a large gap in the history of public opinion

Box 2.5   Effeminate Versus Manly Rhetoric

Margaret Thatcher. (Photo courtesy of the Margaret Thatcher Foundation, © Terence Donovan)

In her book on the history of speechmaking, Kathleen Hall Jamieson includes a section on the problematics of women's speech. She notes first that

between the development of the art of public speaking and the next major technique: the invention of the *printing press* (see Figure 2.3). Introduced in the sixteenth century, the printing press enabled the formation of modern publics. In other words, the publication of newspapers, books, and pamphlets made it possible for large numbers of dispersed people to communi-

"womanly discourse" has traditionally been described as "shrill" and without merit:

> For centuries, their opponents argued that women's fundamental irrationality and congenital emotionalism should disqualify them from public speaking and public office. The high pitch of the woman's voice was seen as symptomatic not of physiological differences in the vocal mechanism but of excessive emotionalism. ... Noting that shrillness characterized the voices of eunuchs, women, and invalids, [the Roman rhetorician] Quintilian recommended that men increase the robustness of their voices by abstaining from sexual intercourse. Later theorists were equally concerned that men not sound womanish. "Some have a womanish squeaking Tone," wrote John Mason in *An Essay on Elocution and Pronunciation* (1748), "which, Persons whose Voices are shrill and weak, and overtrained, are very apt to fall into." ... Eager to mute the inference that their voices signaled irrational or emotional natures, female politicians, Margaret Thatcher [former prime minister of Great Britain] among them, have sought voice retraining. Under the supervision of a tutor from the National Theatre, Mrs. Thatcher lowered the natural pitch at which she spoke in public.

Yet Jamieson also points out that the "feminine" rhetorical style so thoroughly disdained throughout history can be very effective in the age of television. She argues that President Ronald Reagan's success (he was often called "the great communicator" in the press) was due in part to his employment of a traditionally female rhetorical style—one based on self-disclosure and emotional display. About oratory over the airwaves, Jamieson writes:

> Television invites a personal, self-disclosing style that draws public discourse out of a private self and comfortably reduces the complex world to dramatic narratives. Because it encompasses these characteristics, the once spurned womanly style is now the style of preference. The same characteristics comprise a mode of discourse well suited to television and much needed in times of social stress or in the aftermath of divisive events. By revivifying social values and ennobling the shared past, epideictic or ceremonial discourse helps sustain the state.

SOURCE: Kathleen Hall Jamieson, *Eloquence in an Electronic Age: The Transformation of Political Speechmaking* (New York: Oxford University Press, 1988), quoted passages from pp. 78–79, 84.)

cate with each other. Before printing, one could only communicate with neighbors and those one met during travel (which was uncommon among ordinary citizens). With the introduction of printed materials about public affairs, however, people could ally themselves with causes, ideas, and organizations. The invention of printing was revolutionary in many respects,

FIGURE 2.3 "A True Representation of a Printing House with the Men at Work." The printing press enabled the development of modern "publics"—geographically dispersed people who shared the same interests or points of view. Depicted in this engraving is a 1752 printing house. John M. Lewis, *Anatomy of Printing: The Influences of Art and History on Its Design* (New York: Watson Guptill Publications, 1970).

but its importance to public opinion expression cannot be overestimated. Thomas Jefferson once said about newspapers in a letter to a friend, "Were it left to me to decide whether we should have a government without newspapers, or newspapers without a government, I should not hesitate a moment to prefer the latter."[18] Tocqueville and Bryce noted the importance of newspapers in nineteenth-century America, but their influence began much earlier in the European monarchies of the seventeenth and eighteenth centuries.

Printing made possible the mass distribution of knowledge itself. Common citizens, especially those in rural areas, could get access to ideas about politics, religion, and the arts. And the fact that so many inexpensive pamphlets, newspapers, and books were in circulation boosted the literacy rates in European nations. The explosion of printed materials was not accompanied by freedom of the press, of course, since monarchs could and did shut down newspapers when such publications threatened their rule. Indeed,

FIGURE 2.4   Lloyd's Coffeehouse in London, 1798. Coffeehouses and taverns served as forums for political debate in the seventeenth and eighteenth centuries. Such sites exist today, although during this earlier period people went to coffeehouses for the express purpose of learning about—and talking about—public affairs. SOURCE: Heinrich Eduard Jacob, *Coffee: The Epic of a Commodity* (New York: Penguin Books, 1935).

there are multiple historical cases of printers being tortured and executed for publishing newspapers that criticized the state.

Interestingly, printing enabled the mobilization of groups for political causes, the suppression of others, and served as a catalyst for the development of other public opinion communication techniques. The newspapers themselves carried opinions and letters to the editor, but they also served as a starting point for discussion among citizens. In the seventeenth and eighteenth centuries, for example, newspapers and books were vital to the evolution of two important opinion technologies: the *coffeehouse* and the *salon*.

Coffeehouses were popular places in England during the centuries following the introduction of printing (see Figure 2.4). Admission to these forums was cheap, and one could spend hours in coffeehouses reading newspapers and political tracts and arguing about ideas with other patrons. Eighteenth-century descriptions of coffeehouses noted that the mix of individuals in attendance varied greatly, with judges, journalists, and lawyers sharing tables with tradesmen, workers, and even the occasional thief or pickpocket. Perhaps the sociologist Lewis Coser best describes the importance of the coffeehouses as a technology of public opinion:

> A common opinion cannot be developed before people have an occasion to discuss with one another, before they have been drawn from the isolation of lonely thought into a public world in which individual opinion can be sharpened and tested in discussion with others. The coffeehouse helped to crystallize a common opinion from a multitude of individual opinions and to give it form and stability. What the newspaper had not yet been able to accomplish was achieved to a large degree by the coffeehouse.[19]

During the period in which coffeehouses were established, another forum for discussion and debate about public affairs became popular in France. Salons—gatherings of intellectuals, statesmen, and artists—were extraordinarily important to the development of political discourse in seventeenth- and eighteenth-century France. Salons were in many ways less "democratic" than coffeehouses, which were open to all for a tiny entrance fee. The salons were run with an iron hand by bourgeois women who decided who should be invited and what topics should be discussed. Much has been written about the exclusivity of the salons, but the effects of the conversations within these gatherings were tremendous. It was in the salons of ancien régime Paris that Rousseau developed the ideas for his *Social Contract*, an essay often cited as laying the philosophical groundwork for the French Revolution. Many writers and artists fine-tuned their ideas in the salons before they wrote books for mass distribution. But salons, like all public opinion technologies, were also technologies for public opinion measurement. There is substantial evidence that kings and their courtiers visited the salons on a regular basis in order to gather "data" about public opinion. These data reflected only a small, elite sampling of French opinion, yet since the ideas generated in salons were destined for diffusion throughout France and the world, such information was extraordinarily valuable to those interested in public opinion.[20]

Perhaps this is a good moment to reflect on one of the troubling issues in the field of public opinion raised in Chapter 1. *Who* is a member of the public is always shifting, depending upon historical context and the agendas of those measuring public opinion. In terms of developing economic policy in the eighteenth century, for example, it was not as important to the king of France to gather public opinion from the French countryside as it was to monitor the way influential bankers and businessmen talked in the salons. This may seem to be a very elitist way of thinking about the public and public opinion (i.e., public opinion is the discourse of rather exclusive salon meetings), yet it is the most accurate meaning of public opinion *for that particular period*. We mentioned in Chapter 1 that the meaning of public opinion is contested in contemporary American politics, and the same was true in Europe and England in the seventeenth and eighteenth centuries. Some believed public opinion to be the exclusive banter of the salons, whereas others argued that the discourse of the more egalitarian coffeehouse was more representative and therefore more meaningful as an indicator of public opinion.

The seventeenth and eighteenth centuries also witnessed the evolution of other interesting techniques for communication of public opinion. Two closely related ones are the *petition* and the *public rally*. Beginning as early as 1640, citizens of England petitioned Parliament about a number of public affairs, from taxes and monopolies to social issues and peace. Petitions were a very effective means of focusing legislators' attentions on topics of importance to common folk. Petitions were presented peaceably at times, but very often an angry mob delivered its petition to Parliament in person. In a colorful description of violent petitioning during the first English civil war (1642–1646), a British writer noted how women—who were often the leaders in petitioning for peace—presented their demands. The women, he said,

> kepte knockinge and beatinge of the outwarde dore before the parliament house, and would have violently forced the same open, and required Mr Pym, Mr Strode, and some other members . . . and threatened to take the rounde heades of the parliament whome they saide they would caste into the Thames [River]. . . . These women were not any whit scared or ashamed of their incivilities, but cryed out so much the more, even at the doore of the house of Commons, Give us these Traytors that are against peace, that we may teare them in pieces, Give us Pym.[21]

Not all petitioners were angry mobs, but so much violence accompanied the presentation of petitions to Parliament that in 1648, legislators passed a bill against unruly petitioning. This was ineffective, so Parliament then limited the number of people who could present a petition to twenty. Even this did not deter violence in conjunction with petitioning, so in 1699, all petitioners were required to give their petition to their representative in advance of parliamentary debate so that he could present it for them.

This series of incidents in British history could be interpreted in several ways. One might argue that the petitioners were too unruly to engage in the sort of rational political dialogue necessary for the construction of public policy. Alternately, we can read this as an attempt by Parliament to squash the intensity of public opinion by erasing the emotion underpinning the demands of petitions. Historians' interpretations of these events, as well as other acts of citizens during the English civil wars, are interesting and varied.[22]

Why add *rioting* and *demonstrations* to our list of opinion technologies, since the process of people gathering together to express their desires might be seen as a fundamental human activity? Although crowds gathered in the ancient city-states of Greece and throughout the ages, rioting escalated as a form of public opinion expression in seventeenth-century England. Most of these "popular disturbances" (as they were called at the time) centered on economics: Rioters protested fiscal policies of the Parliament as well as the food shortages and food price hikes resulting from those policies. In a 1938 book, British scholar Max Beloff reports on his archival research concerning the food riots of the late seventeenth and early eighteenth centuries. In late-twentieth-century America, we are not accustomed to food rioting, but such demonstrations were common during this period. Beloff writes of 1708:

> The steepness of the rise in [grain] prices was indeed sharper in these years than at any other time in the period under discussion. . . . The populace was not slow to react. In May of 1709 it was reported from Essex that mobs of women amounting to hundreds were on the move and had threatened to 'fire divers houses, and shoot several persons, by reason they have been dealers in corn to London, on pretense they make the same dear.'[23]

Rioting is one of the most obviously *public* of public opinion technologies: Although one can often get "lost in a crowd," those involved in riots expect to be recognized and heard. In contemporary American politics, we often witness demonstrations, strikes, and marches. Yet the intensity of these gatherings pales in comparison to the series of violent protests over government economic policy in seventeenth- and eighteenth-century England.

The next important opinion technology worthy of mention in this brief historical overview is the *general election*. There is evidence that elections were used in the early Greek democracies, although participation was limited only to male citizens, so they are not considered "general" in any contemporary sense.

Elections are interesting from the standpoint of public opinion history because they represent a turning point in public expression itself. Until the emergence of the secret ballot—generally used in democratic elections—opinion expression was public and attributed. One could not cast a vote anonymously and therefore had to take a certain amount of responsibility in one's local community for holding a particular opinion. With the diffusion of the general election, the anonymous communication of beliefs became possible on a large scale. Although not all were allowed to vote (e.g., slaves and women), general elections for the presidency in America began in the early nineteenth century. It is not surprising that *straw polling* emerged shortly thereafter.

Straw polling is "nonscientific" polling conducted with pen and paper, over the telephone, or by less formal means (e.g., a "show of hands"). In the early nineteenth century, journalists, party operatives, and citizens would poll people in their communities about upcoming elections. Major newspapers, like the *New York Times* and the *Chicago Tribune,* would publish polls from their reporters who were often traveling around the country covering political rallies and speeches. Many journalists conducted straw polls on long train or boat rides in order to get a sense of public opinion in the local community. Although straw polls are still conducted today (e.g., "call-in polls" on radio or television stations), most serious polling after 1936 utilized the sample survey or scientific poll.

Were these straw polls accurate? Probably not, but it is difficult to tell from our vantage point in the late twentieth century. Claude Robinson, a professor at Columbia University, conducted an analysis of straw polling in 1932 and found much variance. Straw polls conducted in person tended to be more accurate than the sort that asked readers to cut a ballot from the newspaper and mail it back. Yet even the in-person interview did not always yield accurate forecasts of upcoming elections.[24]

We believe that the accuracy of these straw polls is the least interesting aspect of the phenomenon. Straw polls were important in the nineteenth and early twentieth centuries because they were a vehicle for getting citizens involved in politics. First, straw polls made elections seem like "horse races." On the surface this may sound like a negative assessment, but it can be argued that news articles emphasizing the *contest*—who is ahead and who trails—get voters excited about an upcoming election. Second, people often conducted their own straw polls (see Figure 2.5) instead of waiting for journalists to poll them or their neighbors. This is another way that straw voting, as a formal political endeavor, increased citizen involvement. Finally, there is historical evidence that straw polling was accompanied by political discussion: When people were polled, it usually followed or preceded a debate about the issues and the campaign. Thus, straw polling prompted people to engage their neighbors and coworkers in discussions of public affairs. Do today's scientific polls serve the same function of inspiring public discourse? It is a difficult question to answer but an important one for students of public opinion to ponder.

Opinion polling was so popular and useful throughout the nineteenth and early twentieth centuries that marketing researchers, political analysts, academics, and statisticians all worked intensely on developing a more accurate and rigorous way of assessing public opinion. In 1936, a year when a popular magazine called the *Literary Digest* mistakenly predicted that Alf Landon would defeat Franklin Roosevelt in the presidential election, a young man named George Gallup predicted just the opposite. Gallup, using a mathematical approach called random sampling, did not determine the election outcome perfectly (he was off by 7 percentage points), but his method was far better than the *Digest*'s or any other straw poll.

For Bryan and the County Jail.

To the Editor of The New-York Times:

On a south-bound train on the Delaware and Hudson Railroad last Thursday, in one car an enthusiastic drummer took the now popular straw vote to determine the political affiliations of the passengers. The poll showed the 23 occupants divided—18 for McKinley, 5 for Bryan. This was satisfactory, but more was to come. When the train halted at Ballston, among those who got off were the five Bryan sympathizers, and then it was seen that they were handcuffed together, and were a gang of prisoners on their way to the county jail at that place.

SOUND MONEY.

BALLSTON, N. Y., Oct. 5.

FIGURE 2.5　In the nineteenth century, citizens would often poll their friends, neighbors, and coworkers about upcoming presidential races. Often, businessmen who were traveling around their own region would poll strangers in train cars and on steamers. This humorous poll, sent to the *New York Times* in 1896 during the contest between McKinley and Bryan, comes from a McKinley supporter who watched one of his fellow passengers poll the riders on a New York train.

The key to Gallup's success was sampling theory, which dictates that one use methods of random selection to choose respondents for a poll (see Box 2.6). If one carefully chooses members of a sample using this method and response rates are reasonably high, the sample should "simulate" the opinions of the population at large. The *Literary Digest* did not use sampling methods; it simply relied upon various lists of citizens (gathered from phone directories and auto registration records) and sent out millions of ballots, asking citizens to mark their preference for the upcoming election. From 1916 through 1936, the *Digest* used this method. After Gallup embarrassed the *Digest* by predicting the election more accurately than it had, the *Digest* issued a public apology and eventually shut down operations.

Our history of public opinion stops here because the introduction of representative sampling was the last revolutionary change in how we think about and measure public opinion. Petitions, rioting, and demonstrations are still influential means of expressing and assessing public opinion, but scientific polling is now the preeminent tool for communicating opinion.

Box 2.6   George Gallup on Polling in a Democracy

George Gallup, an early pollster who did much to popularize the opinion survey. (Photo courtesy of the Gallup Organization)

George Gallup's success as a pollster was primarily due to his early use of random sampling. His pioneering methodological spirit was only part of the reason for his success: He had an almost religious belief that polling could strengthen democracy in America and beyond. In 1940, he and Saul Rae wrote:

The kind of public opinion implied in the democratic ideal is tangible and dynamic. It springs from many sources deep in the day-to-day experience

(continues)

Box 2.6   *(continued)*

of individuals who constitute the political public, and who formulate these opinions as working guides for their political representatives. This public opinion listens to many propagandas, most of them contradictory. It tries in the clash and conflict of argument and debate to separate the true from the false. It needs criticism for its very existence, and through criticism it is constantly being modified and molded. It acts and learns by action. Its truths are relative and contingent upon the results which its action achieves. Its chief faith is a faith in experiment. It believes in the value of every individual's contribution to political life, and in the right of ordinary human beings to have a voice in deciding their fate. Public opinion, in this sense, is the pulse of democracy.

SOURCE: George Gallup and Saul Forbes Rae, *The Pulse of Democracy: The Public-Opinion Poll and How It Works* (New York: Simon and Schuster, 1940), quoted passage at p. 8.)

Since Gallup's earliest polls, a variety of technical improvements in the collection and analysis of survey data have made preelection polling much more accurate. Polling on issues—how people feel about health care reform, foreign policy, and other current affairs—is still extraordinarily difficult and complicated. Sampling and survey design will be addressed in Chapter 3, where you will be introduced to that method as well as to several other methods of assessing public opinion.

The story of public opinion is a long one, beginning with the ancient Greek philosophers who thought and wrote so much about popular sentiments and the meaning of those sentiments in a democracy. Some periods have seen more interest in public opinion than others due to the predominance of certain forms of government: In autocratic regimes, public opinion is important only in that it must be tamed or controlled, whereas in democratic states, the nature of public opinion (in theory) determines the direction of public policy. In every era, new democracies emerge—the most recent set appearing in Eastern Europe—and the same enduring questions about public opinion arise: Who composes the public? And how might we know its desires? As we saw in Chapter 1, these questions are difficult to answer. Yet no democratic state can evolve if its leaders and citizens fail to grapple with such monumental theoretical and practical issues.

Notes

1. Ernest Barker, *Greek Political Theory: Plato and His Predecessors* (London: Methuen 1918), pp. 38–39, cited in Paul Palmer, "The Concept of Public Opinion

in Political Theory," in C. Wittke, ed., *Essays in History and Political Theory in Honour of Charles Howard McIlwain* (New York: Russell and Russell, 1964).

2. Robert Minar, "Public Opinion in the Perspective of Political Theory," *Western Political Quarterly* 13 (1960):31–44.

3. Thanks to Professor Jean Goodwin of Northwestern University for her translation and insights.

4. *The Prince*, trans. and ed. N. H. Thompson (Buffalo, NY: Prometheus Books, 1986), pp. 57–58.

5. Quoted in Palmer, "The Concept of Public Opinion in Political Theory," p. 239.

6. Alexis de Tocqueville, *Democracy in America*, ed. and trans. J. P. Mayer (New York: Anchor Books, 1969), p. 255.

7. Ibid., p. 435.

8. C. J. Arthur, ed., *The German Ideology* (New York: International Publishers, 1984), pp. 65–66.

9. James Bryce, *The American Commonwealth* (London: Macmillan and Co., 1891), p. 265.

10. See, for example, David Protess et al., *The Journalism of Outrage: Investigative Reporting and Agenda Building in America* (New York: Guilford Press, 1991).

11. Bryce, *The American Commonwealth*, p. 267.

12. Terry N. Clark, ed., *Gabriel Tarde: On Communication and Social Influence* (Chicago: University of Chicago Press, 1969), p. xx.

13. Arthur N. Holcombe, "Roundtable on Political Statistics," *American Political Science Review* 19 (February 1925):123–124.

14. For a more detailed discussion of these trends in the history of public expression, see Susan Herbst, *Numbered Voices: How Opinion Polling Has Shaped American Politics* (Chicago: University of Chicago Press, 1995).

15. "Speaking Your Mind Without Elections, Surveys, or Social Movements," *Public Opinion Quarterly* 47 (1983):465.

16. "Public Opinion," in Edwin Seligman, ed., *Encyclopaedia of the Social Sciences* (New York: Macmillan, 1930), p. 671.

17. Kathleen Hall Jamieson, *Eloquence in an Electronic Age: The Transformation of Political Speechmaking* (New York: Oxford University Press, 1988), p. 5.

18. Quoted in Michael and Edwin Emery, *The Press and America: An Interpretive History of the Mass Media* (Englewood Cliffs, NJ: Prentice Hall, 1988), p. 90.

19. Lewis Coser, *Men of Ideas: A Sociologist's View* (New York: Free Press, 1970), p. 20.

20. On salons and their place in political history, see Susan Herbst, *Politics at the Margin: Historical Perspectives on Public Expression Outside the Mainstream* (New York: Cambridge University Press, 1995).

21. Quoted in Patricia Higgins, "The Reaction of Women, with Special Reference to Women Petitioners," in Brian Manning, ed., *Politics, Religion, and the English Civil War* (London: Edward Arnold, 1973), pp. 190–191.

22. See Manning, *Politics, Religion, and the English Civil War*, or Maurice Ashley, *England in the Seventeenth Century* (Baltimore: Penguin Books, 1968). On

petitioning and political meetings in British history, see Cecil Emden, *The People and the Constitution* (London: Oxford University Press, 1956).

23. Max Beloff, *Public Order and Popular Disturbances 1660–1714* (London: Oxford University Press, 1938), p. 68.

24. Claude Robinson, *Straw Votes* (New York: Columbia University Press, 1932).

Chapter Three

Methods for Studying Public Opinion

By now you might have guessed that public opinion is difficult to measure. Because it is a very complex force with so many psychological and sociological dimensions, there are many ways to think about the concept. Researchers have puzzled over the best way to measure public opinion since the early decades of the twentieth century and have debated the pros and cons of many techniques for evaluating this rather "slippery" concept.

Despite continuing debates over how to measure public opinion, there is some consensus among scholars, policymakers, interest group leaders, and journalists. These parties use a variety of techniques to assess the public mood: election returns, consumer behavior, stock market fluctuations, public meetings and demonstrations, and other such behavioral indicators. But when leaders or journalists want to understand the attitudes that drive behavior, they often turn to four methods of opinion assessment: survey research or polling, focus groups, experimental research, and the analysis of mass media content. In this chapter, we introduce each of these methods in order to give you a general overview of them. Our introduction to these methods is not intended to make you an expert on them, as this is not a methodology textbook. We do hope, however, that you will refer to the many methodological texts on public opinion, including those referenced in this chapter.

Survey Research: Aggregating Individual Opinions

Survey research has significantly shaped our view of publics and their opinions. We have seen in previous chapters how social theory in the early twentieth century grew more concerned with the concept of mass publics. A tool was needed that would empirically test notions of how large, dynamic groups of individuals thought and behaved. Sociologists had earlier been accustomed to carefully interviewing people in smaller group situations, such as the workplace or in discrete neighborhoods. Early social researchers analyzed their findings more from a qualitative than a quantitative perspective, not having accurate enough measures to reliably "count" public opinion trends across citizen populations. Informal preelection straw polls and "person-in-the-street" interviews by journalists were common, though notoriously unscientific and unreliable. In both cases, reporters simply asked people they knew or people they happened to run into whom they were going to vote for.

The main formal "counting" tool was the U.S. census, which every ten years tried to provide an actual head count and some raw demographics for the population as a whole. The most meaningful measures of public opinion were election results. Obviously, neither indicator provided the kinds of subtleties needed to show what people were thinking about public issues, let alone why they were thinking what they did.

The initial impetus to find ways of doing large-scale summations of people's attitudes and behaviors was heavily influenced by the growth of broadcast media in the 1920s and 1930s. Broadcasters needed ways of letting advertisers know how many people "out there" in the then poorly defined audience areas were listening. Concepts borrowed from probability sampling theory allowed measurement of smaller samples drawn from much larger populations, with the results representative of the whole. In effect, application of sampling theory allowed the findings of surveys of small samples picked from bigger populations to be *generalized* to those populations. We will explain how this works later.

In those early years, door-to-door interviewing was required to get close to a fair sampling of a population, and that process was—and remains—exorbitantly expensive and time-consuming. Polling by telephone tended mainly to reach the wealthier, who could afford telephones, and mail surveys suffered from lack of valid address lists. Nonetheless, early survey efforts yielded at least some representative indications of early radio audiences. Preelection polls also became more formal, although still primitive by today's standards.

By the late 1930s and into the 1940s, many elements came together to make large-scale opinion surveys the more reliable tool they are today. For one thing, people became easier to find, with increased telephone ownership and more sophisticated telecommunications networking, more accurate mailing lists, and population movement to urban areas. Equally important were advances in statistical theory and, later, the application of computers to statistical modeling. Computerizing both survey sampling and analytic techniques made surveys far more efficient and cost-effective.

Moreover, the birth of academic survey research centers at such places as the University of Chicago and the University of Michigan spawned many innovations in survey procedures and added greatly to their validity. Survey research today is a multibillion dollar industry, with studies of nearly every type imaginable being conducted by academicians, market researchers, mass media, governmental agencies, and political pollsters. Without survey research, most of this book could not have been written.

It seems curious that after over a half century of such experience, surveys are still assumed to be more complicated than they actually are by the people they study. Many people have misconceptions about what surveys can and cannot show and about how their results can be interpreted. We will outline some basic principles below, with particular attention to survey applications in public opinion research.

The Survey Process

Surveys consist of several entwined components, all strongly affecting one another. Key elements include:

1. The *population* of people that the survey is to provide data about.
2. The kind of *sample* of individuals that will be drawn from that population.
3. The method of *data gathering* to be used—usually involving personal, phone, or mail interviews.
4. The kind of *questionnaire* or interviewing instrument used.
5. The kinds of *analyses* done and *inferences* drawn.

The nature of the population is usually the one constant that the rest of the survey needs to be designed around. Sampling, data gathering, and other components will vary considerably depending on the composition of the population. Strategies will differ according to whether the population includes, for example, all U.S. adults, Democrats likely to vote in Ohio, chief executive officers of biotechnology companies, or freshmen students at a Midwestern state university.

The purpose of the survey obviously influences the kinds of analyses to be done and the inferences drawn. If our purpose is preliminary and exploratory—perhaps to get some broad ideas about how the Internet may affect political views of college students—we may begin with a rather small sample of students we know in one dormitory at a large university just to try out some questions. We might also use focus groups, described later in this chapter, to get a better fix on the situation. If, however, our goal is to predict a month ahead who is leading in a governor's race and why, our sampling needs to be larger and more representative of likely voters, and our items should be better formed and precise. Or if our purpose is to test the more formal hypothesis that television leads to less public social interaction, we had better have several well-validated indicators of television viewership, social interaction, and related variables. It may not be so important that our sample represents the U.S. population as a whole as that it adequately reflects types of people and situations that have bearing on the hypothesis.

Types of Surveys

Several types of surveys exist. We first define a *survey* as a research technique for measuring characteristics of a given population of individuals. Some surveys are done to count or describe characteristics of a population; others are more concerned with explaining why characteristics occur and how they relate to others. Simple descriptive surveys are sometimes called *polls,* when they are conducted more for political or election forecasting purposes. For instance, CNN might do a preelection poll to see who is ahead in a presidential contest, whereas during the same time period, the University of Michigan would be doing more extensive surveys to find out why people are choosing to vote as they are and what the consequences of those behaviors are for the body politic.

We can also distinguish among three broad types of surveys by looking at which people out of the population are actually counted or interviewed. *Census* surveys attempt to count every person in the population, as the federal government does every ten years. *Sample surveys* take a smaller sampling of people out of the population to measure. *Probability sample surveys* (also more loosely called "scientific" surveys) use statistical methods to select who is to be included in the sample. Using probability sampling methods lets us *generalize* our findings to the larger population, meaning that we can with some confidence assume that the findings will be approximately what we would have gotten had we interviewed the whole population. To be cost-effective, surveys attempt to choose the smallest, most accessible sample possible that will still allow meaningful generalizations to be made about the entire population.

Surveys are typically *cross-sectional,* meaning that they are done at one point in time to provide a "snapshot" of public views at that particular time. *Panel* surveys reinterview the same people over time to get a better picture of how opinions may change over months or even years. Surveys are often a main element in *field experiments,* in which samples may be divided into "experimental" or "control" conditions and are then subjected to different stimuli: One community, for example, may receive a particular public health information campaign, while another does not. Surveys may then be done to compare whether the recipient community gains in knowledge over the nonrecipient.

Sampling

Samples can be either probability or nonprobability based. Nonprobability samples cannot be viewed as representative of any larger population, but they can nonetheless be useful in certain instances. Intensive case studies of families or other small units, for example, can generate significant knowledge about specific social concepts or processes that may be overlooked in broader-scale survey efforts. That is, we can learn a lot in such case studies about how a particular family works, but we cannot be sure that family is typical of others. Nonprobability surveys may be useful in helping to develop concepts and measures to be tested later in larger samples.

"Person-in-the-street" or "mall-intercept" nonprobability interviews are favored by some marketing researchers. This method usually involves interviewers positioning themselves in a shopping mall or other well-traveled location and trying to interview as many people in desirable age or gender categories as possible. Although the information gained may be useful for some marketing purposes, the sampling is typically sloppy enough to avoid using the results for valid generalizations about any population. We simply have no way of knowing whether the people interviewed are typical of the larger community or even typical of other shoppers at a particular mall.

Probability sampling, by contrast, assumes that each person within a given population has a certain known chance of being included in a sample. In the most rigorous case of *simple random sampling*, each person in the population has the exact same chance as every other person of being sampled. Note that this is a far more demanding definition of "random" than we use in everyday talk, where the term usually implies doing things "by chance" or *un*systematically. Rather, strict probability sampling methods carry systematic selection to an extreme. Sophisticated random number tables are often used to try to assure that the selection of each person for a sample is independent of the selection of every other person. The analogy often used is continuously shaking a bin of numbered balls, as in lottery drawings, between selections of the numbered balls. This effort to make each selection independent of every other selection helps assure that each unit chosen for the sample has the same chance of selection as any other unit in the sample.

The underlying assumption is straightforward: If you choose a sample from a population using probability techniques, you can generalize or make inferences from that sample back to the population by using the same probability techniques. Put another way, if you know the chances or odds that people in the population have of being included in the sample, you also know the chances or odds that whatever you measure in the sample also occurs in the population.

Suppose that you read a story in *USA Today* that a national probability sample survey of U.S. adults found that 66 percent support a balanced federal budget; another 24 percent do not, and 10 percent are undecided. The story also reports that the "error margin" for the findings is plus or minus 3 percent and that the sample size was 1,000. This means that because 66 percent of the sample supported a balanced budget, we can infer with 95 percent confidence that in the larger population somewhere between 66 percent plus 3 percent or 66 percent minus 3 percent (or between 63 percent and 69 percent) would have supported the balanced budget if they had been asked.

If we dissect this a bit, what we are saying first is that we can only generalize the 66 percent statistic to the larger population within a certain range of error. In this case, that range is plus or minus 3 percent. Thus, if the statistic is 66 percent, the true population percent (or *parameter*) is likely to be within plus or minus three percentage points of 66 percent. This error range is known as *sampling error*, or the error that results when we try to generalize or infer results from a sample to the larger population.

We can estimate sampling error because when probability sampling is used, we know the probability of each person being drawn into the sample in the first place. Using appropriate mathematical formulas, we can retrace those probabilities after the survey to estimate sampling error.*

Note that we have no way of absolutely knowing or proving what the true population value is. If we wanted to know "really" whether exactly 66 percent of the actual population supported a balanced budget, we would have to ask every one of the more than 200 million adults in the United States. Being unable or unwilling to do that, we hedge our bets. We specify what the odds are—or how confident we are—that the true population value is within that plus or minus 3 percent error range.

This *confidence level* is the final factor that concerns us in understanding probability sampling. The conventional confidence level associated with nearly all sample surveys is 95 percent: In the *USA Today* example, we estimate that there is a 95 percent chance that the true population value of balanced budget support lies within that plus or minus 3 percent error range. To put the notion behind confidence level another way, if we had drawn 100 random samples of 1,200 citizens each and interviewed all of them, we would expect that in 95 out of those 100 samples, somewhere between 63 and 69 percent would have supported the balanced budget. In sum, the larger the sample size, the lower the sampling error, given the same confidence level. Population size for the most part has little effect on sampling error.

---

*Strictly speaking, the sampling error is calculated from a value called the standard error, which is added to or subtracted from the population mean or percentage value. We do this theoretically, because we of course don't really know what the population mean or percentage really is (if we did, we wouldn't have to draw the sample!). So in truth, we never know in the distribution of all possible samples we might have drawn exactly where our own sample lies.

As a general rule of thumb, sample sizes of around 1,000 are often adequate to provide descriptive public opinion data for populations of around 100,000 or more—including the U.S. adult population of 200 million. Responses from samples of this size will usually yield a sampling error of roughly 3 to 4 percent. Sample sizes of 300 or so may often provide useful information about certain large populations—if a somewhat sloppy sampling error rate of 5 to 7 percent or more does not cause problems. (Consider that if a preelection poll has a sampling error of 5 percent and one candidate is found to have the support of 40 percent of the sample and the other has 45 percent, the race is statistically a dead heat.)

Several specific probability sampling methods may be used, depending on the nature of the population, the kind of sample needed, and whether respondents will be contacted in person or by phone or mail. In many cases, *stratified sampling* methods or oversampling are used, meaning that the sample is purposively weighted to better represent one population group or another. (For example, if the purpose of a study is to compare opinions of black versus white citizens on racial issues, a higher proportion of black respondents than would be drawn by chance alone may need to be included in the sample to have adequate numbers for statistical comparisons with whites.)

The Problem of Survey Participation

A key problem in survey research is that people statistically chosen to be included in a sample do not always choose to participate. Some individuals are more difficult to reach than others, and some are more willing to cooperate than others. Well-run professional general population telephone surveys often get *response rates* of 70 to 80 percent, meaning that 70 to 80 percent of the people included in the initial sample have been successfully interviewed.

The impact of low response rates on how well we can generalize findings to the population is a major concern. Many researchers argue that as long as it can be shown that those not participating in the survey are essentially the same as those who are, the problem is minimal. Most opinion surveys are able to compare the demographics of their respondents with U.S. census demographics (gender, age, race/ethnicity, and so on) of the populations of interest, and often they are highly similar; and even if they are not, weighting can be done before results are reported.

Other researchers argue, however, that even if demographics are similar, we can never really know how well the interviewed respondents stack up against the general population in terms of their public views, involvement, and behaviors. (If we knew in the first place, there would be no reason to do the survey!) There is the suspicion that people who agree to be interviewed may be somewhat more interested in public affairs, perhaps more knowledgeable, and more active; hence, such surveys may not represent the full range of public views. Thus, samples may be *biased* to overrepresent some population characteristics at the expense of others.

However, it is clear that people are more willing to participate when they sense the study is legitimate (e.g., not a sales promotion), when they are interested in the subject area, and when they are given additional inducements, such as payment for their time. Paying respondents raises concerns about people who need money being more represented or about paid respondents wanting to provide answers they think will please the interviewer.

Methods of Gathering Survey Data

The three most common methods of getting survey data from respondents are in person, by telephone, and by mail. Each has advantages and disadvantages, and choosing a method again depends on how well it fits with other components of the survey.

In-Person Interviews.   Most researchers would ideally prefer to do in-person, face-to-face interviews for nearly all surveys. One-on-one in-person interaction makes it easier for interviewers to build rapport with respondents. Better rapport can increase the quality of answers to questions in terms of both accuracy and completeness, especially in studies dealing with the more sensitive issues. Greater rapport can also promote longer, more detailed interviews. Interviewers are also able to note more emotive aspects of responses through facial expressions and body language. Another main advantage is that more complex and in-depth questions can be asked by using visual aids and other explanatory tools. Questions about campaign advertising, for example, can be asked by showing the actual ads, on portable VCRs, if appropriate.

A decided disadvantage of in-person interviews is their often excessive cost, and for this reason, they are quite sparingly used. The cost per interview for, say, a twenty-minute in-person survey can average over $200 (versus one-fourth that amount or less for comparable telephone or mail interviews). Multiply this amount by the 300 to 1,200 respondents needed for most public opinion studies, and you quickly see that only the most well-endowed projects can afford personal interviews.

Much of the expense is due to interviewer time in tracking down, soliciting, and completing interviews in the respondents' home or workplace. Sampling costs are also higher, given the need to coordinate the actual physical location of respondents rather then relying only on lists of phone numbers or addresses. National population surveys cause special problems in this regard.

Telephone Interviews.   Telephone interviewing is by far the most-used public opinion survey technique, and it has cost effectiveness and interviewer convenience on its side. A twenty-minute telephone survey might run $50 or upward per interview, with most survey organizations having volumediscounted phone lines that minimize long-distance charges. As a result, a survey of 600 adults drawn from across the United States may not cost significantly more than the same survey carried out locally within a given city.

Most general population telephone samples are drawn by so-called *random digit dialing* techniques. Telephone numbers to be called are probability-sampled from computerized lists of all possible telephone exchanges in the population area. As calls are made, nonworking numbers and business and other nonhousehold numbers are systematically excluded, leaving what is usually an excellent representation of all private household telephones within the specified geographic area. Software that automatically dials the selected numbers is now commonplace as well, easing tedious labor. Random-digit dialing methods are not only more cost-efficient but avoid biases associated with telephone directories reaching unlisted numbers.

Telephone surveys are fast and flexible—hence the reliance on telephones for quick-reaction opinion polls on major news events, candidate debates, and the like. It is not unusual for an organization such as CNN to commission a national poll on reactions to a president's speech and to air the results within a few hours or less. Use of *computer-assisted telephone interviewing (CATI)* techniques has boomed, with interviewers posted at terminals that dial the numbers and allow interviewers to enter answers as respondents give them. Computation of results is in effect on-line, speeding up the process even more.

Although telephone surveys do not allow the rapport of personal interviews, they do a better job of it than the far more impersonal mail surveys to be discussed below. The telephone questionnaire format does need to be relatively simple, however, with easy-to-read and comprehend questions and response categories. The most effective maximum length for telephone surveys is about fifteen minutes, and anything over twenty minutes can be quite wearing on respondents, risking lower-quality data and the respondent hanging up before completion of the survey. Increased uses of answering machines and call screening devices by the public adds to the response rate problems of using telephone surveys.

Mail-Administered Surveys.   Collecting public opinion data by mail surveys has long been derided as a last resort, often not worth the trouble. Although this is typically the cheapest method—printing and postal costs are all that is needed—response rates can border on the horrific. General population mail surveys have been known to achieve response rates of less than 5 percent, usually nowhere near the minimal 50 percent or so needed for any statistical acceptability. Indeed, some mail "surveys" are often nothing more than promotional gimmicks, such as the questionnaires sent out by candidates, officeholders, or special interest groups to "gauge" public opinion, when the real reason is to build public awareness or to raise money.

Nonetheless, using the mails to assess opinion has its legitimate place. Mail surveys can be quite effective in collecting data from smaller, more specialized population groups. (One example of such a group is college faculty, who routinely receive polls regarding their own areas of interest, academic policy, and student interests. Faculty typically respond in respectable numbers to these—whether this response is more a result of altruism, curiosity, compulsiveness, or self-interest is another issue.)

Physicians, civil servants, business executives, or just about any other occupational or interest segment can be successfully targeted—*as long as the survey topic is of relevance and interest to members of that particular group.* Such surveys also require careful planning and administration. Advance notices that the questionnaire is en route, careful explanation of survey purposes, and repeated mailings to nonrespondents are needed to gain respectable response rates. The added costs of such inducements can approach those of telephone surveys, or even small-sample personal interviews.

Mail surveys have the added advantage of allowing more complex questions than telephone surveys, provided that appropriate visual aids are used. Desktop publishing techniques can provide highly attractive and readable formats that add to a questionnaire's appeal.

Alternative Techniques.   Multiple data collection techniques are now more in use. For example, mail questionnaires might be sent out first, with a telephone follow-up to nonrespondents. Conversely, a telephone interview might be used to gather basic data and to try to talk the respondent into allowing a more detailed mail survey to be sent or a personal interview to be scheduled. Workplace-related interviews now depend more on fax machines and E-mail. Internet web pages gather data by counting hits as acknowledgments of interest or opinion.

Questionnaire Design

Writing appropriate questionnaire items requires solid understanding both of the survey's subject matter and of the respondents' views of the world and their verbal skills. On average, the general U.S. adult population has had about a year of college beyond high school and is unlikely to know as much as researchers do about any given subject area. Survey designers need to explain topics and options clearly, in everyday, user-friendly terms.

As an example of a not-so-user-friendly item, take this question: "Do you agree or disagree that U.S. foreign policy should give more sympathetic consideration than it has in the past to Bosnian Serb appeals for greater autonomy?" We can simplify this question into the following: "Do you agree or disagree that the United States should side more with the Bosnian Serbs?" This puts it into the type of everyday language that most respondents will more readily understand. However, it also blunts the subtleties of the issue. This is a common trade-off for survey researchers: precision of meaning versus getting the general message across to a broad audience (see Box 3.1).

This question in either its complex or more simple form is also a "true" opinion or attitudinal question, as opposed to knowledge or behavior questions. Such opinion items are often the most difficult kind to ask and produce the least reliable assessment of responses—unless they are very carefully worded and placed in a proper context. Many people have a tendency to give their opinions about virtually anything, no matter how much they may know or not know about it. A respondent could easily answer "agree" to the Bosnia question, yet know next to nothing about what U.S. Bosnia policy actually is. One way around this problem is to first ask questions determining how much respondents know about the issue; another is to describe the issue more fully before asking opinion questions so that all respondents share similar information before answering. Questions asking people what they know about an issue or about how they behave or act—as in voting or other forms of political participation—are usually easier to write, as well as to answer, and tend to be more valid and reliable than opinion questions.

For similar reasons, surveys should try to avoid hypothetical questionnaire items. Asking questions on the order of "What would you think if the U.S. invaded Ireland tomorrow" or "What would you do if you lost your job" often leads to highly speculative answers with little grounding in reality.

Even clear, simple, and specific items can lead to biased answers. A *leading* question such as "Do you agree that the property tax should be raised by only 1 percent to fund a new high school" will most likely generate more agreement than if worded "Do you agree or disagree . . . ," with the "only" dropped. So-called *double-barreled* questions are another common problem: "The United States would be better off cutting welfare spending and using the money saved training more police." Some people might agree with welfare cuts but not to fund more police; others might want more police but more welfare as well. The result is that the survey results will indicate more "no opinion" answers, more confused responses, and less-valid, misleading data overall.

Questions also need to be worded to avoid respondents' wanting to give socially desirable responses or answers that they think are more socially acceptable to the interviewer. A common technique is to list for the respondent a range of statements that "other people have made" about an issue and ask respondents to choose the one closest to their own views. This opens the range of "acceptable" responses for interviewees, as does assuring the respondent that there are no "right" or "wrong" answers to opinion questions.

Question order effects can be a problem as well. For example, beginning an interview by asking respondents whom they will vote for in an upcoming

---

Box 3.1   Questionnaire Wording and the Holocaust Denial Controversy

In 1992, a well-respected survey research firm, the Roper Organization, fielded a national survey on attitudes of Americans toward the Holocaust and its impact on Jews and on the subject of intolerance more generally. To assess knowledge of the Holocaust, or more precisely, belief that the German government under the Nazis had purposively killed several million Jews in the 1940s, Roper asked the following question: "The term Holocaust usually refers to the killing of millions of Jews in Nazi death camps during World War II. Does it seem possible or does it seem impossible to you that the Nazi extermination of the Jews never happened?"

The findings appeared surprising, if not shocking, to many—because 22 percent of the respondents said it was "possible" the mass killings had not happened, 12 percent said they "didn't know," and 65 percent said it was "impossible" that the event had not happened. That nearly one-fourth of U.S. adults denied that the Holocaust had happened and that nearly one-third either denied it or did not know whether it had happened or not raised serious questions about the quality of knowledge about recent history. It also raised concerns of an anti-Semitic undercurrent involving rumors being spread at the time by some white supremacist and other extremist groups that the Holocaust had indeed been a hoax perpetrated by Jewish groups to gain sympathy and political favor.

Although news of the findings made headlines and focused on the denial and ignorance of much of the public, other survey researchers keyed in on the confusing, double-negative wording of the question and its possible impact on the responses. Criticisms included that the question was misleading and too hypothetical or that some people might have been led to respond that "anything's possible" and that technically, the Jews had not been fully "exterminated," as the question may have implied.[1]

The Roper Organization immediately admitted these possible problems and worked with a larger research team to do a more definitive study of the issue.

---

election can force them into an attitudinal commitment for the rest of the questions: They may answer the remaining questions more in the way they think a supporter of that candidate should rather than as they would have ordinarily. Similarly, beginning an interview by asking respondents whether they had recently been victims of crime and then asking what they thought the most important problems facing the country were would likely bring the crime problem higher onto their issue agendas.

A key problem particular to opinion questions is to devise ones that adequately tap the range, depth, and complexity of public thinking about political issues. In many cases, we need to use more than single-item measures

(In fact, the question that was asked replaced an earlier version that was recognized as even more biased: "Does it seem possible to you that the Holocaust never happened?") The new study—and a number of others that followed up on the topic—demonstrated the way in which minor wording changes can influence responses to questionnaire items. The new items also restored some faith in the knowledge and values of the American public. A few examples follow, drawn from a detailed account of the controversy by Tom W. Smith.[2] In each case, the question is introduced by this sentence: "The Holocaust is a term used to describe the extermination of the Jews in World War Two."

"Some people have said it is possible it never actually happened. In your own mind, are you certain that the Nazi extermination of the Jews happened, or does it seem possible to you that it never happened?" (93 percent "certain it happened"; 4 percent "possible it never happened"; 4 percent "don't know")[3]

"Do you think the Nazi extermination of millions of Jews actually took place, or not?" (90 percent "yes, took place"; 4 percent mixed, maybe (volunteered); 3 percent "no, did not take place; 5 percent "don't know")[4]

"Do you doubt that the Holocaust actually happened, or not?" (9 percent "yes, doubt it"; 87 percent "no, don't doubt it"; 4 percent unsure, etc.)[5]

---

1. Tom W. Smith, "Review: The Holocaust Denial Controversy," *Public Opinion Quarterly* 59 (1995):269–295.
2. Ibid.
3. May 1993 Bruskin polling organization telephone survey; see Smith, "Review: The Holocaust Denial Controversy."
4. January 1994 CBS telephone survey; see Smith, "Review: The Holocaust Denial Controversy."
5. January 1994 Gallup telephone survey; see Smith, "Review: The Holocaust Denial Controversy."

of public opinion: Groups of items, often analyzed by highly sophisticated statistical techniques, may be needed to more fully appreciate the complexity of public viewpoints. One example involves a controversy over how to measure "latent opinions" regarding broad political value concepts such as "postmaterialism." Latent opinions are assumed to be core values that underlie more obvious and observable opinions about issues like welfare, affirmative action, and so forth. Such latent opinions are difficult to tap using single survey opinion questions, so multiple indicators or varied groups of questions that may at first seem quite unrelated are asked. Responses to those are then analyzed using sophisticated response clustering techniques to try to tease out the underlying concept. This issue and related ones, and some of the controversies over them, will be discussed in more detail in later chapters.

Two key summary concepts in questionnaire design are validity and reliability. *Validity* generally refers to how well the questions measure what they are supposed to measure. For example, if we want to find out whether a person plans on voting for the Democratic or the Republican candidate for governor, simply asking the respondent about party membership would not be too valid an indicator of the person's planned vote, given what we know about party crossover voting. A more valid indicator would be to directly ask for whom the respondent planned to vote; that measure would also likely become more valid the closer it was asked to election day. *Reliability*, however, refers to how stable or consistent a measure is in getting the same result when asked again and again over time. More precise, unambiguous questions are usually more reliable: Asking a person's birth date is apt to be a more reliable item than asking, say, how much that person agrees or disagrees on a ten-point scale with current U.S. policy toward welfare reform.

Interviewer training is also a critical ingredient for in-person and telephone surveys. Most reputable survey organizations maintain permanent staffs of experienced interviewers who are expert at eliciting both cooperation and answers that are as honest and unbiased as possible from respondents. The best interviewers act as professional communicators, or information brokers, between researcher and respondent—and *not* as persuaders, helpers, teachers, or confidants in their calls. Good interviewers are alert, interested, and appreciative of the respondent's time but do not approve or disapprove of answers or prompt or imply what answers are expected.

Issues in Survey Research

Survey research over the years has generally proven its value as a tool for better understanding mass social processes and as a device for more accurately describing public moods and behaviors with respect to politics, mass media, marketing, and lifestyle. As with any technique, inappropriate uses of it, and overreliance on it, can cause problems.

A major complaint against political uses of surveys is that pollsters can ask questions in biased or distorted ways—or use inappropriate samples—to get the answers they want to prove their own points. Hardly a major election campaign goes by without such charges being leveled at one candidate or another—and often there is at least a grain of truth in the charges. Most responsible news media now refuse to report polls unless they can include the exact questions used and provide detail on how the survey was carried out. Many journalism organizations refuse to publish results of any

---

Box 3.2   Push Polls

The 1992 and 1994 election campaigns saw an increased use of so-called push polls, or polls used by candidates or special interest groups to purposively promote their own agenda to respondents. More commonly, this takes the form of slamming the opposing candidate or viewpoint by asking questions that imply the opposition holds views that are generally unacceptable to voters.

An extreme example would be for Candidate A to conduct a phone survey that emphasized a question on the order of the following: "Candidate B (the opponent) has called for a federal law bringing back racial segregation in public schools. Do you agree with that position, disagree, or aren't you sure?" Obviously, the purpose is not to gather useful data but rather to use the phone poll format as a campaign technique to put out false and damaging information about the opposing candidate. Perhaps less offensive but equally disreputable from a professional polling perspective is using surveys that may ask some legitimate questions but that also promote the views of a given candidate. In either case, respondents are being misled as to the purpose of the survey.

Such uses of polls are difficult to track down, and candidates often deny any such doings. In truth, sometimes the line between data gathering and promotional efforts can be a fine one. Legitimate polls may provide some citizens with information about candidates they had not been aware of. The use of push polls may have declined in 1996 because of pressure from professional organizations such as the American Association for Public Opinion Research, which upholds strict standards against such practices by its members.

---

polls except their own or those of other news media or of relatively unbiased public agencies. A recent extension of this problem has been the rise of so-called "push polls," or telephone surveys on behalf of one candidate in which views of opposing candidates are purposively misrepresented to respondents (see Box 3.2). Consumers of polls should carefully look for exact questionnaire wording—and the nature of the sampling, response rate, and survey sponsorship—before putting too much stock in the findings of any study.

A broader issue is the reliance on survey data by policymakers in general—whether in government, private industry, or academia. Critics charge that too much dependence on surveys results in a leadership vacuum—with officeholders, for example, willing to recommend or do only what polls show that the public wants. Such dependence may reduce innovativeness in policy building or diminish leaders' willingness to recommend strategic but unpopular options.

In political campaigns, polls may well lead to candidates telling voters what they want to hear, as opposed to candidates revealing the truth of their own views, as will be discussed in Chapter 12. Still, in both of the above cases, policymakers and politicians at the least have access to a far broader spectrum of public views, far more than they would have listening only to their own advisers, lobbyists, and those few citizens who speak out at hearings and forums. Access to such information can enlighten judgment and lead to more effective communication with the public.

As a social research tool, surveys can also be faulted for turning too much attention to public opinion in the aggregate, with emphasis on mass social processes and without enough weight given to individual motivation and activity, and especially to the dynamics of smaller group interactions. As you will see, a central point of this book is that we need to take as holistic a view as possible of the public opinion environment. More studies now regard surveys as only one component of the research process and combine them with focus groups, content analyses, participant observation, and in some cases even intensive clinical psychological examinations. By taking this wider view, findings from surveys can be more validly interpreted in the full context of social behavior and interaction.

Focus Groups: Using Group Dynamics to Measure Public Opinion

Although survey methods continue to dominate public opinion research, alternative methodologies are also gaining wide acceptance. One reason for this is that researchers have come to recognize that since public opinion is complex and multifaceted, it is necessary to explore it using multiple methods. One methodology that is being rediscovered is focus group interviewing.[1] Focus groups are "carefully planned discussion[s] designed to obtain perceptions on a defined area of interest in a permissive, nonthreatening environment."[2] The roots of this method can be traced to sociologist Robert Merton's examination of propaganda during World War II, but it is a method of social inquiry that had been largely ignored in public opinion research. However, today focus groups are enjoying a modest resurgence, most notably in the areas of market research and campaign consulting but increasingly in journalism and academia as well.

Unlike survey methods that typically ask individual subjects to answer a series of closed-ended questions, focus groups involve open discussion among a group of subjects. The typical focus group discussion includes between six and ten participants, though as few as four and as many as twelve are not uncommon. Researchers vary considerably with respect to how many focus groups they conduct for particular projects. Participants are selected in a variety of ways, but unlike survey research, projects seldom strive for a true random sample of the target population. Most focus group projects include some form of standard paper-and-pencil questions, allowing, at a minimum, the collection of basic demographic and attitudinal information.

The discussions themselves follow a loosely structured protocol that a moderator uses as a guide, though this "script" is seldom stuck to completely. Conversations often take an unexpected but potentially valuable turn, and the moderator may decide to deviate from the protocol to pursue new terrain. Usually the protocol serves as a checklist to assure that by the discussion's end, all of the key points have been addressed. The typical focus group discussion lasts from one to two hours.

Individual groups are usually constructed so that participants share some specific demographic or attitudinal characteristic. This allows people to speak their mind without feeling intimidated or defensive. For example, in her analysis of attitudes toward gender roles, Roberta Sigel ran separate groups for men and women, also stratifying several groups further by age, class, and occupational status.[3] Participants in Pamela Conover, Ivor Crewe, and Donald Searing's study of perceptions of citizenship, discussed in more detail below, were stratified not only by citizenship (British or U.S.) but also by place of residence (rural or urban) and, in Britain, by social class.[4]

The structure of the focus group discussions has changed little from those conducted in earlier years by sociologist Robert Merton. Researchers attempt to put participants at ease by making the setting as natural and informal as possible. In the case of group meetings held in a public setting like a university, this usually means selecting a conference room that is comfortably appointed, providing refreshments, allowing people to move about with some freedom, and so forth. Sometimes, discussions are held in the home of a researcher or one of the participants.

Information generated by focus groups can be analyzed qualitatively (employing critical interpretation, as one might do with an in-depth interview) or quantitatively (through systematic content analysis, described in the next section). This information can stand alone as a way of providing insights into opinion formation and sometimes allows for cautious generalizations. Focus groups are also useful in conjunction with other methods such as participant observation, in-depth interviews, experiments, and surveys. These qualities make the focus group methodology well-suited to helping explore the complexities of public opinion by bridging the gap between more qualitative, interpretive methodologies and other more conventional social scientific methods. By offering some of the qualities of each, they are also ideal for studying the fluid and dialogic aspects of opinion formation.

It is also important to note that focus groups have certain limitations when compared to other methods of inquiry. The setting is less natural than participant observation. The researcher has less control than in an in-depth individual interview or an experiment. Results are less easily analyzed and generalized than in survey research. Nevertheless, focus groups have some significant advantages over these other methods. They allow one to examine the role of social interaction in opinion formation and expression. They combine the probing and flexibility of in-depth interviews with the ability to talk to a larger number of people. They help guard against research bias and shortsightedness by guaranteeing that interaction is not exclusively with the researcher alone and by allowing enough open-endedness for unanticipated views to emerge from the discussion. And they strike a compromise between the generalizability of quantitative analysis and the depth of qualitative analysis.

Focus groups are particularly well suited to examine the fluidity and dynamics of attitude and opinion formation. They also allow one to examine politics in a communal setting and to focus on how citizens interact with each other in discussing public issues: "The hallmark of focus groups is the explicit use of the group interaction to produce data and insights that would be less accessible without the interaction found in the group."[5] As focus group research has become more common, the kinds of questions for which they are suitable has become clearer.

What Focus Groups Tell Us About Public Opinion

Focus groups have been used to address a wide range of substantive topics. Despite this diversity, however, focus group findings are quite similar in their conclusions about the general process of opinion formation and expression. These conclusions suggest that public opinion is exceptionally dynamic and complex, that opinions are constructed and reconstructed in ways that make them impossible to separate from the context from which they emerge, and that opinions emerge from a synthesis of personal, social, and mass-mediated information. Perhaps most important, in contrast to much survey research, focus group research paints a picture of a thoughtful citizenry. When it comes to the formation of public opinion, focus groups indicate that citizens can be—with some prompting—active, critical, and reasonably sophisticated. Focus group research does not always challenge the conclusions drawn from more traditional research methods, but it does illuminate and enrich them in valuable and unique ways. In fact, focus group methodologies have been used in at least two different ways in public opinion research: as a check on or supplement to traditional survey methods and as a method that can stand on its own and cast light on aspects of public opinion formation ignored by more traditional methods.

Supplementing Traditional Survey Methods.   Among the first researchers to reintroduce focus groups to the study of political psychology were Roberta Sigel and Cliff Zukin. They conducted six focus groups on the topic of gender relations. The groups were intended to serve two related purposes: to help in the construction of closed-ended survey questions measuring attitudes about gender relations and gender roles and to generate hypotheses to be tested with more quantitative techniques. The focus groups proved useful for these purposes, but Sigel also found them helpful in fleshing out the findings of subsequent quantitative analyses: "Notwithstanding their limitations, focus group observations . . . greatly enriched our understanding of men's and women's perceptions of gender relations. In fact, we found them to 'deliver' much more than we had anticipated. Originally conceived mainly as guides to questionnaire construction, it soon become obvious that they had an independent contribution to make."[6] There are other examples of using focus groups to supplement quantitative projects. For example, Conover, Crewe, and Searing, in their comparative study of citizenship, used focus groups as a "critical first step" in a larger survey research project.

Although they have their own potential for bias, focus groups do provide some checks on the danger, found in both depth interviews and survey questions, that the researcher's prior expectations will unduly influence the expression of public opinion. As Conover, Crewe, and Searing note, the focus group format assures that "participants talk to one another in their own language, rather than simply reacting to the questions and language of an interviewer in a one-to-one situation."[7] This, in turn, increases the likelihood of new, often unexpected conclusions emerging from focus group analyses.

The Unique Contributions of Focus Groups.   The uses described above are enough to recommend focus groups as a method of inquiry. However, their greatest utility lies less in what they have in common with other methods than in what is unique about them. Focus groups can illuminate aspects of public opinion that are less accessible through traditional methods. In particular, focus groups are valuable in revealing the process of opinion formation, in providing glimpses of usually latent aspects of this process, and in demonstrating the social nature of public opinion.

Opinions, from this perspective, are not fixed constructs that are "stored" and "retrieved" like data in a computer. Rather, they are continuously constructed through cognitive processes involving a myriad of complex schemata. Yet in spite of creative research designs and sophisticated data analyses, traditional methods of measuring opinions are not always able to capture this dynamism. For example, closed-ended survey items often reify opinions by forcing respondents to present them as self-contained and preexisting objects. The cross-sectional nature of most surveys adds to this static quality. Even panel studies and experimental designs encourage a mechanistic mode, in which opinions are measured, new information is introduced, and opinions are remeasured. Focus groups, by contrast, can be "catalyst[s] for the individual expression of latent opinion . . . for free-associating to life."[8] By essentially forcing people to "think out loud," they become windows through which to observe the process of opinion formation.

Researchers who use focus groups often do so because this method is suited to modeling these social processes. For example, Conover, Crewe, and Searing argue convincingly that given their interest in "discovering the commonplace meaning of political terms" such as citizenship, focus groups were an appropriate choice of method because they allow social scientists to study the actual language and categories people use in discussing political issues related to citizenship.[9] Tamar Liebes and Elihu Katz also consider the conversational and social nature of focus groups to be their greatest asset. In particular, they argue that focus groups are effective in illustrating "the processes of collective meaning-making" because they permit tentative interpretations to be floated by someone and shot down by someone else, because they permit bullies to try to impose themselves on the others, because expert opinion is sought out for guidance, and because interpretations are molded and twisted to fit the underground loves and hates that permeate interpersonal relations. This is what happens in life. They further argue that focus groups succeed because they replicate the kinds of exchanges that citizens actually have: "We were, in effect, operationalizing the assumption that the small-group discussion following the broadcast is a key to understanding the mediating process via which a program such as this enters into the culture."[10]

There are limits to the comparison of focus groups to "real life," however. As William Gamson correctly notes, "Most people do not spontaneously sit down with their friends and acquaintances and have a serious discussion for more than an hour on different issues in the news."[11] Gamson goes on to compare the exchanges that occur in focus groups with two other forms of discourse. Public discourse involves "speaking to the gallery," whereas sociable interaction is the informal, private conversation that occurs among friends, family members, and the like. Focus groups as usually constructed in academic research are a blend of these two types of communication. On the one hand, participants know that they are "speaking for the record" and that their views are being recorded, and thus they are being recorded and being expressed for an academic "gallery." On the other hand, the conversational format, the familiarity of participants with each other, and the relaxed setting in which they take place give the discussions elements of sociable interaction as well. Gamson labels this blend of public and private exchange "sociable public discourse."

This semipublic nature of focus group discussions may make them problematic for studying some kinds of discourse. However, though admittedly artificial, they are often less contrived than most experimental or survey-based research. Consider, for example, the dynamics of a telephone interview: At one moment, a person is sitting at dinner, watching TV, conversing with family members, and so forth and the next, engaged in a formal interview with a stranger answering questions about a variety of issues with no time to think about them. In addition, it is arguable that the way people talk about politics is closer to sociable public discourse than to either public discourse or sociable interaction. This is especially true when it occurs outside the home but holds to some degree regardless of where the conversation occurs or what the relationship of the people conversing. Rather, it is driven by the public nature of the topic. Viewed in this light, focus groups seem an especially appropriate method for studying how people talk—and therefore think—about politics (see Box 3.3).

Focus Groups and the Construction of Public Opinion

Our last example of focus group research draws on Michael Delli Carpini and Bruce Williams's exploration of the role of television in shaping discourse about public issues.[12] As a way of demonstrating the utility of focus groups for exploring the dynamics of public opinion formation, we focus here on two observations that emerged from their studies. The first is the fluid, often inconsistent nature of public opinion and the ways in which people construct rather than retrieve their views on complex issues. And the second is the role of the mass media, especially television, in this process of opinion formation.

Delli Carpini and Williams conclude from their close reading of the focus group transcripts that people regularly construct rather than retrieve their views on complex issues. The focus group methodology was central to this observation in several ways. Freed from the forced constraints of closed-ended surveys and from the self-consciousness of the one-on-one interviews, the contextual, fluid, and often inconsistent nature of opinions was presented in bold relief. And although this inconsistency partially reflects the participants' lack of information, interest, and so forth, the transcripts make clear that it also reflects the "inherent contestability" of most important public issues. Examining the complete set of comments made by a single participant regarding a particular topic demonstrated that even the most thoughtful citizens express views that are contradictory. Indeed, often the most consistent views were expressed by those who clearly were uninterested in and unreflective about the issues under discussion.

It was common for the same person to express opinions at different points in the conversation that, when placed back to back, appear incompatible. For example, consider the following two comments by one subject (Kara): "I think it definitely is [possible to protect the environment in today's world]. I mean, to think there's all these big rains and all this big money for making things, surely they can come up with some way to make them in a safe manner, or to protect the public, or the land or animals." Yet later in the conversation, she says: "There's just a lot of other stuff you

---

Box 3.3   An Illustration of Focus Group Research

Like many other researchers, William Gamson uses groups as a method for studying the interplay of mass-mediated and interpersonal communications. Gamson argues that despite survey results documenting low levels of political knowledge, people are neither "passive" nor "dumb." Rather, they "read media messages in complicated and sometimes unpredictable ways, and draw heavily on other resources as well in constructing meaning."[1] To demonstrate this active negotiation process and explore implications, Gamson conducted thirty-seven "peer group conversations." He was interested in the way "working people"—a term that emerged from the participants' own self-references—talk about politics and how talk is translated into the potential for collective political action. The 188 individuals who participated in his peer group discussions were about equally split between men and women and between whites and blacks.

Drawing on social movement theory, Gamson argues that for citizens to turn "talk into action," they need "collective action frames."[2] These frames allow groups to see that an injustice has occurred, that they have the power—the agency—to address the injustice, and that they have a clear identity that distinguishes "us," the victims, from "them," the perpetrators. The mass media are obviously critical in determining how public issues are framed, and based on an extensive content analysis of several different news media, Gamson concludes that the extent to which the media use the frames of injustice, agency, and identity varies significantly from issue to issue. He also finds that the extent to which citizens use these frames in their own discourse is connected to the prevalence of these frames in the media.

More interesting, however, is his finding that this connection between media coverage and citizens' opinions is much looser and more complex than a simple persuasion or agenda-setting model would anticipate. Although often unable to construct their own injustice frames, citizens were able to resist some of those constructed by the media. For example, Gamson found that the media often presented the Japanese as the source of injustice regarding America's industrial problems. However, citizens seldom followed this cue, tending instead to discuss the Japanese with great admiration.

---

have to deal with . . . I mean, you would just have to take over the world pretty much, it would have to be every person in the United States, every company, every—I just don't think it would be possible [to protect the environment in today's world] . . . I hate to be Miss Negative, but I just don't think so." What is Kara's view of the possibility of addressing the nation's problems? Delli Carpini and Williams argue that Kara's "true" opinions do not reside in one or the other of her statements. Rather, her opinions are to be found in the full set of statements made about a particular issue and can

Gamson, like others, supports his conclusions through a combination of tables, verbal summaries, and direct quotes from transcripts. Through a careful reading of the transcripts, Gamson has discovered that in discussing public issues, citizens draw on a much wider range of media discourses than the news and therefore have a somewhat wider range of frames upon which to draw. For example, in discussing affirmative action, individuals in several groups referred to public service advertisements they had seen (for example, to the United Negro Fund's slogan "A mind is a terrible thing to waste"). Similarly, in discussing nuclear power, the movies *Silkwood* and *The China Syndrome* were both referenced to make points.

Besides the media, citizens drew upon two additional "conversational resources" for construction-shared frames: "experiential knowledge" and "popular wisdom." Experiential knowledge was based on personal experiences or the experiences of relatives, friends, coworkers, and so forth. Popular wisdom transcended personal experience and was based on cultural "truisms" to be accepted at face value. They were often introduced or concluded with phases such as "As everyone knows" or "It's human nature." Establishing shared frames from discussing public issues allowed group members to find a common language, but it did not mean that the conversations were always consensual.

Gamson concludes that although the working people in his groups generally lacked political consciousness, they did have "the elements necessary to develop [it]." Further, the more participants could draw on integrated resources to frame their discussions, the better able they were to develop the collective action frames necessary for political consciousness. It is Gamson's reasonable suspicion that frames based on integrated strategies are also the most robust and are thus resistant to shifting media frames. And although the ability to draw on such an integrated strategy varies, Gamson argues that "media dependence . . . is only partial and is heavily influenced by the issue under discussion."[3]

---

1. William Gamson, *Talking Politics* (Cambridge: Cambridge University Press, 1992), p. 6.
2. Ibid., pp. 6–7.
3. Ibid., p. 17.

be understood only in the specific context in which they are made. More important, they argue that citizens play an active, if limited, role in the construction of these opinions and do so in part through ongoing conversations with other people and the mass media.[13]

At the same time that subjects recognized their dependence on the media, they often seemed troubled and ambivalent about the potential such dependence has for selectively shaping their perception of the importance of various political issues. Although the media may set the agenda, the public's concern over this process is often overlooked by researchers using more traditional methodologies, as is revealed in the following quote from the participant Mark:

> You know, I think that, in a way, most everybody says that we're definitely concerned, I mean, I think I'm concerned, but then on the other hand, I think I spend very little time thinking about it until I see something like this [gestures to the blank screen] or I see the oil wells burning out of control or something to bring it home . . . I think we need to have more hard facts put before us. I think we need to be bombarded with more things to make us think about it and hopefully therefore to make us act.[14]

Some subjects moved beyond simple ambivalence to an understanding of the reasons for the shifting nature of media coverage. Such sophisticated understandings pen up the possibility of maintaining a critical distance between the media's definition of what is important and other hierarchies of importance. As the participant Paul said:

> One problem with the media is that . . . if they talk about some issue then two weeks later if it's not changed, they really don't want to do the story again . . . They don't want to do the same thing over and over, they think the viewers are going to get bored and change to something else. I wonder if the media's attention to environmental concerns is going to be fad like and then they're going to find something else to focus on six months form now. That can be a problem . . . when you involve the media.[15]

The Focus Group Alternative

The traditional survey methods are valuable tools for public opinion research. However, these methods, like any attempt to simplify something as complex as human thought and action, also miss a good deal of what is important in the formation and expression of public opinion. Focus groups offer an alternative method that, either in conjunction with more traditional methods or on their own, help avoid the oversimplification of these cognitive, social, and political processes.

Ultimately, this is more than an issue of methodology. One might argue that what survey research treats as "public opinion" might better be termed "private opinion." Citizens are viewed as isolated, individual decisionmakers consuming information and privately choosing at specific points in time among competing elites, parties, or ideas. In this "citizen as consumer" metaphor, politics is a marketplace (or more accurately, a mail order catalogue or home shopping network), and opinions are the currency with which public goods are purchased.

In contrast, focus group research emphasizes the inherently ambiguous nature of politics, leading to a significantly different conceptualization of public opinion than the one that emerges from mainstream research. Focus group studies assume that public opinion is about public issues that are discussed in public. It is through "conversations" that political opinions are continuously created and recreated. The need to consider seriously the position of others is what distinguishes private life from public life and private opinion from public opinion. Focus groups represent a methodology ideally suited to study these conversational aspects of public opinion.

Experimental Methods and Opinion Research

Since the 1940s, psychologists with an interest in public opinion have employed laboratory and field experiments in an attempt to understand political attitude change among citizens. Some of the earliest and most interesting work along these lines was conducted by a team of psychologists led by Carl I. Hovland and commissioned by the U.S. Army during World War II. Psychologists were asked to evaluate a series of films, produced by the American filmmaker Frank Capra to train American soldiers, to see whether these movies did influence enlistees. Capra had been asked to make the films, called the *Why We Fight* series, in order to boost the confidence of soldiers and educate them about the political importance of the war effort. Hovland and his associates took the opportunity to explore important issues in psychological theory and, at the same time, provide a "nuts and bolts" assessment of the films' effectiveness. As in many experiments, the researchers divided the soldiers into two groups—an "experimental group" and a "control group." As those familiar with psychological experiments know, an experimental group receives the "treatment" or "stimulus" of interest to researchers—in this case, the Capra films under evaluation. The control group does not see the films. Both groups in this series of experiments were given questionnaires before and after the days the films were actually shown—although remember that only the experimental group watched them. Hovland and his colleagues found that the films did indeed have an effect on these men, who would be risking their lives in the Atlantic and Pacific theaters of battle. The films were most effective in teaching soldiers about the events leading up to the war. Yet the effects were disappointing on the whole: The films did not boost the motivation levels of the men who would fight. Why no effects on motivation were found is a complex issue, tied to both the experimental design and historical circumstance. Nonetheless, psychologists were inspired to try and figure out how mass media might change attitudes, and they focused on the laboratory as a site for such studies.[16]

These days, political psychologists still conduct experimental research in an attempt to understand how people form their opinions and how these opinions might be manipulated. For example, Shanto Iyengar and Donald

Kinder have conducted laboratory experiments to see whether media can effectively "prime" or stimulate thought about issues in the minds of participants. They have also explored whether media can force people to think about certain issues as more important than others ("agenda-setting effects"). Their findings generally support the notion that media are highly effective in shaping the nature of individual cognition toward political leaders, events, and issues. The Iyengar and Kinder experiments are part of a long history in mass communication research, but they are far more sophisticated than the early wartime studies. Psychologists have become much more careful about controlling the experimental setting and designing the procedures of the experiments.[17] And perhaps it is valuable to quote Iyengar and Kinder about the value of experimentation. In the passage that follows, they emphasize issues of control and also of "random assignment"— the process of mixing up people across control and treatment groups so that these groups match each other in terms of demographic and attitudinal composition:

> For us, the essence of the true experiment is control. Experiments of the sort we have undertaken here are distinguished from other systematic empirical methods in the special measure of control they give to the investigator. In the first place, the experimenter *creates* the conditions under investigation, rather than waiting for them to occur naturally. In the second place, the experimenter *randomly assigns* individuals to those conditions, thereby superseding natural processes of selection. By creating the conditions of interest, the experimenter holds extraneous factors constant and ensures that individuals will encounter conditions that differ only in theoretically decisive ways. By assigning individuals to conditions randomly, the experimenter can be confident that any resulting differences between individuals assigned to varying conditions must be caused by differences in the conditions themselves.[18]

In Iyengar and Kinder's experiments, the researchers show their groups of participants a variety of news stories in order to manipulate the ideas and attitudes of citizens.

Iyengar has also conducted further research on the nature of television news itself and how it frames political issues. In particular, he uses content analytic and experimental procedures to demonstrate that television news stories can be either "thematic" or "episodic." Thematic news frames highlight larger issues and general trends, using analysis to extend the viewer's understanding of a political issue. Many news stories, however, tend to be episodic, concentrating on particular life stories of individual citizens in order to illustrate a social problem or trend. Unfortunately, Iyengar argues, although episodic frames are entertaining, they often cause audiences of such stories to "blame the victim"—to hold individuals and not political leaders responsible for a social problem. Take the issue of unemployment, for example. Journalists have a choice of many news frames. They can do a very analytical segment on unemployment trends and data, emphasizing policy change. Or they might focus on the vivid story of one unemployed homeless man in New York City. The former news frame enables viewers to think about public policy on unemployment, whereas the latter news frame plays to viewers' emotions and focuses them on the plight of one individual. Which is more educational for citizens? And which sort of story enables them to assess political options more effectively? These are interesting questions, and Iyengar demonstrates how they can be explored through laboratory experimentation.[19]

Some experimental projects focus on the effects of particular sorts of media content (e.g., the frames of news stories), but others concentrate on the media technology itself. For example, W. Russell Neuman, Marion Just, and Ann Crigler have conducted experiments to find out whether citizens learn more about political issues from television, newsmagazines, or newspapers. They found that their experimental subjects gained more knowledge about issues from television and magazine news reports than from newspapers. This finding may be rooted in the different journalistic techniques used by reporters for different media, or it may have something to do with the way people actually *use* media—the way these various sources for news fit into peoples' lives and daily information-gathering patterns. Regardless, experiments can help researchers understand the ways that media formats influence political thinking, in addition to helping them study content itself.[20]

In all of the experiments mentioned, researchers were very cautious about maintaining both "internal" and "external" validity. These are scholarly terms, describing crucial criteria for good experiments. Experimental procedures must measure the concepts they are *intended* to measure (internal validity). Yet strong experiments must also *simulate* aspects of the world outside the laboratory by making stimulus materials that are professionally produced and by making sure that the experimental "protocol" (what the subjects must do) is a reasonable imitation of real life. For example, in Iyengar and Kinder's work, the researchers were sure to produce news programs (editing together existing news stories) that looked professional. And they made the laboratory more like a living room than a sterile experimental environment so that subjects felt comfortable. The arrangement is not quite like watching television at home, but at least some of the tension created by being in an experiment is reduced.

Yet there are other experiments in attitude formation and public opinion as well that are not necessarily keyed to media or how journalists present the world. One example is Kathleen M. McGraw and Clark Hubbard's work on persuasion. They were interested in how people process communications from public officials—particularly the way people accept or fail to accept politicians' accounts of their actions in the legislature. They found that citizens' predispositions and characteristics influence the ways they "read" persuasive accounts of their leaders. In these experiments, subjects were randomly assigned to various groups and given materials containing persuasive communications as well as a battery of tests about their own knowledge levels, sophistication, and personal characteristics. This sort of research is very important because it tests hypotheses that rhetoricians have generated for centuries. Since the time of the ancient Greek city-states, leaders and scholars have pondered the nature of political persuasion: Which messages persuade which segments of the population and why? Rhetoricians have done an excellent job in detailing the different forms political speeches can take, but we still need more research on the effects of political talk. The laboratory is one environment where researchers can control what people see or hear and then measure their responses to these stimulus materials. Hence, public opinion formation is studied *in process*: Experimentalists can observe effects very closely and very rigorously.[21]

There is one last sort of experiment in the area of public opinion that should be mentioned in this very brief look at some experimental designs. Some researchers have combined the idea of an experiment with survey research, creating multiple forms of a survey or survey question in order to see whether such manipulation changes the sorts of opinions citizens express. Some of the best work in this area has been conducted by Kinder and Lynn M. Sanders. In their work on race and racial prejudice, they demonstrate how the frame of a survey question affects people's answers to that question. Although the nature of the answers to any question is tied in part to a respondent's background and attitudes, the frame of the question still affects the kinds of opinions they give. Kinder and Sanders focus on affirmative action and on welfare, documenting how the rhetorical nature of a question—the words and phrases used—tend to stimulate people to think in particular ways about those issues.[22]

The advantages of experimentation are very clear. Experiments enable the researcher to have close control over the project and the subjects. It is the researcher who determines the subject pool, the sorts of procedures followed by subjects, and the exact timing of attitude measurement. And it is also important that because so much control is possible, researchers can draw inferences about "causal order" of variables. This is difficult to do. We always wonder, for example, whether conservative talk programming makes people more conservative, or whether conservatives are simply drawn to conservative programming. Media effects such as these may be easier to study in the controlled situation of the lab than they are outside the lab, where an enormous number of events cloud our vision of particular communication processes. On the down side, experiments tend to have very narrow foci and can only take into account a limited number of variables at a time. Internal and external validity often present problems, and there are also challenges associated with what we call "demand characteristics." Were the experimental subjects somehow able to figure out the hypotheses of the researchers? If they do figure out the hypotheses, in either a specific manner or a more vague one, this is a dangerous occurrence: Experimental subjects tend to want to help and to please the researcher, so they may answer questions dishonestly just to be polite and cooperative. This sort of effect is to be avoided at all costs, of course, since experimental researchers are looking for people's honest opinions. The final problem with experiments is that they tend to document short-term effects only. Experimental subjects are queried either right after the experiment or (in rare cases) a few weeks later. But researchers rarely know whether a persuasive communication, news program, or political advertisement has long-term effects. Do the effects still hold long after the experimental subjects have left the lab? This is one of the central challenges of experimental work in the area of public opinion.

Content Analysis of Mass Media: "Archives" of Public Opinion

When we think about measuring public opinion, we usually turn to research methods that ask citizens how they feel about a particular social or political issue. This seems a most direct and efficient way to evaluate the public mood. Yet as we have seen, both survey research and focus group testing—two popular methods for measuring public opinion—are problematic: How one asks a question, the mood state of respondents, whether the sample is a representative one, and a variety of other factors make such research challenging for students of public opinion. One way to measure public opinion that does not appear as often as polls or focus groups is *content analysis,* which is the systematic (and usually quantitative) assessment of media texts. Media researchers have performed such analyses on all sorts of mass-produced communications over the years—magazine and newspaper articles, advertisements, television programming, comic strips, radio talk shows, company newsletters, and even forms of dialogue on the Internet. Some scholars believe that content analysis simply demonstrates what the producer of that content (e.g., a journalist or a screenwriter) thinks. Yet we believe that media content represents much more than one individual's view of the world: The content of the mass media can reveal valuable evidence about public opinion.

Popular texts are popular because they somehow resonate with cultural norms, values, or sentiments. In a capitalist economy such as our own, it is crucial that mass media products resonate with public opinion: If they fail to appeal, they will not survive in a highly competitive world of images and discourse. Although we believe there are multiple ways to understand the public mood, it is often helpful to focus on the mass media texts that citizens "consume" during a typical day. If we can figure out what people like to read, listen to, and watch, we will have a good sense of their attitudes and opinions on public affairs.

It may seem obvious that you immediately learn something about citizens by knowing their public affairs media habits. If a friend reads the *National Review* and *Commentary*, for example, we know that he or she is probably politically conservative. Alternately, another friend might subscribe to the *Nation* or *In These Times*. Such media consumption indicates that person's leftist or possibly liberal approach to the world. Yet beyond media consumption that directly focuses on public affairs, it is also useful to study the more entertainment-oriented texts that citizens are drawn to. In the early 1990s, for example, a situation comedy called *Roseanne* focused on the problems of a working-class family in the Midwest. The program was extraordinarily popular, and audiences found it hilarious. There were many characters on the program who were created solely to elicit laughs from the audience. Yet the various episodes of *Roseanne* also touched upon some of the most controversial social and political issues of our time. Among these issues were the role of unions, economic worries faced by small businesses, abortion, and the rights of homosexuals.

Content analysis of texts—whether they are newspaper reports on a global conference or hilarious situation comedies—is complex and demands much subtlety and care. There are critics who believe that texts are "read" in so many different ways by so many different people that finding meaning about the public's mood in such texts is impossible. Yet the large majority of media and public opinion scholars feel that this sort of research is both possible and enormously revealing. Content analysis is very labor intensive and often very costly. Yet it provides rich, textured public opinion data that students of politics and social life find useful and enlightening.

Content analysis is often called an "unobtrusive" or "nonreactive" way to measure public attitudes. It is a method that does not involve a conversation with citizens and therefore does not "intrude" on their time or space. Content analysis does not cause people to "react" in particular ways that may affect the research project. There are many advantages to unobtrusive measurement, since it avoids the inevitable problems that a researcher must face when interviewing members of the public. In other words, certain sorts of "errors" that are often unknowingly introduced into research by respondents and interviewers are avoided altogether.

How Is Content Analysis Done?

In this chapter, we concentrate on systematic, quantitative content analysis. There are other forms of textual analysis that involve interpretive tools from the humanities—literary criticism and rhetoric, in particular. Here, however, we focus on methods most commonly used by communication researchers, political scientists, and sociologists who study media content in hopes of learning about public opinion.

There are normally nine steps in the process of content analysis. At every stage in this process, the researcher must make crucial decisions. As long as those decisions can be justified through logical argumentation, they are acceptable.

Step 1: Select a Topic. The first stage in a content analysis project is the selection of a topic. Topics are diverse and can represent all kinds of scholarly inquiry. Suppose we chose drug legalization as our topic, in an attempt to understand public opinion about this fascinating debate in American politics. The topic comes up on a regular basis, and a variety of intellectuals, policymakers, and citizens have debated it in many different forums.

Step 2: Develop a Hypothesis. Before collecting data, one must have some distinct hypotheses that can be tested through content analysis. In the case of drug legalization, one might put forth the following two hypotheses: (1) "Advocates for drug legalization tend to receive negative coverage for their positions in the mass media," and, relatedly, (2) "Advocates for drug legalization get less coverage than those who advocate tougher antidrug laws and strict enforcement of present laws." By confirming or disproving these hypotheses, we learn about public opinion: If drug legalization is generally demeaned in the popular press as a policy option, it is likely that a large and influential segment of the population shares this negative stance toward the proposition.

Step 3: Operationalize Your Terms. There are key terms in these two hypotheses that need to be operationalized or defined before content analysis can begin. How shall we define "negative," for example? One way would be to list negative adjectives that might be used to describe a legalization policy, such as "unworkable" or "dangerous." After creating such a list of negative terms, along with a list of positive ones, the researcher knows exactly what to look for when beginning the actual analysis of text. In terms of amount of attention received by advocates for drug legalization, one could count how much space (newspaper columns in inches or number of minutes during a television news broadcast) is actually devoted to one position versus the other.

Step 4: Decide on a Sample. If we were interested in coverage of the drug legalization debate during a particular year, we could not look at every article published or every news broadcast aired that year. This would be far too time-consuming and is not necessary in order to test our hypotheses. Instead, we could choose a random sample of these texts that represents the discourse more generally. Just as 1,000 people are often polled in order to represent national public opinion, a small number of texts can be analyzed and used as a basis for broader generalization. In the case of drug legalization, we might want to randomly select 50 or 60 media texts, from a variety of sources: newsmagazines, news broadcasts, and large regional and national newspapers, as well as specialty public affairs magazines (e.g., the *New Republic*, *Harper's*, and so on).

Step 5: Construct a Coding Sheet. A simple coding sheet is necessary, if the analyst is to organize the data properly. In our example (Figure 3.1), the coding sheet filled out for each text (newspaper article, for example) is rather simple.

This coding sheet is just one possible scheme for analyzing the articles. Before the research begins, the analyst should collect a small sample of texts and try the coding scheme first, to see whether it will be helpful in assessing the larger sample of articles. In the coding sheet in Figure 3.1, there may be a problem with "negative statements made by the journalist." It could be the case that an article contains a large number of negative statements about legalization, but they are not made by the journalist: The journalist's sources make the negative statements, which have simply been quoted in the article. If this is the case, one might need to develop two questions—one that assesses journalists' statements and one that assesses the statements of their sources.

Step 6: Train Coders. It is best that a researcher get help in coding the articles in the sample. In the ideal case, the researcher who draws up the hypotheses does not in fact code the individual articles or news broadcasts. In any case, those who are evaluating each text must be trained: They must know what they are looking for. What is a negative statement and what is a positive one? Coders must be in agreement about these basic issues if they are to use the same tools and achieve consistency.

Step 7: Perform Coding. Coding may sound simple, once the difficult work of developing hypotheses and coding sheets is finished. Yet there are many conflicts among coders that arise during the study, and those conflicts in analyzing texts must be discussed. Often, a coding scheme must be changed mid-analysis because there is too much conflict among different coders evaluating the same texts, and researchers must go back and recode the sample.

Step 8: Analyze Data and Calculate "Intercoder Reliability."° After the coding sheets are filled out, the analyst must see how much agreement or disagreement existed among the coders. There are a variety of ways to figure this out, and there are many books that contain useful discussions of

Coding Form

Name of coder _____

Text (publication/date/page) _____

Number of positive and negative statements made by journalist about drug legalization:

Positive _____

Negative _____

Number of paragraphs describing the prolegalization position vs. the antilegalization position:

Prolegalization _____

Antilegalization _____

FIGURE 3.1   Sample Content Analysis Coding Form

this elementary statistical calculation. High intercoder reliability means that a researcher has tested the hypotheses with confidence. Low intercoder reliability means that there was so much disagreement about the coding scheme that the study was not a strong test of those hypotheses.

Step 9: Report Results.   This is by far the most enjoyable part of content analysis. The researcher can determine whether the hypotheses were confirmed and how strongly they were supported (see Box 3.4). If it is the case that those who advocate drug legalization get a tiny proportion of coverage and that the coverage is largely negative, this would reflect the general public bias against such a solution to our illegal drug consumption and trafficking problems.

Problems Associated with Content Analysis

There are many benefits in performing content analysis of popular texts in order to understand public opinion. It is subtle, unobtrusive, and provides rich information about Americans' mood and values. Yet there are some problems associated with the method as well, and these problems (like the problems with survey research and focus group testing) must be acknowledged by the researcher, since they present limitations to a study conducted this way.

First, and most obvious, a researcher must be very cautious when putting together the sample of texts. If one "oversamples" from conservative or liberal magazines, the results of the content analysis will be suspect. Much

Box 3.4   An Example of Content Analysis

One interesting study of media content took up the issue of environmental waste. In an attempt to build theory about the news media, scholars W. Lance Bennett and Regina Lawrence looked for evidence of concern about the environment in the *New York Times*. They produced the following chart, which demonstrates how dramatically the mentions of words like "recycling" and "environment" increased from the early 1980s through 1990. One might argue that the growing number of mentions of such environmentalism "keywords" is evidence that the public was becoming more concerned with environmental issues and that concern of the public is reflected in the pages of the *New York Times*.

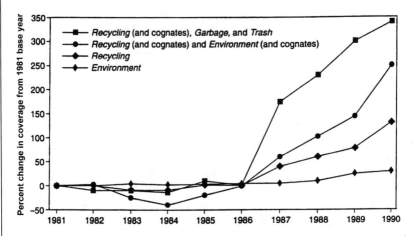

Creating a News Icon: Changing Rates of Word Use. SOURCE: W. Lance Bennett and Regina G. Lawrence, "News Icons and the Mainstreaming of Social Change," *Journal of Communication* 45 (Summer 1995), figure 1, p. 32.

thought should be given to the range of texts one collects, since a severely biased sample will yield useless results. The same problem is faced by survey researchers: The citizens who serve as respondents in their studies must represent the larger population on all relevant dimensions.

Second, the researcher must be sure to develop a coding scheme that is objective and fair. A coding scheme can reflect a researcher's biases, and this is dangerous. For example, a researcher who personally feels that drug legalization is a useful and necessary policy might slant the coding scheme in order to find more positive coverage than really exists. This biasing of coding schemes almost always happens without the researcher realizing it.

The third and most problematic limitation of content analysis is that it focuses on the *manifest* and not the *latent* content of media. Content analysis can only tell the researcher about surface-level meanings of media text—what *can* be readily counted, not the deep, often unconscious effects that a newspaper article or television program could have on a reader or viewer. In politics, it is reasonable to measure manifest content, since that is the content most often prompting policy debate, lobbying, and citizen participation. However, there is a feeling among many communication researchers that visual content of media may have subtle effects on the audience and that these effects are not readily noticed in the evaluation of manifest content of media. Research on how visual imagery represents and affects the public mood is only in its infancy, however, so media scholars have not as yet developed methods for coding latent meanings of visual content.

Conclusion

This chapter has explored four of the most common means for assessing public opinion, but there are others as well—analysis of election results or movement of the stock market, for example. The student of public opinion must decide upon the most effective means for understanding popular moods, and the tools chosen must fit the research question at hand. Do keep in mind that all the methods discussed here assume certain conceptions or dimensions of public opinion. In conducting a poll, a researcher is arguing that public opinion can reasonably be defined as the aggregation of individual opinions, anonymously and scientifically collected. Yet if focus groups are used, the researcher wants to witness the *processual* nature of public opinion: how people develop opinions and change them, especially when they articulate their opinions in the presence of others. The survey researcher understands that a respondent's opinions have been influenced by others as well (in conversations before the survey), but the focus group researcher wants to watch how those opinions are formed. All of the approaches to understanding public opinion discussed in this chapter are valid, if used with care and rigor. And it is important to note that they are not mutually exclusive. In fact, the best research project would evaluate public opinion using multiple methods. But this is often unnecessary and also quite expensive, so researchers must make the best choices they can, based upon their theoretical concerns, the possibilities for collecting data, and budgetary constraints.

Notes

1. Much of this section is based upon Michael X. Delli Carpini and Bruce A. Williams, "The Method Is the Message: Focus Groups as a Method of Social, Psychological, and Political Inquiry," in Michael X. Delli Carpini, Leonie Huddie, and Robert Shapiro, eds., *Research in Micropolitics* (J.A.I. Press, 1994), pp. 57–85.

2. Ronald Krueger, *Focus Groups: A Practical Guide for Applied Research* (Newbury Park: Sage Publications, 1988), p. 18.

3. Roberta Sigel, *Caught Between Ambition and Accommodation: Ambivalence in the Perception of Gender Relations* (Chicago: University of Chicago Press, 1996).

4. Pamela Conover, Ivor Crewe, and Donald Searing, "The Nature of Citizenship in the United States and Great Britain: Empirical Comments on Theoretical Themes," *Journal of Politics* 53 (1991):800–832.

5. David Morgan, *Focus Groups as Qualitative Research* (Newbury Park, CA: Sage Publications, 1988), p. 12.

6. Sigel, *Caught Between Ambition and Accommodation*, p. 13.

7. Conover, Crew, and Saring, "Nature of Citizenship," p. 805.

8. Tamar Liebes and Elihu Katz, *The Export of Meaning* (Oxford: Oxford University Press, 1990), p. 28.

9. Conover, Crew, and Saring, "Nature of Citizenship," p. 805.

10. Liebes and Katz, *Export of Meaning*, p. 82.

11. William Gamson, *Talking Politics* (Cambridge: Cambridge University Press, 1992), p. 17.

12. Michael X. Delli Carpini and Bruce A. Williams, "Methods, Metaphors, and Media Research: The Uses of Television in Political Conversations," *Communication Research* 21 (1994):782–812.

13. Ibid., pp. 801–802.

14. Ibid., p. 804.

15. Ibid.

16. Some of the experiments are recounted in Carl I. Hovland, Arthur A. Lumsdaine, and Fred D. Sheffield, *Experiments in Mass Communication* (Princeton: Princeton University Press, 1949).

17. The Shanto Iyengar and Donald R. Kinder book is titled *News That Matters: Television and American Opinion* (Chicago: University of Chicago Press, 1987).

18. Ibid., p. 6.

19. Shanto Iyengar, *Is Anyone Responsible? How Television Frames Political Issues* (Chicago: University of Chicago Press, 1991).

20. W. Russell Neuman, Marion R. Just, and Ann N. Crigler, *Common Knowledge: News and the Construction of Political Meaning* (Chicago: University of Chicago Press, 1992).

21. Kathleen M. McGraw and Clark Hubbard, "Some of the People Some of the Time: Individual Differences in Acceptance of Political Accounts," in Diana C. Mutz, Paul M. Sniderman, and Richard A. Brody, eds., *Political Persuasion and Attitude Change* (Ann Arbor: University of Michigan Press, 1996), pp. 145–170.

22. Donald R. Kinder and Lynn M. Sanders, *Divided By Color: Racial Politics and Democratic Ideals* (Chicago: University of Chicago Press, 1996). For another important book on race, which involves experimentation with survey forms and also presents arguments in opposition to Kinder and Sanders, see Paul Sniderman and Thomas Piazza, *The Scar of Race* (Cambridge: Harvard University Press, 1993).

Part Two

Theories of Public Opinion

Chapter Four

Psychological Perspectives

Although many early democratic theorists contemplated the nature of public opinion, many of the earliest discoveries about public opinion in the social sciences came from the study of psychology. Psychologists and sociologists alike attempt to account for the variations in people's opinions. Why do some people favor prayer in schools while others do not? Why are some people convinced O. J. Simpson is guilty while others are just as convinced that he is innocent? How do people decide which candidate to vote for? How do our internalized thoughts become our public opinion? Psychologists consider how our individual mental states, such as our moods, our attention span, or our thinking ability, affect the opinions we express. Sociologists, whose work we will explore in the next chapter, explore how social factors like group membership and social norms affect the expression of public opinion.

We have to approach the study of public opinion from many different directions because public opinion expression is made up of so many different psychological factors and social experiences. The formation of public opinion can be seen as a merging of individual beliefs, values, and attitudes in a situational context. Ideally, a public opinion scholar should be familiar with ideas and techniques from several fields—psychology, sociology, political science, and communication. Here, we will introduce you to some of the most important contributions from the study of psychology.

What Psychology Can Tell Us

Psychologists offer us insight into some of the most basic building blocks of public opinion. The concepts developed in this field help us to understand how elements of our psychological makeup can be altered by new information and yet affect the processing of new information. This research also suggests that psychological factors affect our behavior, although the links between what we think and what we do are often weak. Although this sort of research would seem to have a great deal of practical applicability, especially in designing persuasive messages (and resisting them!), public opinion researchers sometimes neglect these theories. Remember that here we are focusing on what goes on within the individual who is formulating an opinion. In Chapter 6, we will explore how social and psychological factors interact to produce expressions of public opinion.

Speaking the Language: Beliefs, Values, Attitudes, and Opinions

A traditional place to start when describing attitude research is by defining the basic concepts. Definitions of the terms *beliefs, values, attitudes,* and *opinions* have been debated and discussed by scholars through the years. Regardless of the definitions, scholars agree that there are cognitive and social foundations for these concepts. In the sections that follow, we will offer brief descriptions of the terms that summarize this extensive debate.

Beliefs

Beliefs are the cognitive components that make up our understanding of the way things are, that is, "the information that individuals have about objects or actions."[1] Beliefs are often hard to identify, especially when they are widely shared. Such beliefs are the assumptions by which we live our lives, and we presume that others think of the world the same way that we do. Western Christian philosophies contain the belief that people are perfectible—that they can improve themselves or be improved. Given this assumption, it is difficult for Westerners to fathom the caste system, a structure that supports the belief that individuals do not rise above, or sink below, their origins.

Some beliefs are totally distinct, but many are grouped together as belief systems. These belief systems may be quite simple, consisting of only a few items, or they may be enormously complex, involving thousands of beliefs. A belief system, ideally, is internally and psychologically consistent. Clear examples of systems of this kind can be found in religion, in which large numbers of beliefs are interrelated to form a network guiding one's thought and action.

We often see conflicts between belief systems. In politics, for example, belief systems common to one party clash with belief systems typical of another party. In early 1996, President Clinton's belief system came into conflict with the belief system of the Republican majority in Congress. As a result, the U.S. government was shut down for several weeks, unable to reach agreement on the country's budget. Sometimes an individual's own belief systems clash, producing a state of psychological tension known as cognitive dissonance. Beliefs are the building blocks of attitudes and opinions.

Values

Values are ideals. Beliefs represent our understanding of the way things are, but values represent our understanding of the way things should be. According to Richard Perloff, values "are overarching goals that people strive to obtain." He says that values are "more global and general than attitudes."[2]

According to psychologist Milton Rokeach,[3] there are two kinds of values. Terminal values are the goals we want to reach. Instrumental values are the means we endorse to reach our goals. Terminal values might include end states like freedom, equality, or peace. Instrumental values might encompass honesty, responsibility, and loyalty.

Leaders of social movements often invoke values, sometimes incorporating them into a motto that describes the movement to others. Thus, the leaders of movements attempt to connect their activity to a desired goal. Mottoes like Patrick Henry's "Give me liberty or give me death" helped to frame the American Revolution in terms of the value of freedom. Individual liberties and personal accomplishment have been important characteristics of American culture. The French Revolution was built on a slightly different set of values: "Liberty, equality, fraternity." It is worthwhile to note that both revolutions were built on the more fundamental belief that people are perfectible, that they can improve themselves.

Because values, like beliefs, tend to be taken for granted or are treated as if they were universal characteristics, it is often difficult for us to comprehend that other cultures may have different values. One of the most upsetting things that can occur when you travel to a foreign land is the discovery that some of your values are not shared by the host culture.

One of the authors of this text once taught at a university in a foreign culture in which collective and societal attainment is an important value rather than the individual accomplishment valued in the United States. The professor confronted a student for cheating on an exam by getting answers from the person in front of her. The student said very little, except that she was "ashamed." The professor did not realize that this situation reflected a difference in values until she discussed the incident with another student. "Yes," the other student agreed. "I'd be ashamed as well. . . . Getting caught that easily is a very silly thing to do." The student explained, "It is not wrong to cheat, but it is very embarrassing not to cheat correctly."

Attitudes

Most scholars agree that attitudes are "general and enduring positive or negative feeling about some person, object or issue."[4] Psychologists describe attitudes as having three components: cognitions (or beliefs), affect (or feelings), and behavior.[5]

A major difference between attitudes and beliefs is that attitudes have a strong "affective," or emotional, component. Beliefs are primarily cognitive; they are the mental constructs by which we know the world. However, many beliefs are evaluative in nature. You may believe that a particular television program is funny, that your friend looks good in her nose ring, or that buying imported goods hurts the U.S. economy. If these are your beliefs, you perceive these evaluations as inherent characteristics of the objects of your beliefs. Attitudes, in contrast, reflect your personal likes and dislikes: that you enjoy *Seinfeld,* that you admire your friend's taste, that you dislike buying imports. These are attitudes because you recognize them as your own orientation toward objects rather than as characteristics that are somehow part of the objects themselves.

However, attitudes are only "predispositions to respond and/or react [and are] directive of behavior."[6] Changing people's attitudes does not always change their behavior. In fact, there is some evidence that under certain conditions, attitudes do not predict behavior at all!

In their simplest form, our attitudes are positive or negative feelings toward something. Nevertheless, attitudes can combine in complex patterns, and the outcome may be unpredictable. For example, I may like pizza and dislike anchovies, but my attitudes about each ingredient separately may be quite different from my attitude about both ingredients together. Perhaps I like anchovies only when they are on pizza, or I might just dislike pizza that has anchovies on it.

We might consider a more complex example. I may have a friend whom I like very much. However, I may strenuously disapprove of people who live off welfare. If my friend goes on public assistance, I may decide that I no longer like him or that people on public assistance are not so bad. Or, I may live with the logical discontinuity.

Attitudes are built upon our beliefs and values. Our beliefs form the cognitive foundations for our attitudes (anchovies are too salty; people are basically good). Attitudes are also the manifestation of our values as they come into contact with the physical world and take specific form (people should be allowed to eat what they want; people should be responsible for their own lives).

Opinions

When an attitude is expressed, either verbally or through behavior, it is called an opinion. However, there is often confusion in the literature about the difference between attitudes and opinions. Although the terms are often used interchangeably, many researchers do see a difference. Opinions express attitudes, but not all attitudes are expressed. Attitudes are only predispositions to respond; opinions are the responses. Thus, attitudes are seen

Opinions	I support equal rights for women. I wouldn't support a tax increase. I favor increased immigration.
Attitudes	I respect most people. I value public schools. I distrust censorship.
Values	We should respect diverse viewpoints. People should be free. Everyone should have the opportunity to succeed.
Beliefs	People are basically good. All people are created equal. Human beings can be perfected.

FIGURE 4.1 Beliefs, Values, Attitudes, and Opinions: A Cognitive Hierarchy. This figure shows how beliefs form the basis for values, values for attitudes, and attitudes for opinions.

as broader, more enduring, and less consciously held than opinions. They are "deeper" inside a person than opinions are.[7]

If you give it some thought, you will see that the same attitude can result in two different opinions, depending on the circumstance and the object being evaluated. For example, I may like small children enormously. However, after eight hours of caring for several rambunctious tots, I may opine, "I've had enough!" My attitude toward small children as essentially good, even wonderful, people has not changed, but my opinion has, at least temporarily. Nonetheless, if I go for several weeks without seeing my little friends, I may miss them a great deal.

Opinions are usually, but not always, consistent with the attitudes to which they are related. I may believe that members of Congress in general are disreputable but have a lot of faith in the representative from my own district.

Figure 4.1 summarizes what we have been discussing in this section. Notice how attitudes are built upon beliefs and values and are finally expressed as opinions. Notice, too, that the same beliefs and values may produce divergent opinions that may even seem contradictory.

Early Theories of Attitude Formation and Change: The Legacies of Behaviorism

When we study changes in attitudes, we are faced with an unusual problem. It is very difficult to determine whether beliefs or attitudes existed in a person prior to an experimental or survey-based research study. As researchers, we cannot be sure whether we are measuring existing attitudes or actually causing new ones to be formed. Thus, scholars often use the term "attitude change" quite broadly to mean either attitude formation or attitude change, or both. The distinction is not critical, since what really matters is the process. Psychologists who study "attitude change" are interested in how perception and other processes occurring in people's heads bring about the expression of an opinion.

Some of the earliest theories about how attitudes are formed and changed and about how they affect behavior were based on the assumption that people functioned like animals. Animals responded to stimuli without much thought. Researchers found that animals could be "conditioned" to respond in a certain way to a specific stimulus, and they believed people could be conditioned in much the same way.[8] This perspective is known as behaviorism, and the theories relevant to public opinion that derive from it are known as conditioning theories.

Early twentieth-century psychologist Ivan Pavlov's work with dogs provided researchers with the first clues that conditioning theories might explain the behavior of both animals and people.[9] Researchers such as Arthur and Carolyn Staats[10] thought that if the same stimulus were to produce more or less the same response in everybody, it might be possible to isolate the reasons people form certain attitudes and opinions. They felt that if stimuli received by the brain could be controlled, then, presumably, the attitude structure, the personality, and even the behavior of individuals could also be controlled.

Two variants of conditioning theories have been of special interest to public opinion scholars: classical conditioning and operant conditioning.

Classical Conditioning

Classical conditioning is a way to study attitude change from a stimulus-response perspective. Classical conditioning is said to occur when an initially neutral stimulus (the conditioned stimulus, or CS) is associated with another stimulus (the unconditioned stimulus, or UCS) that is connected inherently or by prior conditioning to some response (the unconditioned response, or UCR).

Pavlov's[11] classic study provides a good example. In that study, shown in Figure 4.2, a hungry dog is given a piece of meat (the UCS), which causes the dog to salivate (the UCR). When a bell is rung (the CS—an initial neutral stimulus) whenever the dog is given the meat, a CS-UCS pairing occurs. That is, by pairing the bell with the delivery of the meat, Pavlov eventually created a situation where the ringing of the bell alone caused the dog to salivate. By repeatedly ringing a bell when meat was presented to the dog,

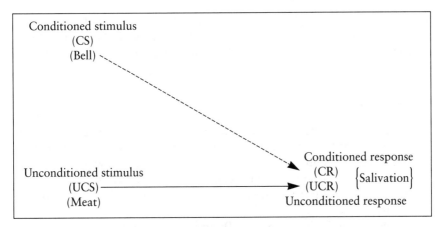

FIGURE 4.2   An Example of Classical Conditioning. SOURCE: R. E. Petty and J. T. Cacioppo, *Attitudes and Persuasion: Classic and Contemporary Approaches* (Dubuque, IA: William C. Brown Company Publishers, 1981), p. 41.

Pavlov created a conditioned response (CR). The salivation was the result of conditioning rather than the result of a link between the initial stimulus (the meat) and the response (salivation).

Attitude researchers believe that work by social psychologist Arthur Staats was paramount in stimulating research on conditioned responses as it pertains to attitudes.[12] Staats[13] was interested in whether animals (and by extension, people) could be conditioned to develop a negative emotional response toward certain words, arguing that people may acquire attitudes in a manner similar to Pavlov's dogs. For example, as Alice Eagly and Shelly Chaiken[14] describe, a child eventually learns the evaluative meaning of the words "good" and "bad" if these conditioned stimuli are repeatedly paired with unconditioned stimuli such as food or physical punishment.

Theoretically, after an attitude has become associated with words such as "good" and "bad," the words can be used as unconditioned stimuli to establish attitudes toward other stimuli. Eagly and Chaiken describe how a child might acquire a negative attitude toward some minority group on the basis of these principles:

> Imagine that the child hears a number of negative adjectives (e.g., bad, dirty, stupid) paired with the name of a particular minority group (e.g., blacks, Jews). In this application, the minority group name is the CS, and the negative adjectives are the UCSs. The UCSs are assumed to regularly evoke UCRs—in this case implicit negative evaluative responses ... With repeated pairings of the CS and the various UCSs, the minority group name comes to elicit a CR ... the CR is an implicit negative evaluative response, or negative attitude toward the minority group.[15]

Prejudice is an important attitude in the study of public opinion, for it can lead to expressions of public opinion about other social groups, about candidates and leaders who represent those groups, and about social policies which affect them.

Operant Conditioning

Operant conditioning is based upon the supposition that people act to maximize the positive and minimize the negative consequences of their behavior.[16] We may come to adhere to attitudes that yield rewards and to reject attitudes that result in punishments.[17] Figure 4.3 illustrates how such operant conditioning might work for individuals who are being indoctrinated into a cult.

Numerous studies in the late 1950s and 1960s investigated the effects of such social reinforcement on the conditioning of attitude statements. Typically in these studies, subjects might be asked to construct sentences, converse informally with the experimenter, or answer specific questions asked by an experimenter. The experimenter would reinforce certain verbal responses either positively or negatively.

A classic example of conditioned responses appears in a study conducted by Joel Greenspoon,[18] in which he used verbal rewards to change what people would say. Greenspoon was able to increase the frequency with which a subject used a plural noun by responding with "good," "mm-hmmm," or an approving head nod whenever the subject used a plural noun. Likewise, Greenspoon would react negatively with "bad," "humph," or a disapproving head movement or might not even react at all when the subject emitted an incorrect response (such as a singular noun). Many studies since have used this approach.[19]

A number of studies on the verbal conditioning of attitudes suggest that people actually do change their attitudes as a result of rewards and that these attitudes persist.[20] However, no one has been able to explain why this works. Some studies suggest that attitudes change not as an automatic and unconscious consequence of reinforcement but because of "cognitively mediated social influence" (such as information or norms presented through one's culture). That is, people do not merely react to a stimulus. They actually think, and think strategically, about how to behave. Social factors as well as thought processes may interfere with the linkage between stimulus and response. For example, behavioral conditioning may result not in attitude change but in compliance. That is, subjects may not actually alter their opinions; they may merely "go along" with the experimenter.

Can this operant conditioning response be seen at work in more generalized public opinion situations? Operant conditioning might have been one of many complex factors at work in Nazi Germany during the 1930s,

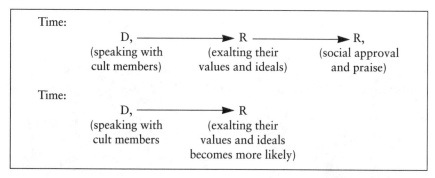

FIGURE 4.3   An Example of Operant Conditioning. SOURCE: R. E. Petty and J. T. Cacioppo, *Attitudes and Persuasion: Classic and Contemporary Approaches* (Dubuque, IA: William C. Brown Company Publishers, 1981), p. 48.

where German citizens were heavily rewarded for those activities one might think of as patriotic (e.g., saluting, joining a political party, attending a political rally [Figure 4.4]) and for feelings of historical greatness (costumes reflecting medieval customs, and so on). "Incorrect" responses in these situations (e.g., being against Hitler or the Nazi Party) were severely punished. Regardless of whether these public expressions of opinion represented compliance or genuine attitude change, the policies they supported had dramatic consequences for Germany and for the world.

For many years, behavioral approaches to human psychology were prevalent. However, this perspective turned out to have important drawbacks, as you have probably already begun to see. Since behaviorism was predicated on the idea of acting without thinking, it was very difficult to explain why people did what they did. Much of the later psychological research into public opinion can be usefully categorized by the ways it addresses the failings of the behavioral perspective. Before we begin to elaborate on these shortcomings of the behavioral approach, you should recognize what is perhaps the most important contribution of behaviorism to understanding public opinion. Most people do not think very much about the opinions they express. Asked questions on a survey or in an exit poll, they are likely to answer without thinking.[21] These relatively automatic responses to a stimulus resemble in important ways the original vision of behaviorism.

Nevertheless, behavioral approaches have at least five significant drawbacks that later researchers have tried to remedy with other kinds of theories. First, although it is true that people often do not think very much before expressing an opinion, there are some cases where they think carefully and others where they do not. Information processing models try to diagram key elements of people's cognitive work before they respond to a

FIGURE 4.4   A Mass Rally in Nazi Germany. Large rallies such as this one were common public opinion displays during the Nazi ascent to power. (Photo courtesy of the Library of Congress)

stimulus. Other processing models try to describe some of the cognitive shortcuts people use to make sense of a complex, fast-moving world. Second, attitudes and opinions come in packages, and sometimes the way we respond to a stimulus is affected by a whole group of attitudes, beliefs, and values. Furthermore, different people package attitudes in different ways. Notice that this problem also stems from the fact that people actually engage in some cognitive work to produce an opinion rather than just responding to a stimulus. Cognitive consistency theories try to explain how the elements in a package of attitudes interact when people are asked to express an opinion. Judgmental theories try to explain how people's current attitudes affect the processing of new information and the likelihood of attitude change. A third problem behavioral approaches do not take into account is that two people may hold the same attitude for different reasons. Functional theories try to explain why people hold the attitudes they do. Fourth, behavioral theories cannot explain why people often do not behave in accordance with their attitudes. Social scientists believe there may be many reasons for this, and the theory of reasoned action attempts to explain the relationship between attitudes and behavior. Finally, emotions can play an important role in the formulation and expression of public opinion.

All of these later theories reject one of the central ideas of behaviorism: that people presented with the same stimulus will respond in the same way.[22] They are also informed by one of the most important recent findings about public opinion: People do not just remember their opinions and recite them when asked. They actually construct these opinions based on what they are thinking about at the time they are asked.[23] Let us consider some of these classic and contemporary theories in more detail.

Cognitive Processing: What Happens When People Think

Many scholars believe that if they can understand how a person cognitively processes a message, they can better understand the impact the message has on the individual's attitudes and behavior. Two main approaches have developed to explain how message processing occurs: cognitive processing models and cognitive response theories. Both of these approaches reject behaviorism's model of unthinking response to a stimulus, but both also recognize that the world is a complex place and people do not devote equal attention to all aspects of it. A third approach, the study of "heuristics," or mental shortcuts, also attempts to account for the fact that people can only make limited use of the information available to them.

Cognitive response theories assume that the brain is a "noisy" place. The basic idea behind these theories is that the brain is always active, trying to make sense of the information it is receiving, checking the accuracy of the information it is processing, and so forth. According to this model, the idiosyncratic thoughts—the cognitive responses that recipients generate, rehearse, and learn—interfere with various other mental activities. Therefore, ongoing cognitive activity interacts with incoming information in complex ways.

These responses are especially important in persuasion attempts.[24] According to the cognitive response model, people connect the information in persuasive messages to their existing feelings and beliefs about the message topic. The model suggests that message and information processing is a very active and interactive process; the complexity of the process suggests that cognitive responses mediate the effect of persuasive messages, determining both the direction and extent of attitude change.[25] One of the most important implications of this model for persuaders is that it suggests that people are easily distracted. Messages must often be repeated before they have any persuasive effect.

There are several cognitive processing models, but we have chosen to discuss the elaboration likelihood model (ELM)[26] as an example of models of this type. We have chosen this model in part because it has generated more research than other similar models but also because it was developed in response to the perceived shortcomings of the cognitive response approach.

In developing the model, Richard Petty and John Cacioppo felt that the cognitive response approach failed to consider the many ways in which people engage in thinking about issues relevant to the message. "Elaboration" thus refers to "the extent to which a person thinks about the issue-relevant arguments contained in a message."[27]

In the model, elaboration is described as falling on a continuum that ranges from complex thought processes to mainly superficial thoughts. People's reactions to a persuasive message can range from unthinking acceptance or rejection to active counterargumentation.

Petty and Cacioppo argue that a recipient of a persuasive message studies, analyzes, and evaluates issue-relevant information, comparing it to information already available in memory. Sometimes the recipient engages in a great deal of scrutiny about the central issues. In these situations, elaboration is high and the recipient will tend to ignore "peripheral matters" such as the credibility of the source. Other times, the recipient of the message does not (or cannot) engage in processing the message in any depth, and elaboration is low. The recipient may then rely on peripheral factors (such as source credibility) to form or change attitudes about the message and its content.

In their model, Petty and Cacioppo try to describe some of the conditions under which elaboration is likely to be high and situations where it is likely to be low. When people are motivated to think about a message—either because it seems directly relevant to them since they feel a sense of personal responsibility about the topic or simply because they like to think—then elaboration will be high. People will contemplate the message in issue-relevant ways. The same is true for messages that are repeated often to audiences that are relatively undistracted and have some knowledge of the issue. By contrast, when people are not motivated or able to process issue-relevant information, elaboration will be low, and the audience is likely to respond to simple cues in the message rather than giving it careful consideration.[28]

The diagram of Petty and Cacioppo's[29] elaboration likelihood model is presented in Figure 4.5. As the figure shows, the ELM process begins with a persuasive communication and ends with a negative or positive attitude change. For the most part, the central route, which depicts high elaboration, is presented on the left side of the figure. The peripheral route, representing low elaboration, appears on the right. Interconnections between the two routes are indicated in the figure. The final outcome is based on the individual's motivation and ability to process the message, which in turn influences the person's choice of processing strategy.

Consider the implications of this model for public opinion scholars and for those who design persuasive messages. The ELM suggests that there are

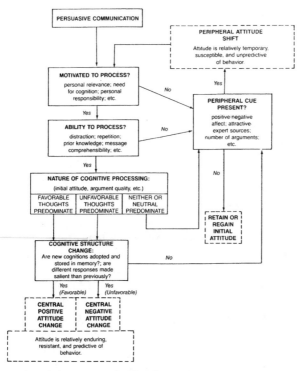

FIGURE 4.5   The Elaboration Likelihood Model. SOURCE: R. E. Petty and J. T. Cacioppo, "The Elaboration Likelihood Model of Persuasion," figure 1, p. 126, in L. Berkowitz, ed., *Advances in Experimental Social Psychology* (San Diego: Academic Press, 1986).

two ways to produce attitude change: (1) by encouraging people to do a great deal of thinking about the message (the central route), or (2) by encouraging people to focus on simple, compelling cues (the peripheral route). The effectiveness of the message will depend on people's ability and willingness to process it. Campaign messages for a high-profile race such as the presidential campaign may succeed by encouraging high elaboration. The same kinds of messages may fail miserably in a low-profile race for county supervisor, where voters may follow a peripheral path. The same may be true for policy debates. Think of how differently people are likely to process messages about arms control policy versus messages about abortion. Alternatively, large national campaigns like the presidential race may need messages that encourage low elaboration, since the voters who will go to the polls may not be very motivated to learn about the issues. Local races, where only the very dedicated turn out to vote, may do better by assuming that voters will follow the central route. Although Petty and

Cacioppo's model seems simple enough, applying it effectively to the real world can be complex.

Notice that the ELM serves primarily as a descriptive rather than an explanatory model. That is, the model does not explain "why certain arguments are strong or weak, why certain variables serve as (peripheral) cues, or why certain variables affect information processing."[30] Nevertheless, as Eagly and Chaiken note, "the model represents a powerful and integrative empirical framework for studying persuasion processes."[31]

Theories about the use of mental heuristics also tend to describe rather than explain, but they have proved useful in exploring important aspects of public opinion and behavior. Samuel Popkin (see Chapter 8) makes important use of this concept in his discussion of "low information rationality." The term *heuristic* is described from a Greek word meaning "to discover," and a heuristic is a device or an argument for letting someone personally discover the truth. The idea of the brain using heuristics is simply that even though certain procedures would appear to be the most logical ways of arriving at a solution to a problem, the brain may use fast, simple methods that are usually, but not always, the most clear-cut or the most likely to be correct.

Thus, we find that when people process heuristically, they use a subset of available information so that they can employ fairly simple rules and decisionmaking procedures to formulate a reasonably accurate decision.[32] The most important thing to note about heuristics and their use in attitude change is that some relatively simple rules might be the best representations of people's attitude judgments.[33] Like most of the more recent theories about the psychological processes involved in attitude formation and change, theories involving mental heuristics assume people think about their opinions but that they do not think about them very much.

Consistency and Judgmental Theories: Attitudes Come in Packages

Attitudes are neither formed nor changed in a vacuum. The attitudes that we hold now affect the ways in which we process new information and assess persuasive messages. Existing attitudes form a frame of reference, a basis of comparison, for new ideas. Further, changing one attitude may result in changing a whole network of related attitudes. Although information processing models do not completely ignore this aspect of attitude change, the interconnectedness of attitudes is not something these models focus on.

Some theories about attitudes make the interconnections central in explaining why people's attitudes change and why people resist changing their attitudes. Consistency theories describe the ways in which attitudes are networked and how that networking is likely to affect opinion expression and attitude change. Judgment theories emphasize the ways that existing attitudes color the interpretation of new information. Let us consider each in turn.

Consistency Theories

All consistency theories share several concepts in common. First, they all describe cognitions (beliefs, values, attitudes, and so on) as being consistent, inconsistent, or irrelevant to one another. According to Leon Festinger,[34] two cognitions are consistent when one follows from the other (e.g., the cognition "I love ice cream" is consistent with plans to buy ice cream cones daily at the local dairy bar). Two cognitions are inconsistent (dissonant) when the opposite of one cognitive element follows from the other (e.g., the cognition "I eat lots of ice cream" is dissonant with the public health statement that too much ice cream results in high cholesterol levels). Finally, two cognitive elements can be irrelevant when knowledge of one tells you nothing about what you might expect regarding the other (e.g., the announcement that smoking can cause lung cancer has nothing to do with the expectation that five hurricanes will hit Florida in the year 2000). Relations among cognitions (elements) are determined by a person's subjective expectations regarding what will happen in these relationships rather than by the actual, logical interrelationships between the elements.

Balance Theory. Many of you may already be familiar with balance theory, especially if you have taken a class in psychology. Balance theory, originally formulated by Fritz Heider,[35] provides a way to describe attitudes held by the individual and the relation of these attitudes to each other. This theory is often relevant to students because it deals with a triadic relationship and students often find themselves in this type of situation. Recently, a student advisee came to my office to discuss a problem she was having with her roommates. For simplicity's sake, let us say she had only two roommates, although she really had many more.

My student liked both roommates a great deal, and they, in turn, liked her. However, her two roommates disliked each other. Obviously, this would create a miserable situation for all concerned—it would create a state of imbalance.

According to Heider, a strain would arise because there is psychological pressure to restore balance. In this particular situation, there are several things that could be done. My student could: (1) play the role of peacemaker and work with the roommates on their relationship, hoping the roommates would change their attitudes and begin to like each other; (2) develop a dislike for one of the roommates and shift the imbalance;

(3) move to a different apartment and leave the situation altogether (this is the solution my advisee decided upon).

Heider[36] presented these relationships as shown in Figure 4.6. Heider used the symbols P, X, and O to illustrate relationships of this kind, in which P is the perceiver, O is some other person, and X is either a third person or some attribute of O. The plus and minus signs in the figure indicate an attitude or sentiment. For example, P plus O indicates that P likes O. P minus O indicates that P dislikes O.

The general rule for determining whether a given situation is balanced or imbalanced is to multiply all the signs in the triad, algebraically. Thus, a plus times a plus yields a product that is a plus; a minus times a minus yields a plus; a plus times a minus equals a minus. If the product of the three signs is a plus, the triad is balanced. If the product of the three signs is a minus, the triad is unbalanced.

It is clear that there are limits to the value of balance theory because it explains attitudes and relationships in relatively simple terms. However, it has been useful not only for understanding hypothetical situations in which people must react but also in field studies and experimental situations. Political scientists and public opinion scholars have applied the principles of balance theory when attempting to understand voters' perceptions of candidates' positions on issues and other public opinion phenomena. For example, Jon Krosnick[37] found that perceptions of political candidates' positions can be biased by perceiving that liked candidates agree with the voters' own positions on issues whereas disliked candidates disagree. In this case, individual voters seem to be trying to maintain a balanced triad between themselves, their candidates, and their issue positions by deliberately or unconsciously deceiving themselves.

It is clear that the principles of balance theory are enduring ones. Although interest in the theory waned in the late 1960s, it was revived in the late 1970s and 1980s[38] and research using the principles of balance theory continues to be of interest.

Congruity Theory.   One of the major criticisms of Heider's balance theory is that there are no provisions for degrees of liking or belonging between the elements. That is, a positive P and O sentiment is scored as plus 1, regardless of whether we are discussing friends, lovers, or virtual strangers. Congruity theory, as presented first by Charles Osgood and Percy Tannenbaum,[39] attempts to overcome this problem by quantifying gradations of liking. The theory is often considered a special case of balance theory.[40]

Congruity theory focuses on the manner in which we integrate a number of potentially conflicting communications concerning other people (or objects or issues). Rather than viewing problems as having simple yes or no solutions, congruity theory assumes there will be conflicting messages with

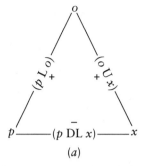

(a)

The given situation is unbalanced:
two positive relations and one
negative relation.

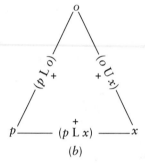

(b)

Change in sentiment relation
resulting in a balance of three
positive relations.

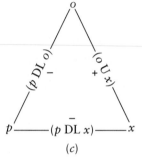

(c)

Change in sentiment relation resulting in a balance of two negative relations and one positive relation.

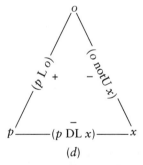

(d)

Change in unit relation resulting in a
balance of two negative relations
and one positive relation.

FIGURE 4.6   An Illustration of Balance Theory. SOURCE: F. Heider, *The Psychology of Interpersonal Relations* (New York: Wiley, 1958), figure 1, p. 208.

shades of gray. Conflicting messages could result in "incongruity," which is a state of cognitive imbalance. This cognitive state causes us to change our attitudes in a way that D. W. Rajecki describes as a compromise between the initial polarities of our attitudes before we heard the communication: "A basic dictum of the model is that when a disliked person endorses a liked other, the resultant attitude will be the same toward both. By reason of association with each other, the person you initially disliked intensely will improve somewhat in your estimation."[41]

Thus, balance theory lets us account for the fact that we sometimes disagree with our friends or our political leaders and yet continue to like and support them. However, over time, if our disagreements become more frequent or more important, we may decide to achieve balance by acquiring new friends or new political leaders whose views are more in tune with our own.

Much of the research on congruity theory has shown that people's attitudes on a particular issue can influence both their attitudes toward a person who expresses opinions on the issue and their attitudes toward other (unrelated) issues on which the person takes a stand. Eagly and Chaiken[42] discovered that the behavior of American politicians reflects their belief that they can enhance their image with voters by (1) associating themselves with popular causes, (2) disassociating themselves from unpopular causes, and (3) remaining mute on issues over which voter opinion is divided. We see an increasing trend in politicians who attempt to avoid all but the most basic issues and find both Republicans and Democrats speaking out primarily on issues on which both parties hold similar stands. This trend is explored further in Box 4.1.

Cognitive Dissonance Theory.　　Cognitive dissonance theory takes the basic foundations of the consistency theories to new levels. First developed by Festinger in 1957, the theory has generated a tremendous amount of research and has become one of the most important attitude change theories of the last fifty years. As Perloff notes, since Festinger's book *A Theory of Cognitive Dissonance* was written, more than 1,000 studies of cognitive dissonance have been published! These studies have "tested different aspects of Festinger's theory, challenged hypotheses derived from the theory and applied it to contexts ranging from marketing to religion."[43]

Festinger[44] carries the examination of the interrelationships between the cognitive elements much further than these relationships are explored in balance theory or congruity theory. However, with balance and congruity theories, the interrelationships among a number of elements can be considered simultaneously to determine whether the structure of the elements is balanced or not. Dissonance theory considers only pairs of elements at a time.

Box 4.1 Abandoning the Faithful: How Candidates Prepare for the General Election

In almost every presidential campaign, after the conventions are over, the major party nominees do something very odd. They endorse policies and positions that are out of character for their party ideology and out of step with the party faithful who nominated them. Consistency theories, especially balance theory, can help us understand why.

The last presidential election provides a useful example. Although the Republican Party platform contained a plank that advocated making abortion illegal, Republican Party nominee Bob Dole softened his antiabortion stand as the general election campaign neared. He said that there was room in the party for both pro-life and pro-choice advocates. On the other side of the aisle, Bill Clinton, the Democratic nominee and incumbent president, signed a tough new welfare law limiting the number of years a person can receive benefits and denying benefits to anyone who is not a U.S. citizen. This would appear to be very out of character for someone representing the Democratic Party.

If we represent Dole's and Clinton's issue stands from the perspective of the party faithful who nominated them, you can see that in each case, these voters experience incongruity.

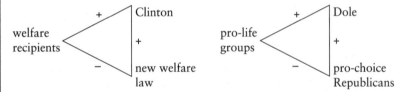

Abandoning the Party Faithful

Why would Clinton and Dole risk producing psychological discomfort in these people who may be instrumental in getting them elected? The key lies in the insights of balance theory. Although pro-lifers may be appalled at the notion of admitting pro-choice advocates and their ideas into the Republican Party, they are unlikely to defect and vote for Clinton, since his stand on abortion is likely to be even less palatable to them. For welfare recipients, the story is much the same. Although they may feel the new welfare law is unfair, they are unlikely to abandon Clinton, because Dole's policies may be even more unfavorable to them. In each case, the candidates are relying on voters' use of balancing tests—the party faithful like the candidate more than they dislike his policy stands.

Now consider what effect these postconvention issue positions may have on voters who are *not* among the party faithful. For example, blue-collar workers

(continues)

Box 4.1 (*continued*)

who voted for Reagan may find Clinton's tough stand on welfare appealing. Women, who have tended to vote for Democrats in recent years, may reconsider Dole in light of his new stand on abortion.

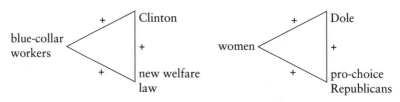

Appealing to the Fence-Sitters

In each case, the new policy positions have produced congruity between candidate, voter, and issue where none (or only a very shaky fit) appeared before.

Candidates change their issue positions, often moderating them, after the conventions. A candidate counts on the party faithful remaining faithful despite the changes and hopes to attract uncommitted voters by adopting issue positions that are more congruous to theirs. One practical effect of this is that the opinions of the party faithful sometimes have less impact than those of the "fence-sitters." African-American voters, for instance, often complain that the Democratic Party does not take account of their interests because it is so sure of their votes. And indeed, a very large percentage of African-American voters do cast their ballots for Democratic candidates.

In this case, congruity theories can help us explain the behaviors of both candidates and voters as the nominees engage in the paradoxical behavior of abandoning their staunchest supporters in an effort to win the election.

One of Festinger's important statements is that an inconsistency between two cognitions (such that one cognitive element implies the opposite of the other) gives rise to the uncomfortable psychological state of "cognitive dissonance." For example, if I love ice cream yet I am aware of the dangers of high cholesterol, I would experience dissonance. Psychologically, it does not make sense to engage in a behavior that would endanger my health.

The magnitude of the dissonance depends on the importance of the cognitive elements to the person. If I value ice cream more than my health or if I am skeptical of the dangers of high cholesterol, it is doubtful that I will reduce my consumption of ice cream. Alternatively, if my health is the most important value for me (for instance, if I have a family history of heart trouble), I may give up ice cream all together. Dissonance is at its most powerful when the two cognitive elements are important and evenly valued—if I am really worried about my health but I really love ice cream.

Of course, if most of us had to live every day experiencing constant cognitive dissonance, it would not be long before we became stressed, mentally imbalanced, or worse! Obviously, something must be done to alleviate the stress associated with such dissonance. Festinger says that because dissonance is so very uncomfortable to us, we will do almost anything to reduce the dissonance in order to achieve consonance. As he notes, there are three ways in which dissonance can be reduced:

1. The individual can change one of the cognitions so that the relationship between the two becomes consonant (e.g., I could decide that eating ice cream is too dangerous so I actually give it up!).
2. The person might "add" consonant cognitions (e.g., I could think up all the reasons why I like ice cream and find these reasons are more important to me than any health concerns).
3. The person might alter the importance of the cognitions (e.g., I might rationalize that I need to eat ice cream every day because it has milk in it—I am getting older, after all, and ice cream might keep me from getting osteoporosis).

It is clear that cognitive dissonance is an important psychological state for researchers to study so they can determine how people react when they are faced with conflicting cognitive elements. In fact, researchers have examined the concept of cognitive dissonance from a number of perspectives, including (1) the requisite conditions needed for dissonance arousal,[45] (2) ways to determine when a person is experiencing cognitive dissonance,[46] or even (3) how cognitive dissonance "feels" to a person.[47]

The theory of cognitive dissonance may have much to contribute to the study of public opinion. But how can students of public opinion apply dissonance theory to public opinion research? Clearly, studies of public opinion over a certain time period are needed to examine the nature of cognitive dissonance and public opinion. We might want to understand, for example, how important, or how dissonance arousing, an issue is to a person before there is any commitment to a point of view. Another interesting question is whether dissonance could be a social-level phenomenon as well as an individual-level phenomenon. Can a group experience dissonance? It also seems possible that dissonance theories could help us explain some important public opinion phenomena, such as the current levels of political cynicism. If individuals believe in their country but not in their leaders, could the cognitive dissonance created by these beliefs be expressed in the form of public cynicism?

It would also be an interesting area in public opinion research to study the formation of dissonance in association with the development of social issues so that we could understand the points at which people become committed to certain views. It is clear that when an issue is relatively new, it may have little direct importance to the public. Little cognitive dissonance could be aroused if the issue were examined or voted on; the public simply would not care enough about the outcome. In later stages, however, members of the public may have chosen sides on the issue and feel committed to those opinions.

Judgmental Theories

The underlying principle of most judgmental theories is that "all stimuli can be arranged in some meaningful order" on a psychological dimension. That is, attitudes toward an object can be arranged from the most negative (unfavorable) to the most positive (favorable) in the same way that people might be arranged in order from most attractive to least attractive, longest hair to shortest hair and so forth. How positive or negative something feels or how it is rated on an attitude scale depends upon the frame of reference.[48] That is, our past experiences play an important role in the ways that we interpret new information.

Adaptation Level Theory.   In adaptation level theory, a person's adaptation level is that point on the dimension of judgment that corresponds to the psychological neutral point. As Petty and Cacioppo explain, "If you were to put your hand in a bucket of very cold water, eventually your hand would adapt to the water temperature so that the cold water would feel neutral or normal. Subsequent judgments of how cold or warm another bucket of water felt would be made relative to the water temperature to which your hand had previously adapted."[49]

Adaptation level is important because other stimuli we experience are judged in relation to this level, which serves as an anchor or reference point. A contrast effect occurs when a new stimulus being judged is displaced, moved away from the adaptation level. For example, many Americans might be shocked at the tenor of debates in the British Houses of Parliament, where members cheer speeches given by others in their party and boo and hiss those given by the opposition. We are used to the more staid and "respectful" debates held in our own legislative chambers, so to us, the British seem rowdy and undignified. Our judgment of their behavior is based on what we are used to rather than on the objective "propriety" of their actions. A number of studies have investigated contrast effects and have demonstrated that these effects do occur in the judgments of both social and physical stimuli.[50]

An interesting study of adaptation level theory was conducted by Philip Brickman, Dan Coates, and Ronnie Janoff-Bulman[51] who tested the proposition that extremely positive events do not increase one's overall level of happiness. To use an example close to home: Recently, an accountant in a department in which one of us works won the state lottery—$18 million. Brickman and associates suggest that this event should raise the accountant's adaptation level so that more common, mundane events become less pleasurable than they used to be.

When Brickman and associates tested this hypothesis, they asked people who had won from $50,000 to $1,000,000 in the Illinois state lottery how pleasant they found seven ordinary events like watching television and eating breakfast. People in a control group of nonwinners were asked the same questions. Lottery winners rated these events as less pleasant than the controls, even though earlier studies had found no differences in overall pleasure ratings between the two groups.

The researchers speculate that the extra pleasure of winning the money is offset by the decline in pleasure from ordinary events. Indeed, when the accountant in our department, who is now able to enjoy the finer things of life, was asked if the pleasure of eating breakfast was reduced since winning the lottery, she answered, "Not on my [new] front porch!"

Social Judgment Theory. Social judgment theory is similar to adaptation level theory in that it also assumes that people tend to arrange stimuli in a meaningful order on a psychological dimension (tall to short, fat to thin, and so forth). However, in social judgment theory, judgments about physical as well as social stimuli are thought to be subject not only to contrast effects but also to assimilation effects. In addition, in social judgment theory, one's own attitude is thought to serve as an internal anchor, and the opinions and attitudes expressed by others may be displaced and moved either toward or away from one's own position.[52] Attitudes that are relatively close to one's own are assimilated (seen as closer than they actually are), but attitudes that are quite discrepant from one's own are contrasted (seen as further away than they actually are).

How do we develop such misperceptions? According to social judgment theory, an attitudinal dimension is composed of three categories or latitudes. The latitude of acceptance includes the person's most preferred position but also includes the range of other opinions on an issue that the person finds acceptable. The latitude of rejection comprises the range of opinions that the person finds objectionable. Finally, the latitude of noncommitment comprises those positions that the person finds neither acceptable nor unacceptable.

Social judgment theory states that people's existing attitudes distort their perception of others' positions. These distortions influence how likely it is that a person's attitude will change. For example, say that you and a friend are discussing the issue of abortion. Assimilating your friend's attitude on abortion toward your own attitude would probably make you regard your friend's statements as "fair," "unbiased," and so forth, increasing the likelihood of attitude change.[53] However, contrast, which causes another's position to be seen as further from one's own point of view, would lead you to regard your friend's statements about abortion as "unfair" or "biased," reducing the likelihood that your attitude will change.

Whether the attitude or message being presented by someone falls within an individual's latitude of acceptance, rejection, or noncommitment determines whether the content is positively or negatively evaluated and also influences whether attitude change occurs. There are many more theories about how people process information in order to form opinions. We have discussed only a few to give you some idea of how the psychology of the individual can have a profound impact on the opinions of the whole, that is, on the formation of public opinion.

Motivational Theories: Same Attitude, Different Reason

When you first think of public opinion, it may not be obvious that there are reasons for holding opinions. Perhaps the foregoing discussion of consistency theories helps to some extent, for these theories imply that we hold opinions not only because they seem logically "right" to us but because they seem consistent with other beliefs, values, and attitudes we find important. But there are many reasons for holding opinions. In the 1950s, two separate groups of investigators developed theories that attitudes serve various psychological needs and have diverse motivational bases. These are known as functional theories. Other theories describe and explain the ways our concern about our appearance to other people affects the attitudes we hold and the opinions we express. One of these theories, impression management theory, is discussed here because of its close links to cognitive dissonance theory. Several of the other theories that deal with this aspect of opinion formation are discussed in Chapters 5 and 6.

Functional Theories

Obviously, there are a number of functions attitudes can serve. They may be convenient summaries of our beliefs, they may help others to know what to expect from us, and they can express important aspects of our personality.[54] Central to functional theories, however, is the notion that there are specific personality functions that attitudes serve for the individual.

The key functional approach described here is Daniel Katz's[55] functional theory of attitudes. However, students should be aware that others such as M. Brewster Smith, Jerome Bruner, and Robert White[56] and Herbert

Kelman[57] have also described functional approaches to the study of attitudes.

Katz's Functional Theory of Attitudes

In his article entitled "The Functional Approach to the Study of Attitudes,"[58] Katz describes four functions that attitudes might serve for a person: the (1) ego-defensive function, (2) value-expressive function, (3) knowledge function, and (4) utilitarian function.

The ego-defensive function describes how attitudes are held to help people protect themselves from unflattering truths about themselves. These attitudes may also be held to protect individuals from unflattering truths about others who are important to them. A simplistic example of the ego-defensive function would be when a person with illegible handwriting states that "bad handwriting is the mark of a true genius." In the value-expressive function, a person holds an attitude in order to express an important value. For example, when people says that they try to vote in every election, they may be promoting the value of democracy.

The knowledge function helps people better understand events and people around them. For example, feeling revulsion and developing negative attitudes about the Oklahoma City bombing may help a person to better understand the militia movement. Finally, in the utilitarian function, attitudes help people gain rewards and avoid punishments. You may decide to take on the attitudes your professor expounds in class, hoping that this helps you to get an A on an exam.

Thus, functional theories explore the notion that changing an attitude requires understanding of its motivational basis. That is, knowing what function an attitude serves dictates the form persuasion attempts should take.[59] For example, suppose you know that I approve of the way Bill Clinton is handling his job as president and that this attitude serves a utilitarian function. All of my friends are Democrats, and liking Clinton is one part of fitting in with the social set to which I belong. You might persuade me to change my mind by telling me that my friends would not really mind if I did not approve of Clinton, or you might convince me that it was more rewarding to belong to another group that favored Republicans. However, if my approval of Bill Clinton is an attitude that serves an ego-defensive function, you may have to use a very different persuasive strategy. Suppose I approve of Clinton because I think I know something about politics and I voted for Clinton for president. If I were to disapprove of Clinton, my image of myself as knowledgeable about politics would be threatened. Your persuasive tactics might include things like telling me that no one could be sure how Clinton would handle his second term or that even political experts are surprised at how poorly he is doing. In this way, you might make it possible for me to change my attitude without damaging my ego. In both cases, the attitude is the same, but the persuasive strategy is different because the same attitude may serve different functions.

Impression Management Theory

A different approach to examining motivations for attitude change is found in studies that use impression management theory. Impression management theory deals with how people present an image to others in order to achieve a particular goal.[60] Most studies of impression management assume that the primary goal is attaining social approval.[61]

In this and other ways, impression management theory differs significantly from the cognitive consistency theories described earlier. In cognitive consistency theories, it is assumed that people are motivated to set their thoughts and actions in order and must decide how to achieve this consistency. Impression management theorists assume that people want to convey, given social constraints, as positive and consistent a public image as possible in order to obtain social rewards—regardless of whether that image is consistent with internalized attitudes.

In fact, James Tedeschi, Barry Schlenker, and Thomas Bonoma,[62] proposed impression management theory as an alternative to dissonance theory. As Schlenker states: "Irrespective of whether or not people have psychological needs to be consistent ... there is little doubt that the appearance of consistency usually leads to social reward, while the appearance of inconsistency leads to social punishment."[63]

Impression management theorists agree with Festinger that tension is produced when people act publicly in a manner contrary to their attitudes, but they do not agree that the tension is produced by dissonant cognitions. Rather, Tedeschi and colleagues,[64] among others, believe that this tension is produced by people's knowledge that they appear inconsistent to others. When people perceive that their attitudes appear inconsistent, they immediately begin to manage more carefully the impression they are making on others by restoring consistency to their actions or in their expression of attitudes.[65]

Because people are often motivated to impress other people and to create a desired effect upon others, they may change or report to have changed their beliefs and attitudes in an effort to create desirable impressions on others.[66] The result of this "false" reporting often leads to a difference between individuals' privately held and publicly held attitudes. I may say that I believe it is everyone's civic duty to report for jury duty, but I may reflect privately that it is an enormous waste of my time to do so. Impression management theory is of importance to the public opinion scholar because of this focus on potential differences between public and private attitudes.

Public opinion researchers often investigate public opinion situations in which discrepancies between these attitudes occur.

Links Between Attitudes and Behavior: What People Think and What They Do

You probably assume that people say what they think and think what they say, act what they think and think what they act. This assumption has been a common one, made not only by researchers but by the general public. After all, how can we interact with those around us if we cannot make some predictions about how people will react in various circumstances?

Being able to predict how people will react is certainly important to public opinion scholars, who often view attitude-behavior linkages as key determinants of a public's opinion on any number of issues. The number of positions in polling firms would be dwindling dramatically and we would not be writing this book if it turned out that attitudes had no bearing on behavior.

Certainly, there are issues and situations that appear to result in clear (though not necessarily strong) relationships between attitudes and behavior. For example, numerous studies of voting behavior have shown that attitudes toward particular candidates predict voting for those candidates with considerable accuracy.[67] However, Howard Schuman and Michael Johnson state that although attitudes do predict behaviors in voting studies, the findings seem to "vary from small to moderate in size."[68]

In other words, the strength of the relationship between attitudes and behaviors is debatable. In fact, research over the years has shown that this linkage is more tenuous than intuition would have us believe. How many friends have you had who feel strongly about issues concerning the environment but could not care less about recycling, would gladly take a spin in a motorboat, or do not think twice about how much gas their car consumes? Or have you ever been involved in a relationship with someone who said you were special but treated you as if you were anything but?

Empirical studies suggesting weak relations between attitudes and behaviors appeared in the 1930s, and such research continues to this day.[69] There may be many reasons for these discrepancies.

Measurement Issues

In addition to all of the other methodological concerns associated with experiments and surveys when they are used to measure public opinion (see Chapter 3 for a discussion), studies that attempt to measure the links between attitudes and behavior have some special difficulties associated with them.

Different methods of data collection seem to produce contradictory evidence regarding the strength of the relationship between attitudes and behavior. For example, Kelman[70] and Schuman and Johnson[71] maintain that whereas weak and even negative relationships between attitudes and behaviors exist in experimental research, positive and moderately strong relationships are found using survey research. One reason for this may be that there is a tendency for survey research to examine "attitudes that are more important and involving and that therefore may be more influential in relation to behavior."[72]

Icek Ajzen[73] describes what he calls the "principle of correspondence." That is, attitude measures that do not correspond to behavioral measures will not predict behavior very well. High correspondence between measures will produce a higher consistency between the measures. For example, a general attitude about environmental protection may not predict the likelihood that someone will donate to the Sierra Club, but it might predict a respondent's overall "environmental concern" (e.g., attitudes about recycling, mass transit use, and so on), especially if that concern were measured over a period of time.

Obviously, you need to make sure that questions on a survey reflect clearly the behavior you want to measure. If you want to predict how much someone is likely to donate to a specific charity, for example, you are better off asking them about their opinion of that specific charity rather than about their general beliefs or values concerning donating, social responsibility, and so forth.

Individual Differences

Individual differences can account for some inconsistencies in attitude-behavior relationships. You probably have some friends who exhibit high consistency between their attitudes and behaviors. If they tell you they think something you can almost rest assured they will back up their purported attitudes with their behaviors. However, you can probably think of just as many or more friends who are known to exhibit inconsistencies between their attitudes and behaviors. They may say one thing and act in a completely different way.

As Perloff notes, your friends who fit the latter category may have a strong attitude about an issue, but "they will keep their opinion to themselves, or they may even argue for the opposite point of view."[74] I have even known some people in group situations who will monitor the opinion "climate" before expressing an opinion—and then they make sure that the opinion they express is contrary to that being expressed by the majority of people in the group!

Perloff[75] describes two key individual differences that influence this consistency (or lack thereof) between attitudes and behaviors: (1) self-monitoring and (2) direct experience.

Mark Snyder developed the self-monitoring concept, which he describes as "the extent to which people monitor (observe, regulate, and control) the public appearances of self they display in social situations and interpersonal relationships."[76] Snyder developed a scale that classifies people as high self-monitors or low self-monitors.

As Perloff notes:

> High self-monitors are adept at controlling the images of self they present in interpersonal situations, and they are highly sensitive to the social cues that signify the appropriate behavior in a given situation . . . low self-monitors are less concerned with conveying an impression that is appropriate to the situation. Rather than relying on situational cues to help them decide how to act in a particular situation, low self-monitors consult their inner feelings and attitudes.[77]

Thus, high self-monitors are more likely to express public opinions that are different from their private opinions. Low self-monitors are likely to have private and public opinions that match.

In addition to self-monitoring, direct experience can influence the attitude-behavior relationship. Perloff[78] and Russell Fazio and Mark Zanna,[79] among others, contend that attitudes based on direct experience will predict behaviors better than attitudes based on indirect experiences.

Fazio and Zanna assert that attitudes based on direct experience are "more clearly defined, held with greater certainty, more stable over time, and more resistant to counter influence."[80] For example, if a five-year-old says he is "never gonna do drugs," he is probably basing this statement on television advertisements he has seen and on comments made by his teachers rather than on the fact that he has actually seen another kindergartner "do drugs." Based on the research by Fazio and Zanna, the statement would be more meaningful and would be more likely to predict his behavior if he had actually witnessed a friend have a bad physical reaction to a drug.

Social and Situational Factors

There are many social factors, including cultural differences and norms, that may also interfere with the linkages between attitudes and behavior. We will explore norms and other social factors that may influence the production and expression of public opinion in Chapters 5 and 6. However, at this point, we want to describe a classic study, shown in Box 4.2, that demonstrates how social norms, such as politeness, can interfere with the expression of some opinions, such as prejudice.

Box 4.2   Traveling America: Weak Links Between Prejudiced Attitudes and Prejudiced Behavior

A classic study by Richard LaPiere serves as an excellent example of the sometimes poor fit between behavior and attitudes. In this study, a number of surprising inconsistencies were found in the attitudes and behaviors of proprietors of hotels and restaurants toward Chinese people.

For the study, LaPiere was accompanied by "a personable Chinese student and his wife" on a trip across the United States. During their travels, the three would stop at restaurants, "auto camps," and hotels. The purpose of this study was to determine whether the proprietors would serve the couple in spite of any underlying prejudice. Notably, because the students were Chinese and because it was the 1930s, when a communist government had recently taken over in China, LaPiere assumed that many Americans would hold negative attitudes toward the couple.

Surprisingly, only one of the proprietors of a sample of 250 hotels and restaurants refused service to the visiting Chinese couple. Yet the proprietors presented quite a different attitudinal response in their answers to a mail questionnaire. As LaPiere notes:

To provide a comparison of symbolic reaction to symbolic social situations with actual reaction to real social situations, I "questionnaired" the establishments which we patronized during the two year period. . . . To the hotel or restaurant a questionnaire was mailed with an accompanying letter purporting to be a special and personal plea for response. The questionnaires all asked the same question: "Will you accept members of the Chinese race as guests in your establishment?"

Although all but one of the hotel and restaurant employees served the Chinese couple, the survey results indicated that a vast majority of the proprietors (92 percent) would not be willing to "accept members of the Chinese race as guests."

Donald Campbell argues that in these situations, people who hold negative attitudes toward minorities may be reluctant to express their attitudes through public behavior because norms of tolerance and politeness are considered to be so important to Americans. More important, Campbell said that social norms may create different thresholds for expressing attitudes, producing apparent discrepancies between attitudes and behaviors, when, in fact, no real discrepancies exist.

There were several methodological problems in this study, including (1) not knowing whether the same person who waited on the Chinese couple was the one who filled out the questionnaire, and (2) the fact that the questionnaire did not evaluate whether the proprietors would accept a white man and a Chinese couple (who were known to be attractive and personable) into their establishment. However, it is also clear that social and situational factors weighed heavily in this case as well.

SOURCES: Richard T. LaPiere, "Attitudes vs. Actions," *Social Forces* 13 (1934):230–237, quoted portions from pp. 232–233; Donald T. Campbell, "Social Attitudes and Other Acquired Behavioral Dispositions," in S. Koch, ed., *Psychology: A Study of Science* (New York: McGraw-Hill, 1963), pp. 94–172.

When do attitudes predict behaviors? It is clear that there are a lot of cognitive and situational factors that must be considered in order to answer this question. A hot topic in psychology pertaining to the attitude-behavior relationship is the concept of "attitude accessibility."[81] That is, attitudes are thought to guide behavior partially through the perception process. Attitudes that are highly accessible (i.e., that come to mind quickly) are thought to be more likely to guide perception and therefore behavior. Studies indicate that more accessible attitudes predict behavior better than less accessible ones, independent of the direction and intensity of attitude expression.[82] Thus, knowing how quickly someone can express an attitude or opinion can provide useful information about how that person is likely to behave.

In addition to studying the attitude-behavior relationship from the perspective of attitude accessibility, researchers have also attempted to focus on this problem by developing more complex models. Martin Fishbein and Icek Ajzen attempted to explain the underlying psychological processes by which attitudes might predict behavior through a model called the theory of reasoned action. Later, Ajzen modified and enlarged the Fishbein-Ajzen model in an alternative theory of planned behavior. Both of these models will be described briefly.

Theory of Reasoned Action

Fishbein and Ajzen actually proposed the theory of reasoned action more than twenty years ago. Since then, the theory has generated a great deal of research in a variety of social science disciplines and has had important impacts in the area of attitude-behavior relations.

The theory of reasoned action specifies, in a mathematical way, the relationship among beliefs, attitudes, and behaviors. The theory is based on the assumption that humans are rational. Because they are rational, they calculate the costs and benefits of engaging in particular actions, taking into account the perceptions significant others might have concerning their actions. The theory specifically concerns voluntary behaviors—behaviors that people perform because they decide (or want) to perform them.

There are four basic components of the theory of reasoned action: (1) attitude toward the behavior (which includes behavioral beliefs and beliefs about the consequences of the behavior), (2) subjective norm (beliefs that specific individuals or groups think the behavior should or should not be performed), (3) behavioral intention (intention to perform a particular behavior), and (4) the actual behavior (see Figure 4.7).[83]

In general, the theory of reasoned action states that people intend to behave in ways that allow them to obtain favorable outcomes and that meet the expectations of others who are important to them. And this seems to

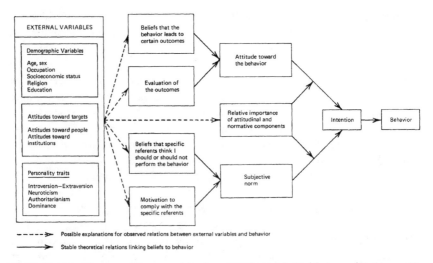

FIGURE 4.7   Theory of Reasoned Action. SOURCE: M. Fishbein and I. Ajzen, *Understanding Attitudes and Predicting Social Behavior* (Englewood Cliffs, NJ: Prentice-Hall, 1980), figure 7.1, p. 84. Reprinted by permission of Prentice-Hall, Inc., Upper Saddle River, NJ.

make sense. Most of us want to get along with others in this world and would also like social, financial, or other rewards. We may find that some of our behaviors are determined by the likelihood of impressing others and achieving such rewards.

However, even though a number of studies have found that behavioral intentions can be predicted from the theory of reasoned action by measuring attitudes toward the behavior and subjective norms, there are some inherent problems. For example, the theory of reasoned action has been criticized because it does not attempt to incorporate many of the more traditional factors that may affect behavioral outcomes such as characteristics of the environment or the situation (e.g., poverty or access to information) or characteristics of the person (e.g., mental or emotional illness). Many studies have found that such characteristics are directly relevant to the linkage between attitudes and behaviors.

In spite of these criticisms, many studies have found the premises of the theory of reasoned action to be useful. These studies have investigated a variety of different topics, including investigations of voting and presidential elections,[84] family planning,[85] and consumer product preferences.[86]

The relevance of the theory of reasoned action to public opinion studies is most clear in relation to public opinion perspectives that take account of individuals' perceptions of others (see Chapter 6). Looking at these per-

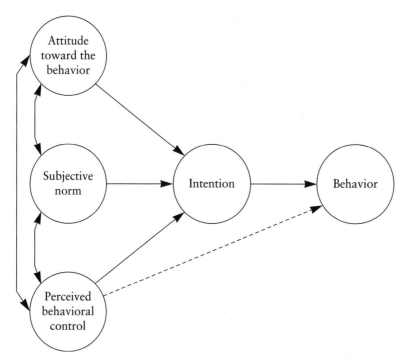

FIGURE 4.8   Theory of Planned Behavior. SOURCE: I. Ajzen, "The Theory of Planned Behavior," *Organizational Behavior and Human Decision Processes* 50 (1991):182.

spectives, it is clear that a person has a concern about the expectations of others and sees certain opinions to be more acceptable than others. Thus, these perspectives are ripe for the inclusion of norms and motivations for opinion expression.

Theory of Planned Behavior

Because of some of the criticisms of the theory of reasoned action, Ajzen proposed an alternative theory of planned behavior that substantially enlarges the original Fishbein-Ajzen model. Basically, Ajzen maintained that the reasoned action model is most relevant when considering voluntary behaviors. He stated that the theory must be revised to account for behaviors not wholly under voluntary control. The theory of planned behavior (see Figure 4.8) was developed to help account for these types of behaviors— behaviors that may be mandated or that may result from situations outside of the person's control.

A major premise of the theory of planned behavior is that all behaviors can be regarded as goals. For example, a behavior as voluntary as voting in an election can be regarded as a goal. However, sometimes these goals cannot be achieved because of experiences or events beyond a person's control. The intention to vote may not result in actually voting if your car breaks down on the way to vote and the tow truck does not arrive on the scene until after midnight.

According to the theory of planned behavior, the ability or inability to engage in the behavior is called perceived behavioral control, defined as one's perception of how easy or difficult it is to perform the behavior. This is a major difference between this theory and the theory of reasoned action. Thus, as shown in Figure 4.8, perceived behavioral control affects behavior in two ways: It influences intention to perform the behavior, and it may have a direct impact on the behavior.

In the area of public opinion research, the theory of planned behavior may help focus attention on the goal of the person giving the opinion. In some ways, then, it is similar to functional theories, except that it focuses on the goal of expressing the opinion rather than the motivation for holding the opinion. If, as we discussed with the theory of reasoned action, a person's goal is to be accepted among others, we may make very different predictions about the result of an opinion poll than we might make if we assume that most people's goals are to get the interview over with as quickly as possible. These issues have remained untouched by most current perspectives in public opinion.

Emotions and Attitudes

Your first reaction to the title of this section may be something like "What do emotions have to do with public opinion?" Previous texts on public opinion would probably answer, "Nothing." However, in recent years, researchers have been studying mood and emotions from many different perspectives and backgrounds. These scholars have been finding that emotions play a crucial role in how we act, what we think, and who we are. In short, emotions have a great deal to do with public opinion and the expression of our selves.

Early Conceptions of Emotion

Although much of our knowledge of emotions has been accrued during the past ten years, the founders of psychology and social psychology prescribed a crucial role for emotion in understanding psychological processes. William James's classic text, which defined the field of psychology,[87] included a number of chapters describing the role of emotion in various psychological processes. However, with the rise of behaviorist theories and interpretations in the field of psychology during the 1920s and continuing through the 1950s and 1960s, very little research dealt with the concept of mood or emotions. Researchers concentrated on specific aspects of observable behavior, or, when it became necessary for them to describe aspects of mental operations, they relied on the notion of cognition as a kind of logical, almost mathematical operation.

When the influence of behaviorism began to wane during the 1950s, the computer analogy became the dominant model in psychology, and, as you might guess, there was little room for emotions in a computer model of the mind! The emphasis was on logic and logical consistency, as well as on the development of efficient algorithms to simulate decisionmaking and other processes.

By the 1970s, however, psychologists began to realize the need for incorporating emotions into psychology and the field has grown over the last twenty years to include many different ideas and perspectives. A number of these perspectives are important to help us understand emotions. However, we will limit this discussion to two major contemporary approaches to emotion and how our understanding of emotion may be applied to public opinion: the cognitive and the social approaches to emotion.

Cognitive Approaches

Cognitive approaches to emotion seek to determine how emotions develop and how they interact with what we typically think of as cognition, or logical, conscious thought processes. One of the most important of these approaches is developed in the work of Robert Zajonc, who is primarily interested in the relationship between thinking and feeling, or affect:

> There are practically no social phenomena that do not implicate affect in some important way. Affect dominates social interaction, and it is the major currency in which social intercourse is transacted. The vast majority of our daily conversations entail the exchange of information about our opinions, preferences, and evaluations. And affect in these conversations is transmitted not only by the verbal channel but by nonverbal clues as well—clues that may, in fact, carry the principal components of information about affect. It is much less important for us to know whether someone has just said "You are a friend" or "You are a fiend" than to know whether it was spoken in contempt or with affection.[88]

Public opinion research might profit from an examination of emotion as described by Zajonc.[89] For example, he notes that one often knows how one feels about something long before one has a thoughtful opinion about it. If Zajonc's conceptualization is correct, the implications for public opinion polling are staggering! Many polls about particular issues are taken in which people are asked their opinions, some of which may be in the early stages of development.

If affect and cognition are two different systems, these polls may in fact be tapping two different things—opinions, among those who have decided, and feelings, among those who have not thought enough about the issue to develop a cognitive appraisal leading to an opinion. It is interesting to note that the wording in many public opinion polls suggests that the researcher is inherently aware of the problem, as such polls often ask not for an opinion but instead ask how a person feels about an issue.

Researchers are also suggesting that emotions and cognition may not be separate systems but may work in tandem in motivating our attitudes and behavior. Lyn Ragsdale has studied people's emotional reactions to presidents. Ragsdale found that people seem to weigh the emotional aspects of evaluation at least as strongly as the presidents' stands on issues or their economic situation. In fact, statistical tests from Ragsdale's studies suggest that emotions are actually better predictors of presidential evaluation than more "rational" (less emotional) explanations.[90]

Social Approaches

A very different perspective on emotions is provided by social psychologists who examine what are called the "social emotions." These include embarrassment, pride, and shame. Charles Cooley[91] was among the first to describe the social role of emotions. Cooley centered on pride and shame as managing devices that helped maintain a social bond and even hold the social system together. Much more recently, Rowland Miller and Mark Leary[92] and Thomas Scheff[93] suggest that many emotions are in fact social emotions, as they usually arise from interactions with other people. In addition, Miller and Leary describe the social sources and functions of embarrassment.

These social emotions depend on the implied presence and attention of others: They depend on our concern for what others are thinking of us and would not occur if we were unaware of others' presence or did not care what others thought.[94] Undoubtedly, such current perspectives as the "looking-glass perception," "false consensus," pluralistic ignorance," and the "spiral of silence" (see Chapter 6 for a discussion) could not be developed and the phenomena they describe could not occur except as social acts involving interactions with self and interactions with others.

As Miller and Leary[95] suggest, social emotions would not occur if we did not care what others thought. Similarly, the public opinion phenomena described above would not occur without the very same assumption. It is intriguing that these social emotions remain uninvestigated within these perspectives.

FIGURE 4.9 Doonesbury on Polling the Public Mood. SOURCE: DOONESBURY © 1980 G. B. Trudeau. Reprinted with permission of Universal Press Syndicate. All rights reserved.

Whether one proceeds from a cognitive or a social perspective, there is clearly a need for describing the role of emotion in public opinion research and theory (see Figure 4.9). It is interesting to note that both social and cognitive perspectives suggest the important link between emotions and the separation of humans from other animals. It is no coincidence that one of the first scientists to describe the role of emotion in both cognitive and social perspectives was Charles Darwin,[96] who devoted an entire book to the interplay of biology, emotion, and communication. It is clear that emotion—always closely related but seldom, if ever, investigated in public opinion research—is destined to play a stronger and stronger role in future research efforts.

Notes

1. Richard M. Perloff, *The Dynamics of Persuasion* (Hillsdale, NJ: Lawrence Erlbaum, 1993), p. 29.

2. Ibid.

3. Milton Rokeach, *The Nature of Human Values* (New York: Free Press, 1973).

4. Robert B. Cialdini, Richard E. Petty, and John T. Cacioppo, "Attitude and Attitude Change," *Annual Review of Psychology* 32 (1981):357–404; Daryl J. Bem, *Beliefs, Attitudes, and Human Affairs* (Belmont: Brooks/Cole, 1970); Stuart Oskamp, *Attitudes and Opinions* (Englewood Cliffs, NJ: Prentice-Hall, 1977).

5. Perloff, *Dynamics of Persuasion*; Milton J. Rosenberg and Robert P. Abelson, "An Analysis of Cognitive Balancing," in Milton J. Rosenberg et al., eds., *Attitude Organization and Change* (New Haven: Yale University Press, 1960), pp. 112–163.

6. Bernard C. Hennessey, *Public Opinion*, 5th ed. (Belmont, CA: Brooks/Cole, 1985).

7. Michael Corbett, *American Public Opinion: Trends, Processes, and Patterns* (New York: Longman, 1991).

8. Clark L. Hull, *Principles of Behavior: An Introduction to Behavior Theory* (New York: Appleton-Century-Crofts, 1943); Edward L. Thorndike, *The Fundamentals of Learning* (New York: Teacher's College Press, 1932).

9. Alice H. Eagly and Shelly Chaiken, *The Psychology of Attitudes* (Orlando, FL: Harcourt Brace Jovanovich, 1993).

10. Arthur W. Staats and Carolyn K. Staats, "Attitudes Established by Classical Conditioning," *Journal of Abnormal and Social Psychology* 57 (1958):37–40.

11. Ivan P. Pavlov, *Conditioned Reflexes* (London: Oxford University Press, 1927).

12. Arthur W. Staats, "Paradigmatic Behaviorism: Unified Theory for Social-Personality Psychology," in Leonard Berkowitz, ed., *Advances in Experimental Social Psychology* (San Diego: Academic Press, 1983), pp. 125–179; see also Eagly and Chaiken, *Psychology of Attitudes*; Chris T. Allen and Thomas J. Madden, "A Closer Look at Classical Conditioning," *Journal of Consumer Research* 12 (1985):301–315.

13. Staats, "Paradigmatic Behaviorism."

14. Eagly and Chaiken, *Psychology of Attitudes*.

15. Ibid., p. 400.

16. B. F. Skinner, *The Behavior of Organisms* (New York: Appleton-Century-Crofts, 1938).

17. Richard E. Petty and John T. Cacioppo, *Attitudes and Persuasion: Classic and Contemporary Approaches* (Dubuque, IA: William C. Brown Company, 1981).

18. Joel Greenspoon, "The Reinforcing Effect of Two Spoken Sounds on the Frequency of Two Responses," *American Journal of Psychology* 68 (1955):409–416.

19. For example, see Leonard Krasner, "Studies of the Conditioning of Verbal Behavior," *Psychological Bulletin* 55 (1958):148–170; Leonard Krasner, "The Therapist as a Social Reinforcement Machine," in Hans H. Strupp and Lester Luborsky, eds., *Research in Psychotherapy* (Washington, DC: American Psychological Association, 1962), pp. 61–94; Leon H. Levy, "Awareness, Learning, and the Beneficent Subject as Expert Witness," *Journal of Personality and Social Psychology* 6 (1967):365–370; Richard D. Singer, "Verbal Conditioning and Generalization of Prodemocratic Responses," *Journal of Abnormal and Social Psychology* 63 (1961):43–46.

20. See, for example, Petty and Cacioppo, *Attitudes and Persuasion*.

21. John Zaller, *The Nature and Origins of Mass Opinion* (New York: Cambridge University Press, 1992).

22. Staats and Staats, "Attitudes Established by Classical Conditioning."

23. Michael X. Delli Carpini and Bruce Williams, "The Method Is the Message: Focus Groups as a Method of Social, Psychological, and Political Inquiry," *Research in Micropolitics* 4 (1994):57–85.

24. Eagly and Chaiken, *Psychology of Attitudes*; Anthony G. Greenwald, "Cognitive Response Analysis: An Appraisal," in Richard E. Petty, Thomas M. Ostrom, and Timothy C. Brock, eds., *Cognitive Responses in Persuasion* (Hillsdale, NJ: Erlbaum, 1981), pp. 127–133.

25. Ibid.

26. Richard E. Petty and John T. Cacioppo, "The Elaboration Likelihood Model of Persuasion," in Berkowitz, ed., *Advances in Experimental Social Psychology*, pp. 123–205.

27. Ibid., p. 182.

28. Ibid.

29. Ibid., p. 126.

30. Ibid., p. 192.

31. Eagly and Chaiken, *Psychology of Attitudes*, p. 323.

32. Shelly Chaiken, "The Heuristic Model of Persuasion," in Mark P. Zanna, James M. Olson, and C. Peter Herman, eds., *Social Influence: The Ontario Symposium* (Hillsdale, NJ: Erlbaum, 1987), pp. 3–39.

33. Eagly and Chaiken, *Psychology of Attitudes*.

34. Leon Festinger, *A Theory of Cognitive Dissonance* (Evanston, IL: Row, Peterson, 1957).

35. Fritz Heider, "Attitudes and Cognitve Organization," *Journal of Psychology* 21 (1946):107–112.

36. Fritz Heider, *The Psychology of Interpersonal Relations* (New York: Wiley, 1958).

37. Jon A. Krosnick, "Psychological Perspectives on Political Candidate Perception: A Review of Research on the Projection Hypothesis," paper presented at the meeting of the Midwest Political Science Association, Chicago, 1988.

38. Eagly and Chaiken, *Psychology of Attitudes*.

39. Charles E. Osgood and Percy H. Tannenbaum, "The Principle of Congruity in the Prediction of Attitude Change," *Psychological Review* 62 (1955):42–55.

40. Petty and Cacioppo, *Attitudes and Persuasion*.

41. D. W. Rajecki, *Attitudes*, 2d ed. (Sunderland, MA: Sinauer, 1990), p. 64.

42. Eagly and Chaiken, *Psychology of Attitudes*.

43. Perloff, *Dynamics of Persuasion*, p. 220.

44. Festinger, *Theory of Cognitive Dissonance*.

45. Philip E. Converse, "The Nature of Belief Systems in Mass Publics," in David Apter, ed., *Ideology and Discontent* (New York: Free Press, 1964), pp. 206–261; Anthony G. Greenwald and David L. Ronis, "Twenty Years of Cognitive Dissonance: Case Study of the Evolution of a Theory," *Psychological Review* 85 (1979):53–57.

46. Festinger, *Theory of Cognitive Dissonance*.

47. Joel Cooper, Russell H. Fazio, and Frederick Rhodewalt, "Dissonance and Humor: Evidence for the Undifferentiated Nature of Dissonance Arousal," *Journal of Personality and Social Psychology* 36 (1978):280–285; Joel Cooper, Mark P Zanna, and Peter A. Taves, "Arousal as a Necessary Condition for Attitude Change Following Induced Compliance," *Journal of Personality and Social Psychology* 36 (1978):1101–1106.

48. Petty and Cacioppo, *Attitudes and Persuasion*.

49. Ibid., p. 96.

50. Albert Pepitone and Mark DiNubile, "Contrast Effects in Judgments of Crime Severity and the Punishment of Criminal Violators," *Journal of Personality and Social Psychology* 33 (1976):448–459; Marshall Dermer et al., "Evaluative

Judgments of Aspects of Life as a Function of Vicarious Exposure to Hedonic Extremes," *Journal of Personality and Social Psychology* 37 (1979):247–260.

51. Philip Brickman, Dan Coates, and Ronnie Janoff-Bulman, "Lottery Winners and Accident Victims: Is Happiness Relative?" *Journal of Personality and Social Psychology* 36 (1978):917–927.

52. Muzafer Sherif and Carl I. Hovland, *Social Judgment: Assimilation and Contrast Effects in Communication and Attitude Change* (New Haven: Yale University Press, 1961).

53. Eagly and Chaiken, *Psychology of Attitudes*, p. 368; Muzafer Sherif and Carolyn W. Sherif, "Attitude as the Individual's Own Categories: The Social Judgment-Involvement Approach to Attitude and Attitude Change," in Carolyn W. Sherif and Muzafer Sherif, eds., *Attitude, Ego-Involvement, and Change* (New York: Wiley, 1967), p. 130.

54. M. Brewster Smith, Jerome S. Bruner, and Robert W. White, *Opinions and Personality* (New York: Wiley, 1956); Daniel Katz, "The Functional Approach to the Study of Attitudes," *Public Opinion Quarterly* 24 (1960):163–176; Petty and Cacioppo, *Attitudes and Persuasion*.

55. Katz, "Functional Approach to the Study of Attitudes."

56. Smith, Bruner, and White, *Opinions and Personality*.

57. Herbert C. Kelman, "Compliance, Identification and Internalization: Three Processes of Attitude Change," *Journal of Conflict Resolution* 2 (1958):51–60.

58. Katz, "Functional Approach to the Study of Attitudes."

59. Ibid.; Eagly and Chaiken, *Psychology of Attitudes*.

60. Erving Goffman, *The Presentation of Self in Everyday Life* (New York: Anchor Books, 1959).

61. Robert M. Arkin, "Self-Presentation Styles," in James T. Tedeschi, ed., *Impression Management Theory and Social Psychological Theory* (London: Academic Press, 1981), pp. 311–333.

62. James T. Tedeschi, Barry R. Schlenker, and Thomas V. Bonoma, "Cognitive Dissonance: Private Ratiocination or Public Spectacle," *American Psychologist* 26 (1971):685–695.

63. Barry R. Schlenker, *Impression Management: The Self-Concept, Social Identity, and Interpersonal Relations* (Monterey, CA: Brooks/Cole, 1980), p. 204.

64. Tedeschi, Schlenker, and Bonoma, "Cognitive Dissonance."

65. Petty and Cacioppo, *Attitudes and Persuasion*.

66. Schlenker, *Impression Management*.

67. Eagly and Chaiken, *Psychology of Attitudes*; Angus Campbell et al., *The American Voter* (New York: Wiley, 1960).

68. Howard Schuman and Michael P. Johnson, "Attitudes and Behavior," *Annual Review of Sociology* 2 (1976):167.

69. For example, Bernard Kutner, Carol Wilkins, and Penny Rechtman Yarrow, "Verbal Attitudes and Overt Behavior Involving Racial Prejudice," *Journal of Abnormal and Social Psychology* 47 (1952):649–652; Richard T. LaPiere, "Attitudes vs. Actions," *Social Forces* 13 (1934):230–237; Irwin Deutscher, *What We Say/What We Do: Sentiments and Acts* (Glenview, IL: Scott, Foresman, 1973); Allan W. Wicker, "Attitudes Versus Actions: The Relationship of Verbal and Overt Be-

havioral Responses to Attitude Objects," *Journal of Social Issues* 25, 4 (1969): 41–78.

70. Herbert C. Kelman, "Attitudes Are Alive and Well and Gainfully Employed in the Sphere of Action," *American Psychologist* 29 (1974):310–324.

71. Schuman and Johnson, "Attitudes and Behavior."

72. Eagly and Chaiken, *Psychology of Attitudes*, p. 157.

73. Icek Ajzen, "Attitudes, Traits and Actions: Dispositional Prediction of Behavior," in Julius Huhl and Jurgen Beckmann, eds., *Action Control: From Cognition to Behavior* (New York: Springer-Verlag, 1987), pp. 11–39.

74. Perloff, *Dynamics of Persuasion*, p. 85.

75. Ibid.

76. Mark Snyder, *Public Appearances/Private Realities: The Psychology of Self-Monitoring* (New York: Freeman, 1987).

77. Perloff, *Dynamics of Persuasion*, p. 85.

78. Ibid.

79. Russell H. Fazio and Mark P. Zanna, "Direct Experience and Attitude-Behavior Consistency," in Berkowitz, ed., *Advances in Experimental Social Psychology*, pp. 161–202.

80. Ibid., p. 185.

81. Jon A. Krosnick, "Attitude Importance and Attitude Accessibility," *Personality and Social Psychology Bulletin* 15 (1989):297–308.

82. Russell H. Fazio and Carol J. Williams, "Attitude Accessibility as a Moderator of the Attitude-Perception and Attitude-Behavior Relations: An Investigation of the 1984 Presidential Election," *Journal of Personality and Social Psychology* 51 (1986):505–514.

83. Icek Ajzen and Martin Fishbein, *Understanding Attitudes and Predicting Social Behavior* (Englewood Cliffs, NJ: Prentice-Hall, 1980), p. 6.

84. Martin Fishbein and Icek Ajzen, "Acceptance, Yielding and Impact: Cognitive Processes in Persuasion," in Petty, Ostrom, and Brock, eds., *Cognitive Responses in Persuasion*, pp. 339–359.

85. Martin Fishbein et al., "Predicting and Understanding Family Planning Behaviors: Beliefs, Attitudes, and Intentions," in Icek Ajzen and Martin Fishbein, eds., *Understanding Attitudes and Predicting Social Behavior* (Englewood Cliffs, NJ: Prentice-Hall, 1980), pp. 130–147.

86. Martin Fishbein and Icek Ajzen, "Predicting and Understanding Consumer Behavior: Attitude-Behavior Correspondence," in Ajzen and Fishbein, eds., *Understanding Attitudes and Predicting Social Behavior*.

87. William James, *The Principles of Psychology* (New York: Holt, Rinehart and Winston, 1890).

88. Robert B. Zajonc, "Feeling and Thinking: Preferences Need No Inferences," *American Psychologist* 35 (1980):153.

89. Ibid.

90. Lyn Ragsdale, "Strong Feelings: Emotional Responses to Presidents," *Political Behavior* 13 (1991):33–65.

91. Charles H. Cooley, *Human Nature and the Social Order* (New York: Scribner, 1902).

92. Rowland S. Miller and Mark R. Leary, "Social Sources and Interactive Functions of Emotion: The Case of Embarrassment," in Margaret S. Clark, ed., *Review of Personality and Social Psychology* (Newbury Park, CA: Sage Publications, 1992), pp. 202–221.

93. Thomas J. Scheff, *Microsociology: Discourse, Emotion and Social Structure* (Chicago: University of Chicago Press, 1990).

94. Miller and Leary, "Social Sources and Interactive Functions of Emotion."

95. Ibid.

96. Charles R. Darwin, *The Expression of the Emotions in Man and Animals* (London: Murray, 1972).

Chapter Five

Sociological Perspectives

In Chapter 4, we considered the ways in which mental processes affect public opinion. In this chapter, we will examine the ways in which social forces affect public opinion formation and expression. It may seem strange to think of social factors influencing public opinion. American culture places a high value on individualism, and we tend to think in individualistic terms. The democratic ideal envisions an independent actor acquiring information, weighing choices, and rendering an evaluative judgment, all more or less without interference from the rest of the citizenry or from politicians.

This vision of the independent actor is further supported by the way that we most commonly measure public opinion. When we take a survey, we ask each individual, anonymously and privately, to express opinions on a variety of issues. Those individual responses are aggregated, and the result is called public opinion. However, reality is often not like what we try to measure in survey research. People interact and acquire information from each other and influence each other; they are socialized into particular ways of thinking about social problems, and they often feel constrained by norms or standards of "correct" behavior in our society.

Unfortunately, much of what we know about public opinion is based upon the investigation of what goes on within the individual, because this individual perspective has guided most empirical public opinion research. In recent years, however, scholars have determined that public opinion is a phenomenon far more complex than the aggregation of individual opinions suggests. Once again, scholars have turned their attention to the social and group factors that influence the formation and expression of public opinion.

Literally dozens of social alliances can affect public opinion: culture, political affiliation, socialization, and group dynamics, for a start. Rather than attempt an encyclopedic approach to this area of research, we want to introduce you to some of the more important theories available to the public opinion scholar from the field of social psychology. To begin with, we will consider the ways in which our own beliefs about others affect public opinion by reviewing attribution theory and stereotyping. Then we will consider at length how social norms—the rules and values that govern our social behavior—can also affect the opinions we form and the ways in which we express them.

One of the most important ideas that runs through this chapter is the concept of groups and group identity. You probably belong to dozens of groups. You are a member of your family, of a racial or ethnic group, of a gender group, of a social class. You may also affiliate with sororities, fraternities, sports teams, or *Star Trek* fans. You may even be a member of groups you are not aware exist, such as demographic groups created by survey researchers. For example, in the late 1980s, survey research identified a group of people who came to be known as "DINKs," which stood for "double income, no kids." It is unlikely that people who fit this description realized that they were part of a group until the group was "discovered" by the researchers. However, if you do recognize yourself as having some important characteristic in common with others, you probably *identify* with that group, even if you have never met another member. The fact that we tend to think of ourselves as members of some groups and nonmembers of others has important implications for public opinion, as you will see.

Attribution Theory

Attribution theories emphasize how people's inferences about the reasons behind other people's behaviors or attitudes affect their own agreement with these behaviors or attitudes. Interest in attribution theory began in the 1960s with research conducted by Daryl Bem. Bem stated that people infer their own and others' attitudes by observing the behavior of others.[1] He also said that people infer underlying characteristics of others, including others' motivations and intentions, from the verbal and nonverbal behaviors they observe. Thus, "when there appears to be an obvious reason for some behavior, people confidently attribute that behavior to that cause."[2]

Attitudes toward an issue will change to the extent that people view a message being presented as conveying the "truth" about the issue. The change will not take place if the message is attributed "to factors that compromise truth value."[3] For example, information that appears in a news story is more likely to be believed than information that appears in an advertisement, even if it is the same information. We know that advertisers have an interest in selling a product or a candidate or an idea. Information that appears in the news is usually perceived as more objective than that which appears in ads, since news derives its value from being "true" information. For this reason, if the nightly news report says that aspirin may help prevent heart attacks, you are more likely to believe it than you would be if a company that made aspirin put the same information into one of its ads.

As Eagly and Chaiken point out, the information people take into account in inferring the meaning behind messages will often include salient "contextual cues" such as the "communicator's personal circumstances and the audience the communicator is addressing."[4] In evaluating the truth value of a message, we may try to ascertain the reason the communicator is conveying the information and why we are the targets of the message. In the case of product advertising, a company is communicating with us in order to encourage us to buy its product, and we are targets of the message because we have resources (namely, money) that the company wants. No wonder we are often somewhat mistrustful of such messages.

Several researchers have found consistent biases in the ways we attribute our own and other people's statements and behavior. For one thing, we have a tendency to attribute our own negative behavior to aspects of the situation we are in. For example, if you fail to complete an assignment on time, you may attribute this to your busy schedule.

By contrast, we may attribute others' negative behavior to their personality. Your professor, receiving your late assignment, may attribute your lateness to your lack of commitment to that particular class. These biases often extend themselves to cover the groups to which we belong. That is, we tend to attribute negative behaviors of members of our own group to situational factors. We attribute negative behaviors of other groups to their personal characteristics.

Taxpaying citizens may see welfare mothers as lazy and undisciplined women who have children out of wedlock and leave others to pay the tab. The mothers may see themselves as poorly treated by men who abandoned them and by a society that does not provide them with adequate job training or child care. Attributions of this kind can clearly have important impact on public opinion. People who believe that welfare mothers are lazy and undisciplined are unlikely to support social welfare programs to aid these women. People who see these women as victims of circumstance are more likely to favor such programs.

Stereotyping

Stereotypes are generalizations about people "based on category membership."[5] That is, stereotypes are beliefs that all members of a group have the same qualities or characteristics. As social psychologists Michael Hogg and Dominic Abrams[6] note, a specific group member is assumed to be, and is often treated as, identical to other members of the group. The group, in turn, is perceived and treated by others as homogeneous.

Conceptually, most social psychologists define stereotypes as *"socially shared sets of beliefs about traits that are characteristic of members of a social category"* (emphasis ours).[7] Stereotypes tend to be shared by many members of a society, and it is not unusual for large portions of a society to agree on the stereotypes of particular groups—both in the language used to describe the group and in the way the group is treated by members of the larger society. These stereotypes are not always the product of direct experience. Many come to us indirectly from what we are told by other people or by the media.

Researchers have explored the issue of stereotypes from a number of perspectives and by investigating different stereotyped groups. Daniel Katz and Kenneth Braly[8] were among the first to study the stereotypes people hold concerning specific social groups. In these studies, respondents would select, from a long list, adjectives that they "believed to be typical of certain ethnic groups (in the United States)," groups such as Jews, Irish, and Turks.[9] The respondents would then indicate five adjectives that appeared to be most characteristic of each group. Often, more than 80 percent of responses indicated a general agreement between the respondents on what constitutes the stereotype of certain social groups.[10]

Think of the number of stereotypes you hold and how they affect your perceptions of others. It is clear that stereotypes often guide us in our attitudes toward and treatment of others. As an illustration, examine Table 5.1. Ask a friend, acquaintance, or parent to say whatever words or phrases come to mind when you say the words in the first list. Odds are very high that the response you get will be representative of stereotypes associated with each of these ethnic groups.

Now read the second list—the individual names—and jot down what is said about each of the people named. Compare the two results. How many descriptions of individuals matched a description of the general category to which they belong? The odds are that the phrases associated with the general category would not be very helpful in describing the individuals, even though each individual "fits" within one or more particular categories. It is clear that our notions of stereotypes require us to generalize certain characteristics so that it is often difficult to find an individual who matches the stereotype.

The early research of Katz and Braly[11] resulted in a number of descriptive studies on stereotyping. These studies ranged from explorations of gender and race stereotypes to studies on how we stereotype famous (as opposed to nonfamous) people, people in various professions, and people who live in certain parts of the United States. Descriptive studies on stereotyping are important because they aid us in establishing the stereotypes people hold of particular groups, understanding how strongly these stereotypes are held, and so forth. However, descriptive approaches do not help us understand underlying processes.

Stereotypes can have profound impact on people's lives and may influence decisions on personnel evaluations, job applications, and university admissions. These are decisions that can result in unintended discrimination.[12] The use of stereotypes in discrimination can result in very negative

TABLE 5.1   Sample Lists for Generating Generalized and Individual Responses

List 1: Generalization	List 2: Individual
Jew	Albert Einstein
Californian	Richard Nixon
Professor	O. J. Simpson
Farmer	Janis Joplin
Texan	Jimmy Carter
Actor	

Linkages: Albert Einstein, Jew; Richard Nixon, Californian; O. J. Simpson, actor and Californian; Janis Joplin, Texan; Jimmy Carter, professor and farmer.

SOURCE: M. A. Hogg and D. Abrams, *Social Identifications: A Social Psychology of Intergroup Relations and Group Processes* (London: Routledge 1988), p. 76.

outcomes. Certainly you would not like to enter the workforce knowing that your skin or hair color, your gender, or even the part of the country in which you were born could affect hiring decisions. However, consciously or unconsciously, employers sometimes make decisions based on stereotypes.

Stereotypes are also a social force in the sense that they can have profound influence on how we deal with those around us. They can have tremendous impact on public opinion, but they can also affect measurements of public opinion. We know from research on survey taking, for example, that people are more likely to give an opinion on an issue if they perceive that the interviewer is of their own race.* This, of course, is the result of the stereotypes we have of people of our own race and people of other races. A person who is white and of Anglo-Saxon descent in the United States has ideas about other white Anglo-Saxon Americans and other ideas about black African-Americans, and still other ideas about white Africans.

The very notion of stereotypes probably evokes a negative image in your mind. Typically, we think of stereotypes as bad, and we fear that if we stereotype, we are being narrow-minded or bigoted. But is this always the case? Stereotypes are quite cognitively complex, often containing both positive and negative elements. Although attitudes imply consistent evaluative responses, as Anthony Greenwald and Mahzarin Banaji note, a stereotype may "encompass beliefs with widely diverging evaluative implications." An example these researchers use is the stereotype of cheerleaders, which may "simultaneously include the traits of being physically attractive (positive) and unintelligent (negative)."[13]

Furthermore, in his classic discussion of stereotypes, Walter Lippmann argued that in some sense, stereotyping is a necessary condition for functioning in this world. He notes:

---

*Athey, Coleman, Reitman and Tang, 1960; Hatchett and Schuman, 1975–1976; Schuman and Converse, 1971.

There is neither time nor opportunity for intimate acquaintance. Instead, we notice a trait which marks a well-known type, and fill in the rest of the picture by means of the stereotypes we carry about in our heads. He is an agitator. That much we notice, or are told. Well, an agitator is this sort of person, and so *he* is this sort of person. He is an intellectual. He is a plutocrat. He is a foreigner. He is a "South European." He is from Back Bay. He is a Harvard Man. How different from the statement: he is a Yale Man. He is a regular fellow. He is a West Pointer. He is an old army sergeant. He is a Greenwich Villager: what don't we know about him then, and about her? He is an international banker. He is from Main Street.[14]

One of the most fascinating and elaborate stereotypes ever developed was the so-called criminal type. Many fiction writers, average people, and even criminologists of the late nineteenth and early twentieth centuries believed you could tell a criminal by physical appearance alone (see Box 5.1).

Lippmann says the most pervasive of all influences are those that "create and maintain the repertory of stereotypes."[15] He states:

We are told about the world before we see it. We imagine most things before we experience them ... Were there no practical uniformities in the environment, there would be no economy and only error in the human habit of accepting foresight for sight. But there are uniformities sufficiently accurate, and the need of economizing attention is so inevitable, that the abandonment of all stereotypes for a whole innocent approach to experience would impoverish human life.[16]

Stereotypes are a "cognitive consolidation" of how the world works. They are so fundamental to the way that we make sense of the world that we often do not realize we are using them at all. Just think: Every time you observe, "People would rather die than ask directions" or "Politicians are all crooked," you are stereotyping.

The alternative to using stereotypes is to treat each individual as a unique person, having nothing in common with anyone else. In other words, stereotypes are necessary if we are going to generalize about others. Without stereotypes, we cannot even begin to discuss culture, which is a reflection of all the characteristics a group of people has in common. For example, we can talk about an "American" culture, which may include "African-American" culture, "Hispanic-American" culture, and "Irish-American" culture. The cultures, in a sense, reflect certain real aspects of the stereotype, and the stereotypes reflect certain real aspects of the culture.

Therefore, if stereotypes are necessary in order for us to consolidate information about our world, why do we cringe with embarrassment if someone says we are stereotyping a person or group? Because, as Lippmann says, it is important to consider the character of the stereotypes and "the gullibility with which we employ them."[17] Stereotypes are not necessarily evil and need not be offensive if we understand that our stereotypes are ways of coding information. We must realize that our stereotypes are merely that, and we should be willing to change these viewpoints when we find out that they are inaccurate. We should also adjust our stereotypes when we find that by using them, we are hurting others or are misusing stereotypes to our benefit.

One of the most troubling aspects of stereotyping is that we tend to stereotype groups we are members of (in-groups) in ways that result in *positive* evaluations but stereotype groups that we do not identify with (out-groups) in ways that result in *negative* evaluations. For example, you might describe members of the sorority you belong to as "extremely intelligent" but describe the members of the sorority across the street as "serious party types."

Sometimes, these stereotypes seem to develop according to what Henry Tajfel calls an "accentuation principle."[18] Tajfel believed that people stereotype objects by bringing into sharper focus certain aspects of the environment that have special importance for those people. He hypothesized that people tend to engage in "perceptual accentuation," which makes them more aware of similarities *within* groups and differences *between* groups.

Take, for example, perceptions of height differences in men and women. Tajfel hypothesized that there would be an accentuation of *differences* in height between the two groups (men would be seen as taller, women as shorter than they really are) and an accentuation of *similarities* within each of these groups (differences in height between men and differences in height between women would seem less than they really are). An example of perceptual accentuation is illustrated in Figure 5.1.

Often, we not only perceive that others possess certain stereotypical traits but also *act* toward individuals or groups of people as if they possess these traits. You may, for example, find yourself treating the sorority members across the street with disdain and talking to them sarcastically. If you see one of them drinking a beer on the front porch you might turn to one of your own "sisters" and say, "See, that's all they do is party over there."

In fact, researchers have found that stereotypes can be "self-fulfilling prophecies" through a process called "behavioral confirmation." According to Rajecki, behavioral confirmation occurs "when a holder of a stereotype behaves consistently with that attitude and elicits the expected behavior from" the individual about whom the attitude is held, whether or not the individual being stereotyped "really has a personal disposition to act in that fashion."[19]

Mark Snyder, Elizabeth Tanke, and Ellen Berscheid[20] attempted to investigate whether behavioral confirmation occurs by looking at the social stereotype "What is beautiful is good" (described by Rajecki).[21] In their study, men and women were put in individual rooms and were told that the experimenter was "studying the acquaintance process."

Box 5.1   Lombroso's Criminal Types

Modern criminology has its roots in the work of a nineteenth-century Italian doctor named Cesare Lombroso. Lombroso believed that there was in fact a "criminal type." His theory was based on Charles Darwin's studies of evolution, then a novel idea, and the beliefs in "higher" and "lower" races that were also popular at the time. Lombroso argued that many criminals were actually genetic throwbacks to earlier evolutionary stages of man: These people were uncivilized and uncivilizable—born to a life of crime.[1]

Among Lombroso's most famous research efforts were his attempts to define the physical characteristics of the born criminal. He argued that many criminals had physical features reminiscent of those found in apes and other animals:

> Thus was explained the origin of the enormous jaws, strong canines . . . and strongly developed orbital arches [brow line] which he had so frequently remarked in criminals, for these peculiarities are common to carnivores and savages who tear and devour raw flesh. Thus also it was easy to understand why the span of the arms in criminals so often exceeds the height, for this is a characteristic of apes. . . . The other anomalies exhibited by criminals—the scanty beard as opposed to the general hairiness of the body, prehensile foot, diminished number of lines in the palm of the hand, cheek pouches, enormous development of middle incisors and frequent absence of the lateral ones, flattened nose and angular or sugarloaf form of the skull, common to criminals and apes; the excessive size of the orbits [eye sockets], which, combined with the hooked nose, so often imparts to criminals the aspect of a bird of prey, the . . . supernumerary teeth (amounting in some cases to a double row as in snakes) . . . all these characteristics pointed to one conclusion, the . . . criminal . . . reproduces physical, psychic, and functional qualities of remote ancestors.[2]

Criminals supposedly had sharp teeth, like rats, and, Lombroso claimed, some had the vestiges of a tail. They were more likely to be left-handed than "normal" people. It is from Lombroso's work that we derive the old saying that criminals have "shifty" eyes, "difficult to describe but . . . nevertheless apparent to all observers."[3]

Lombroso even argued that one could tell which sorts of crimes a born criminal might commit by looking at his or her physical characteristics:

> The lips of violators of women and murderers are fleshy, swollen, and protruding. . . . Swindlers have thin, straight lips. . . . Dark hair prevails especially in murderers, and curly and woolly hair in swindlers. . . . Those guilty of crimes against the person have short, clumsy fingers and especially short thumbs. Long fingers are common to swindlers, thieves, sexual offenders, and pickpockets.[4]

These images probably seem quite familiar to you. Writers of both fiction and nonfiction became fascinated with this vision of the born criminal, and echoes of Lombroso's work appear in many popular texts of that era, including Sherlock Holmes stories. Even today, fictional villains often have many of the characteristics of the "born criminal."

FIG. 4

HEAD OF CRIMINAL

HEAD OF CRIMINAL

According to Lombroso, these men display the typical physical characteristics of criminals. SOURCE: G. Lombroso-Ferrero, *Criminal Man According to the Classifications of Cesare Lombroso* (1911; Montclair, NJ: Patterson-Smith, 1972).

Lombroso's descriptions confirmed and expanded existing stereotypes people had about what criminals looked like. His daughter explained why: "Like the little cage-bird which instinctively crouches and trembles at the sight of the hawk, although ignorant of its ferocity, an honest man feels instinctive repugnance at the sight of a miscreant and thus signalises the abnormality of the criminal type."[5] Lombroso did modify his theory over time to take environmental factors into account, but consider the impact of these "scientific" stereotypes on the public! Would you offer a job to someone with thin lips and long fingers? Would you walk on the same side of the street at night with someone with dark hair and stubby hands?

Today, Lombroso's analysis of environmental contributions to criminal behavior still seem prescient, but his descriptions of the physical characteristics of "criminal man" are actually offensive. Nevertheless, the concept of the born criminal has not completely died away. As we write this, the Supreme Court is considering the constitutionality of a Kansas law that permits the state to continue the incarceration of "sexual predators" after they have served their sentences. The law is based on the argument that "sexual predators" cannot be rehabilitated and remain a threat to society. In other words, sexual predators are born criminals. However, there is one important difference we should note. One possible reason that many Kansans would favor such a law is that they believe sexual predators look just like the rest of us.

1. Leonard D. Savitz, introduction to Gina Lombroso-Ferrero, *Criminal Man According to the Classification of Cesare Lombroso* (1911; Montclair, NJ: Patterson Smith, 1972); Lombroso-Ferrero, *Criminal Man According to the Classification of Cesare Lombroso.*

2. Lombroso-Ferrero, *Criminal Man According to the Classification of Cesare Lombroso,* pp. 7–8.

3. Ibid., p. 14.

4. Ibid., pp. 14, 18, 20.

5. Ibid., p. 51.

REALITY

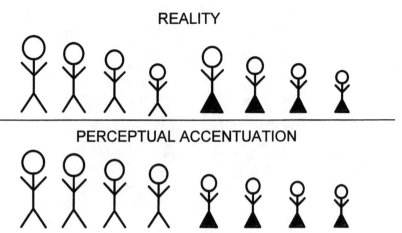

PERCEPTUAL ACCENTUATION

FIGURE 5.1 Perceptual Accentuation: Height Differences Between Men and Women. Stereotypes make us 'see' larger differences than are there.

The experimenter then explained to the men and women that they would be interacting socially with each other on the telephone. Prior to the telephone conversations, the researcher asked these men and women to write down general background information on a form, stating that the forms were to be exchanged as an aid to getting acquainted.

Each man received a woman's form with a photograph attached. The women, however, only received the form. Each man naturally assumed that the photograph was of the woman he would talk to on the telephone, but in reality it was not—it was the picture of a paid model. Of importance as well, half of the men taking part in this experiment were given photographs of women with low "attractiveness ratings," while half were given photographs of women with high "attractiveness ratings."

The researchers found that men with photographs of attractive women judged them to be "sociable, poised, humorous and socially adept."[22] Men who had photographs of unattractive women saw them as "unsociable, awkward, serious and socially inept." Behavioral confirmation occurred in that the men who subsequently talked to "attractive" women on the telephone treated them very differently during the telephone conversation from the way "unattractive" women were treated by the men they talked to on the telephone. This in turn affected the way in which the respective women communicated with the men. The way the men talked to the women "behaviorally confirmed" the stereotypes of attractive and unattractive women.

The findings of Snyder and his colleagues[23] have implications for everyday interactions. For example, if you think that people with red hair have bad tempers, you may treat a red-haired friend more gingerly than you

TABLE 5.2 Individual and Social Functions of Stereotyping

Individual Functions	*Social Functions*
Cognitive	Social causality
(well-differentiated and sharply	(explanation of widespread and
"focused" world)	distressing social or physical events)
Value	Social justification
(relatively positive self-evaluation)	(rationalization or justification of
	treatment of social groups)
	Social differentiation
	(accentuation and clarification of
	differences between social groups)

might a blonde friend. And, you might assume (because of stereotypes) that your blonde friend is not a math whiz and (perhaps equally incorrectly) that a Chinese friend is brilliant in math!

These perceptions, in turn, may affect whom you work with on projects or with whom you do homework. You may find that such stereotyping leads to disastrous results. But even if you end up flunking a math exam because you trusted your Chinese friend and found out that your blonde friend received an A on the math exam, would this cause you to change your stereotypes of Chinese or blondes concerning brilliance in math? Probably not.

Even animals are not immune from our stereotypes. You probably have stereotypes for certain breeds of dogs or for how various species of animals will behave. Dobermans are vicious and aggressive; collies are loyal and friendly. Grizzly bears have nasty tempers; dolphins are intelligent. Even though it might cause you to stop and think, one interaction with a friendly Doberman or a nasty dolphin would probably not change your stereotypes of these creatures very much!

Tajfel[24] offers a list of the functions that stereotypes serve for the individual and for society as a whole that offers us insights into both how stereotypes work and how they affect public opinion. They also serve as a summary of some of the positive and negative aspects of stereotyping that we have discussed above.

As indicated in Table 5.2,[25] individual functions of stereotyping include the cognitive function and the value function.

Cognitive Function

In this function, stereotyping serves an accentuation function, bringing the world into "sharper focus" for the individual. As we said, this can help people make sense of the complex world that they live in, but it can have negative effects if our stereotypes are inflexible.

Value Function

When stereotypes serve an evaluative function, they directly influence one's own value system and perception of oneself. They achieve this by contrasting the attributes of one's own group with the attributes of other groups. There is also an interest in preserving the "superiority" of the in-group and in retaining consistent exclusion of out-group members. Although we could think of examples of this type of exclusion occurring (girl scouts; men-only clubs), Tajfel[26] takes these examples one step further by citing a number of extreme historical events, such as the witch-hunts of Europe and the anti-Semitism of Nazi Germany. Such cases of out-group stereotyping resulted not only in exclusion but in mass murder and genocide. These cases were also known as powerful public opinion events! Unfortunately, the principle continues to surface periodically, with more recent events including insidious movements toward "ethnic cleansing" in Eastern Europe and the rise of neo-Nazis in Europe and the United States.

Tajfel describes some functions stereotypes serve for society, too. These are social causality, social justification, and social differentiation.

Social Causality

According to Tajfel, social causality is the search for an understanding of "complex and usually distressing large-scale social events" resulting in "scapegoating."[27] Out-groups are seen as the "cause" of the distress. Tajfel describes the use of Scots in Newcastle and Catholics in Oxford as scapegoats for the seventeenth-century plague in Britain as examples of social causality. Poor sanitation and a lack of quarantine practices had much more to do with spreading the disease.

Recently, public opinion about economic problems in the U.S. has been directed against the Japanese, for "causing" trade imbalances, and Mexicans, for "taking" American jobs (even though both countries are experiencing economic problems of their own). While there may be some connection between our economic difficulties and the behavior of other nations, social causality is at work to the extent that blame is placed on the others rather than on aspects of our own system that might explain the situation.

Social Justification

Tajfel uses the term social justification to refer to the use of specific stereotypes of a group in order to justify actions against that group. As an example, Tajfel describes "the way that colonialist powers of the last century constructed derogatory stereotypes (dim-witted, simple, lazy . . .) of exploited races (e.g., British stereotypes of the Irish)."[28] As Hogg and Abrams[29] note, such "dehumanization of a group makes its exploitation seem justified, natural and unproblematic" to individuals doing the stereotyping.

In the United States, a strong and very popular segment of the music industry at the end of the nineteenth and the beginning of the twentieth century took a decidedly racist turn, aimed at maintaining status differentials and segregation between whites and African-Americans, with heavy use of derogatory stereotypes in lyrics and titles in such chart-topping songs as "Stay in Your Own Backyard," "The Bully," and "All Coons Look Alike to Me."

Recordings of all three songs were major "hits" between 1900 and 1920. "Stay in Your Own Backyard" was a ballad in which a "mammy" directed her child (a "pickaninny") not to play with the white children; "The Bully" described a particularly "nasty nigger" who carried a razor for anyone who got in his way; and "All Coons Look Alike to Me" was a comic recording that depended on stereotyping for its humor. Songs like these helped reinforce existing laws and social rules that segregated African-Americans, kept them from voting, and prevented them from joining unions or obtaining many kinds of jobs.

Social Differentiation

According to Tajfel,[30] social differentiation is the tendency for ethnocentrism (enhancing one's own social group) to occur through stereotyping. Social differentiation tends to be accentuated under conditions in which the uniqueness or distinctiveness of one's own group appears to be eroding or "when social conditions are such that low status is perceived to be illegitimate and changeable."[31] Clearly, one reason for the popularity of the racist recordings of the early twentieth century described above was the tremendous strides in civil rights that were being made at the time; because of the uncertainty of future status differentials, white people were feeling threatened, and social differentiation was used to attempt to maintain the status quo.

A similar tack was taken in the 1950s when rock and roll was beginning to develop, and black and white teenagers were beginning to socialize together. Educators and parents joined forces in denigrating the African influences on popular music, calling it the "devil's music" and referring to the "low" station from which it sprang. On national television, Steve Allen ridiculed Elvis Presley's performance of "Hound Dog" (a song first written for and recorded by African-American blues singer Big Mama Thornton) by having him perform the song in a tuxedo, singing to a real hound dog.

The implications of social differentiation for public opinion formation, though potentially vital, have not been researched in any consistent fashion. Part of the problem is that social change must be examined over a relatively long period of time, an expensive option for public opinion scholars. An outcome of social differentiation in the 1950s, for example, may have been a "boomerang" effect. That is, the differences between young and old (the so-called generation gap), which exhibited themselves in speech, dress, and lifestyle divergence between the generations, contributed to protests and other events a decade later, shaking the country's basic values and causing tremendous strife and turmoil in everyday life. However, this cause-and-effect relationship is difficult to prove because so little public opinion data have been collected in a consistent way over time.

In general, the effects of stereotyping on public opinion have been understudied by scholars, but our discussion should give you some idea of the major impact this human tendency may have on public opinion outcomes.

Social Norms

A norm is "a principle of right action binding upon the members of a group and serving to guide, control and regulate proper and acceptable behavior."[32] Much like stereotypes and other group processes, social norms can profoundly influence public opinion formation and change. In fact, according to Hogg and Abrams norms have been defined as "the *stereotypic* perceptions, beliefs, and modes of conduct associated with a *group*" (emphasis ours)[33] Think of how norms influence the way you behave, dress, and even talk to those around you! If a student stood up in a large lecture class and began shrieking for no reason, you would probably be shocked. This behavior would be counter to the norms in our society—you have been taught that you should not shriek in class (unless it is an acting class). It is perfectly "normal," however, to stand up and shriek at a football or basketball game. The norms for the two situations are very different, and our public actions reflect that difference.

Similarly, when someone asks whom you plan to vote for in an upcoming presidential election, it is relatively "normal" to answer by naming either a Republican or a Democratic candidate. For certain elections, a third-party candidate (e.g., John Anderson in 1980, Ross Perot in 1992) is acceptable and considered a serious candidate by the public. Very rarely in the United States would someone even consider naming someone from the Communist Party, the Nazi Party, the Vegetarian Party, or any other political party. Part of the reason for this hesitation is that the norm in our society is for the U.S. political system to function as a two-party system, even though many viewpoints are omitted from consideration by both of those parties. The norm is so entrenched among most of us that most people do not take third-party candidates seriously.

Research on social norms has been around for a while. In fact, interest in norms dates back to the late nineteenth and early twentieth centuries, when scholars began attempting to measure the force of custom and tradition on society[34] or concerned themselves with mechanisms (such as norms) that lead to the influence of others and to compliance with the will of groups or individuals.[35] Often, scholars emphasized the usefulness of social norms for society.[36] Muzafer Sherif,[37] for example, says that norms "fulfill the function of ordering, simplifying, and regulating interaction"[38] and that once created, norms continue to influence group interaction even after the original members of the group are gone. In this section, we will discuss how norms develop, how they affect public opinion formation and expression, and how they are enforced.

Generating Norms

Many social norms are of such long standing that we rarely think about them at all. Violations of them seem quite strange. The social norm against public nudity is one we in the United States do not often consider. Other norms, however, develop and change frequently, such as norms about appropriate skirt lengths for women. We should also note that norms are created by groups, including cultures. Sunbathing topless in America violates a social norm. Sunbathing topless in Norway does not.

Some of the earliest studies of group norms explored the ways in which such norms develop. Sherif[39] conducted the first social psychological studies of norms. His classic experiments took advantage of what is called the "autokinetic phenomenon." Subjects shown a point of light in a darkened room, with no point of reference for it, will perceive the light to be moving even though it is stationary. Sherif showed such a light to groups of experimental subjects. He found that in this situation, people interacted socially to resolve the ambiguity of the light "movement." Eventually, members of the group "converged upon a consensual group decision concerning the supposed movement of the light."[40]

There have been a number of autokinetic studies since the initial experiment conducted by Sherif. These studies consistently find that (1) a norm is a product of social interaction, (2) the reality of a norm is rooted in perceptions of the physical and social world, (3) a norm is a quality of the group rather than of individuals in the group, and (4) a norm "exacts" conformity from those who join the group.[41] The studies reveal that norms are negotiated among members of a group and that different groups develop different norms. Thus, the norms belong to the *group*. If you are a member of several groups, you are likely to obey different norms in each of them. By the same token, if you join a new group, you are subject to its norms, although they may be different from the norms of other groups you belong to.

Norms are often very persistent. We may obey the same rules for behavior and think with the same preconceptions for long periods of time. But norms can change, too. The historian Ken Cmiel, who has documented some of the changes in the norms for polite behavior that occurred during the 1960s, has found that African-Americans who staged sit-ins at lunch counters in the South both upheld the norms of politeness by behaving in the same way any other customer would and at the same time defied the norms of polite behavior by violating the norm that African-Americans and whites could not share the same public spaces. The hippie counterculture argued that a new norm of politeness based on authentic expressions of one's true feelings rather than social rules of etiquette should be established. The result of these and other struggles over the norms for politeness resulted in an informalization of American culture, Cmiel argues.[42] Norms about language, dress, sexual behavior, and other social activities became less rigid. New behaviors from growing sideburns to smoking pot became more acceptable in polite society.

When norms are in transition, people are often uncomfortable. Norms about social exchanges between men and women are currently changing, and both groups seem somewhat touchy on the subject. Should men hold doors open for women? Pick up the checks at restaurants? Some men feel that such behaviors represent courtesy and respect. Some women feel demeaned by them, arguing that to engage in such behaviors suggests that women are incapable of doing these things for themselves. These interpersonal encounters can have larger social ramifications as well, as women file claims of discrimination or even sexual harassment against men.

Social Norms and Public Opinion.   Several studies have found that social norms can play an important part in opinion formation and expression. For example, Theodore Newcomb[43] found that women from a conservative background who attended Bennington College were rapidly influenced by the liberal political norms of that college. Newcomb said that "conservative" juniors who were members of sororities with liberal seniors rapidly conformed to the more liberal norms. He also found that these effects persisted after graduation from Bennington and, in fact, were still present more than twenty years later.[44] Obviously, expressions of opinions on social issues and vote decisions are influenced and sustained by norms, and it is findings such as these that make the concept of norms fascinating for public opinion scholars.

However, despite a long history of research and extensive use of the concept, there is still no consensus about the explanatory and predictive value of social norms—nor is there a consensus on a common definition of social norms.[45] As Robert Cialdini, Carl Kallgren, and Raymond Reno[46] note, there are, on the one hand, "those who see the concept as crucial to a full understanding of human social behavior."[47] On the other hand, there are those who view the concept as vague, overly general, often contradictory, and ill suited to empirical testing.[48]

Two Perspectives: Consensus and Conflict.   Two major perspectives we should discuss concern the roles norms play in our society: the "consensus" view of society and the "conflict" view of society. According to the *consensus* view, norms "embody the socially acceptable modes of action to achieve society's goals."[49] Thus, taking the consensus perspective, norms are responsible for uniformities of social behavior. Norms "arise to govern and ensure smooth and predictable social interaction and thus enable society to exist as a cohesive and stable entity. They suppress strife and conflict by furnishing consensus and agreement on an acceptable *modus operandum* for social life."[50]

Often, consensus norms are invisible in studies of public opinion. By definition, these norms are accepted by such a large proportion of the population that asking survey questions about them does not seem like a worthwhile activity. As Hogg and Abrams observe: "Norms can be concretized, through legislation, as the laws and rules of society, or more often they are so pervasive and so saturate society that they are 'taken for granted' and are invisible. They are the 'hidden agenda' of everyday interaction, the background to our behavior, the context within which things happen."[51]

Nevertheless, norms of this kind are very important. For example, as you will see in Chapter 7, a basic consensus on democratic principles is necessary in order for our political system to function. In fact, in our society, the norm of democratic decisionmaking is a powerful consensus norm. We adopt the model of our national government in many of our private activities, and the norms of democratic decisionmaking are seen as the legitimate way to make decisions in these spheres. Unions, condominium associations, and many other private groups use democratic models to govern their interaction. Officers or leaders are elected, and frequently, issues are voted on by the group as well. Majority rule is the rule of thumb. Yet there is no reason that makes it necessary for these groups to employ this model for organizing themselves. They are simply responding to an important social norm.

The *conflict* view of norms sees society as a "heterogenous collection of different groups of different sizes which stand in power and status relations to each other."[52] That is, different norms are seen as attached to different groups. Norms become the set of expectations concerning the attitudes, beliefs, and behaviors of particular groups. They also become the social uniformities that result in distinguishing characteristics among groups.

According to the conflict view, norms *describe* and evaluate the typical behavior of a typical member of a particular group or social category. In addition, norms *prescribe* by pointing out to people or groups that they ought to behave in a particular "circumscribed" manner.

Deborah Tannen has explored the different norms that govern men's and women's conversational styles and has investigated what happens when people of opposite genders try to converse together.[53] One important difference is in the norms that govern what Tannen calls "troubles talk." Both men and women engage in talk about the difficulties they experience in life, but the norms governing appropriate responses to such talk are very different for each group. Women respond to troubles talk by confirming the feelings of the speaker. Such responses are interpreted as a way of building rapport between the conversants. Women's responses say, "I understand." Men respond to troubles talk by dismissing the troubles of the other and telling stories of their own troubles. Such responses are interpreted as a way of respecting the vulnerability of the teller by not usurping his status or being condescending. Men's responses say, "Hey, I'm no better than you are." When men and women converse together, their different conversational norms produce unsatisfying outcomes. Women who tell their troubles feel that men are unsympathetic.

Tannen's research into the differences between men's and women's conversational styles also has important implications for opinion expression. She argues that it is a difference in conversational style that may prevent women from being heard in male-dominant environments. Men may treat women as equals, as being as free to speak out in meetings or other public forums as the men are. Women, however, may not be comfortable with "competing for the floor." They are treated as equals, but the outcome is unequal. Tannen suggests that both genders have a responsibility to take the other's conversational norms into account.[54]

It is clear from both the consensual and conflict views that norms fulfill a critical function for the individual: "They simplify, render predictable, and regulate social interaction. Without them social life would be unbearably complex and stressful: the individual would collapse beneath the tremendous cognitive overload involved in interaction."[55]

It is useful at this point to consider how both consensual and conflictual views of norms can help us understand public opinion formation and expression. For one thing, norms can create a common perspective from which to view social problems. Emile Durkheim, who viewed society as consensual, called such common perspectives "collective representations." Serge Moscovici, who focused on the conflict view of society, called them "*social representations.*"

Moscovici[56] notes that we derive only a small fraction of our knowledge and information from direct interactions between ourselves and the world.

Instead, most of our knowledge is supplied to us by communication, which affects our way of thinking and creates new content via social representations.[57] According to Moscovici, then, social representations refer to *the ideas, thoughts, images and knowledge that members of a collectivity share.*[58]

Through these representations, members of a society are able to construct "social reality."[59] The concept of social representations subsumes stereotypes and normative beliefs, highlighting the function of norms for furnishing an explanation that accounts for events and experiences we have in our lives. As a society, for example, we must choose to act on certain social problems and to not act on others. To a large extent, our shared perceptions of these problems (our social representations) determine the amount of effort we put into their resolution. Thus, to the extent that our perceptions of certain issues and events are similar, we can talk about a specific social problem. These social problems become public issues that can be debated and discussed and that eventually may be slated for public action. To the extent that we all share these perceptions, our society can coordinate its efforts and set priorities. Communication scholars have explored the ways in which media guide us in building social representations, a concept they call "framing" (see Chapter 11).

The theory of social representations has a certain amount of appeal for public opinion researchers, even though it is vague, imprecise, and difficult to understand. For example, Pierre Bourdieu[60] believes that public opinion is nearly impossible to measure because there is so much variety among social representations. He argues that unless the researchers and the respondents see an issue in more or less the same way, survey questions make no sense to the respondents and survey answers do not measure what researchers think they do. There appears to be much potential here for further study and refinement. We refer the interested student to works by Moscovici.[61]

Several other theories take a more explicitly conflictual view, as they describe the ways in which group norms affect the interaction among groups, social behavior, and public opinion. Tajfel's notion of *social categorization* attempts to explain how social norms aid in determining the ways people classify themselves and others as members of distinct categories and reference groups.[62] Social categorization research has shown that the simple act of classifying others into social categories is enough to provoke discrimination between in-group and out-group members.

This classification results in a variety of effects, including discriminatory group behavior, intragroup cohesion, and ethnocentric biases.[63] By simply defining a group, we appear to create a competition between "them" and "us," even when the distinction means nothing. After we have classified people as "them" or "us," we appear to look for (and find) differences, and the general weight of the differences is that "we" are better than "they" are.

Box 5.2   Group Identity and Group Polarization:
The Stanford Prison Study

In the early 1970s, a group of researchers at Stanford University wanted to find out how prison conditions affected the people who lived and worked in them. Many people believed that prisons were harsh places because only the worst kinds of people were locked up there. Others believed that prisons were bad because those who chose to become guards often had a sadistic streak. Craig Haney, W. Curtis Banks, and Philip Zimbardo demonstrated that the group dynamics of the prison setting played a key role in making their mock prison an extremely uncomfortable place. This is what they did.

First, they prescreened a group of men for their psychological stability. Then, they selected the twenty-two who were the most psychologically "normal" for the study. These men were randomly assigned to be either a prisoner or a guard in a simulation that was to last two weeks. All subjects were told that "prisoners" would be guaranteed "a minimally adequate diet, clothing, housing and medical care"[1] for the duration of the study. Both "prisoners" and "guards" were paid $15 per day for their participation. Those who became prisoners were "arrested" at their homes by the Palo Alto police and taken to the "prison," which was built into the basement of a building on the Stanford campus. They remained in prison twenty-four hours a day until the experiment ended. The "guards" worked eight-hour shifts and spent the other sixteen hours each day doing what they normally did. Each group was given no real instructions about what its role was to be, though the experimenters did engage in several procedures that were designed to dehumanize the "prisoners," such as "delousing" them when they arrived at the "prison" and giving them uniforms with "prisoner numbers." The "guards," who were also issued uniforms to promote group differences, met with the experimenters the day before the "prisoners" arrived to create a set of rules for the prison. The experimenters imposed one cardinal rule: "Guards" were not to use violence against "prisoners." The researchers reported that all other "prison rules" were developed by "guards" and experimenters together.

The results of the experiment were stunning. "Prisoners" and "guards" became so involved in their roles that within days, several prisoners had to be released because they were in so much emotional distress. The researchers decided to end the experiment early. Haney, Banks, and Zimbardo report:

> The most dramatic evidence of the impact of the mock prison upon the participants was seen in the gross reactions of five prisoners who had to

---

One clear example of social categorization occurs in the abortion issue, where individuals have tended to align themselves as either "pro-life" or "pro-choice." As is clear from current headlines and news stories, both sides see their own group as "clearly in the right," as having morals somewhat superior to the opposing group. Another striking example was the result of an experiment on prison life conducted at Stanford University (see Box 5.2).

be released from the study because of extreme emotional depression, crying, rage, or acute anxiety. The pattern of symptoms was quite similar in four of the subjects and began as early as the second day of imprisonment. The fifth subject was released after being treated for a psychosomatic rash which covered portions of his body. . . . When the experiment was terminated prematurely after only six days, all the remaining prisoners were delighted by their unexpected good fortune; in contrast, most of the guards seemed to be distressed by the decision to stop the experiment. It appeared to us that the guards had become sufficiently involved in their roles so that they now enjoyed the extreme control and power they exercised and were reluctant to give it up.[2]

Haney, Banks, and Zimbardo demonstrated that even "normal" people react in inhumane ways to the conditions of prison life. They also demonstrated that group norms are powerful and quick to develop. In only six days, "prisoners" and "guards" had adopted group norms and group identities that encouraged both polarization and inhumane treatment on the part of the "guards." Routine bodily functions like eating or going to the bathroom became privileges for the "prisoners," to be earned with good behavior. The "prisoners" began to lose self-esteem and respect for each other. The "guards" developed a group norm of never questioning another guard's treatment of a "prisoner," no matter how harsh.

The development of these norms at the Stanford prison both regulated behavior and maximized the differences between "prisoners" and "guards." The researchers report, "Not to be tough and arrogant was taken as a sign of weakness by the other guards." The "prisoners," by contrast, developed a norm of passivity as a means of coping with the arbitrary authority of the "guards." The results of the Stanford prison study tell a cautionary tale about the power of groups and group identity. As one "prisoner" in the study put it, "I learned that people can easily forget that others are human."[3]

SOURCE: Craig Haney, W. Curtis Banks, and Philip G. Zimbardo, "Interpersonal Dynamics in a Simulated Prison," in M. Patricia Golden, ed., *The Research Experience* (Itasca, IL: F. E. Peacock Publishers, 1976), pp. 157–177.

---

1. Haney, Banks, and Zimbardo, "Interpersonal Dynamics in a Simulated Prison," p. 159.
2. Ibid., p. 164.
3. Ibid., pp. 173, 170.

When individuals classify themselves and others into categorical groups, there are perceptual effects: There is increased perception of differences among groups (polarization) and decreased perception of differences within groups (homogenization). These effects can result in standardization of public opinion within groups and an exaggeration of differences in public opinion among groups.

Group polarization is conformity to a polarized norm that defines one's own group in contrast to other groups within a specific social context.[64] Under conditions that render an in-group psychologically salient, people conform to the in-group norm, the position perceived as most "consensual."[65] In some circumstances, the group norm will be the position that is the average for the in-group distribution—the position that minimizes the differences between in-group members.

However, it is equally likely that the norm of the in-group will not be the group mean but some other point in the distribution. The resultant norm occurs because groups do not exist in isolation but in a wider social frame of reference that encompasses both in-groups and out-groups. The defining features of a group—its norms and stereotypes—not only characterize the in-group's qualities but also distinguish the in-group clearly from relevant other groups, thus maximizing differences between in-groups and out-groups.[66] As you can see, these norms can also have an impact on perceptions of public opinion, maximizing differences between the in-group and the out-group.

For example, we might expect to see group polarization effects when loggers and environmentalists interact, even though both groups ultimately wish to see the forest survive. Environmentalists, in the face of opposition from loggers, may come to argue that the forest must be preserved in a pristine state and that no logging activity is acceptable. They may take this position even though many of their members once believed that some logging was compatible with saving the forest and they may even have worried about the loggers losing their jobs. The loggers, by comparison, may come to argue that jobs are more important than saving the forest and advocate clear-cutting and replanting, even though many of their members once believed that preserving old-growth trees was a worthy goal.

The actual position of the in-group norm is often a trade-off between minimizing intragroup differences and maximizing intergroup differences. The homogenization of group members' opinions becomes a part of the polarization effect as members seek to differentiate themselves from the out-group.

Vincent Price[67] suggests that news reports cue their recipients to think about the reported issue in terms of their particular group perspective. This perspective leads to polarized or exaggerated perceptions of group opinions, finally leading to expression of personal opinion consistent with the exaggerated perception of the group norm. Price interprets his data as indicating that media reports emphasizing group conflicts may play a role in the formation of public opinion. Thus, groups may affect public opinion even when no interpersonal interaction occurs within them.

Two Functions: Descriptive and Injunctive Norms.   Cialdini, Kallgren, and Reno[68] distinguish two types of norms. Norms that characterize what is commonly done (the perception of what most people do) are *descriptive* *norms*; the norms that characterize the perception of what most people approve or disapprove (what ought to be done) are *injunctive* norms. Descriptive norms have an informational function, whereas injunctive norms have a sanctioning function.

Descriptive norms motivate people by providing evidence of effective or appropriate actions (e.g., "If everyone is doing or thinking or believing it, it must be a sensible thing to do or think or believe"). Descriptive norms are important to consider when studying public opinion as perceptions of what others might be doing or thinking. At this moment in American business history, many people are investing in mutual funds. This behavior has become, in some ways, normative. For some, investing in mutual funds may be something they do rationally, because interest rates are low or because it will be many years before they retire. However, for others, these investments are a normative behavior. They invest in mutual funds because others do so and appear to reap rewards. These norms are tied to other descriptive norms regarding the overall health of the American economy.

Festinger's[69] social comparison theory (see Chapter 6 for a more complete discussion) suggests an important role for descriptive norms in providing the comparison base by which individuals validate their opinions. Opinions that are normative for the group provide a validity check for individuals, because others (who were already judged to be similar to the individual) hold a particular opinion norm.[70] According to Festinger, the opinion norm thus provides the closest thing to an "objective" measure of what is real, true, or the "correct" opinion to hold. For instance, opinion norms about the future of the American economy are the closest we can come to "knowing" what will happen to the economy in the next few years. Thus, descriptive norms play an important role in opinion formation.

In contrast, injunctive norms specify what ought to be done, that is, they are the "moral rules of the group."[71] These norms can affect public opinion expression through a phenomenon known as "social desirability." Injunctive norms help people determine whether it would be "wrong" for them to reveal what they really think.[72] (For a further discussion of social desirability phenomena, see Chapter 6.)

People might be asked for their opinions on an issue related to racial unrest, for example, and a certain percentage of respondents might want to give a particular opinion but might perceive that such an opinion would probably be considered racist by others. The injunctive norm at work here—that racism is bad—would stifle opinion expression, though it might not stifle the opinion itself. An example of the role of injunctive norms in public opinion expression is provided by Barbara Anderson, Brian Silver, and Paul Abramson, who suggest that survey respondents often "exaggerate their conformity with socially approved norms": "However well theoretical concepts are defined, survey questions are formulated and data are analyzed, the data are the product of an interview. The interview involves an interaction between the interviewer and respondent in which the stimulus is not just the 'question' as it is written in the survey booklet, but also the social context in which the question is asked."[73]

One way to think about the relationship between these two types of norms and public opinion is to recognize that descriptive norms tend to influence opinion *formation*, whereas injunctive norms tend to influence opinion *expression*.

Enforcing Norms

Group conformity (and the enforcement of group norms) is of interest to public opinion scholars who examine how and why people conform to group pressure when forming and expressing their opinions. Conformity is the mechanism by which norms affect public opinion. Thus, understanding group conformity can be critical to understanding the relationship of norms to the public opinion process.

Solomon Asch conducted some of the first studies that attempted to look at the pressure that groups can exert on individuals to conform. In these studies, groups of seven to nine people would sit in a semicircle. The subjects were then shown lines of clearly varying lengths and were asked which lines were the longest and which were the shortest.

Only the last person to respond in the group was a true "naive" subject. All of the other members of this "group" were confederates (people who were "planted" in the group by the experimenter). When it was their turn to speak out loud, the confederates would give a unanimous *incorrect* judgment.[74]

Obviously, Asch was interested in how the subjects would respond to group pressure, since in reality there was only one clearly correct answer (the lines varied significantly in size) (see Figure 5.2). However, it is interesting to note that the subjects accepted the incorrect group position about one-third of the time.

The fact that some people conform more than others has led to a great deal of research on establishing whether there may be a "conformist syndrome" or a "conformist personality."[75] For example, conformists appear to have low self-esteem,[76] a high need for social approval,[77] low IQ, high anxiety, insecurity, and so forth.[78] Stanley Milgram's[79] experiments, however, showed that "average" people conform to authority when they are placed in situations where that authority seems relevant.

Actually, people may conform publicly without changing their attitudes. Eagly and Chaiken[80] suggest that when influence is of an injunctive nature (when it is socially desirable to conform), social pressures may produce public agreement with other group members but provide little or no private acceptance. For example, imagine that you and some friends are watching

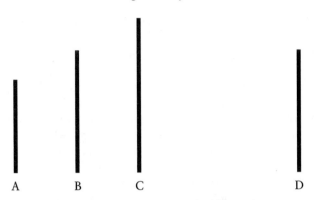

FIGURE 5.2   The Asch Lines. Which line is longer?

TV and a show you particularly enjoy comes on. One of your friends says that the show is "really stupid," and another person quickly agrees. Another chimes in, then asks you what you think. Faced with feeling different, many people in this kind of situation will verbally conform to the group norm—not liking the program—while not actually changing their attitude toward the program at all.

Paul Nail[81] has distinguished four possibilities in the compliance-acceptance situation. We will take each in turn:

1. Conforming privately and publicly (conversion). In this case, the individual becomes convinced that the group norm is the "correct" or best opinion to have on the matter and changes his or her own attitude toward the subject (private acceptance) as well as agreeing with the group verbally (publicly).
2. Conforming publicly but not privately (compliance). This behavior is like the example above regarding the TV program. In this case, the individual is willing to alter personal opinion publicly but will not change his or her attitude about the topic (privately).
3. Conforming privately but not publicly (anticompliance). This is the odd situation in which the individual agrees with the group norm in private but will not say so in public. This situation may be found when a person is very committed to a position but does not want to admit the possibility of being wrong and therefore maintains the original position long after not believing in it anymore.
4. Nonconformity at both private and public levels (independence). In this case, the individual simply does not care what others think and will assert an opinion publicly even when it contradicts the group norm.

Thus, although many researchers use the term conformity to refer to public agreement, Nail suggests that conformity may not be an accurate label for what occurs.[82] The idea of private and public aspects of conformity should have considerable interest for researchers in public opinion and provides an important consideration for research on public opinion and norm conformity. Expression of an opinion that is in keeping with a social norm does not necessarily indicate that behavior or even an individual's belief on the subject is consistent with what was expressed.

Michael Hogg and John Turner argue that issues such as those of private and public aspects of conformity can be integrated and simplified in order to arrive at a distinction between two forms of social influence that "share the burden of explanation": normative influence and informational influence.[83] According to Morton Deutsch and Harold Gerard,[84] normative influence results from the individual's need for social approval and acceptance. It creates conformity that "is merely public compliance with, rather than private acceptance or internalization of, the group's attitudes, beliefs, opinions or behaviors."[85] Conformity in this case is not associated with true internal change. The individual will go along with the group, however, to be accepted by the group, to avoid punishment, and so forth.

Normative influence can arise under conditions in which the group (or individual) is perceived to have coercive power (e.g., the power to criticize, threaten, and so on) or the ability to reward (such as the power to give affection or praise). An important precondition for normative influence is the perception of surveillance by the group. Individuals are unlikely to comply with norms they have not internalized unless they believe they might get "caught."

Hogg and Turner also suggest that normative influence may be powerful if the reference group is very important to the individual.[86] Because reference groups are implicitly defined in terms of emotional attachment (such as liking and admiration),[87] pressures for uniformity within such groups will be powerful, based on a strong desire for approval or acceptance. Thus, we would expect that a person would be more likely to conform to the norms within a tight circle of friends than among strangers. We simply are more concerned about what the people we care about think than we are about what strangers think of our behavior.

Unlike normative influence, informational influence results from the individual's need to be correct.[88] It is "true influence" in that it results in private acceptance or internalization of beliefs, attitudes, and behaviors.

According to Hogg and Abrams, the power of informational influence "resides in the perceived expertise or expert power (i.e., possession of knowledge that others repeatedly need to draw upon), or the informational power (possession of a specific piece of information that is needed) of others. The precondition for informational influence is subjective uncertainty or lack of confidence in the validity of one's beliefs, or opinions."[89]

In most circumstances, normative and informational influence "operate together to create conformity." However, there are those individuals who will fight or resist these influence attempts, especially if they are perceived to threaten individual freedoms.

Public opinion scholars have begun to use conformity research as a basis for some of their theoretical work on public opinion formation. For example, Elisabeth Noelle-Neumann asserts that much of her research on the spiral of silence is based on conformity studies. Her "fear of isolation" concept is based in part on the experimental work of Asch[90] and Milgram.[91] Noelle-Neumann states that people often fear isolation because of their need to be associated with others; they have a strong need to conform in order to be accepted (for a more complete discussion, see Chapter 6).

Conclusion

Public opinion scholars seldom attempt to understand the influence of social and institutional forces (such as laws, courts, and social value systems) on public opinion processes, and vice versa. Instead, much like research in collective behavior,[92] public opinion research is a field that presents a perfunctory image of the social process but relies heavily on individualistic explanations. Most public opinion scholars approach the study of public opinion as individual behavior while paying lip service to the collective or sociological aspects of public opinion.

Certainly, sociological factors are critical to the understanding of public opinion processes and functions, and it would be useful if more research were conducted that examined this phenomenon from a sociological perspective.

For example, one decidedly sociological public opinion phenomenon is what sociologists refer to as collective behavior. Collective behavior can include organized expressions of opinion such as strikes, sit-ins, or letter-writing campaigns. It also includes disorganized expressions of opinion such as riots, fads, and episodes of "mass hysteria." Although these phenomena are clearly social in nature, much of the research on collective behavior has focused on psychological aspects of it.

Most notably, scholars have worked for years to understand what motivates people to act on their opinions. For example, many acts of collective behavior are undertaken by groups agitating for civil rights. Such rights would be bestowed on all members of a social group regardless of their participation in the collective behavior. When the right to vote was extended to women, it was extended to all women, not just to the suffragettes. So why would a woman risk jail, public disgrace, or worse to obtain these rights if she would gain them anyway by letting others take such risks? In the case of an episode of mass hysteria, scholars have been interested in the psychological differences between those who were caught up in the panic and those who were not.

Other sociological aspects of collective behavior have often been neglected as well, especially as they relate to opinion expression. Few studies have explored such issues as the relationship of group organization to opinion expression.

One potentially fruitful area of research is what Thomas Scheff says is the most crucial human motive, the "maintenance of social bonds."[93] Scheff suggests that secure social bonds are the force that holds a society together. An intact social bond balances the needs of the individual with the needs of the group. Scheff suggests that social scientists need to study the social bond if they are ever to understand human behavior. In Scheff's view, much of human behavior is motivated by the maintenance of the social bond. A number of ideas related to public opinion are clearly relevant to this approach, including social desirability effects in interviewers, Noelle-Neumann's idea of "fear of isolation," the "false consensus," and "pluralistic ignorance" phenomena (see Chapter 6), and many other concepts described in this book. We encourage students of public opinion to explore the potential of sociological theory in understanding public opinion processes.

Notes

1. Daryl J. Bem, "Self-Perception Theory," in Leonard Berkowitz, ed., *Advances in Experimental Social Psychology* (San Diego: Academic Press, 1972), pp. 1–62.

2. Richard E. Petty and John T. Cacioppo, *Attitudes and Persuasion: Classic and Contemporary Approaches* (Dubuque, IA: William C. Brown Company, 1981), p. 163.

3. Alice H. Eagly and Shelly Chaiken, *The Psychology of Attitudes* (Orlando, FL: Harcourt Brace Jovanovich, 1993), p. 351.

4. Ibid.

5. Michael A. Hogg and Dominic Abrams, *Social Identifications: A Social Psychology of Intergroup Relations and Group Processes* (New York: Routledge, 1988).

6. Ibid.

7. Anthony G. Greenwald and Mahzarin R. Banaji, "Implicit Social Cognition: Attitudes, Self-Esteem, and Stereotypes," *Psychological Review* 102, 1 (1995):14.

8. Daniel Katz and Kenneth W. Braly, "Social Stereotypes of One Hundred College Students," *Journal of Abnormal and Social Psychology* 28 (1933):280–290.

9. Hogg and Abrams, *Social Identifications*, p. 67.

10. Katz and Braly, "Social Stereotypes of One Hundred College Students."

11. Ibid.

12. Greenwald and Banaji, "Implicit Social Cognition."

13. Ibid., p. 14.

14. Walter Lippmann, *Public Opinion* (New York: Harcourt, Brace, 1922), p. 59.

15. Ibid.

16. Ibid., pp. 59–60.

17. Ibid., p. 60.

18. Henry Tajfel, "The Anchoring Effects of Value in a Scale of Judgments," *British Journal of Psychology* 50 (1959):294–304; Henry Tajfel, "Social and Cultural Factors in Perception," in Gardner Lindzey and Elliot Aronson, eds., *Handbook of Social Psychology* (Cambridge: Addison-Wesley, 1969), pp. 30–45.

19. D. W. Rajecki, *Attitudes*, vol. 2, 2d ed. (Sunderland, MA: Sinauer, 1990), p. 282.

20. Mark Snyder, Elizabeth D. Tanke, and Ellen Berscheid, "Social Perception and Interpersonal Behaviour: On the Self-Fulfilling Nature of Social Stereotypes," *Journal of Experimental Social Psychology* 11 (1977):1–13.

21. Rajecki, *Attitudes.*

22. Ibid., pp. 282–285.

23. Snyder, Tanke, and Berscheid, "Social Perception and Interpersonal Behaviour."

24. Henry Tajfel, *Human Groups and Social Categories: Studies in Social Psychology* (Cambridge, England: Cambridge University Press, 1981).

25. Hogg and Abrams, *Social Identifications*, p. 76.

26. Tajfel, *Human Groups and Social Categories.*

27. Hogg and Abrams, *Social Identifications*, p. 77.

28. Ibid.

29. Ibid.

30. Tajfel, *Human Groups and Social Categories.*

31. Hogg and Abrams, *Social Identifications*, p. 77.

32. *Webster's New Collegiate Dictionary* (Springfield, MA: G. and C. Merriam Company, 1981), p. 776.

33. Hogg and Abrams, *Social Identifications.*

34. Walter Bagehot, *Physics and Politics* (1869; New York: Knopf, 1946); William G. Sumner, *Folkways* (Boston: Ginn, 1906).

35. Edward A. Ross, *Social Control: A Survey of the Foundations of Order* (New York: Macmillan, 1901).

36. Robert K. Merton and Alice S. Kitt, "Contributions to the Theory of Reference Group Behavior," in Robert K. Merton and Paul F. Lazarsfeld, eds., *Studies in the Scope and Method of "The American Soldier"* (New York: Free Press, 1950), pp. 40–105.

37. Muzafer Sherif, "A Study of Some Social Factors in Perception," *Archives of Psychology* 27 (1935):1–60; Muzafer Sherif, *The Psychology of Social Norms* (New York: Harper and Brothers, 1936).

38. Hogg and Abrams, *Social Identifications*, p. 160.

39. Sherif, "Study of Some Social Factors in Perception"; Sherif, *Psychology of Social Norms.*

40. Sherif, "Study of Some Social Factors in Perception"; Vincent Price and Hayg Oshagan, "Social-Psychological Perspectives on Public Opinion," in Theodore L.

Glaser and Charles T. Salmon, eds., *Public Opinion and the Communication of Consent* (New York: Guilford Publications, 1989), pp. 177–216; Muzafer Sherif, B. Jack White, and O. J. Harvey, "Status in Experimentally Produced Groups," *American Journal of Sociology* 60 (1955):370–379.

41. Hogg and Abrams, *Social Identifications*, p. 161.

42. Kenneth Cmiel, "The Politics of Incivility," in David Farber, ed., *The Sixties: From Memory to History* (Chapel Hill: University of North Carolina Press, 1994), pp. 263–290.

43. Theodore M. Newcomb, *Personality and Social Change: Attitude Formation in a Student Community* (New York: Holt, Rinehart and Winston, 1943).

44. Theodore M. Newcomb et al., *Persistence and Change: Bennington College and Its Students After Twenty-five Years* (New York: Wiley, 1967).

45. Carroll J. Glynn, "Public Opinion as a Normative Opinion Process," in Brant R. Burleson, ed., *Communication Yearbook 20* (Thousand Oaks, CA: Sage Publications, 1996), pp. 157–183.

46. Robert B. Cialdini, Carl A. Kallgren, and Raymond R. Reno, "A Focus Theory of Normative Conduct: A Theoretical Refinement and Reevaluation of the Role of Norms in Human Behavior," in Mark P. Zanna, ed., *Advances in Experimental Social Psychology* (San Diego: Academic Press, 1991), pp. 201–234.

47. Sherif, *Psychology of Social Norms*; David J. McKirnan, "The Conceptualization of Deviance: A Conceptualization and Initial Test of a Model of Social Norms," *European Journal of Social Psychology* 10 (1980):79–93.

48. Dennis L. Krebs and Dale T. Miller, "Altruism and Aggression," in Lindzey and Aronson, eds., *Handbook of Social Psychology*, vol. 2, pp. 1–72; Margaret M. Marini, "Age and Sequencing Norms in the Transition to Adulthood," *Social Forces* 63 (1984):229–244.

49. Hogg and Abrams, *Social Identifications*, p. 159.

50. Ibid.

51. Ibid.

52. Ibid.

53. Deborah Tannen, *You Just Don't Understand: Women and Men in Conversation* (New York: Random House, 1990).

54. Ibid.

55. Hogg and Abrams, *Social Identifications*, p. 159.

56. Serge Moscovici, "On Some Aspects of Social Representations," paper presented at the symposium on "Representations" of the American Psychological Associations, Anaheim, CA, 1983.

57. Glynn, "Public Opinion as a Normative Opinion Process."

58. Serge Moscovici, *La psychanalyse, son image et son publique* (Paris: Presses Universitaires de France, 1961); Serge Moscovici, "The Coming Era of Representations," in Jean-Paul Codol and Jacques-Philippe Leyens, eds., *Cognitive Analysis of Social Behavior* (The Hague: Martinus Nijhoff, 1982), pp. 115–119.

59. Glynn, "Public Opinion as a Normative Opinion Process."

60. Pierre Bourdieu, "Public Opinion Does Not Exist," in Armand Mattelart and Seth Siegelaub, eds., *Communication and Class Struggle*, vol. 1 (New York: International General, 1972), pp. 124–130.

61. Serge Moscovici, "On Some Aspects of Social Representations"; Moscovici, *La psychanalyse*; Moscovici, "Coming Era of Representations"; Serge Moscovici, "On Social Representations," in Joseph P. Forgas, ed., *Social Cognition* (London: Academic Press, 1981), pp. 80–95.

62. Price and Oshagan, "Social-Psychological Perspectives on Public Opinion"; Henry Tajfel, "The Social Psychology of Intergroup Relations," *Annual Review of Psychology* 33 (1982):1–39; John C. Turner and Penelope J. Oakes, "Self-Categorization Theory and Social Influence," in Paul B. Paulus, ed., *Psychology of Group Influence* (Hillsdale, NJ: Lawrence Erlbaum Associates, 1989), pp. 233–278.

63. John C. Turner, "Towards a Cognitive Redefinition of the Social Group," in Henry Tajfel, ed., *Social Identity and Intergroup Relations* (Cambridge, England: Cambridge University Press, 1982), pp. 15–40; John C. Turner, "Some Comments on . . . 'the Measurement of Social Orientations in the Minimal Group Paradigm,'" *European Journal of Social Psychology* 13 (1983):351–367.

64. Michael A. Hogg, John C. Turner, and Barbara Davidson, "Polarized Norms and Social Frames of Reference: A Test of the Self-Categorization Theory of Group Polarization," *Basic and Applied Social Psychology* 11, 1 (1990):77–100.

65. John C. Turner et al., *Rediscovering the Social Group: A Self-Categorization Theory* (Oxford and New York: Blackwell, 1987).

66. Hogg, Turner, and Davidson, "Polarized Norms and Social Frames of Reference."

67. Vincent Price, "Social Identification and Public Opinion: Effects of Communicating Group Conflict," *Public Opinion Quarterly* 53 (1989):197–224.

68. Cialdini, Kallgren, and Reno, "Focus Theory of Normative Conduct."

69. Leon Festinger, "A Theory of Social Comparison Processes," *Human Relations* 7 (1954):117–140.

70. Glynn, "Public Opinion as a Normative Opinion Process."

71. Cialdini, Kallgren, and Reno, "Focus Theory of Normative Conduct," p. 203.

72. Glynn, "Public Opinion as a Normative Opinion Process."

73. Barbara A. Anderson, Brian D. Silver, and Paul R. Abramson, "The Effects of the Race of the Interviewer on Race-Related Attitudes of Black Respondents in SRC/CPS National Election Studies," *Public Opinion Quarterly* 52, 3 (1988):290.

74. Solomon E. Asch, *Social Psychology* (Englewood Cliffs, NJ: Prentice-Hall, 1952).

75. Hogg and Abrams, *Social Identifications*.

76. Milton J. Rosenberg and Robert P. Abelson, "An Analysis of Cognitive Balancing," in Milton J. Rosenberg et al., eds., *Attitude Organization and Change* (New Haven: Yale University Press, 1960), pp. 112–163.

77. Philip R. Costanzo, "Conformity Development as a Function of Self-Blame," *Journal of Personality and Social Psychology* 14 (1970):366–374.

78. Richard S. Crutchfield, "Conformity and Character," *American Psychologist* 10 (1955):191–198.

79. Stanley Milgram, "Nationality and Conformity," *Scientific American* 205, 6 (1961):45–51.

80. Eagly and Chaiken, *Psychology of Attitudes*.

81. Paul R. Nail, "Toward an Integration of Some Models and Theories of Social Response," *Psychological Bulletin* 83 (1986):603–627.

82. Ibid.

83. Michael A. Hogg and John C. Turner, "Social Identity and Conformity: A Theory of Referent Information Influence," in Willem Doise and Serge Moscovici, eds., *Current Issues in European Social Psychology* (Cambridge: Cambridge University Press, 1987), pp. 139–182.

84. Morton Deutsch and Harold B. Gerard, "A Study of Normative and Information Social Influence upon Individual Judgment," *Journal of Abnormal and Social Psychology* 51 (1955):629–636.

85. Hogg and Abrams, *Social Identifications*, p. 166.

86. Hogg and Turner, "Social Identity and Conformity."

87. Hogg and Abrams, *Social Identifications*; Harold H. Kelley, "Two Functions of Reference Groups," in Guy E. Swanson, Theodore M. Newcomb, and Eugene L. Hartley, eds., *Readings in Social Psychology* (New York: Holt, 1952), pp. 410–414.

88. Deutsch and Gerard, "Study of Normative and Information Social Influence upon Individual Judgment"; Harold H. Kelley, "Two Functions of Reference Groups."

89. Hogg and Abrams, *Social Identifications*, p. 167.

90. Solomon E. Asch, "Effects of Group Pressure upon the Modification and Distortion of Judgments," in H. Guetzkow, ed., *Groups, Leadership, and Men* (Pittsburgh, PA: Carnegie Press, 1951), pp. 177–190.

91. Milgram, "Nationality and Conformity."

92. H. Lee, "A Study of Spiral of Silence Theory," Master's thesis, University of Wisconsin–Madison, 1987.

93. Thomas J. Scheff, *Microsociology: Discourse, Emotion, and Social Structure* (Chicago: University of Chicago Press, 1990).

Other References

Athey, K. R., J. E. Coleman, A. P. Reitman and J. Tang (1960). "Two experiments showing the effect of the interviewer's racial background on responses to questionnaires concerning racial issues." *Journal of Applied Psychology*, 44: 244–246.

Hatchett, S., and H. Schuman (1975–1976). "White respondents and race of interviewer effects." *Public Opinion Quarterly*, 39:523–528.

Schuman H., and J. Converse (1971). "The effects of black and white interviewers on black respondents in a national survey." *Public Opinion Quarterly*, 35: 44–68.

Chapter Six

Perception and Opinion Formation

You have probably heard it before: It is not reality that matters but rather the perception of that reality. Nothing could be more true. A homeless man on the street corner may be perfectly harmless, but if you perceive him as a threat, that becomes the reality. You will cross the street to avoid passing him. As Perry Hinton[1] writes, we are more than "simply recorders of information . . . we are processors of information." That is, we do not simply take in information through our eyes and ears; we make inferences and derive meaning from that information.

We make judgments about other people all the time, and we base these judgments on our perceptions. Think of the many times you rely on your perceptions. If a recent acquaintance walks past you without saying hello, you may perceive the action as coming either from rudeness or preoccupation. You may perceive a fellow student who expounds loudly and extensively in class as being either obnoxious or extremely intelligent. You may perceive that people are angry or sad, that they are dishonest or sincere.

And these perceptions can be very important. Perceptions of O. J. Simpson's character, as well as the character of the many Los Angeles police officers involved in that highly publicized case, influenced jury members and obviously affected the outcome of the trial. When you apply for a job, the employer's perception of you can provide you with a job opportunity or keep you in the ranks of the unemployed.

Our perceptions help us understand the world around us. We try to predict what others will do or say and rationalize others' motives in order to provide explanations for their behaviors. We constantly perceive our world, and we rationalize what is going on in that world based on our perceptions. In many ways, these perceptions provide the foundation for a public's opinion.

As Walter Lippmann describes, there is a world outside and there are the pictures in our heads. He argues:

FIGURE 6.1   How Do People Perceive the Opinions of Those Around Them?
SOURCE: © Tom Tomorrow. *Greetings from This Modern World* (New York: St. Martin's Press, 1992).

> Whatever we believe to be a true picture, we treat as if it were the environment itself . . . the real environment is altogether too big, too complex, and too fleeting for direct acquaintance . . . the analyst of public opinion must begin then, by recognizing the triangular relationship between the scene of action, the human picture of that scene and the human response to that picture working itself out upon the scene of action.[2]

This chapter will concentrate on the theories and perspectives that deal with perceptions of other's opinions and the roles these perceptions play in the public opinion process. Almost every psychology text deals with perception as the processing of information received through the five senses. For this textbook on public opinion, we will use the term "perception" in a very different way, in a use closer to its conversational meaning. That is, "perception" here means a summary attitude that is based on all of our past and present sensory information.

There are a number of perspectives we will discuss, among them "pluralistic ignorance," "the spiral of silence," and "looking-glass perception." For each of the perspectives we discuss, perceptions of others' opinions are the principal focus; for some, communication plays a particularly important role.

It is at this point that we ask students of public opinion to turn their attention to the fascinating world of perception—a world that is both internal and external to ourselves, a world that not only influences what we think or say but how we act. In essence, the perceptual world is the world of public opinion (see Figure 6.1).

The Limits of Perception

As we discussed in previous chapters, early social-psychological theories of attitude and behavior change argued that human beings were not much different than animals. That is, responses were thought to be spontaneous. Instinct, heredity, and social evolution were thought to be the main factors influencing an individual's attitudes and behavior.

Obviously, humans are more complex creatures than researchers originally thought. Charles Cooley argued that humans are different from other animals because of their greater inherent potential for complex thought processes and capacity for "mental sharing."[3] However, humans, like other animals, face physical, spatial, and other limitations when attempting to perceive and interpret the actions of others.

For example, we obviously experience a variety of sense limitations. As George McCall and J. L. Simmons note, the "physical characteristics of our sense organs impose limitations on both the breadth and the acuity of our perceptions."[4] You can only see so far, and the clarity with which you can see things (say, for example, small objects which are far away) is quite limited. In addition, our perceptions are limited by the perspective or position from which we do the observing. If we are looking ahead of us we obviously cannot see behind us. If we look to our left we cannot see to our right.

McCall and Simmons also note that even more important than these sensory limitations and the limits imposed by the position of the perceiver are other cognitive limitations—the selective attention and inattention of the perceiver.[5] People tend to pay attention to social objects (people and events) that are most relevant to their lives.

If you look outside one of your classroom windows, you might notice a group of soldiers walking by. Their presence might barely register with you—because it is probably a group of ROTC students. If you were in Bosnia, the sight of soldiers might be of grave concern to you—perhaps signaling life-threatening danger.

McCall and Simmons note that the perceptions we have of others are always incomplete and are usually less than accurate.[6] In fact, Bruner comments:

In the interest of economizing effort we do three things . . . we narrow the selectivity of attention more or less to those things that are somehow essential to the enterprises in which we are engaged. . . . Secondly, we "recode" into simpler form the diversity of events that we encounter . . . Sometimes these recodings of information serve their economical function but lead to a serious loss of information . . . Not only is information lost, but misinformation is added. . . . Finally, we deal with the overload of information provided by the environment . . . by the use of technological aids.[7]

These processes are so basic to the way we live that it is difficult to provide an example in which these things do not occur. Suppose we were to have a discussion with a friend while attending a soccer game. If we wanted to talk during the game, we would have to narrow our focus so that we could alternate our attention to develop the conversation we were trying to have but also keep track of the main occurrences during the game—the things that Bruner describes as "essential to the enterprise."

According to Bruner, we then alter the information we receive from the game in order to make it simpler to keep track of both things at the same time. We might, for example, begin to clap at an almost subconscious level each time the people around us clapped and cheered. Most of the time, we would not even know what we were clapping about (because we were paying attention to the conversation, not the game). In accord with Bruner's suggestion that we then turn to technological aids, we might begin to watch the scoreboard more carefully to see who was ahead and how many minutes were left to play so that the scoreboard would become an aid in keeping track of the game for us. Perceptual limitations of this kind can also restrict, confine, and help define public opinion on any particular issue.

Perception and Opinion:
Socialization and Social Comparison

In spite of the limitations of our perceptual abilities, our perceptions play critical roles in the formation of our opinions—and in the formation of a public's opinion. In fact, many of the perspectives we will discuss in this chapter are based on the fundamental principle that comparison of ourselves to others and our perceptions of others' opinions are critical aspects of our lives.

It is obvious that human activity does not occur in isolation. It is true that we have our own unique personalities and the formation of our opinions will be limited in part by the individual intellectual and emotional characteristics of our personalities. Indeed, our perceptions of the world around us are influenced by these intellectual and emotional factors. However, our perceptions are not formed simply by the combination of our innate intelligence, our unique personalities, and our senses. Equally important to our opinion formation and our perceptions is the contact we have with others in our physical and social world through processes such as *socialization* and *social comparison*. Who these others are and their effect on our perceptions and opinions are obviously elements that change as we go through life.

Socialization

A great deal of attention has been spent in the political and social sciences on understanding how what we learn and what we perceive as we go through various life stages affect our beliefs, opinions, and even behaviors in later life. In some sense, this process, known as *socialization*, includes the transmission of culture from one generation to the next. One critical aspect of socialization is the way that perceptions of what important others think affect our lives.

There are many forms of socialization, for children learn about all sorts of things from their parents and other influential adults. However, in this book, we are most interested in *political socialization*—how it is we develop particular ideological orientations and policy preferences. Political socialization is enormously difficult to study because it is very hard to track individuals over time, from their earliest political experiences (e.g., shaking a congressperson's hand at age eight) to their adult voting choices. In addition, political culture is always shifting, so even when children imitate or reject their parents' political orientations, it is challenging to sift out these reactions from reactions to political events or more general changes in the political environment.

Several scholars have tried to document the political socialization process.[8] For example, political scientist Paul Abramson has studied the ways that party identification, feelings of political efficacy, and trust in government change over the course of one's life span. He concludes that party loyalty is fairly stable over time: We tend to keep our ideological affiliations even as we grow older, find partners, and advance in our careers. Abramson finds, in his analysis of survey data, that there is little evidence to support the notion that people shift to the Republican Party or become more conservative as they age. Interestingly, he finds that young adults feel more efficacious (able to influence the course of government) than do older adults. These findings are tentative, however, and we do need more study of how political attitudes change over the course of one's life. But it is obvious that our parents or those who raised us play a major role in shaping our belief systems and the development of our values. Even when we live apart from these individuals—so vital in our socialization to the world—their ideas tend to stay with us, shaping our perceptions.

Social Comparison

Festinger[9] provides us with an interesting discussion of the importance of *social comparison* and perception for opinion formation and public opinion. In fact, his discussion is so relevant and important for this chapter that we have provided a summary of his major points in Box 6.1.

According to Festinger, we like to use objects in the physical world to test the correctness or appropriateness of our opinions. However, there are many situations where the use of the physical world is not possible. As Festinger notes:

> One could . . . test the opinion that an object was fragile by hitting it with a hammer, but how is one to test the opinion that a certain political candidate is better than another or that war is inevitable? Even when there is a possible immediate physical referent for an opinion, it is frequently not likely to be employed. The belief, for example, that tomatoes are poisonous to humans (which was widely held at one time) is unlikely to be tested.[10]

When we are not able to evaluate or compare our opinions to concrete events in the physical world, we will resort to comparing ourselves, our opinions, and our beliefs with the opinions and beliefs of others around us. As you can see from Festinger's[11] hypotheses in Box 6.1, the importance, use, stability, and so forth of our opinions based on these comparisons depends upon a number of social factors. Festinger particularly underscores the important role that consensus plays as an information base for our perceptions and opinions.

Many of the perspectives we will discuss in this chapter attempt to look at some of these important social underpinnings in order to explain how perceptions of others' opinions influence and affect our lives. That is, these perspectives attempt to discern the connections between the psychological, or the self, and the social, or the other. Such comparisons between self and other are the very essence of public opinion, for public opinion does not exist in the absence of a social system. Indeed, public opinion reflects the essence of our social system—the idea that people live with and accommodate others. However, please keep in mind that much work still needs to be done in these important areas.

Perceiving Others' Opinions

Hinton describes five social factors that influence our perceptions: (1) the information from the actor, (2) the influence of the perceiver on this information, (3) the relationship between the perceiver and the actor, (4) the social context, and (5) the cultural setting.[12] The student of public opinion needs to consider each of these.

Box 6.1 Festinger's Social Comparison Theory

When he first outlined social comparison theory, Leon Festinger developed a number of hypotheses and derived their corollaries. These formed the essential basis of his theory and suggested many of its implications for public opinion. Here are some of his hypotheses and corollaries that have proved especially useful:

Hypothesis 1: There exists, in the human organism, a drive to evaluate his opinions and his abilities.

Hypothesis 2: To the extent that objective, non-social means are not available, people evaluate their opinions and abilities by comparison respectively with the opinions and abilities of others.

Hypothesis 3: The tendency to compare oneself with some other specific person decreases as the difference between his opinion or ability and one's own increases.

Hypothesis 6: The cessation of comparison with others is accompanied by hostility or derogation to the extent that continued comparison with those persons implies unpleasant consequences.

Hypothesis 7: Any factors which increase the importance of some particular group as a comparison group for some particular opinion or ability will increase the pressure toward uniformity concerning that ability or opinion within that group.

Corollary 7a: The stronger the attraction to the group the stronger will be the pressure toward uniformity concerning abilities and opinions within that group.

Corollary 7b: The greater the relevance of the opinion or ability to the group, the stronger will be the pressure toward uniformity concerning that opinion or ability.

Hypothesis 9: Where there is a range of opinion or ability in a group ... those close to the mode of the group will have stronger tendencies to change the positions of others, relatively weaker tendencies to narrow the range of comparison and much weaker tendencies to change their own position compared to those who are distant from the mode of the group.

This last hypothesis has been modified by other researchers. Some studies have found that in order to maintain a distinctive group identity, groups sometimes adopt an opinion that is more extreme than that of the mode of the group. This more extreme opinion helps the group differentiate itself from other groups. However, many of Festinger's hypotheses have been tested with great success. These studies clearly show that social comparison is an important factor in opinion formation.

SOURCE: Leon A. Festinger, "A Theory of Social Comparison Processes," *Human Relations* 7 (1954):117–140.

First, the information the actor presents to us can influence our perceptions in profound ways. This information can include unusual behaviors, style of dress, or formal information such as a résumé. Second, our own expectations can influence our perceptions about the actor. We might expect someone of Italian descent to act differently than someone of Irish descent. In other words, these expectations can form the basis for stereotyping those around us. Third, the relationship we have with those we perceive can affect our perceptions. Our perceptions will differ if the action we observe is performed by a friend, a stranger, or a colleague at work. A hug by a friend we have not seen in a long time will be taken quite differently from a hug by a stranger. Fourth, the social context can influence our perceptions. We would perceive someone laughing loudly in church very differently than we would if the person laughed at a raucous sorority party. And finally, the cultural setting needs to be considered. For example, in the United States, people from states in the South are often thought to be warmer and more "touchy" than are people who were raised in the Northeast.

Our perceptions of the actions and opinions of others will depend upon factors such as these. Our reactions and formation of our own opinions will also be affected by these factors.

New Approaches to Public Opinion Formation

As Carroll Glynn, Ronald Ostman, and Daniel McDonald[13] note, the past two decades have seen the development of a number of new approaches that include the study of perception as it pertains to public opinion formation. Each of the perspectives described in this chapter is based on certain assumptions: that individuals care what others think about public issues, form perceptions of what others think, and, to an extent, modify their own opinions or behaviors, or both, on the basis of these perceptions. Each perspective we will discuss attempts to make some use of the factors spelled out by Hinton[14] in the previous discussion. Many of these perspectives make it clear that our everyday lives are rich tapestries of "interwoven roles, groupings and social norms to which the individual continually adapts, obtains information and provides information for others."[15]

In this chapter, there are eight public opinion perspectives with which we will concern ourselves: (1) looking-glass perception, (2) pluralistic ignorance, (3) disowning projection, (4) conservative/liberal/ideological biases, (5) false consensus effect, (6) impersonal impact and unrealistic optimism, (7) the third-person effect, and (8) the spiral of silence.

These perspectives, or frameworks, all include perceptions of others' opinions in one form or another. As you read this chapter, notice how different perspectives on public opinion examine different parts of the process and, in fact, define public opinion in different ways. Some perspectives appear to present public opinion as the majority opinion; others present it as generated within individuals. Although many dimensions of the perspectives we will discuss are compatible, in some instances, they reveal differences that simply cannot be resolved or incorporated within a common framework. It is also important for you to note which of the many components of public opinion—a spoken opinion, a perception of the majority opinion, or the aggregation of spoken opinion—are considered to be most relevant for each perspective.

Because public opinion studies subsume a number of academic disciplines, including sociology, social psychology, political science, and communication, some of these perspectives result from the investigation of similar processes in different fields. Often, public opinion scientists from one field who are studying these processes are unaware of the similarities of their own approaches to those in other fields!

Where confusion is a possibility because different labels mean essentially the same thing, we have combined discussion of some of these processes or we use the most commonly used label. It is important for you to remember not to limit your literature explorations to one field when conducting your own investigations or writing papers dealing with public opinion. Much rich understanding can come from incorporating the ideas of scholars working in a variety of disciplines.

Many of the perspectives presented later in the chapter focus on individuals' comparisons of their own opinions with actual groups of others (although, typically, specific individuals within these groups remain unnamed). However, as Ruben Orive[16] notes, there is a more implicit type of comparison that can occur when individuals do not or cannot compare their opinions with actual others. That is, Orive says that in the absence of knowledge of others' actual opinions, consensus will in effect be "self-generated." Individuals will make educated guesses about what others' opinions might be, based upon such things as group characteristics and the individual's own opinion. The psychological mechanism through which the person fabricates this consensus is termed "social projection."

The typology developed by Glynn, Ostman, and McDonald,[17] shown in Figure 6.2, should help you understand the differences in these approaches, and you should refer to it frequently during the discussion of each approach.

One corner of this typology deals with people to whom Glynn and associates refer as "hard core." These are people who hold minority views and are aware of the fact that most people disagree with them. Because this chapter is primarily concerned with how others' opinions affect our own, we will not consider "hard-core" people here.

Looking-Glass Perception

Looking-glass perception is a phenomenon that is said to structure perceptions of the opinions of others on social issues.[18] Basically, the looking-glass

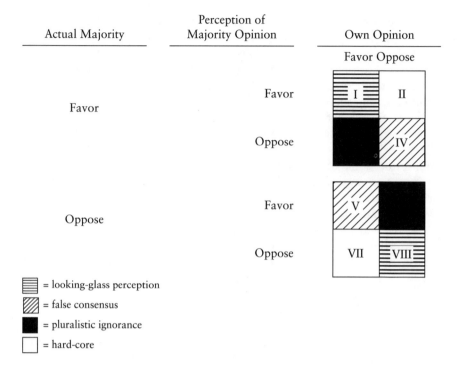

Actual Majority	Perception of Majority Opinion	Own Opinion	

FIGURE 6.2 The Distribution of Public Opinion on an Issue. SOURCE: Carroll J. Glynn et al., "Opinion, Perception, and Social Reality," in Theodore L. Glasser and Charles T. Salmon, eds., *Public Opinion and the Communication of Consent* (New York: Guilford Press, 1995), figure 10.1, p. 269.

perception occurs when *people see significant others as holding the same opinions on issues that they themselves hold.*[19] It appears from most research findings on looking-glass perception that in many situations and for many public or social issues, people will feel that most other people have opinions similar to their own.

When someone has a looking-glass perception on a particular issue or when a group of people are found to have engaged in looking-glass perception, this may, in fact, be the "correct" perception. That is, looking-glass perception tends to occur for issues that are noncontroversial or that people simply do not care much about and for which there seems to be (and actually is) almost universal agreement. If someone asks you your opinion about whether you think freedom of speech should be a basic right and then whether you think others believe there should be a right to free speech, you would probably find that both answers are essentially the same. This finding would not be surprising.

However, looking-glass perception can also occur when the "true" opinion is exactly the *opposite* of one's own, for instance, when (1) there is an issue or behavior that is divisive, and (2) one misperceives others as in "agreement with oneself," when in fact there may not be agreement.[20] Sometimes this occurrence results in "false consensus" (see the discussion later in this chapter).

Extensive research has not been conducted on the looking-glass hypothesis, and what research there is has tended to focus on whether or not the phenomenon occurs rather than on why it occurs, under what conditions, and so forth. If more research were conducted, we might understand some of the psychological and social factors leading to this outcome. As Glynn and associates note, there are no conditions detailed for when this phenomenon will or will not occur or when it will affect some people and not others.

Pluralistic Ignorance

According to Glynn, Ostman, and McDonald,[21] pluralistic ignorance is one of the more researched concepts in the perceptual influence literature.[22] Pluralistic ignorance occurs when *the majority position on issues is incorrectly perceived to be the minority position*[23] (see Figure 6.2). Richard Schanck[24] originally labeled this phenomenon "misperceived consensus" or "misperceived sharing."

In public opinion research, studies of pluralistic ignorance are most concerned with "perceptual accuracy," in which the researcher analyzes the role of social perception in public opinion and the accuracy of this perception. Pluralistic ignorance occurs when individuals underestimate the proportion of others who think, feel, or act as they themselves do.

Hubert O'Gorman and Stephen Garry describe pluralistic ignorance as the "false ideas held by individuals regarding the groups, social categories and collectivities to which they belong." They found that even members of "small and relatively cohesive groups frequently misjudge the values and attitudes of other members." They also note that this phenomenon is apt to occur in larger, more impersonal settings and that in times of "accelerated social change it tends to become extensive" (although why this is so is not articulated).[25] In general, pluralistic ignorance can be seen as a special case of inaccurate perceptions of majority opinion.[26]

For example, you may believe that abortion is wrong yet perceive that all your friends think abortion is appropriate in most situations. If, in fact, most of your friends "really" think abortion is wrong in most situations, this is a case of pluralistic ignorance. In this particular situation, you would be misperceiving the majority position of your friends on the abortion issue.

Often, pluralistic ignorance is tested by asking someone's opinion on a particular issue and then subsequently asking the same individual his or her perceptions of majority support. For example, in one study, O'Gorman and Garry[27] asked white respondents their opinions on segregation, followed by questions about their perceptions of majority support. As shown in Table 6.1, most white respondents did not personally support segregation. However, when respondents were classified by demographic characteristics, as is done in Table 6.1, perceptions of segregationist support were greatly over-estimated. That is, regardless of sex, age, education, income, and so forth, there was a marked tendency among white respondents to overestimate support for segregation.

Glynn and associates note that in research on pluralistic ignorance, the major assumption is that people have an inherent perception of others' opinions that is often inaccurate. Little or no explanation is provided in research for why or how these perceptions are inaccurate. "Pluralistic ignorance merely describes the coincidence of an issue with inaccurate perceptions."[28]

Researchers such as Dale Miller and Cathy McFarland suggest that fear of embarrassment is one of the key motivating factors behind pluralistic ignorance.[29] This fear could inhibit individuals from expressing true opinions on issues, resulting in pluralistic ignorance. If you believe you have a socially unacceptable opinion about an issue, you will respond to a question about that issue in the opposite direction from the way you feel. However, you may "project" your true opinion onto others. Pluralistic ignorance will be the outcome. This special case of pluralistic ignorance sometimes takes the form of a *disowning projection*.

Disowning Projection.   In 1947, Cameron, discussed disowning projections in a book entitled *The Psychology of Behavior Disorders*.[30] This phenomenon has not been dealt with much in research since then, but its occurrence is probably quite common. Cameron notes that disowning projection occurs when an individual *"tends to attribute selfish motives, evil intent and stupid attitudes to others and to disclaim them for oneself, even though objectively the reverse of this may seem true to an impartial observer"* (emphasis ours).[31] In many ways, disowning projections are a special case of attribution theory, which we discussed in Chapter 5.

As Cameron describes:

> A child accused by a playmate of some act, attitude, motive or characteristic which his peers condemn or ridicule commonly denies it and immediately ascribes it to his accuser—"I am not! *You* are!"—or shifts the accusation at once to a scapegoat whom everyone dislikes ... the average adult still uses direct denial and counteraccusation when he is surprised into it, and when he is frightened or angry. When a person is normally on guard and neither angry nor frightened, his denials, counteraccusations and scapegoating are carried out by indirect techniques—by implication, by stressing opposite trends, by distracting others, etc.[32]

TABLE 6.1   Whites in Favor of Racial Segregation and Whites' Perception of White Support for Racial Segregation, by Status Characteristics

Status Characteristics	North[a] (N)	(1)[c] (%)	(2)[d] (%)	(3)[e] (%)	South[b] (N)	(1)[c] (%)	(2)[d] (%)	(3)[e] (%)
Sex								
Male	(215)	13	47	24	(88)	36	86	55
Female	(251)	11	53	27	(133)	27	70	41
Age								
18–29	(119)	5	52	20	(67)	16	79	50
30–39	(78)	3	46	25	(40)	36	82	52
40–49	(83)	25	45	29	(40)	36	73	42
50–59	(71)	12	51	30	(24)	35	60	40
60 and older	(114)	16	56	26	(49)	37	79	45
Education								
Grammar school	(104)	23	65	32	(52)	49	84	54
High school	(223)	12	52	28	(115)	27	76	48
College	(138)	4	36	16	(53)	18	70	36
Income								
Less than $3,000	(54)	16	69	31	(30)	40	80	44
$3,000–$5,999	(60)	14	64	40	(41)	32	56	38
$6,000–$8,999	(127)	8	52	22	(74)	32	84	42
$9,000–$14,999	(125)	12	47	26	(42)	29	83	57
$15,000 and over	(84)	13	31	14	(23)	5	74	53
Occupation								
White-collar	(169)	8	40	19	(72)	25	75	47
Blue-collar	(146)	19	66	34	(56)	34	79	47
Religion								
Protestant	(272)	10	49	25	(196)	31	76	45
Catholic	(130)	15	56	28	(14)	17	75	58
Political party								
Democrats	(169)	15	54	26	(97)	37	74	43
Republicans	(138)	13	43	26	(46)	13	76	45
Independents	(150)	7	53	25	(78)	32	80	52

[a] All states except the Deep South and the Border South.

[b] Deep South and Border South.

[c] Favors racial segregation.

[d] Believes that half, most, or all of the whites in area favor racial segregation.

[e] Believes that most or all of the whites in area favor racial segregation.

SOURCE: Hubert O'Gorman and Stephen L. Garry, "Pluralistic Ignorance: A Replication and Extension," *Public Opinion Quarterly* 40 (1976), table 2, p. 254.

We have all known someone who engages in disowning projection at one time or another. You may, for example, have known a young man who complained constantly about how competitive other people in his classes were, when in fact he was the most competitive student of all! Although disowning projection can obviously be used by people without mental health problems, Cameron takes disowning projection a step further by noting that schizophrenic and paranoic individuals engage in this type of projection. Cameron states that schizophrenics engage in disowning projection by "reacting to their own behavior as if it were the behavior of others," such as when a schizophrenic says, "They say I am the Blessed Virgin."[33]

The O'Gorman and Garry study we described earlier[34] may have uncovered disowning projection on the part of its respondents as well, given that this study was conducted in the early 1970s. Attitudes toward segregation may not have been changing as rapidly as laws or public opinion about segregation may have been perceived as changing faster than it actually was. Perhaps respondents felt safer reflecting their own points of view through their perceptions of what others were thinking!

Survey researchers refer to this sort of phenomenon as "social desirability." Respondents believe that there is a "right" answer to the question—for example, that they should be opposed to segregation. When asked about their own opinion, they give the socially desirable answer. If asked about others' opinions, they respond by telling the interviewer what they think the real distribution of opinion is, and if a disowning projection is occurring, what their own opinion is as well. The social desirability of some responses to survey questions can make true opinion hard to measure.

Conservative, Liberal, and Ideological Biases.   Instances of conservative and liberal (or ideological) bias could also be considered instances of pluralistic ignorance, if they involve misperceptions of others' opinions on issues. These biases occur when individuals see others' opinions as either more liberal or more conservative than their own, regardless of whether this is actually the case.

For example, James Fields and Howard Schuman[35] investigated the perceptions of racial opinions of Detroit, Michigan, residents. In this study, the researchers asked white respondents their perceptions of others' opinions on several interracial issues by asking them to consider hypothetical, but very feasible, situations. For example, in one question they outlined the following scenario:

One day a six-year-old asks her mother if she can bring another girl home to play. The mother knows that the other girl is a Negro, and that her own daughter has only played with white children before. What should the mother do? Here are three possible responses:

A. She should tell her daughter that she must never play with Negroes;
B. The daughter should be told that she may play with Negro children in school, but not at home; or
C. The Negro child should be permitted to come to the home.[36]

This question was repeated when asking respondents' perceptions of what most people in "this neighborhood" and most people "in Detroit" thought about this particular issue. (You should note that in 1956, when this question was first asked, "Negro" was an approved racial term, and as the authors indicate, "even in 1971 the term was still probably the most suitable for interviews with whites.")

The authors also asked questions on other racial issues and on two civil liberties issues (including whether an atheist should be permitted to speak on a college campus and whether a child should be allowed to refuse the pledge of allegiance in school).

Most of these issues probably seem quite foreign to you now, and in fact, most of you would find it hard to believe that opinions and perceptions on these issues would vary much at all! However, at that time, Fields and Schuman found that for most of these issues, perceptions of others' opinions tended to "lean in a conservative direction," as respondents seemed to assume that others held more conservative opinions than their own.[37] That is, respondents would tend to answer "C" in the question above while they perceived that others would respond "A" to the same question. Some of their results are shown in Table 6.2.

If study respondents thought others would say it is not appropriate for a white child to play with an African-American child but, in fact, a majority of respondents feel that it is appropriate, pluralistic ignorance has occurred.

TABLE 6.2   Perceptions of Majority Opinion

	% Distribution of Actual Opinion	% Believing Alternative to Be Majority Opinion in Detroit Area	% Believing Alternative to Be Majority Opinion in Own Neighborhood
Never play with Negroes	2	11	12
Play only at school	22	56	50
OK to play at home	76	33	38
Total	100	100	100
N	(617)	(543)	(505)

SOURCE: James M. Fields and Howard Schuman, "Public Beliefs About the Beliefs of the Public," *Public Opinion Quarterly,* 40 (1976), p. 430.

In a study of neighbor perceptions of others' opinions on local, state, and national issues, Glynn[38] found evidence of disowning projection and conservative bias. However, she also discovered that in some situations, there can be a "liberal bias" where respondents see others as having more liberal opinions than their own.

In Glynn's study, individuals in specific geographic neighborhoods within a city were asked their perceptions of what others thought about eight issues salient for that particular point in time: two each from the national level (national defense spending and wilderness development), the state level (nuclear power plant bans and death penalty approval or disapproval in the state in which the data were collected), the local level (providing a late-night cab fare subsidy for women and closing underused schools in the city), and the neighborhood (building a home for the mentally retarded in the neighborhood and petitioning against a neighbor's solar panel).[39] Her results are shown in Table 6.3.

Glynn notes that

> on every issue without exception, respondents viewed individuals living in the city as having more "liberal" opinions than their own, regardless of whether it was a national, state or local issue. On the other hand, with only one exception, respondents viewed their neighbors as having more "conservative" opinions on issues than their own ... [providing] considerable evidence for ... the existence of a "conservative bias" at least at the local level ... [the findings also suggest] that respondents can, and do, have differing perceptions about different groups of people.[40]

Glynn's findings are remarkable because the people she interviewed were residents of both the neighborhoods and the city. They believed opinion in their city was more liberal than their own and that opinion in their neighborhood was more conservative than their own, even though they themselves were the elements composing the "public" they were speculating about.

Glynn notes that there is difficulty in using the labels "liberal" and "conservative" bias because "such terms are subject to much change in interpretation over time." Instead, she recommends using the term "ideological bias" to indicate discrimination among groups based upon "perceived ideological differences."[41]

False Consensus Effect

As if things were not confusing enough, researchers also consider that there are situations where individuals perceive their own opinions and behaviors as "normal" and all other opinions and behaviors as strange. That is, individuals overestimate the number of other people who agree with their

TABLE 6.3   Perceived Ideological Differences

Issue	More Liberal (%)	Same (%)	More Conservative (%)
Wilderness			
Neighbors	21	42	37
City	27	47	26
National defense			
Neighbors	21	41	39
City	35	41	24
Nuclear power			
Neighbors	28	42	31
City	36	37	27
Death penalty			
Neighbors	30	40	30
City	43	35	22
Taxicab subsidy			
Neighbors	20	46	33
City	29	46	25
School closing			
Neighbors	29	49	22
City	34	39	27
Home for the retarded			
Neighbors	5	34	61
Solar enegry panel			
Neighbors	10	51	39

SOURCE: Carroll J. Glynn, "The Communication of Public Opinion," *Journalism Quarterly* 64 (1987), table 2, p. 695.

views. Sometimes false consensus is nothing more than a special case of looking-glass perception.[42] Conceptually, "false consensus" refers to the tendency for individuals *"to see their own behavioral choices and judgments as relatively common and appropriate to existing circumstances while viewing alternative responses as uncommon, deviant and inappropriate"* (emphasis ours).[43]

Typically, false consensus occurs when a person engaging in a given behavior estimates that same behavior to be shared by a larger proportion of others in a group than is estimated for that same reference group by a person engaging in the alternative behavior.[44] Lee Ross, David Greene, and Pamela House found that false consensus is a relatively common phenomenon.[45] These researchers studied a group of college students to determine the extent of false consensus on a variety of issues. For example, as you can see in Table 6.4, college students who thought about dying estimated that 44 percent of all college students also thought about dying. However, college students who reported that they did not think about dying estimated

TABLE 6.4 Some Examples of False Consensus Effects Among College Students

Questionnaire Item: Category 1 (Category 2)	Raters' Estimates of Percentage of College Students in Category 1		Direction of Difference (+ Predicted; − Opposite to Predicted)	t
	Mean Estimates by Raters Placing Themselves in Category 1	Mean Estimates by Raters Placing Themselves in Category 2		
Personal traits and views				
Shy (not shy)	45.9	35.9	+	2.66‡
Optimistic (not)	61.9	50.4	+	2.58†
Competitive (not)	75.1	69.9	+	1.35
Politically left of center (not)	59.7	58.0	+	<1
Supporter of women's lib (not)	57.3	33.4	+	3.96§
Unweighted mean of five items	60.0	49.5		
Personal preferences				
Brown (white) bread	52.5	37.4	+	3.26‡
To be alone (with others)	36.0	30.7	+	1.18
Italian (French) movies	51.6	43.4	+	2.00†
City (country) life	51.4	49.8	+	<1
Basketball (football)	36.7	37.7	−	<1
Unweighted mean of five items	45.6	39.8		
Personal characteristics				
Male (female)	58.7	57.1	+	1.01
Brown (blue) eyes	58.3	54.5	+	1.63
Subscribe (don't) to magazines on list provided	56.9	42.7	+	2.76‡
First-born (laterborn) child	42.2	37.1	+	1.57
Hometown more (less) than 200,000	58.2	51.9	+	1.68*
Unweighted mean of five items	54.9	48.7		
Personal problems				
Think about dying? yes (no)	44.0	25.6	+	2.87‡
Hard to make friends? yes (no)	38.7	35.1	+	<1
Difficulty controlling temper? yes (no)	42.1	27.9	+	3.26‡
Frequently depressed? yes (no)	55.1	39.2	+	3.25‡
Emotional needs satisfied? yes (no)	52.9	42.2	+	2.29†
Unweighted mean of five items	46.6	34.0		

(continues)

TABLE 6.4 *(continued)*

Questionnaire Item: Category 1 (Category 2)	Raters' Estimates of Percentage of College Students in Category 1		Direction of Difference (+ Predicted; − Opposite to Predicted)	t
	Mean Estimates by Raters Placing Themselves in Category 1	*Mean Estimates by Raters Placing Themselves in Category 2*		
Personal activities				
Watch TV 30 hours/month? yes (no)	49.2	40.9	+	<1
Play tennis once a week? yes (no)	33.0	30.3	+	<1
Attend religious service once a month? yes (no)	26.5	27.5	−	<1
Donate blood once a year? yes (no)	22.6	21.2	+	<1
Long distance phone call once a week? yes (no)	50.7	45.0	+	1.06
Unweighted means of five items	36.4	33.0		
Personal expectations				
Marriage by age 30? yes (no)	74.5	71.9	+	<1
Better financial status than parent? yes (no)	68.3	61.8	+	1.86*
Live outside U.S. for one year in next 20? yes (no)	37.4	36.9	+	<1
Great satisfaction from job or career? yes (no)	53.5	43.3	+	<1
Death before 70th birthday? yes (no)	57.6	43.9	+	2.81‡
Unweighted mean of five items	58.3	51.6		
Political expectations				
Removal of Nixon from office? yes (no)	deleted			
Woman in Supreme Court within decade? yes (no)	63.3	34.6	+	6.19§

SOURCE: Lee Ross et al., "The 'False Consensus Effect': An Egocentric Bias in Social Perception and Attribution Processes," in the *Journal of Experimental and Social Psychology* 13 (1977), table 3, p. 287.

that only 25.6 percent thought about dying. This same false consensus occurred for a number of issues ranging from perceptions of shyness or optimism to preferences for brown versus white bread.

Steven Sherman, Clark Presson, and Laurie Chassin[46] suggest three motivations for false consensus: self-enhancement, motivation to view the other as oneself, and need for social support and validation. Basically, they argue that false consensus is the product of a need to feel confident in one's own views and behaviors.

Ross describes two possible explanations for false consensus: (1) False consensus could represent an unintentional perceptual distortion that results from a selective exposure to and recall of other people who agree with oneself, or (2) false consensus could represent a motivated and intentional strategy to appear normal, appropriate, and rational.[47] In other words, false consensus could be a product of the perceptual limitations discussed earlier in this chapter. Alternatively, false consensus could occur for people who, out of fear or embarrassment, want to believe that what they feel or do is most appropriate for the situation.

It is not easy to separate out these two explanations. For example, a student who took a test that seemed very difficult may perceive that most other students thought the test was very difficult, even though most students in the class may have thought the test was easy. Ross's first explanation for this false consensus phenomenon would be that the student associates with other students who studied in a similar fashion and who also probably thought the test was difficult.[48] Using the second explanation, however, we might suggest that the student is embarrassed by not having done well and so saves face by perceiving that others felt the test was difficult.

Although false consensus is a product of individuals' perceptions of the climate of opinion, it can have major impact on public opinion formation and on public debate. In the case of the abortion debate, public discourse was radically altered by a case of false consensus (see Box 6.2).

It might be easiest to see the differences and similarities between the looking-glass perception, ideological biases, false consensus, and pluralistic ignorance through an example. Suppose that the campus paper at your university reported that one of the most famous researchers there had a very large grant to study cancer and was using dogs in his studies. Suppose that the dogs underwent painful operations and were exposed to a number of toxic chemicals before being killed. The issue of animal experimentation would probably become a major topic at your university. Now, if you spend the weekend at your parents' home and a relative asks how most of the students at your school feel about the issue, what would you reply?

According to the "looking-glass" perception, you would most likely respond that the students feel the same way you feel about the issue. However, if you are very conservative by nature and you see the students as very liberal in comparison, the "ideological bias" might influence you to suggest that most of the students feel exactly the opposite of the way you do. If, in fact, the majority feel the same way you do but ideological bias comes into play, we may find a state of pluralistic ignorance—the minority position will be perceived as the majority position. Alternatively, you may see your own opinion as being very typical of college students and think that your

Box 6.2   A Case of False Consensus: Mobilizing the Pro-Life Movement

One of the most remarkable examples of the effects of false consensus in contemporary times is the case of the pro-life movement. Prior to the Supreme Court's 1973 decision in *Roe v. Wade,* there were many activists involved in trying to make abortions easier to obtain legally, but there was almost no grassroots movement opposed to abortion. Kristin Luker argues that this is because most people who opposed abortion believed that theirs was the majority view:

> Perhaps the most important reason why pro-life activists were not well prepared to resist abortion reform was that they simply couldn't believe such a movement would get very far. They tacitly assumed that the unsavory connotation of abortion rested on a deep belief in the sacredness of embryonic life, and they found it hard to understand how such a belief could be changed so quickly. They counted on public opinion to be outraged and were stunned when most of the public was either unaware or unconcerned.

Luker's qualitative interviews with pro-life activists show that this case of false consensus stemmed from their selective exposure to the social world. Most pro-lifers had never had abortions themselves, nor did they know anyone who had experienced an abortion. Thus, they believed that it was an uncommon event. These people also misperceived the "unsavory connotation of abortion":

> In particular, they interpreted the relative social invisibility of abortion prior to the 1960s as proof that their opinion was the common one. And in a way, their assumption was plausible. If people didn't talk about abortion very much (or talked about it only in hushed tones in back rooms), wasn't that because most people believed it was the taking of an innocent life, hence morally repugnant? What these early pro-life activists did not understand was that for many people abortion was "unspeakable" not because it represented the death of a child but because it represented "getting caught" in the consequences of sexuality. Sex, not abortion, was what people didn't talk about.

Because of this false consensus effect, the pro-life movement did not become well-organized or prominent until after the *Roe v. Wade* decision was handed down, and its early years were rocky ones. People who opposed abortion were so surprised to find themselves in the minority that they had difficulty formulating persuasive arguments to support their opinions:

(continues)

Box 6.2   *(continued)*

Their belief that everyone accepted a common definition of the meaning and moral nature of abortion left these pro-life people with few arguments to use against the abortion reformers. They tried to appeal to what they thought was the commonly shared value, but when it turned out to be not so common after all, they were literally at a loss for words.

As you can see, false consensus can have both psychological and social consequences. In this case, the shape of public debate was altered by people's perceptions of majority opinion.

SOURCE: Kristin Luker, *Abortion and the Politics of Motherhood* (Berkeley: University of California Press, 1984), quoted passages from pp. 128–131.

---

opinion is the "norm" for your college, even when it is, in fact, the minority view. In this case, we would have a situation in which there is false consensus about the issue.

Impersonal Impact and Unrealistic Optimism

The basic thesis underlying research on impersonal impact and unrealistic optimism is that *individuals often see themselves as being somehow different from others in terms of the probability of good or bad things happening to them.* That is, when people estimate the likelihood that they will be involved in certain life events (such as having car accidents, getting cancer, and so forth), they tend to be unrealistically optimistic.[49] People tend to think they are invulnerable (especially young people!). As Neil Weinstein says, people "expect others to be victims of misfortune, not themselves."[50]

According to the unrealistic optimism hypothesis, you will tend to believe that negative events are less likely to happen to you than to others and to perceive that positive events are more likely to happen to you than to those same others.[51] Researchers have found that this phenomenon occurs across a wide range of topic areas from perceptions of being murdered to perceptions of winning the lottery.[52]

Although impersonal impact and unrealistic optimism have been considered two different research areas, the differences between them are quite subtle. In order to avoid confusion, we will discuss the broad, underlying assumptions for both rather than confuse you by discussing the small differences.

Tom Tyler and Fay Cook[53] note that there is a major assumption to consider when investigating impersonal impact and unrealistic optimism: that people can and do distinguish between two possible levels of judgment—personal and societal.[54] Individuals' beliefs about their own degree of risk from life's hazards form the personal level of judgment. Individuals' beliefs about groups of others and their likelihood to experience these events form a "societal" level of judgment.

For example, Weinstein conducted a study that looked at college students' perceptions of future life events and the extent to which students expressed unrealistic optimism about these life events.[55] Table 6.5 presents some of his results.

As you can see from this table, for college students, unrealistic optimism is alive and well. When you read the table, note that a positive value in the first column indicates that the students tended to believe their chances were greater than average that a good thing would happen to them; a negative value indicates that students believe their chances are less than average that a bad thing would happen to them.

The numbers in the second column indicate the ratio of optimistic to pessimistic responses. For example, students felt that their chances were greater than those of their classmates for liking their postgraduation job—the ratio of optimistic to pessimistic responses was almost 6 to 1 (5.93).

Another important consideration for both the impersonal impact and unrealistic optimism hypotheses is the effect the media have on these perceptions. Tyler and Cook state that mass-mediated messages affect people's perceptions of how often certain problems or risks occur in general but do not affect people's perceptions of their own personal risks. For example, they found that people who had seen a television newsmagazine story about fraud in home health care services were more likely afterward to view the problem as serious. However, they were still equally confident in their own ability to secure good home health care for themselves or their relatives.

Third-Person Effect

The third-person effect essentially occurs when *people think that the media will have greater impact on others than on themselves.* Sociologist W. Phillips Davison was the first to coin the term "third-person effect" in an article he wrote in *Public Opinion Quarterly* in 1983.[56] Davison is a wonderful storyteller and writer, and he introduced his discussion of this effect by describing an incident that happened to a historian while "combing through cartons of U.S. Marine Corps documents from World War II."

Davison documents the following:

> There was a service unit consisting of Negro troops with white officers on Iwo Jima Island in the Pacific. The Japanese learned about the location of this unit and sent planes over with propaganda leaflets. These leaflets stressed the theme that this was a white man's war and that the Japanese had no quarrel with colored peoples. They said, more or less, "Don't risk your life for the white man.

TABLE 6.5   Unrealistic Optimism for Future Life Events

	Measures of Optimism	
Abbreviated Event Description	_Mean Comparative Judgment of Own Chances vs. Others' Chances (%)[a, b]_	_No. of Optimistic Responses Divided by No. of Pessimistic Responses[b, c]_
Positive events		
Like postgraduation job	50.2[f]	5.93[f]
Owning your own home	44.3[f]	6.22[f]
Starting salary > $10,000	41.5[f]	4.17[f]
Traveling to Europe	35.3[f]	2.25[f]
Starting salary > $15,000	21.2[e]	1.56[d]
Good job offer before graduation	15.3[e]	1.42
Graduating in top third of class	14.2	1.02
Home doubles in value in 5 years	13.3[d]	1.78[d]
Your work recognized with award	12.6[d]	1.72[d]
Living past 80	12.5[e]	2.00[e]
Your achievements in newspaper	11.3	1.66[d]
No night in hospital for 5 years	8.5	1.23
Having a mentally gifted child	6.2[d]	2.26[e]
Statewide recognition in your profession	2.1	1.00
Weight constant for 10 years	2.0	.82
In 10 years, earning > $40,000 a year	− .7	.64[d]
Not ill all winter	− .7	.89
Marrying someone wealthy	− 9.1	.36[d]
Negative events		
Having a drinking problem	−58.3[f]	7.23[f]
Attempting suicide	−55.9[f]	8.56[f]
Divorced a few years after married	−48.7[f]	9.50[f]
Heart attack before age 40	−38.4[f]	5.11[f]
Contracting venereal disease	−37.4[f]	7.56[f]
Being fired from a job	−31.6[f]	7.56[f]
Getting lung cancer	−31.5[f]	4.58[f]
Being sterile	−31.2[f]	5.94[f]
Dropping out of college	−30.8[f]	3.49[f]
Having a heart attack	−23.3[f]	3.18[f]
Not finding a job for 6 months	−14.4[f]	2.36[f]
Decayed tooth extracted	−12.8	2.22[f]
Having gum problems	−12.4[e]	1.39
Having to take unattractive job	−11.6[d]	1.84[e]
Car turns out to be a lemon	−10.0[d]	2.12[e]
Deciding you chose wrong career	− 8.8	1.43

(continues)

TABLE 6.5   *(continued)*

Abbreviated Event Description	Measures of Optimism	
	Mean Comparative Judgment of Own Chances vs. Others' Chances (%)[a, b]	*No. of Optimistic Responses Divided by No. of Pessimistic Responses*[b, c]
Tripping and breaking bone	− 8.3[d]	1.66[d]
Being sued by someone	− 7.9	2.38[f]
Having your car stolen	− 7.3	2.94[f]
Victim of mugging	− 5.8	3.17[f]
Developing cancer	− 4.4	1.28
In bed ill two or more days	− 3.2	1.75[d]
Victim of burglary	2.8	1.21
Injured in auto accident	12.9[d]	.80

[a] In making a comparative judgment, students estimated the difference in percent between the chances that an event would happen to them and the average chances for other same-sex students at their college. N = 123 to 130, depending on rating form and missing data. Student's t was used to test whether the mean is significantly different from zero.

[b] For positive events, the response that one's own chances are greater than average is considered optimistic, and the response that one's own chances are less than average is considered pessimistic. For negative events, the definitions of optimistic and pessimistic responses are reversed.

[c] Significance levels refer to a chi-square test of the hypothesis that frequencies of optimistic and pessimistic responses are equal.

[d] $p < .05$.

[e] $p < .01$.

[f] $p < .001$.

SOURCE: Neil D. Weinstein, "Unrealistic Optimism About Future Life Events," *Journal of Personality and Social Psychology* 39 (1980), table 1, p. 810. Copyright 1980 by the American Psychological Association. Reprinted with permission.

Give yourself up at the first opportunity, or just desert. Don't take chances." The next day that unit was withdrawn.[57]

This is a classic example of the third-person effect. There was no apparent evidence that the propaganda had an effect on the troops at all. Rather, the effect of the propaganda appeared to be on the white officers who withdrew their troops.

As Davison notes:

in its broadest formulation, this hypothesis predicts that people will tend to overestimate the influence that mass communications have on the attitudes and behaviors of others . . . more specifically . . . individuals who are members of an audience that is exposed to a persuasive communication . . . will expect the communication to have a greater effect on others than on themselves.[58]

The third-person effect is very similar to the idea of unrealistic optimism, only instead of a concern with good or bad things occurring, concern is about the perceived effects of the mass media. Davison's ideas have generated a good deal of research.

Jeremy Cohen, Diana Mutz, Vincent Price, and Albert Gunther studied the third-person effect by asking people to read defamatory newspaper articles. They found that readers who were exposed to these newspaper articles estimated that others would be significantly more affected by the messages than they themselves had been.[59]

James Tiedge, Arthur Silverblatt, Michael Havice, and Richard Rosenfeld conducted an interesting study that investigated the third-person effect in specific messages.[60] For example, they examined whether the third-person effect occurred when buyers saw advertising slogans such as "Buy Now While Supplies Last." In this clear-cut case of third-person effect, respondents expected others to run out and buy when they saw these ads. In fact, the others might have been running, but the respondents themselves were running right along with them.

Dominic Lasorsa studied the third-person effect as it pertained to the airing of a controversial miniseries called *Amerika*.[61] The program was controversial because it contained what George Kennan[62] noted were false suggestions—that the dangers of a Soviet takeover of the United States with the help of the United Nations were "quite real."[63]

Lasorsa notes that "despite rising expectations of blockbuster ratings, just before the show aired one of the program's primary sponsors pulled its multimillion-dollar advertising campaign, apparently worried that the juxtapositioning of the program's controversial message with its own 'Pride in America' advertising campaign might cause viewers to turn away from its products."[64]

In his detailing of the third-person effect, LaSorsa also discusses how the third-person effect seems to be

> driven by a belief that others are unlike me in important ways that relate to their inability to evaluate "correctly" a mass medium message. I reason that others may not be as insightful, as experienced, as interested—as knowing, generally—as I am and, therefore, I believe they are more susceptible than I am to media influence. Ironically, however, it may be I who, in an indirect yet important way, am most susceptible to the influence of the message.[65]

Glynn and Ostman did not find evidence for the third-person effect until they investigated responses in specific subsets of the population under study. They note, "These two groups [those who perceive a third-person effect and those who do not] might be very different from each other in the way they view public opinion and public opinion processes."[66] They suggest that one important difference might be in the way people seek out and use information about others' opinions. Most people would seem to be somewhat susceptible to the third-person effect. How many times have you watched a television show, only to turn the set off at the end and say, "Boy, people are sure going to be upset about that!"

Spiral of Silence

Last but not least, we will discuss one of the most researched and controversial approaches to understanding public opinion. This theory (or model) was developed in the mid-1970s by Elisabeth Noelle-Neumann, a German political scientist and pollster. Charles Salmon and Chi-Yung Moh note that her work is "predicated on the notion that society is a potentially intimidating environment for the individual, a setting in which intense social pressure can be brought to bear on the person who dares to test the boundaries of the crowd."[67]

Noelle-Neumann first observed what she labeled the spiral of silence phenomenon during the 1965 elections in the Federal Republic of Germany. The election was being held between two political parties, the Christian Democrats and the Social Democrats. Noelle-Neumann found that public perceptions of who would win the election showed a steady, "independent movement"[68] despite the polls, which showed equivalent levels of support from December until September. Then, during the final days of the election, 3 to 4 percent of the voters shifted their alliances in the direction of the candidate the public perceived as the winner. During the 1972 election, Noelle-Neumann noticed the same phenomenon occurring. Because these findings were so surprising to Noelle-Neumann, she decided to investigate, and her research on the spiral of silence began.

Since that time, more public opinion research has been conducted on the spiral of silence than on almost any other single public opinion approach, thesis, or question.[69] Carroll Glynn and Jack McLeod[70] note that the spiral of silence theory is important because it describes how, through social interaction, people influence each other's willingness to express opinions. The social nature of humans is an important component of the spiral of silence theory.

Noelle-Neumann relies heavily on the studies of Asch,[71] whose work we discussed in Chapter 5, to describe the relationship of conformity to her spiral of silence theory. Indeed, much of Asch's research, as well as that of Sherif[72] and Milgram,[73] provides evidence that people may be so affected by their perception of what others think that they feel pressured to conceal their own opinions.

The theory of the spiral of silence states that one's perception of the distribution of public opinion affects one's willingness or unwillingness to express opinions.[74] Individuals who notice that their personal opinions are spreading will voice these opinions self-confidently in public; those who notice their opinions are "losing ground" will be inclined to adopt a more reserved attitude and remain silent. These perceptions of reality are transformed into reality as those who feel that their opinions are not popular remain quiet and those who believe their opinions are growing in popularity hear their own views more and more often. The result is a spiral of silence.[75]

Although the label "spiral of silence" does not carry with it the implied sophistication of most social-psychological theories, the term is quite appropriate. One can envision a swirling tornado of opinion spiraling into dust and silence.

The spiral of silence theory is based on the assumption that our relationships with others are so critical to us that we will do anything, even change our opinions or become silent about them, to be accepted by others. Noelle-Neumann states that to the individual, "not isolating himself is more important than his own judgment."[76] We want others to like us, and we want to continue our relationships with others. To most of us, this is far more important than expressing an opinion that may deviate from those of our friends.

Although it is impossible here to present the details of research conducted on the spiral of silence, it is important to mention that there are four key elements that need to be considered when examining this theory: (1) one's own opinion on an issue, (2) one's perception of the predominant public opinion, (3) one's assessment of the likely future course of public opinion, (4) one's willingness to support one's opinion with action, verbal statements, or other signs of commitment.[77]

According to the spiral of silence theory, one's opinion and one's assessment of the predominant public opinion are both assumed to influence one's judgment of the future course of opinion. Willingness to express one's opinion depends on an interaction between these two variables. That is, one's opinion (majority or minority) and one's perception of the future trend in public opinion will affect the likelihood that one will speak up on any number of issues.

The spiral of silence theory attempts to describe impacts on public opinion that go far beyond interpersonal interaction. Noelle-Neumann also ascribes importance to the mass media's impact on the formation and presentation of the public's opinions. According to Noelle-Neumann, the key factors the media bring into play in the spiral of silence are that they are both "ubiquitous" and "consonant" with one another.[78]

And what does this mean? Noelle-Neumann says that the media are everywhere (ubiquitous) and that they repeat the same messages over and over (consonance). Clearly, this is a simple but important truth. The media are constantly bombarding us with information, constantly framing our social reality. And we constantly hear the same message—on the radio and television, in newspapers and magazines. These same messages are repeated from reporter to reporter, from medium to medium. Thus, according to Noelle-Neumann, we learn most of our societal norms, customs, and so forth from the media. What we should believe is constantly being reinforced because of these media messages.

Noelle-Neumann states that part of the problem with the ubiquitous and consonant nature of the mass media is that journalists tend to be more liberal than the rest of society.[79] These journalists share common norms and values and reflect their liberal points of view in the messages they present in the media.

It is clear that the spiral of silence is an important theory that the student of public opinion should understand. Although many researchers have found flaws or problems with the theory,[80] most scholars agree that the spiral of silence theory contributes immensely to public opinion theory. If anything, the most simple of its premises attest to its importance: We are social; others are important to us; we want others to like us, and we want to fit in. These factors clearly influence public opinion formation.

Of all the approaches discussed in this chapter, Noelle-Neumann's spiral of silence theory comes closest to being an actual theory. However, this theory and the other approaches mentioned earlier all have serious flaws that limit their usefulness. For example, none of them specifies clearly the roles that social and reference groups can play in opinion formation, there is no discussion of cultural influences, and there is little consistent theoretical thread in the research.

Implications for the Future

It is clear that we need to develop useful theoretical approaches in public opinion research. For the most part, we know that psychological, social, and political factors can change or motivate public opinion outcomes, but we are not sure what these factors are or exactly when these outcomes will occur. We know that the media are important in the formation of public opinion, but we do not know enough about how people are influenced by these powerful transmitters of information.

Politicians know there are ways to manipulate the public through the media; yet public opinion scholars do not know enough about the public opinion process to be able to determine how and when this manipulation will occur. The public is more vulnerable and more susceptible because of this lack of research in this important area.

A few scholars have turned their attention to the process of public opinion formation and change. Most of these scholars believe that social factors, including communication and perceptions of others' opinions, are critical components of the public opinion process. For example, Vincent Price and Donald Roberts[81] and W. Philips Davison[82] attempt to model public opinion processes at the social level. There are some important similarities in the elements they consider critical and in their definitions of public opinion.

Davison views communication as crucial to opinion formation. He traces the public opinion process as it expands from the level of the primary group (a group of individuals who converse together on an issue) to the wider society.[83] Most potential issues, he observes, never make it out of the primary group. Those that do find "leadership transcending the original primary group."[84] These leaders are frequently in the business of "mass manipulation" and have means of publicizing the issue at their disposal. Leaders simplify and generalize issues so that they will appeal to the largest possible audience. If many in that audience accept the new idea, public opinion may develop. Face-to-face discussion proceeds in other primary groups, and these new discussions lead to more public communication about the issue. This process is circular.

As public discussion of the issue increases, individuals begin to develop expectations about what others' opinions are likely to be. These expectations may develop as a result of individuals' "sampling" of group opinions, from social projection of one's own opinion onto others or from individuals' belief that they "know" how members of a group are likely to respond to an issue. Individuals use these expectations to determine where relevant reference groups stand on an issue. They then determine their own opinion relative to the opinions of salient others. Davison argues, "A process is set up in which expectations produce behavioral adjustments, and these in turn reinforce expectations. When this has happened, public opinion has been formed."[85]

Price and Roberts agree with this assessment and observe that many people "deciding their stand on a public issue are not so much deciding their own opinion (or *where* they stand on the matter) but instead deciding on their social loyalties (in other words, *with whom* they stand)" (emphasis ours).[86] They call public opinion a social process and, more specifically, a communication process. They argue that communication allows a group of people to "think together," even as individual cognition often involves "talking to yourself." Public opinion is not the distribution of opinions in a population. Instead, it is a process in which ideas are "expressed, adjusted and compromised en route to collective determination of a course of action."[87] The public, then, is formed by the issue, not the other way around. A public is composed of various groups, some of them interpersonal, others broadly social, "attempting through discursive means to resolve a common issue."[88] The process of forming and changing public opinion is a complex one that involves political actors, media, and an interested public, and all these elements attempt to ascertain and influence opinions on social issues. The public opinion process is a process of social accommodation.

Public opinion is clearly more than responses to public opinion polls. It is a verbal expression of culture, of social interactions, of psychological processes. Students of public opinion should understand the approaches described in this chapter but should also make sure they have a solid grasp of theories developed in other fields, especially sociology, social psychology, and psychology. It is important that we understand how public opinion works so that we can go beyond mere speculation or description. The field is young and exciting, and there is much left to learn. Public opinion scholars of the future can help us understand this important and fundamental social process that is vital to our very survival.

Notes

1. Perry R. Hinton, *The Psychology of Interpersonal Perception* (London: Routledge, 1993).

2. Walter Lippmann, *Public Opinion* (New York: Harcourt, Brace, 1922), pp. 4, 11.

3. Charles H. Cooley, *Human Nature and the Social Order* (New York: Scribner, 1902).

4. George J. McCall and J. L. Simmons, *Identities and Interactions: An Examination of Human Associations in Everyday Life*, 2d ed. (New York: Free Press, 1978), p. 104.

5. Ibid.

6. Ibid.

7. Jerome S. Bruner, "Social Psychology and Perception," in Eleanor E. Maccoby, Theodore M. Newcomb, and Eugene L. Hartley, ed., *Readings in Social Psychology* (New York: Holt, Rinehart and Winston, 1958), p. 86.

8. Paul R. Abramson, *Political Attitudes in America: Formation and Change* (San Francisco: W. H. Freeman and Co., 1983); M. Kent Jennings and Richard G. Niemi, *Generations and Politics: A Panel Study of Young Adults and Their Parents* (Princeton: Princeton University Press, 1981); Roberta L. Sangster and Robert W. Reynolds, "A Test of Inglehart's Socialization Hypothesis for the Acquisition of Materialist/Postmaterialist Values: The Influence of Childhood Poverty on Adult Values," *Political Psychology* 17 (1996):253–269.

9. Leon Festinger, "A Theory of Social Comparison Processes," *Human Relations* 7 (1954):117–140.

10. Ibid., p. 119.

11. Ibid.

12. Hinton, *Psychology of Interpersonal Perception*.

13. Carroll J. Glynn, Ronald E. Ostman, and Daniel G. McDonald, "Opinions, Perceptions and Social Reality," in Theodore L. Glasser and Charles T. Salmon, eds., *Public Opinion and the Communication of Consent* (New York: Guilford Press, 1995), pp. 249–277.

14. Hinton, *Psychology of Interpersonal Perception.*

15. Glynn, Ostman, and McDonald, "Opinions, Perceptions and Social Reality"; Carroll J. Glynn, "Public Opinion as a Normative Opinion Process," in Brant R. Burleson, ed., *Communication Yearbook 20* (Thousand Oaks, CA: Sage Publications, 1996), pp. 157–183.

16. Ruben Orive, "Social Projection and Social Comparisons of Opinions," *Journal of Personality and Social Psychology* 54, 6 (1988):953–964.

17. Glynn, Ostman, and McDonald, "Opinions, Perceptions and Social Reality."

18. Ibid.

19. James M. Fields and Howard Schuman, "Public Beliefs About the Beliefs of the Public," *Public Opinion Quarterly* 40 (1976):427–448.

20. Glynn, Ostman, and McDonald, "Opinions, Perceptions and Social Reality."

21. Ibid.

22. Frank H. Allport, *Social Psychology* (Cambridge, MA: Riverside Press, 1924); Richard Louis Schanck, "A Study of a Community and Its Groups and Institutions Conceived of as Behaviors of Individuals," *Psychological Monographs* 43, 2 (1932) (whole issue); Hubert O'Gorman and Stephen L. Garry, "Pluralistic Ignorance—A Replication and Extension," *Public Opinion Quarterly* 40 (1976): 449–458; Dale T. Miller and Cathy McFarland, "Pluralistic Ignorance: When Similarity Is Interpreted as Dissimilarity," *Journal of Personality and Social Psychology* 53, 2 (1987):298–305; D. Garth Taylor, "Pluralistic Ignorance and the Spiral of Silence: A Formal Analysis," *Public Opinion Quarterly* 46 (1982):311–355.

23. O'Gorman and Garry, "Pluralistic Ignorance."

24. Schanck, "A Study of a Community and Its Groups and Institutions."

25. O'Gorman and Garry, "Pluralistic Ignorance," p. 450.

26. Glynn, Ostman, and McDonald, "Opinions, Perceptions and Social Reality."

27. O'Gorman and Garry, "Pluralistic Ignorance."

28. Glynn, Ostman, and McDonald, "Opinions, Perceptions and Social Reality," p. 262.

29. Miller and McFarland, "Pluralistic Ignorance."

30. Norman Cameron, *The Psychology of Behavior Disorders: A Biosocial Interpretation* (Boston: Houghton Mifflin, 1947).

31. Ibid., p. 168.

32. Ibid.

33. Ibid., p. 169.

34. O'Gorman and Garry, "Pluralistic Ignorance."

35. Fields and Schuman, "Public Beliefs About the Beliefs of the Public."

36. Ibid., p. 430.

37. Ibid.

38. Carroll J. Glynn, "Perceptions of Others' Opinions as a Component of Public Opinion," *Social Science Research* 18 (1989):53–69.

39. Ibid.

40. Ibid., p. 63.

41. Ibid., p. 64.

42. Glynn, Ostman, and McDonald, "Opinions, Perceptions and Social Reality."

43. Lee Ross, David Greene, and Pamela House, "The 'False Consensus Effect': An Egocentric Bias in Social Perception and Attribution Processes," *Journal of Experimental Social Psychology* 13 (1977):280.

44. Brian Mullen et al., "The False Consensus Effect: A Meta-Analysis of 115 Hypothesis Tests," *Journal of Experimental Social Psychology* 21 (1985):262–283.

45. Ross, Greene, and House, "'False Consensus Effect.'"

46. Steven J. Sherman, Clark C. Presson, and Laurie Chassin, "Mechanisms Underlying the False Consensus Effect: The Special Role of Threats to the Self," *Personality and Social Psychology Bulletin* 10, 1 (1984):127–138.

47. Lee Ross, "The Intuitive Psychologist and His Shortcomings: Distortions in the Attribution Process," in Leonard Berkowitz, ed., *Advances in Experimental Social Psychology* (New York: Academic Press, 1977), pp. 150–195.

48. Ross, Greene, and House, "'False Consensus Effect.'"

49. Roger A. Drake, "Lateral Asymmetry of Personal Optimism," *Journal of Research in Personality* 18, 4 (1984):497–507.

50. Neil D. Weinstein, "Unrealistic Optimism About Future Life Events," *Journal of Personality and Social Psychology* 39, 5 (1980):806.

51. Ibid.

52. Hugh M. Culbertson and Guido H. Stempel, "Media Malaise: Explaining Personal Optimism and Societal Pessimism About Health Care," *Journal of Communication* 35 (1985):180–190.

53. Tom R. Tyler and Fay L. Cook, "The Mass Media and Judgments of Risk: Distinguishing Impact on Personal and Societal Level Judgments," *Journal of Personality and Social Psychology* 47 (1984):693–708.

54. Glynn, Ostman, and McDonald, "Opinions, Perceptions and Social Reality."

55. Weinstein, "Unrealistic Optimism About Future Life Events."

56. W. Phillips Davison, "The Third-Person Effect in Communication," *Public Opinion Quarterly* 47 (1983):1–15.

57. Ibid.

58. Ibid., p. 3.

59. Jeremy Cohen et al., "Perceived Impact of Defamation: An Experiment on Third-Person Effects," *Public Opinion Quarterly* 52 (1988):161–173.

60. James T. Tiedge et al., "Discrepancy Between Perceived First-Person and Perceived Third-Person Mass Media Effects," *Journalism Quarterly* 68, 1-2 (1991):141–154.

61. Dominic L. Lasorsa, "Real and Perceived Effects of 'Amerika,'" *Journalism Quarterly* 66 (1989):373–378.

62. George Kennan, "TV's Misguided Cold War Games," *New York Times*, January 5, 1987, p. A16.

63. Dominic L. Lasorsa, "Policymakers and the Third-Person Effect," in J. David Kennamer, ed., *Public Opinion, the Press, and Public Policy* (Westport, CT: Praeger, 1994), pp. 163–175.

64. Ibid., p. 165.

65. Ibid., p. 172.

66. Carroll J. Glynn and Ronald E. Ostman, "Public Opinion About Public Opinion," *Journalism Quarterly* 65 (1988):306.

67. Charles T. Salmon and Chi-Yung Moh, "The Spiral of Silence: Linking Individual and Society Through Communication," in J. David Kennamer, ed., *Public Opinion, the Press, and Public Policy* (Westport, CT: Praeger, 1994), pp. 145–161.

68. Glynn, Ostman, and McDonald, "Opinions, Perceptions and Social Reality."

69. Carroll J. Glynn, Andrew F. Hayes, James Shanahan, "Spiral of Silence: A Meta-Analysis," *Public Opinion Quarterly* 61, 3 (1997):452–463.

70. Carroll J. Glynn and Jack M. McLeod, "Implications of the Spiral of Silence Theory for Communication and Public Opinion Research," in Keith R. Sanders, Lynda Lee Kaid, and Dan D. Nimmo, eds., *Political Communication Yearbook* (Carbondale, IL: Southern Illinois University Press, 1985), pp. 43–68.

71. Solomon E. Asch, *Social Psychology* (Englewood Cliffs, NJ: Prentice-Hall, 1952).

72. Muzafer Sherif, *The Psychology of Social Norms* (New York: Harper and Brothers, 1936).

73. Stanley Milgram, "Nationality and Conformity," *Scientific American* 205, 6 (1961):45–51.

74. Carroll J. Glynn, "The Communication of Public Opinion," *Journalism Quarterly* 64 (1987):688–697.

75. Elisabeth Noelle-Neumann, *The Spiral of Silence. Public Opinion—Our Social Skin* (Chicago: University of Chicago Press, 1984).

76. Elisabeth Noelle-Neumann, "Turbulences in the Climate of Opinion: Methodological Applications of the Spiral of Silence Theory," *Public Opinion Quarterly* 41 (1977):143–158.

77. Taylor, "Pluralistic Ignorance and the Spiral of Silence."

78. Noelle-Neumann, *The Spiral of Silence;* Elisabeth Noelle-Neumann, "Return to the Concept of Powerful Mass Media," *Studies in Broadcasting* 9 (March 1973):67–112.

79. Ibid.

80. Glynn, "Perceptions of Others' Opinions as a Component of Public Opinion"; Lasorsa, "Real and Perceived Effects of 'Amerika'"; Salmon and Moh, "The Spiral of Silence"; Glynn, Hayes, and Shanahan, "The Spiral of Silence: A Meta-Analysis" *Public Opinion Quarterly* 61, 3 (1997): 452–463; Glynn and McLeod, "Implications of the Spiral of Silence Theory"; Carroll J. Glynn and Jack M. McLeod, "Public Opinion du Jour: An Examination of the Spiral of Silence," *Public Opinion Quarterly* 48, 4 (1984):731–740; Charles T. Salmon and F. Gerald Kline, "The Spiral of Silence Ten Years Later," in Keith R. Sanders, Lynda Lee Kaid, and Dan D. Nimmo, eds., *Political Communication Yearbook* (Carbondale, IL: Southern Illinois University Press, 1985), pp. 3–30; Charles T. Salmon and Hayg Oshagan, "Community Size, Perceptions of Majority Opinion and Opinion Expression," *Public Relations Research Annual* 2 (1990):157–171; Wolfgang Donsbach and Robert L. Stevenson, "Challenges, Problems and Empirical Evidence of the Theory of the Spiral of Silence," paper presented at the International Communication Association Conference, San Francisco, 1984; Frank L. Rusciano, *Isolation and Paradox: Defining "the Public" in Modern Political Analysis* (New York: Greenwood Press, 1989).

81. Vincent Price and Donald F. Roberts, "Public Opinion Processes," in Charles R. Berger and Steven H. Chaffee, eds., *Handbook of Communication Science* (Beverly Hills, CA: Sage Publications, 1981), pp. 781–816.

82. W. Philips Davison, "The Public Opinion Process," *Public Opinion Quarterly* 21 (1957):103–118.

83. Ibid.

84. Ibid., p. 106.

85. Ibid., p. 113.

86. Price and Roberts, "Public Opinion Processes," p. 800.

87. Ibid., p. 784.

88. Ibid., p. 803.

Chapter Seven

Basic Beliefs, Democratic Theory, and Public Opinion

BRUCE WILLIAMS AND JILL A. EDY

Although understanding public opinion is important for many reasons, it is essential for the analysis of politics, especially democratic politics. Whatever else we may include in a definition of democracy, at root it must include the idea of a government responsive to the polity. Since public opinion is one way of understanding the political attitudes and beliefs of the polity, it is central to democratic politics. In this chapter, we begin to analyze the connection between public opinion and politics.

First, we will explore the position occupied by public opinion in various kinds of political systems, including democracies. Second, we will examine some of the debates about the role public opinion *should* play in democratic governance. Third, we will survey some of the more basic and enduring features of American public opinion that are relevant to understanding democratic politics. These basic beliefs about government, the economy, and the structure of opportunity in the United States are widely shared and underlie more diverse opinions about proximate political issues like candidates in elections or views on specific policy questions. In this way, they provide the basic structure within which public opinion and politics operate. Often ignored in both academic and popular discussions of public opinion, this basic structure constrains the boundaries of political disagreement and limits what individuals think and say about the political world. In spite of these crucial similarities, differences of opinion exist between key social groups, and we will next turn our attention to some of the more prominent and well-researched political divides. Finally, we will consider the potential for resolving conflicts of opinion about how our consensus values should be realized as public policy.

Public Opinion and the Power to Govern

Democracies are distinguished from other forms of government in part by the formal mechanisms they employ for ascertaining and responding to public opinion. However, it is not the case that the leaders of nondemocratic countries can simply ignore public opinion. Earlier in this book, we discussed the idea that public opinion means more than just survey results or election outcomes. Even in autocratic systems, leaders who completely ignore public opinion may squander a valuable resource known as "legitimacy." Legitimacy—the public's belief that a leader has the right to govern—makes creating and enforcing rules much easier. Without it, leaders must expend more resources to maintain order among the citizenry. Even despots have to have some regard for public sentiment, since revolt is a form of public opinion expression, too. In fact, Benjamin Ginsberg argues, "The fundamental difference between voting and rioting is that voting is a socialized and institutionalized form of mass political expression. The peasant uprising or urban riot is usually a spontaneous affair."[1]

In *The Captive Public*, Ginsberg compares the power of public opinion to influence government both before and after the advent of democratic political regimes. His controversial conclusion is that public opinion may be as powerful or more powerful when it is not channeled through institutional mechanisms like voting but is expressed in ways that the state does not or cannot manage. He observes: "Elections facilitate participation in much the same way that floodgates can be said to facilitate the flow of water. Elections direct mass involvement into formal channels, thus removing many potential impediments to participation, but at the same time diverting it from other courses that may be hazardous to the established political order."[2] However, Ginsberg would probably agree that democracies benefit from stability. He would also probably agree that high-risk opinion expression, such as that of Chinese students in Tiananmen Square in 1989, is not in fact better than the low-risk opinion expression of Americans responding to surveys or going to the polls.

Ginsberg's work is important because it underscores two crucial ideas. First, every political system must, to some degree, take public opinion into account. Second, public opinion in democratic systems may not be as powerful as democratic institutions make it appear.

The Role of Public Opinion in a Democracy

We have shown that there is no simple definition of public opinion to which everyone subscribes. Instead, definitions of public opinion are complex and often contested. This disagreement is not simply a matter of intellectual curiosity. Differences in definitions of public opinion matter because they imply very different ideas about how democratic institutions should be structured and how democratic political processes should function. We will see that this sort of debate has informed not just the study of public opinion but much of American political history.

From the earliest days of our republic, some have held that true democracy requires politically active citizens who make decisions for themselves. These advocates of what is known as *participatory* democracy celebrate New England town meetings and other forms of local and direct self-government. They argue that in America, it is possible to perfect citizens so that they are capable of wise self-government and that "big government" far removed from the people is illegitimate and inherently antidemocratic. This idea that the people can and should govern themselves in the common interest—what James Morone calls "the democratic wish"[3]—recurs frequently in American political thought. In contrast, there have been those who question whether average citizens are likely ever to have enough interest or enough expertise in politics to make wise decisions. These advocates of *representative* democracy believe that citizens ought to delegate decisionmaking authority, through elections or other means, to political leaders who will be able to act on their behalf.

Proponents of participatory and representative democracy have contrasting ideas about the role of public opinion in democratic governance. If, for instance, we conclude that most people are inevitably uninterested and uninformed about politics and only a small proportion of the citizenry can be expected to develop well-informed opinions, we might want institutions that are well shielded from mass opinions. We might also worry, as James Madison did, that self-interested citizens would form what he called a "tyranny of the majority" that could curtail or obliterate the rights of individuals who are not members of the majority. Hence, we might support more representative visions of democracy that severely limit the direct input of the masses in policymaking. In fact, many of the framers of the Constitution had these worries about the limited ability of most citizens to form "enlightened" opinions and tried to design a government that would be insulated from the public.

However, if we believe that public opinion is a reflection of social institutions that do not reward or encourage most people to become informed about politics, we might believe that it is possible to develop a better-informed public capable of formulating enlightened public opinion directed toward the common good. Hence, we might support more aggressive ways of fostering and encouraging the participation of citizens. Once again, this issue has roots in the Constitutional Convention. Many framers thought that the role of government was not to shield officials from uninformed public opinion but rather to enable citizens to make wise decisions.[4]

This debate took on special urgency in the early decades of the twentieth century, with their dramatic social and economic changes. Urbanization, immigration, and technological change, especially in the field of communication with the emergence of the electronic media, seemed to challenge many of the assumptions upon which American democracy had been founded. The best place to start in understanding the current contours of this debate and its implications for how we think about public opinion is by examining the writings of John Dewey and Walter Lippmann (see Box 7.1).

Much public opinion research reveals that most individuals know and care little about politics.[5] Although polls may reveal that a majority of Americans oppose sending troops to Bosnia, upon what are such opinions based? How many of these people understand the issues involved in U.S. interventions abroad and the implications of American involvement for the future of NATO? How many of those surveyed actually have any interest in the issue—except for the fact that it is covered in the media and they have been called upon by a survey to express an opinion? If public opinion is shallow and the public attention span short, then how are we to connect the people's wishes to the political decisions made by policymakers?"[6]

Skepticism about the wisdom and enlightened nature of public opinion is reflected in the design of a variety of representative institutions that seek to insulate policymakers from the public. The modern heirs of those who were most skeptical about the public's ability include many political scientists and public opinion researchers who suggest that only a small proportion of the population can ever be expected to possess the desire or sophistication to actively participate in public discourse. They argue that a well-functioning pluralist political system requires that only a small proportion of the polity be mobilized at any given time; therefore, we need not worry about the lack of political sophistication of the masses and the general failure of the public to participate in politics.

Representative democracy usually employs political parties and elections to solve the problem of lack of political knowledge or attention. Political parties provide a limited number of choices for the public, reducing the complexity faced by citizens. It is not necessary for citizens to understand the intricacies of specific policy issues. They only need choose, on broad ideological grounds, between the parties. In the American case, citizens generally need not decide about the wide range of difficult issues facing the political system; they need only choose between a Democrat and a Republican. Whatever the myriad issues being considered by the political system, a party system reduces the number of alternatives to a manageable few.

In a representative democracy, as opposed to direct or plebiscite systems, the principal activity of citizenship is voting at limited and predetermined times. Elections are a way to periodically allow citizens to select those who will represent them, allowing mass political participation but at the same time shielding politics from the vicissitudes of uninformed public opinion. By providing a limited number of choices at a limited number of well-defined

Box 7.1   Walter Lippmann Versus John Dewey: The Limits and Possibilities of Democratic Politics

In Chapter 2, we discussed the contrasting beliefs of Plato and Aristotle about the value of public opinion. Viewed from another perspective, their debate over public opinion is a debate about the relative value of democracy. Plato, who argued that democracy demands more of most people than they are capable of giving, would probably favor a representative democracy in which leaders are insulated from public opinion. Aristotle, who believed that a public deliberating together could reach better judgments than a single person deciding alone, would probably favor participatory democracy.

In the twentieth century, debate between advocates of participatory and representative democracy found new life in the differences between two of America's most significant "public intellectuals": John Dewey and Walter Lippmann. Lippmann was one of the best known and most respected political columnists in the nation from 1914, when he helped start the *New Republic,* until his death in 1974. He also wrote two seminal books on public opinion: *Public Opinion* in 1922 and *The Phantom Public* in 1925.[1] Lippmann argued that direct democracy was impossible because ordinary citizens could not be expected to make rational decisions about public affairs.[2]

First, Lippmann argued in *Public Opinion* that the amount of knowledge any average individual could be expected to possess was quite limited, especially when compared to the complexity of the modern state, even in 1922.

Walter Lippmann. (Photo courtesy of the Library of Congress)

(continues)

Box 7.1 *(continued)*

John Dewey. SOURCE: John Dewey Papers, Special Collections, Morris Library, Southern Illinois University, Carbondale, Illinois.

Think, Lippmann argued, of how much work it would take for each individual in a society to keep up to date on every public issue. Second, Lippmann observed that the operations of politics were largely invisible and inaccessible to the average citizen, and because of this, the public must depend on the mass media for information. But the media, Lippmann argued, are incapable of providing the sorts of political information citizens need to make wise decisions:

> [T]he audience, tuning in and tuning off here and there, cannot be counted upon to hear, even in summary form, the essential evidence and the main arguments on all the significant sides of a question. Rarely, and on very few public issues, does the mass audience have the benefit of the process by which truth is sifted from error—the dialectic of debate in which there is immediate challenge, reply, cross-examination, and rebuttal.[3]

The result of this is that the best that citizens would be able to do is make very general choices between competing groups of elites.

Especially in *The Phantom Public*, Lippmann used these arguments to develop a theory of elite democracy. He was skeptical about the ability of politicians to make wise choices and thus called upon social science to develop a body of disinterested knowledge that would provide policymakers

(continues)

Box 7.1   (continued)

with the technical information needed to make political decisions in an increasingly complex and demanding world. We will have more to say about elite democracy in Chapter 10.

In contrast, John Dewey, one of this country's most important philosophers and a leader of the Progressive movement in education, argued against Lippmann's elitist views. In one of his most influential political works, *The Public and Its Problems*, first published in 1927, Dewey accepted Lippmann's arguments as a description of the current limited state of public opinion, but he argued that this had nothing to do with any inherent limits of citizenship or democracy.[4] Instead, he contended it was a result of the failures of the political and economic structure of twentieth-century American society. Reflecting a very different view of public opinion, Dewey argued that the political and economic institutions of any society create the social context within which citizens operate. If, as Dewey believed, democracy depended upon the direct participation of its citizens, then what was called for was a remaking of the current democratic institutions to enable such participation:

> The old saying that the cure for the ills of democracy is more democracy is not apt if it means that the evils may be remedied by introducing more machinery of the same kind as that which already exists, or by refining and perfecting that machinery. But the phrase may also indicate the need of returning to the idea itself, of clarifying and deepening our sense of its meaning to criticize and remake its political manifestations.[5]

For Dewey, democratic government required that citizens be given the opportunity to participate in the active and vibrant communal activities that are the defining feature of democratic politics: Communal life, for Dewey, is democracy.[6] Indeed, this idea was reflected in Dewey's educational philosophy, which emphasized that schools must be a principal institution for building democratic life; hence, they should emphasize group participation, seek to limit the arbitrary imposition of authority, and emphasize cooperation rather than individual competition. Social scientific knowledge, an important resource for public decisionmaking, should not become simply a body of knowledge in the hands of elites. Rather, it should be provided to all citizens, for unlike Lippmann, Dewey believed that democracy required the active participation of its citizens.

---

1. Walter Lippmann, *Public Opinion* (New York: Harcourt, Brace, 1922); Walter Lippmann, *The Phantom Public* (New York: Harcourt, Brace and Company, 1925).

2. Our summary of the views of Lippmann and Dewey draws heavily on Robert B. Westbrook, *John Dewey and American Democracy* (Ithaca: Cornell University Press, 1991), pp. 294–318.

3. Walter Lippmann, *Essays in the Public Philosophy* (Boston: Little, Brown and Co., 1955), pp. 128–129.

4. John Dewey, *The Public and Its Problems* (Athens, OH: Swallow Press, 1954).

5. Ibid., p. 319.

6. Ibid.; Westbrook, *John Dewey and American Democracy*.

opportunities, elections and the candidates put up by political parties serve to focus public attention on politics for a brief period of time. Campaigns, so the argument goes, help make otherwise uninterested or uninformed citizens aware of the broad issues confronting the political system. Political parties help to focus and simplify the debate. Rather than having to know about the intricacies of environmental policy, tax policy, welfare reform, and so on, citizens need only have a very general idea about the course they support as outlined by the political parties.

Accepting this limited view of the role of ordinary citizens in politics, Samuel Popkin analyzes the connection between public opinion and elections. He argues that voters use a variety of shortcuts and employ what he calls low information or gut rationality to make reasoned choices about candidates in an election.[7] Rejecting the critiques of some that campaigns simply mislead and misinform a gullible and ignorant public Popkin argues that

> my theory recognizes that voters actually do reason about parties, candidates, and issues. They have premises, and they use those premises to make inferences from their observations of the world around them. They think about who and what political parties stand for; they think about the meaning of political endorsements; they think about what government can and should do. And the performance of government, parties, and candidates affects their assessments and preferences.[8]

Walter Lippmann believed the choice was even simpler than that, arguing that all ordinary citizens can be expected to do is "to support the Ins when things are going well; to support the Outs when they seem to be going badly, this in spite of all that has been said about tweedledum and tweedledee, is the essence of popular government."[9]

However, recent changes in the American electoral system suggest that our institutions may be becoming more participatory and less representative. Some scholars have argued that elections no longer function as they once did. They point to the declining public support for political parties and the rise of candidate-centered campaigns.[10] Far fewer people now consider themselves Democrats or Republicans, and many more claim to be "independents." Candidates often run more as individuals than as representatives of a party. Thus, parties may no longer serve to consolidate and simplify issues for the pubic. Popkin would probably argue that candidate-centered campaigns can still serve to focus issues for the public. Nevertheless, the mass media and public opinion polling may play a distinctly populist role as they constrain the actions of elites by communicating the opinions of the masses.

Public opinion may now have a much greater impact on public policy than it once did as political leaders attempt to maintain public support and keep their jobs, but exactly how public opinion might affect elite behavior is a matter of some scholarly debate. Some political leaders, especially when they are elected by large margins, claim a mandate. That is, they assert that the voters sent them to office to accomplish some specific task. Political scientist Stanley Kelley Jr. observes that modern polling technology makes it possible to discover such mandates, since voters can be queried about why they voted as they did. However, he finds no evidence of mandates because voters' agendas, when they exist at all, seem to be quite diffuse.[11]

A second theory about how public opinion is linked to elite political behavior is called "retrospective voting." Developed by V. O. Key Jr.[12] and later expanded by Morris Fiorina and others,[13] the theory says that voters judge the past political performance of their current leaders, then decide whether to reelect them or to elect new leaders. This vision of voting is quite similar to Lippmann's. Politicians respond to public opinion by *anticipating* citizens' reactions to their decisions. Fiorina notes that retrospective voting is more than a "throw the bums out," knee-jerk reaction. Sometimes voters will leave even leaders who have failed them in office because the alternative seems worse. Thus, even when Democrats preside over a period of rising unemployment, the unemployed seem to vote Democratic, fearing that a Republican majority will be even less advantageous to them.[14] Other scholars point out that retrospective voting would not necessarily require that the public monitor its leaders particularly closely. R. Douglas Arnold describes what he calls a "tax auditor" model of citizen attention. Political leaders live under constant threat of audit, with severe penalties if they cannot account for themselves. Because of that threat, leaders tend to follow the public's wishes, even though they are not constantly monitored by the electorate as a whole.[15] We will have more to say about the links between public opinion and public policy in Chapter 9.

Regardless of the exact mechanism, the rise of the media and the decline of parties as defining features of the political system have forged a direct link between elected leaders and the general public. Leaders' standings in public opinion polls are quite important for their ability to achieve their policy goals and get reelected. Public opinion polling that tracks the popularity of presidents is a staple of news reports and affects the ability of the president to influence Congress and other political leaders. Indeed, syndicated columnist David Broder says, "In reality, the play of public opinion, as reported and magnified by the press, has grown so powerful in the United States that it has become the near preoccupation of government. . . . When a president loses popularity, he also loses the ability to govern."[16]

One result of this need to maintain public support is that elected politicians, presidents especially, must always keep one eye, and sometimes two, on the impact their actions will have on short-run changes in public opinion. This pressure leads to a tendency for chief executives to continue acting as if they were still running for office, even after their election. This results in what is sometimes called "the never-ending campaign."

Thomas Patterson argues that as parties decline in significance, the press becomes the only institution capable of sorting out the underlying ideological issues in elections—a role for which it is ill-suited.[17] Candidates and elections are not able to provide the limited number of ideologically meaningful choices once offered by parties, and once elected, policymakers are not shielded from the vicissitudes of public opinion. Rather, elected policymakers increasingly tailor their words and actions to the results of public opinion polling, reported almost daily in the mass media. Further, we are still faced with the critique of such democratic institutions by scholars like Lippmann. Is it possible to compensate for the limited attention and sophistication of most citizens?

Basic Beliefs

Most of the time, discussions of politics in general and public opinion in particular focus on disagreement and conflict. Indeed, when it comes to choosing candidates in an election or deciding on specific policy issues, conflict and difference seem to be the stuff of public opinion. For example, throughout the 104th Congress, poll results and political debate chronicled the percentage of Americans who agreed with Republican positions on the federal budget and the percentage of those who agreed with the Democratic position.

However, it is crucial to understand that agreement on many things underlies every ongoing set of interactions among human beings. If there were no underlying shared values, then political communities would be much more likely to fragment over disagreements rather than struggle to work them out. Political theorist Robert Dahl, for instance, argues that political communities require shared norms and respect to successfully negotiate more divisive adversarial issues.[18] At minimum, then, a stable political system not in a state of civil warfare requires a basic level of agreement or consensus over things like fundamental political values, the legitimacy of political institutions, and the broad content of policies pursued by government.

Failure to attain sufficient consensus has severe consequences for democratic politics. Even in stable, peaceful societies, the threat of violence and disorder hovers. American history contains many episodes of civil disobedience and mass protest that sometimes led to violence. There are no precise measures of the degree of consensus "sufficient" to allow the ongoing operation of a political system, but in this section, we outline some of the basic issues over which there seem to be broad agreement. There is considerable evidence that large majorities hold these values.[19] Some have attained the status of conventional wisdom, finding expression in the popular press as assertions that need no evidence. Together, they constitute the bedrock values of American politics, a sort of civic religion.[20] Like the fundamental values in an ecclesiastical religion, they are widely held, largely unexamined, and influential in a subtle, continuous, and incomplete way. They constitute the basic belief structure that underlies more specific disagreements in public opinion in the United States.

Capitalism and Democracy[21]

Americans hold distinct and overlapping values about capitalism and democracy (that is, the economy and the political system). There is much consensus in public opinion over the way American economic and political systems should operate and the connection between the public and private sectors.[22] A crucial element of this belief is that politics and economics are separate and largely unconnected.[23]

An overwhelming percentage of Americans believe in self-reliance, the worth of competition, the legitimacy of pursuing material possessions, the pursuit of profit as a legitimate and worthy activity, private property, private ownership (rather than public ownership) of the means of production and free markets rather than government decree as a means of determining prices and guiding economic activity. Together, these principles form the basis for a widely shared belief in the goodness and value of the all-encompassing notion of capitalism.

In the political realm, most Americans share values that can be subsumed in another all-encompassing term: democracy. Americans believe in individual freedoms such as the freedom of speech, assembly, and religion and the right to due process. They believe that the government rules by the consent of the governed, that government should be limited, and that individual rights limit the authority of government. Americans also believe in equality, usually in the form of equality of opportunity (everyone getting an equal chance to exercise rights and obtain rewards) rather than equality of result (everyone receiving equal rewards).

These values are not well defined, nor are they consistent. For instance, one central democratic value—individual equality—partially conflicts with the general thrust of many of the values embodied in capitalism, especially those of private property, competition, and the pursuit of profit. The conflict is somewhat, but not completely, resolved when equality is defined as equality of opportunity rather than equality of result. Thus, even if everyone does not partake equally in economic well-being (equality of result), the notion of equality of opportunity argues that everyone at least had the chance to do so. However, there is no consensus regarding whether equality of opportunity has been achieved.

The conflict between the democratic political value of equality and the principal values of capitalism has produced a continuing debate in American politics.[24] The notion of liberty, for example, applies not just to the economic realm but to the social and political as well. Thus, if people have equal access to public accommodations, then the liberty of restaurant and country club owners to exclude groups they do not like must be curtailed. This debate has not been a sideshow in American politics. In fact, in their major study of elite and mass beliefs about democracy and capitalism, Herbert McClosky and John Zaller conclude that "the tension that exists between capitalist and democratic values is a definitive feature of American life that has helped to shape the ideological dimensions of the nation's politics."[25]

Even though there are tensions between them, it is important to remember that these are still consensus values. It is not the case that some Americans believe in freedom while others believe in equality. Most Americans believe in both, but they may disagree about how to balance these values' conflicting demands. According to Kevin Phillips, this tension helps explain the cyclical character of Democratic and Republican electoral success and the public policies their successes produce. Periods of Republican dominance are characterized by an emphasis on capitalist values and policies designed to provide the best possible environment for the unfettered pursuit of individual liberty and private gain. Although such periods (i.e., the Gilded Age of the robber barons at the end of the nineteenth century; the Roaring Twenties; the Reagan years) are marked by dramatic increases in economic growth and the accumulation of vast wealth by some, they are also marked by increasing levels of inequality and a neglect of those who are not fortunate or wise enough to succeed. The excesses of such periods allow Democrats to gain electoral power by appealing to values like the need for equity, which can only come from an active government working to reduce economic and social inequality.[26]

The ability to maintain an overriding political consensus, despite such tensions, rests to a large degree on a widely shared belief that the U.S. Constitution provides the basis for an ideal government. The Constitution embodies the values of limited government, due process, and individual rights. It promotes the value of equality, however, only if one includes amendments abolishing slavery and extending the rights of citizenship, including the right to vote, to former slaves and to women. The Constitution also sets rules and procedures for the political system and outlines the roles of various political leaders.

Consensus on Official Decisionmakers. There is little disagreement over the roles the president, Congress, and the courts should play in the political system. The legitimacy and power of the Constitution, which establishes these positions and lays out their basic functions, rubs off and gives them legitimacy as well. To Americans, this legitimacy generally seems so obvious that there is no point in mentioning it, yet many bloody civil wars elsewhere attest that acceptance of major political institutions cannot be taken for granted. The catastrophic recent history of the former Yugoslavia, Zaire (now the Democratic Republic of the Congo), Lebanon, and other countries rent by civil war in part because of lack of agreement on who should make decisions teaches this lesson all too well.

Beliefs About Rules and Procedures. Americans express very high levels of support for many of the basic rules and procedures of the political system. Part of the reason for the public's degree of consensus about the role of various leaders is their belief in the processes that elected them and the so-called checks and balances that constrain their authority. Further, when asked in the abstract about rules and procedures covering individual behavior such as freedom of speech, due process, and equality of treatment, overwhelming majorities express support.

The belief in the value of due process carries implications for procedures both within the political realm and sometimes far beyond it. In the United States, the fairness of the procedures used to arrive at a decision sometimes loom as important as its content. Decisions reached using proper and fair procedures are more likely to be seen as good decisions. Often, opposition to an unpopular decision is expressed as criticism of the procedures used to make it: "We weren't notified of the meeting"; "The discussion was not full and free"; "The environmental impact statement was deficient." Thus, if values like equality or freedom to speak and be heard are violated, they become grounds for questioning the procedures employed.

However, support for basic values can drop drastically in the context of specific situations. For example, 97 percent of a sample of the general public said yes when asked, "Do you believe in freedom of speech?" But when asked, "Do you believe in allowing fascists and communists to hold meetings and express their views in the community?" only 22 percent of those who said they believe in freedom of speech said yes.[27] When asked if the United States was meant to be "a Christian nation" or "a country made up of many races, religions, and nationalities," 20 percent chose the first response, 73 percent the second (7 percent declined to choose); but when asked if a community's civic auditorium should be allowed to be used by "Atheists who want to preach against God and religion," only 17 percent said yes, whereas 68 percent thought Protestant groups wanting to hold a revival meeting should be able to use it.[28] These discrepancies are explored more thoroughly in Chapter 10.

The American Dream

Jennifer Hochschild argues that the best way to summarize Americans' core beliefs about their political and social system is to say that there is overwhelming belief in the "American Dream."[29] President Clinton summarized this set of beliefs: "The American dream that we were all raised on is a simple but powerful one—if you work hard and play by the rules, you should be given a chance to go as far as your God-given ability will take you."[30]

Hochschild argues that the American Dream consists of four basic tenets. First, everyone, regardless of class, gender, race, or any other ascriptive characteristics may pursue the American Dream. Second, one may reasonably anticipate success in pursuing the American Dream. Third, success is defined in terms of the fact that people are materially rewarded or punished according to how vigorously they pursue the American Dream. Fourth, the pursuit of success is a sign of goodness.

Public opinion polls consistently reveal widespread support for these propositions.[31] This support cuts across rich and poor and is generally much stronger among Americans than their similarly situated European counterparts. Fewer than one-fifth of Americans view race, gender, religion, or class as significant impediments to getting ahead in life. Further, even two-thirds of the poor believe that they have a good chance of improving their condition. This is a much higher percentage than surveys of the poor in European countries reveal. In 1980, 70 percent of Americans polled believed that there was plenty of opportunity in the country and that individuals who worked hard could go as far as they wanted. In 1983, "only 31 percent of Americans agreed that in their nation 'what you achieve in life depends largely on your family background,' compared with over 50 percent of Austrians and Britons, and over 60 percent of Italians."[32] Additionally, surveys of young Americans reveal that they believe much more than their European peers that people become poor because they do not work hard enough.

This leads to the more widespread belief among Americans than Europeans that individuals should not be protected from the consequences of their actions and that the role of government is to expand opportunities. Thus, American public opinion shows wider support than European opinion for government providing expanded educational opportunities. In contrast, there is much less support in America than in Europe for government programs to reduce income disparity between the rich and poor.

Although there is widespread support for the propositions underlying the America Dream, this does not mean that there is consensus over how to achieve it or that these beliefs square with the realities of opportunity in the United States. Thus, consensus is always limited. Indeed, Hochschild argues that there are severe contradictions among the basic components of the American Dream and that individuals situated differently have very different explanations and understandings of what the problems with the American Dream may be. In some ways, this is another expression of the tensions between equality and freedom.

The Longing for Community

A final set of beliefs shared by many Americans and important for understanding both public opinion and American politics is the longing for community. In the United States, the twentieth century has been marked by dramatic increases in geographic mobility as nuclear families move about in search of jobs and opportunities. How many of you reading this book grew up in the same town or city as your parents? How many of you expect to return to your old neighborhoods when you graduate? In *Habits of the Heart*, using hundreds of in-depth interviews, Robert Bellah and his colleagues document the yearning of the Americans they interviewed for the lost values that spring from attachment to political, religious, and social communities.[33] One effect of such yearnings is that Americans are often suspicious of the threat to their communities posed by the power of "big government" and "big business." Such institutions are seen as threatening individual freedom (both political and economic) and are viewed with great suspicion. This is one of the reasons that we continue to celebrate New England town meetings and other forms of "direct democracy." It also helps explain why attacks on government and the call to return government to the people resonate with so many Americans.

The Great Divides

Although Americans do seem to agree on the basic ground rules for democracy, there are important divisions of opinion about how many essential aspects of democracy should be incorporated into public policy. Most of these debates are not about "whether" but about "how much." For example, very few people believe that the government should do nothing to help poor people, but there are important disagreements about how much help is appropriate and what form that help should take. In the sections below, we describe some of the more important social divisions in public opinion.

Social Class and Public Opinion

Many theories about the relationship of social class to public opinion have their roots in Marxist theory. If you think about it, it seems fairly obvious that the owners of factories and businesses and other "means of production" would have different interests, and therefore different opinions, than the people who work for them. We would expect that workers would favor more government intervention in the economy and policies that promote equality of result by redistributing income from wealthy owners to less wealthy workers. Indeed, most public opinion researchers have found a reasonably consistent relationship between income and support for government redistribution policies. The less money you have, the more likely you are to support redistribution.

But researchers have had a difficult time determining the relationship between social class and public opinion. In part, the problems stem from the researchers' own disagreements about how to define social class. For example, income and social class are not necessarily related. Skilled blue-collar workers may earn more income than white-collar workers or even small-business owners.

The relationship between social class and public opinion has become even more complex in what has been called the "postindustrial age." It is increasingly difficult to split the world neatly into "capital" and "labor," as the manufacturing industries have come to employ fewer and fewer people while service-sector industries have come to employ more and more. More people are self-employed today than ever before, and many more jobs require creativity and problem-solving skills that were not demanded of workers in traditional manufacturing jobs. It is difficult to classify as capital or labor those who work in growing industries such as health care and the "knowledge" industries.

Another problem with trying to view the world through the lens of class, at least when studying democracy in the United States, is that most citizens do not view themselves in terms of class. Most Americans think of themselves as middle class, even though many of them would be placed objectively in the working class or the upper class. Table 7.1 illustrates the difference between the United States and Great Britain with regard to class identification.

Although the actual distributions among the various classes are quite similar, the British citizens are far more likely to see themselves as working class than the Americans are. A further problem with this lack of class identification is that even American workers who do see themselves as members of the working class often do not make the connections between their class identity and the political opinions that would logically be connected to it.[34] This failure to identify with a social class or to connect one's class identity with one's political views probably attenuates sharp class differences in American public opinion.

Nevertheless, it still seems likely that people occupying different positions in the social structure would have different interests and that their opinions on important public issues would be different. Social science researchers have often attempted to classify people by socioeconomic status (SES) in order to understand what those differences might be. SES is based on a person's income, education, and occupation. Some researchers include other factors, such as the person's parents' SES, as well. SES is based on a concept of status more than class. The assumption these researchers make

TABLE 7.1   Class Position and Class Identification in Britain and the United States

	Britain	U.S.
Class Position		
Service (includes professionals, administrators, and managers)	25.6	34.4
Intermediate (includes clerical and sales personnel, small-business owners, farmers, and supervisors of manual workers)	39.7	35.6
Working (includes skilled, semiskilled, and unskilled manual laborers and farm workers)	34.8	30.0
Class Self-Identification		
Middle	27.9	51.0
Working	72.1	49.0

SOURCE: Adapted from Bernadette C. Hayes, "The Impact of Class on Political Attitudes: A Comparative Study of Great Britain, West Germany, Australia, and the United States," *European Journal of Political Research* 27 (1995), table 1, p. 76.

is that the people who occupy similar places in the social structure (college-educated white-collar workers who make about $40,000 per year, for example) are likely to have similar opinions, not simply because their economic interests are similar but because their values are similar. They have a common perspective.

When they study the public opinion differences between these social strata, researchers often divide the issues under consideration into economic (or interest) issues and value issues. The pattern of differences on each group of issues is distinctive, and both contain some surprises. On issues that pertain to government involvement in redistributing income (that is, government intervention to produce equality of result), the relationship between socioeconomic status and support for redistribution is largely what one might expect. People of lower SES are more likely to favor such policies, and as SES rises, support for such policies declines. However, at the highest levels of SES something strange happens: Support for redistribution increases again. That is, the people with the most prestige in terms of income, occupation, and education seem to be more supportive of equality of result than the so-called middle class. A closer look reveals a phenomenon that researchers call *class polarization*. At the highest levels of SES, the opinions of Democrats and Republicans (or liberals and conservatives) diverge as the Democrats' support for redistribution increases dramatically. Figure 7.1 illustrates this phenomenon. Liberalism indicates support for redistribution, whereas conservatism reflects opposition to such policies.

Democrats in this high-SES group are more likely to be professionals, many of whom are in the health care and knowledge industries. Their high level of education is an important factor placing them in this group. Republicans in the high-SES group are more likely to be administrators or to own or manage their firm or business. They have a higher income, on average, than the high-SES Democrats.[35] Thus, the Republicans in large part represent the "capitalists" that Marx's followers have in mind, whereas the Democrats are more likely to represent the postindustrial aspects of the American economy.

On issues that involve individual freedoms and social values, a different pattern emerges. People with higher socioeconomic status seem to place more value on individual rights and freedoms, whereas those of lower SES seem to prefer a more orderly society in which the government has the authority to manage individual behavior. People of higher SES are more likely to favor civil rights for all, including women, African-Americans, and homosexuals. They are also more likely to favor due process by supporting the rights of the accused.[36] However, this relationship is not straightforward, either. Much of the relationship between SES and public opinion on individual freedoms and other values can be explained by education. Not only does more education contribute directly to a higher SES, but it also contributes indirectly. People with more education tend to make more money and have higher-status jobs. In fact, a recent study by Jerome Himmelstein and James McRae found that differences in education were the only individual characteristic that could consistently explain the more liberal attitudes of the higher-SES groups.[37]

Himmelstein and McRae also argue that issues cannot be neatly divided into interest issues and values issues, since there are often moral components in economic policy decisions, and decisions about values often have economic consequences.[38] For example, banning smoking would limit individual freedom, but it would also reduce the costs to society of treating people who suffer from smoking-related diseases and of losing their economic contributions to the community. The relationship between social class and public opinion is clearly complex. Conflicting ideas about the nature of class and about the nature of issues have exposed diverse gaps in the opinions of social groups about how our democracy should be run.

Public Opinion and Political Parties

Although many have argued that political partisanship matters much less now than it ever has before, the Democratic and Republican parties are still forces to be reckoned with in American politics. Further, there are genuine differences of opinion between Republicans and Democrats. In general, the Democrats are usually thought of as favoring economically and socially liberal policies. That is, the goal of their policies is to diminish the social, educational, and income disparities among people while maximizing their individual freedoms. Republicans are generally considered social and economic

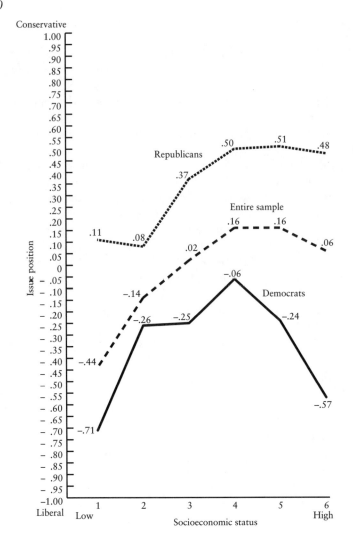

FIGURE 7.1   Class Polarization and Support for Aid to the Poor. SOURCE: Richard D. Shingles, "Class, Status, and Support for Government Aid to Disadvantaged Groups," *Journal of Politics* 51 (1989), figure 1, pp. 946–947, derived from data in a pooled sample of the 1976, 1980, and 1984 NES Surveys of Americans eighteen years and older.

conservatives. They tend to favor economic policies that permit the market-place to work undisturbed while making sure that an orderly society is maintained. As you can see, class interests and party interests are often at odds with each other. As we mentioned earlier, high SES is likely to be associated with more conservative views on economic policy and more liberal views on social policy. Low SES is associated with the reverse. This imperfect fit between socioeconomic status and political partisanship produces what are known as *cross-cutting cleavages*. The public does not divide neatly on either lines of party or lines of class.

An important problem faced by political parties involves the different opinions held by active partisans and more passive party supporters. People who are active in the party, who go to the convention, work for the party, vote in the primaries, and so forth often have opinions that are different in degree, if not in kind, from those who simply turn out in the general election. The result can sometimes be that a party selects a candidate who represents the opinions of the active partisans but not the opinions of the majority of voters who usually support the party. Such a candidate can suffer a crushing defeat at the polls as large numbers of voters defect to the opposition. Parties must sometimes compromise by selecting a candidate who can represent the opinions of party loyalists so that they will continue to work for the party but who will also appeal to the mass of voters, who might ultimately elect the candidate to office. The gap between the opinions of the active partisans and those of the casual party supporters can thus have an important impact on the electoral success of the party.

Public Opinion in Black and White

Unlike class divisions in public opinion, the opinion differences between white Americans and African-Americans are stark. From before the turn of the century until well into the 1960s, race issues could be formulated in terms best described by Gunnar Myrdal in his classic book *An American Dilemma*.[39] Myrdal saw the struggle pitting general American values such as freedom and equality against more specific white prejudices against African-Americans.[40] Of course, Myrdal's analysis could be extended to other ethnic minorities as well. The heart of the issue was whether everyone, regardless of creed or color, had the right to compete for the same jobs, use the same public facilities, be educated in the same schools. Even at that time, there was a tension between values. In order for there to be equal access to facilities and jobs, the liberty of those who owned, for example, businesses or homes had to be curtailed.

Today, the issues surrounding race are still more complex. Prejudice remains a problem, but the laws that condoned segregation and discrimination are gone. Critical issues of race invoke the ongoing tensions in basic American values, such as equality of opportunity, equality of result, and faith in due process and other democratic procedures.

Black Americans and white Americans have deeply contrasting ideas about how the goals of racial equality should be achieved. Although both races seem to agree that everyone should have equal access to education, jobs, and a decent living (in other words, the American Dream), the races disagree profoundly on how such equality is to be achieved. For example, in 1972, 97 percent of Americans agreed that "blacks and whites should have an equal chance at any kind of job." However, just over 50 percent of the white community believes that it is not the federal government's job to ensure fair treatment of blacks in the job market. Only 7 percent of the black community concurs.[41] Kinder and Sanders find evidence of a huge racial divide on issues that touch many of the core values Americans hold, including a struggle over what equality really means and the role of government in society. Table 7.2 displays some of their results.

As you can see, the difference of opinion between blacks and whites is enormous. It is even more pronounced with regard to policies that promote equality of result than it is concerning policies that promote equal opportunities. Kinder and Sanders call this "a divide without peer."[42] Their graph of the divide is shown in Figure 7.2.

On the left are those who agree that the government should do more to aid blacks in six policy instances (five of which are included in Table 7.2). On the right are those who disagree with all six policy statements. The three leftmost categories account for 63 percent of the black community, whereas the three furthest right encompass 36 percent of the white community.[43] Kinder and Sanders's data show that no other demographic groups in America have more different opinions than blacks and whites.

These large disparities are important for both political and social reasons. Not only do we seem to disagree about how to achieve the goals we embraced in the 1960s, but our disagreement may be a source of prejudice rather than a cure for it. Paul Sniderman and Thomas Piazza argue that the policies that were meant to overcome prejudices may instead cause them: "[A] number of whites dislike the idea of affirmative action so much and perceive it to be so unfair that they have come to dislike blacks *as a consequence.* Hence the special irony of the contemporary politics of race. In the very effort to make things better, we have made some things worse. . . . Wishing to close the racial divide in America, we have widened it" (emphasis ours).[44]

The recent trial of O. J. Simpson, who was acquitted of two murders, prompted a host of public opinion polls that revealed another important difference between African-American and white citizens: their faith in the current system of due process. The polls do not reveal disagreement about

TABLE 7.2   Racial Difference in Opinion About Policies to Promote Equality (in percent)

	Whites	Blacks	Difference
Equality of opportunity			
Fair employment			
Government should ensure fair treatment of blacks	46.2	89.8	+43.6
Not the government's business	49.9	7.3	
School desegregation			
Government should see to school integration	35.6	82.9	+47.3
Government should stay out of it	55.2	11.1	
Equality of result			
Federal spending on programs that assist blacks			
Increased	17.6	74.6	+57.0
Stay the same	62.3	21.9	
Decreased	20.0	3.2	
Affirmative action			
Preferential hiring and promotion of blacks			
Favor strongly/favor	15.4	67.7	+52.3
Oppose strongly/oppose	84.6	32.2	
College quotas for blacks			
Favor strongly/favor	29.7	79.7	+50.0
Oppose strongly/oppose	70.3	20.3	

SOURCE: Adapted from Donald R. Kinder and Lynn M. Sanders, *Divided by Color: Racial Politics and Democratic Ideals* (Chicago: University of Chicago Press, 1996), table 2.1, p. 1.

how the justice system *should* work, but they reveal profound disagreements about how the system *does* work, as can be seen in Table 7.3.

Some of these poll results are affected by current events. For example, the results of the March poll that asked whether citizens believe that the police testify truthfully are probably affected by the then recent testimony of Mark Fuhrman, a Los Angeles Police Department officer alleged to hold racist views. Respondents answering questions in October about whether the justice system is biased against blacks were probably responding in part to the verdict in Simpson's trial. However, trend data gathered by the Gallup Organization throughout the trial shows that the important differences revealed here are not simply an artifact of the week's news from Los Angeles.

African-Americans have genuinely different opinions about the overall fairness of the American justice system than white Americans do. Although the results of the surveys above show that many whites believe the system of due process as currently administered discriminates against blacks, these results also show that blacks are much more likely to believe that the sys-

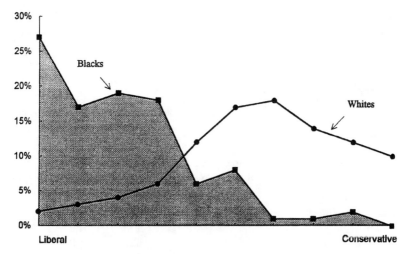

FIGURE 7.2 The "Divide Without Peer": Black and White Opinion on Racial Policy. SOURCE: Donald R. Kinder and Lynn M. Sanders, *Divided by Color: Racial Politics and Democratic Ideals* (Chicago: University of Chicago Press, 1996), figure 2.2, p. 27. This graph displays black and white opinions on race policy based on a composite of six policy questions.

TABLE 7.3 Racial Difference in Opinion About Due Process

	Total	Whites	Blacks	Difference
American justice system biased against blacks (October 1995)	35	33	54	+21
Problem of racist police is widespread (October 1995)	54	52	68	+18
Feel you have been unfairly treated by police because of your race (October 1995)		9	34	+25
Police testify truthfully (March 1995)	66	70	33	−37
Blacks treated more harshly than whites in criminal justice system (July 1995)	49	45	77	+32
White juries more likely to convict black defendants than white defendants (October 1995)	42	40	59	+19
Black juries more likely to convict white defendants than black defendants (October 1995)	33	36	18	−18
Jury reached the right verdict in O. J. Simpson trial (October 1995)	47	42	78	+36

SOURCE: *Gallup Poll Monthly* (March 1995), p. 46; *Gallup Poll Monthly* (August 1995), p. 29; *Gallup Poll Monthly* (October 1995), pp. 4–5, 38–39, 50.

tem is biased against them. Blacks were almost four times as likely as whites to believe that they have been treated unfairly by police because of their race. Almost 80 percent of blacks believe that their race is treated more harshly by the criminal justice system, whereas only 45 percent of whites believe the same. Although the Simpson verdict temporarily narrowed the gap between black and white, in the week that followed the jury's decision, blacks were still far more likely to believe that the system is biased against them.

These differences of opinion about whether the institutions of government operate fairly and about what constitutes being fair have important consequences for both immediate policy outcomes and for the overall viability of the system of government. The legitimacy of the government rests upon the public's acceptance of consensus values and the belief that those values are translated into public policy.

Another important aspect of opinion differences across groups is the attitudes of other minority groups. Although the American social landscape is becoming increasingly multiracial, the vast majority of studies that explore ethnic differences in public opinion have concentrated on the gap between the opinions of African-Americans and whites. Language differences and other impediments have restricted research into the opinions of other ethnic minorities, such as Hispanics and Asians, but as such groups become a larger subset of the American population, public opinion researchers will have to develop new techniques and make a concerted effort to tap the opinions of these groups.

The Gender Gap?

Women are unique among all of the so-called disadvantaged groups in American society. First, since there are more women than men, they do not constitute a minority. Second, women are not isolated from those outside of their group. Unlike ethnic minorities or economic classes, women do not live in distinctive enclaves or neighborhoods; they live with men. We might speculate that women have a distinctive political perspective, but it has taken public opinion researchers a long time to find evidence of one.

Early studies that compared women and men on such dimensions as partisanship and voting found no major differences.[45] However, in the 1980s, a gender gap in voting began to emerge. Women supported Democratic candidates more frequently than men did, and the potential electoral consequences of this sort of gap attracted new attention to the differences between men's and women's opinions. The most obvious difference centers on issues of force and violence. Women are in general less supportive of wars and capital punishment and more supportive of gun control than men are.[46] Women were also less supportive of the war in the Persian Gulf before, during, and after the hostilities (see Box 7.2).

Robert Shapiro and Harpreet Mahajan found that the average difference between men and women's opinions on these kinds of issues is almost 8 percent and that two-thirds of the time, it is more than 6 percent.[47] Such differences may seem minor, but women form the majority of the electorate, so even small differences in opinion can have important policy consequences if those differences lead women to choose different candidates or to become active in specific causes.

Kay Schlozman and her colleagues have indeed found that women are motivated to participate in politics by different kinds of issues than men are.[48] Table 7.4 shows the top five issues that prompted some form of political activism from each gender, according to Schlozman and associates' study. As you can see, men's and women's priorities differ, although not all of these differences are statistically significant and the differences are not that great.

Recall from Chapter 1 that political activism is also a form of public opinion expression. In fact, political leaders may pay more attention to citizen activism than they do to public opinion poll results.[49] Note that these differences of opinion do not necessarily imply disagreement about the core values of the American political system, but they may imply important disagreements about when and how such goals should be achieved. Further, as women have become more involved in politics and more aware of political issues, the gender gap in public opinion may be growing.[50]

Finally, there may be more than one gender gap in public opinion, for the opinions of different groups of women are often more diverse than the opinions of women compared to those of men. Women's lives have changed dramatically since the 1970s. More women now work outside the home, and more have experienced financial and personal independence than at any previous time in history. Women are more educated now than they were in the past. The opinions of women whose lives have followed what might be called a "traditional" trajectory as full-time wife and mother often differ dramatically from the opinions of working women or of women who embrace a more "feminist" perspective. Robert Erikson and Kent Tedin argue that there are two lines of stratification that divide women: level of education and working outside of the home.[51] Differences are often greatest with regard to the issues that concern women the most. For example, Kristin Luker argues persuasively that the differing attitudes of homemakers and working women about legalized abortion are the engine that drives the abortion debate.[52] Whether these dramatic differences between women will be reduced as older generations of homemakers are replaced by more recent generations of women who have always worked outside the home remains to be seen.

Box 7.2   The Gender Gap:
Support for the Persian Gulf War

Women have always been less enthusiastic in their support for wars than men. Public opinion about both the Korean and Vietnam Wars reveals a gender gap, with women being less supportive of both conflicts. Such differences of opinion can have important electoral consequences, for when there is a "shooting war" during an election, the progress of that conflict may be an important element for voters deciding on a candidate.

Public support for the 1991 Persian Gulf War also revealed a gender gap. In December 1990, barely a month before open hostilities began, half of American women believed that "the current situation in the Mideast" was not "worth going to war over." In contrast, 57 percent of men believed it was. A plurality of women (46 percent) believed that the best course of action was to continue the sanctions that were in place, whereas a majority of men (55 percent) believed that war was the best course to follow.[1] Even in the week before hostilities broke out, only 45 percent of women believed that the United States should go to war with Iraq, whereas 67 percent of men supported that course of action.[2] The figure below shows the gender gap in support for the Gulf War while it was ongoing.

(continues)

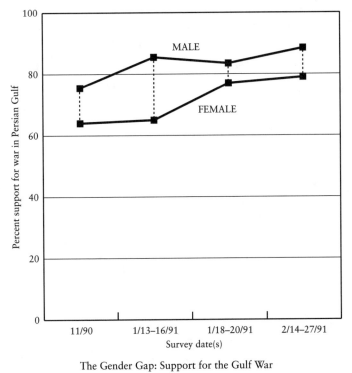

The Gender Gap: Support for the Gulf War

Box 7.2 *(continued)*

Although the gap narrows, it never disappears completely, and it widens again once the war is over.[3]

Scholars have tried to explain the different levels of support for force in a number of ways. Some argue that this difference appears because women are economically disadvantaged compared to men and war policies drain political resources that could otherwise be committed to domestic concerns. Others argue that war and violence are at odds with women's maternal instinct and that women are either socialized or biologically programmed to dislike war more than men. However, Mary Bendyna and her colleagues find little support for either of these hypotheses as an explanation for the gender gap that appeared concerning the Gulf War. Instead, they found that women's greater pessimism about potential negative outcomes of the war explained much of the gap. Women worried more about casualties, both of U.S. servicemen and of Iraqi civilians. They had much stronger emotional reactions to the war than men did, and most of these reactions were negative. Further, it was not the case that women had these negative reactions because they were less informed about what was going on in the Gulf. Bendyna and her associates found that the more women knew about the Gulf War, the wider the opinion gap between women and men became.[4]

As women become more active in politics and occupy more critical decisionmaking roles, will their more negative attitudes toward force and violence result in a substantive change in U.S. policy both at home and abroad? Or will the gender gap close as both women and men adopt more similar attitudes about force as a policy tool and violence as a social problem? Time will tell.

---

1. *Gallup Monthly,* December 1990, pp. 16–17.

2. *The Gallup Poll: Public Opinion 1991* (Wilmington, DE: Scholarly Resources, 1991), p. 16.

3. Mary E. Bendyna et al., "Gender Differences in Public Attitudes Toward the Gulf War: A Test of Competing Hypotheses," *Social Science Journal* 33 (1996):1–22.

4. Ibid.

TABLE 7.4   Issue Concerns Motivating Participation

Women	Percent	Men	Percent
Education	20	Taxes	15
Abortion	14	Education	13
Taxes	12	Economic issues (excluding taxes)	11
Basic human needs	10	Environment	10
Economic issues (excluding taxes)	9	Basic human needs	9
Crime or drugs	9		

SOURCE: Adapted from Kay Lehman Schlozman et al. "Gender and Citizen Participation," *American Journal of Political Science* 39 (1995) table 2, p. 280.

Bridging the Gap? Deliberative Public Opinion

Even though we agree on most of the foundations of our democratic system, it is clear that important disagreements between key social groups remain. The problem of how to bridge differences of opinion has been an ongoing concern to democratic theorists almost from the start. James Madison, in the *Federalist Papers,* argued that "faction" was inevitable. He therefore advocated an elaborate system of checks and balances in order to protect minority groups from majority opinion.[53] But is there a way to bridge differences of opinion rather than simply protecting one group from another?

Rousseau described a concept he called the "general will," the idea that true public opinion is the opinion of a public about what is best for that public *as a whole.*[54] Self-interest and public opinion would not always be the same. Could this be the key to bridging the differences between classes and races that are based on the differing interests of the rich and the poor, of the majority and the minority, of women and men? Could there be agreement on what would be in the best interest of all?

Jane Mansbridge believes that democracies are of two basic types: unitary and adversary. Twentieth-century Americans are used to adversary democracy, which assumes conflicting interests and therefore develops rules and structures that attempt to guarantee equal protection of interests. Majority rule and the secret ballot are the primary decisionmaking structures in such a system.[55] Public opinion is conceptualized as the aggregation of adversarial private opinions. But Mansbridge also offers an alternative vision of what she calls unitary democracy. She argues that many progressive organizations of the late 1960s and early 1970s adopted such a model that is based on friendship and mutual trust rather than conflict and equal protection. Unitary democracy assumes common interests, so its rules and structures attempt to ensure equal respect for all parties. Rather than voting in secret, members of the group meet face-to-face and try to reach consensus decisions. According to Mansbridge, the Athenians of the fifth and sixth centuries B.C. achieved a balance between unitary and adversary democracy. They voted in assemblies to reconcile conflicting interests, but they also continued to believe that on many matters there was a common good that could be revealed through deliberation, decided on by consensus, and acted on in concert.[56] Could the principles of unitary democracy be useful in a huge nation like the United States of the late twentieth century?

James Fishkin has responded to these idealized visions of democracy as well as to complaints about public ignorance and lack of interest with an experiment in democracy that he calls a "deliberative public opinion poll."[57] Fishkin relies on the idea that public opinion is formed through a process of public discussion. If that discussion is both reasonably extensive and reasonably well-informed, the public opinion that develops should be wise and worth listening to if the founding principles of democracy are in fact true.

In a deliberative public opinion poll, a random sample of citizens is brought together in a central location. These citizens will stand in for the electorate as a whole, just as a sample of survey respondents stands in for the public as a whole. The citizens learn about the issues and, in some polls, the candidates, by studying briefing books and attending briefings by experts. They also meet with each other in group discussions about the issues or candidates they are considering. After gathering information and deliberating together, the citizens respond to survey questions that assess their opinions. Polls of this kind have at least two potential advantages. First, the opinions recorded by the poll will be *informed* opinions. Second, the group deliberations suggest that the opinions expressed will take into account the wishes of others, as Rousseau's idea of the general will suggests.

Fishkin argues that deliberative opinion polls model ideal public opinion, unlike standard surveys, which describe existing public opinion:

> An ordinary poll models what the electorate thinks, given how little it knows. A deliberative opinion poll models what the electorate *would* think, if, hypothetically, it could be immersed in intensive deliberative processes. The point of a deliberative opinion poll is prescriptive, not predictive. It has a recommending force, telling us what the entire mass public would think about some policy issues or some candidates if it could be given an opportunity for extensive reflection and access to information. (emphasis in original)[58]

Fishkin, like Dewey, believes that the lack of interest and sophistication shown by most citizens is a problem that must be overcome in a democratic society. He argues that televising deliberative opinion polls is one way to extend the positive impact of informed public deliberation to a wider audience of citizens.

He focuses his proposals on the presidential election process, arguing that the limitations of polling and limited public information and discussion are especially worrisome during the primary process. The process of selecting two individuals who will run for president is exceptionally important, but more than the campaigns themselves, this process is plagued by lack of citizen knowledge and the constant use of polling. It is also in the primary process that the limitations of the mass media, pointed out by Patterson, have the most significant impact on public opinion. Research suggests media effects are most pronounced when citizens have the least information or have not formed strong opinions. Although media coverage may not determine who wins in November, it may have a powerful influence on who runs in that election. In primaries, voters do not have the cue of party affiliation (since all the candidates in the primary are in the same party) and are often undecided until right before the election. Since voters are less informed about the races and may have less well-formed opinions, public opinion is much more vulnerable to manipulation through superficial campaign advertising and the constraining effects of the spiral of silence caused by continuous media coverage of polling results. Compounding these factors is the phenomenon dubbed "momentum," in which candidates develop reputations for electability that outstrip their accomplishments. The subsequent stampede of voters may prevent careful consideration of potential nominees.

But do Fishkin's polls really achieve their potential advantages? Deliberative opinion polls have been held in both the United States and Great Britain. The National Issues Convention (NIC), held in early 1996, brought over 400 citizens together in Austin, Texas, for a weekend of intense engagement with a variety of issues: They received carefully prepared briefing books; heard talks by policy analysts; and engaged in extended discussions with each other. The event was also televised by PBS. Fishkin and his colleagues argue that there was a considerable amount of opinion change as a result of this experiment in deliberative democracy.

Others, however, remain unconvinced. As Dan Merkle points out, the NIC may have fallen short of its goals. One problem was convincing people to come together to deliberate. Only 36 percent of all the people the researchers were hoping to bring to Austin actually came. Although that was more than 400 citizens, the fact that so many people turned them down made some critics worry that the people who went to Austin to deliberate were different from the general public they were supposed to represent. Important social groups were underrepresented. For example, older Americans, perhaps because it was harder for them to travel, were underrepresented in the Austin group. Because deliberation was an important part of the convention, people who could not speak English were also excluded from the Austin group. Interviews with the NIC participants revealed that those who agreed to go to Austin were more interested and active in politics than those who declined the invitation.[59] Thus, some scholars questioned whether the people who participated in the convention were actually representative of the public as a whole.

Another problem in evaluating the deliberative public opinion poll involved the dynamics of the group discussions themselves. In Chapters 5 and 6, we discussed a variety of group factors and processes that can interfere with opinion expression. Participants in the discussion groups may have felt constrained by social norms about desirable opinions, especially in groups whose discussion was videotaped for possible broadcast on PBS. Processes such as spirals of silence may have inhibited group discussion. Observations of some groups showed that "the five most talkative members in each group accounted for over 50 percent of the comments that were made, and the five least talkative members accounted for under 8 percent of the comments."[60]

A final criticism of the deliberative opinion poll was that public opinion did not change all that much as a result. Individuals' opinions changed on many issues, although Fishkin and his colleagues have not yet separated how many of those changes were of degree (from agree to strongly agree, for example) and how many of the changes were of kind (from agree to disagree). Unfortunately, the way the deliberative opinion poll was taken does not allow us to determine how much of that change was due to the discussions in Austin and how much of it was a result of other factors. As Merkle points out, even when people do not engage in discussion or gain new information, their responses to the same survey questions often change over time.[61]

Perhaps even more important, aggregate opinion did not change much after the deliberations. Of eighty-one opinion questions the interviewers asked NIC participants, in only seven cases did majority opinion change after the discussions. The National Issues Convention was a very expensive undertaking, and many critics wondered if the cost was worth the results. It seemed as though the "informed" citizens in Austin recommended more or less the same things that the "uninformed" citizens who had not taken part in the deliberations would have.[62] Perhaps the "top-of-the-head" answers citizens give to survey takers are in fact sufficient.

As Merkle points out, deliberative public opinion polls can still offer some intriguing possibilities. For example, people who participate or observe such polls may develop more reasoned opinions and be less susceptible to manipulation. Deliberative polls could also be helpful in cases where the public knows very little about an issue, as opposed to cases involving well-established public debates. These polls have also been used "as a way of getting citizens involved in framing the issues" or in cases where a researcher wants to combine the advantages of both focus group and survey research.[63] However, it seems unlikely that polls of this sort will replace more traditional survey research.

Conclusion

In this chapter, we have discussed the relationship between public opinion and democratic processes. Consensus about basic democratic values keeps our democratic system stable. However, important differences of opinion among major social groups and doubts about the ability of citizens with very limited interest in public issues to govern a nation raise questions about how public opinion should be integrated into this democracy. Should the public's power be limited to choosing between two major party candidates at elections held every few years, or should public opinion be a factor in public policymaking on a day-to-day basis? Or is the right answer somewhere in between?

In the chapters that follow, we will explore these questions in more detail, as we examine what the public knows about public issues, how (and whether) policymakers respond to public opinion, and the role of the media in these processes.

Notes

1. Benjamin Ginsberg, *The Captive Public: How Mass Opinion Promotes State Power* (New York: Basic Books, 1986), p. 48.

2. Ibid., p. 54.

3. James Morone, *The Democratic Wish* (New York: Basic Books, 1990).

4. On the issue of antifederalists who supported this view, see Jennifer Nedelsky, *Private Property and the Limits of American Constitutionalism: The Madisonian Framework and Its Legacy* (Chicago: University of Chicago Press, 1990); see also Willard Sterne Randall's discussion of Jefferson's approach to this issue and his arguments with other founders about the degree to which enlightened public opinion could be developed (*Thomas Jefferson: A Life* [New York: Henry Holt, 1993]).

5. Michael X. Delli Carpini and Scott Keeter, *What Americans Know About Politics and Why It Matters* (New Haven: Yale University Press, 1996).

6. Iyengar and Kinder, for example, conclude that the mass media set the agenda for public opinion and the result is short-run swings in what the public thinks is important: "All told, our evidence implies an American public with a limited memory for last month's news and a recurrent vulnerability to today's. When television news focuses on a problem, the public's priorities are altered, and altered again as television news moves on to something new." Shanto Iyengar and Donald R. Kinder, *News That Matters: Television and American Opinion* (Chicago: University of Chicago Press, 1987), p. 33.

7. Samuel L. Popkin, *The Reasoning Voter* (Chicago: University of Chicago Press, 1991).

8. Ibid., p. 7.

9. Walter Lippmann, *The Phantom Public* (New York: Harcourt, Brace and Company, 1925), p. 189.

10. See, for example, Martin P. Wattenberg, *The Decline of American Political Parties* (Cambridge: Harvard University Press, 1984).

11. Stanley Kelley Jr., *Interpreting Elections* (Princeton: Princeton University Press, 1993).

12. V. O. Key Jr., *The Responsible Electorate: Rationality in Presidential Voting, 1936–1960* (Cambridge: Belknap Press of Harvard University Press, 1966).

13. Morris Fiorina, *Retrospective Voting in American National Elections* (New Haven: Yale University Press, 1981).

14. Ibid.

15. R. Douglas Arnold, "Can Inattentive Citizens Control Their Elected Representatives?" in Lawrence C. Dodd and Bruce I. Oppenheimer, eds., *Congress Reconsidered*, 5th ed. (Washington, DC: CQ Press, 1993).

16. David Broder, *Behind the Front Page* (New York: Simon and Schuster, 1987), p. 195.

17. Thomas E. Patterson, *Out of Order* (New York: Alfred A. Knopf, 1993).

18. Robert Dahl, *Democracy and Its Critics* (New Haven: Yale University Press, 1989), chaps. 20 and 21.

19. Herbert McClosky and John Zaller, *The American Ethos: Public Attitudes Toward Capitalism and Democracy* (Cambridge: Harvard University Press, 1984). McClosky and Zaller's *The American Ethos* provides an excellent summary of the evidence supporting the assertion that Americans truly do believe in these values.

20. Francis Fox Piven and Richard Cloward, *Poor Peoples' Movements: How They Succeed and Why They Fail* (New York: Vintage Books, 1979), p. 1. A civil religion consists of "an elaborate system of beliefs and ritual behaviors which defines for people what is right and what is wrong and why; what is possible and what is impossible; and the behavioral imperatives that follow from the beliefs."

21. Much of this section is based upon James Eisenstein et al., *The Play of Power: An Introduction to American Politics* (New York: St. Martin's Press, 1995), chap. 2.

22. For a thorough study of the adherence of both the general public and political elites to the values embodied in the notion of capitalism and democracy, see McClosky and Zaller, *American Ethos*. We also rely on Jennifer L. Hochschild, *Facing Up to the American Dream* (Princeton: Princeton University Press, 1995).

23. see McClosky and Zaller, *American Ethos*.

24. For a thorough treatment of the notion of equality in American history and politics, see Sidney Verba and Gary R. Orren, *Equality in America: The View from the Top* (Cambridge: Harvard University Press, 1985).

25. McClosky and Zaller, *American Ethos*, p. 1.

26. Kevin Phillips, *The Politics of Rich and Poor* (New York: Random House, 1990).

27. McClosky and Zaller, *American Ethos*, p. 38.

28. Ibid., pp. 24–25.

29. Hochschild, *American Dream*.

30. President Clinton, speech to Democratic Leadership Council, 1993, cited in Hochschild, *American Dream*, p. 19.

31. Survey results reported in ibid., p. 19.

32. Ibid., p. 23.

33. Robert N. Bellah et al., *Habits of the Heart: Individualism and Commitment in American Life* (Berkeley: University of California Press, 1985).

34. Clem Brooks, "Class Consciousness and Politics in Comparative Perspective," *Social Science Research* 23 (1994):167–195.

35. Richard D. Shingles, "Class, Status, and Support for Government Aid to Disadvantaged Groups," *Journal of Politics* 51 (1989):933–962.

36. Robert S. Erikson and Kent L. Tedin, *American Public Opinion* (Boston: Allyn and Bacon, 1995).

37. Jerome L. Himmelstein and James A. McRae Jr., "Social Issues and Socioeconomic Status," *Public Opinion Quarterly* 52 (1982):492–512.

38. Ibid.

39. Gunnar Myrdal, *An American Dilemma: The Negro Problem and American Democracy* (New York: Harper and Brothers, 1944).

40. Paul M. Sniderman and Thomas Piazza, *The Scar of Race* (Cambridge: Harvard University Press, 1993).

41. Donald R. Kinder and Lynn M. Sanders, *Divided by Color: Racial Politics and Democratic Ideals* (Chicago: University of Chicago Press, 1996), p. 19.

42. Ibid., p. 27.

43. Ibid.

44. Sniderman and Piazza, *Scar of Race,* p. 8.

45. Robert Y. Shapiro and Harpreet Mahajan, "Gender Differences in Policy Preferences: A Summary of Trends from the 1960s to the 1980s," *Public Opinion Quarterly* 50 (1986):42–61.

46. Erikson and Tedin, *American Public Opinion.*

47. Shapiro and Mahajan, "Gender Differences in Policy Preferences."

48. Kay Lehman Schlozman et al., "Gender and Citizen Participation: Is There a Different Voice?" *American Journal of Political Science* 39 (1995):267–293.

49. James B. Lemert, "Effective Public Opinion," in J. David Kenamer, ed., *Public Opinion, the Press, and Public Policy* (New York: Praeger Publishing, 1992), pp. 41–61.

50. Shapiro and Mahajan, "Gender Differences in Policy Preferences."

51. Erikson and Tedin, *American Public Opinion.*

52. Kristin Luker, *Abortion and the Politics of Motherhood* (Berkeley: University of California Press, 1984).

53. James Madison, "Federalist No. 10," in Alexander Hamilton, John Jay, and James Madison, *The Federalist Papers* (Harmondsworth, England: Penguin Books, 1987), pp. 122–128.

54. Jean Jacques Rousseau, *The Social Contract and the Discourses,* trans. G.D.H. Cole (New York: Dutton, 1973).

55. Jane J. Mansbridge, *Beyond Adversary Democracy* (Chicago: University of Chicago Press, 1980).

56. Ibid.

57. James S. Fishkin, *Democracy and Deliberation* (New Haven: Yale University Press, 1991); James S. Fishkin, *The Voice of the People* (New Haven: Yale University Press, 1995).

58. Fishkin, *Democracy and Deliberation,* p. 81.

59. Daniel M. Merkle, "The Polls—Review: The National Issues Convention Deliberative Poll," *Public Opinion Quarterly* 60 (1996):588–619.

60. Ibid., p. 607.

61. Ibid.

62. Ibid.

63. Ibid.

Part Three

Public Opinion in Context

Chapter Eight

Public Opinion and Democratic Competence

COAUTHORED WITH MARK LINDEMAN

Every year, countless polls report the latest findings on "public opinion" about various issues. Viewed through this flood of poll results, public opinion analysis may seem like an endless collection of ever-changing answers to ever-changing questions—and in some ways it is. However, most academic studies of American public opinion pertain to a handful of major debates. And most of these debates speak, directly or indirectly, to what we will call the question of democratic competence.

"Democracy" means "rule of the people." But can "the people" be trusted to rule themselves well? As we noted in Chapter 7, some accounts of representative democracy assume that people need only enough wisdom to vote for responsible political leaders; then it is up to the leaders to govern in the public interest. This line of thought is sometimes called "democratic elitism." Few people fully embrace it. In practice, most voters in most American elections decide only whether to vote for the Democratic or the Republican candidate. They have played little, if any, role in choosing these candidates.[1] If democracy means real popular control over what the government does, then picking a party may not be enough. Perhaps "the people" must have considered opinions on political issues and must be able to ensure that government carries out these wishes.

What are "considered opinions"? This takes us back to the question of whether the people can rule themselves well. What sort of public opinion is worthy of becoming public policy? At least three standards for considered public opinion come to mind: (1) People must have adequate knowledge of the political issues at stake, (2) people must deliberate on these issues, weighing arguments on all sides, to arrive at thoughtful opinions, and (3) people's conclusions must respect crucial democratic norms such as minority rights and free speech, and they should work toward the common good as well as toward people's personal interests. Skeptics insist that many people fail to meet these standards. Many citizens do not know much about the issues, do not think or talk much about the issues, and are not strongly committed to democratic norms and the common interest. Even the most passionate advocates of participatory democracy concede that there is truth in this portrayal—but how much?

Public opinion analysts continually debate how people actually think (or fail to think) about political and social issues—and what the answers mean. If most people do not meet some standard of democratic competence, is healthy democratic government possible? Most analysts believe that it is— but they differ in important ways, both in how they judge public opinion and in their standards for "healthy" government. George Gallup, a father of modern survey research, insisted that "on nearly all major issues of the day the people collectively are competent to make wise judgments, and the mountain of polling data collected during the last forty-four years is proof of this."[2] Walter Lippmann argued, on the contrary, that "the prevailing public opinion has been destructively wrong at critical junctures."[3] What evidence can we bring to bear on this debate?[4]

This chapter considers how social scientists, primarily by using sample surveys, have investigated and debated the evidence that provides "the facts about" public opinion. For the most part, we will trace these debates chronologically, from their origins in the pioneering survey research of the mid-twentieth century. Debates about democratic competence, of course, are much older than this. Many, as we saw in Chapter 2, can be traced back at least to the ancient Greeks. Obviously, social-scientific research is not the only useful way to get at these arguments. Often, it is not even the most useful way. However, in the face of competing claims about "the way people are," social science may help us to gather evidence that will resolve parts of the debate.

Our discussion emphasizes what various debates on "the facts" of public opinion mean for the value-laden question of democratic competence. There is merit and danger in this approach. Value questions can show us why factual debates matter, even as facts may help us settle—or sharpen— the value debate. However, if all debates on public opinion are treated as mainly arguments about democratic competence or popular wisdom, then analysts may be tempted to trim their facts to suit their values. These debates are not simply about whether we "believe in democracy." Instead, they may help us to decide what kind of democracy is both feasible and worthy of support.

The Public's Low Level of Political Knowledge: A Problem?

Widespread public ignorance about politics is often seen as a barrier to democratic competence. In Chapter 1, we discussed survey results that show that many—often most—citizens are ignorant of rather basic political facts. Table 8.1 shows that political knowledge has not grown since the 1940s, even as the average level of schooling in the United States has increased.[5]

As Table 8.1 shows, not even half of survey respondents could correctly provide the name of their congressional representatives, a percentage that has actually declined since 1973. Further, strikingly few knew that the former Soviet Union was not a member of NATO. Americans do better on some of the simplest facts, such as the length of the president's term, and occasionally on "current events" facts that may now seem obscure, such as Charles Lindbergh's views on World War II. Still, overall, especially to those politically knowledgeable people sitting in college classes, the data suggest massive public ignorance.

However, "the facts" here may not be as discouraging as they seem at first. Many analysts argue that these questions amount to trivia quizzes that test people's recall of numbers and names, removed from any political context. In practice, it is more important for people to recognize or find relevant names and facts when they need them, such as before elections or at the ballot box, or when an issue is actually most prominent in the news. If people showed little ability to learn about an issue as it became more salient, that would be discouraging indeed.

Table 8.2 offers reassuring evidence that the public can learn. When the mass media give extended attention to an issue, people learn more about it. Specifically, over time, more Americans learned which side the United States backed in the Nicaraguan struggle between the leftist Sandinista government and the rebel contras (probably even more Americans would have answered correctly if the term "contras" had been used in the question).[6] Nevertheless, barely more than one-half the respondents answered even this question correctly—and some of the right answers must have been lucky guesses. Surely, few Americans ever knew enough about Nicaragua to form what experts would deem "considered opinions" about policy.

Even the most optimistic analysts of public opinion believe that citizens themselves—and the nation as a whole—would be better off if people paid more attention to politics and knew about the details of it. It is hard to take comfort in the argument that it is "rational" for people to be ignorant about politics, a subject we will return to later. True, for most people, tending to family, work, and personal life has greater and more immediate payoffs than studying political issues. Yet if almost everyone ignores politics,

TABLE 8.1   Political Information Among American Adults

Topic (roughly in order of % correct)	Year	Percentage	Survey Organization
Know the length of the president's term	1989	96	SRLVCU
	1947	92	Gallup
Know meaning of "veto" (presidential)	1989	89	SRLVCU
	1947	77	Gallup
Identified governor of home state	1989	74	SRLVCU
	1973	89	Harris
	1945	79	Gallup
Know which party has more members in U.S. House of Representatives	1989	68	SRLVCU
	1947	63	Gallup
Understand Charles Lindbergh's views on on World War II	1941	61, 55	Gallup
Know that there are two U.S. senators from each state	1978	52	NORC
Know what a business (economic) recession is	1989	57	SRLVCU
	1947	51	Gallup
Know term of U.S. House member is two years	1978	30	NORC
	1946	47	Gallup
Identified both U.S. senators of home state	1989	25	SRLVCU
	1973	39	Harris
	1945	35	Gallup
Identified U.S. congressperson from home district	1989	29	SRLVCU
	1973	46	Harris
Know Soviet Union is not a NATO member	1964	38	Gallup
Can explain First Amendment	1979	24	Gallup

KEY: NORC: National Opinion Research Center; SRLVCU: Survey Research Laboratory, Virginia Commonwealth University.

SOURCE: Based on Benjamin I. Page and Robert Y. Shapiro, *The Rational Public: Fifty Years of Trends in Americans' Policy Preferences* (Chicago: University of Chicago Press, 1992), pp. 10–11.

how can the public possibly form sensible policy preferences, much less make sure the government follows these preferences?

Part of the answer, some believe, is that the public performs better as a whole—*collectively*—than most individual citizens do. One reason is that citizens adopt a tacit division of labor. Not only do some know more about politics than others, but different issues engage different people. A multiplicity of "issue publics" exists, each one consisting of people who follow a

TABLE 8.2 Change over Time in Public Knowledge: The Nicaraguan Conflict, 1983–1987 (in percent)

	7/83	11/83	3/85	6/85	3/86	5/87	8/87
Rebels	29	26	37	46	59	52	54
Government	24	24	23	20	13	21	20
Neither	1	<1	1	1	1	1	1
No opinion	47	50	39	34	27	26	24

SOURCE: Benjamin I. Page and Robert Y. Shapiro, *The Rational Public: Fifty Years of Trends in Americans' Policy Preferences* (Chicago: University of Chicago Press, 1992), table 1, p. 13; from data in Richard Sobel, "The Polls—A Report: Public Opinion About United States Intervention in El Salvador and Nicaragua," *Public Opinion Quarterly* 53, p. 120; ABC News/*Washington Post* surveys: QUESTION: "Do you happen to know which side the U.S. is backing in Nicaragua: the rebels or the government?" Sample size ranges from 1148 to 1509.

particular issue. Moreover, as we see in Table 8.2, issue publics can grow; more people can learn about an issue as it becomes (or remains) prominent. We will return to the debate on whether issue publics resolve the problem of democratic competence.

The First Great Debate About Voting: The Columbia and Michigan Models

Voting, despite its limitations, may be the most important political expression of "public opinion." Appropriately, public opinion analysts have long debated how people decide their votes. Between 1940 and the mid-1960s, two university-based institutions, the Bureau of Applied Social Research at Columbia University and the Survey Research Center at the University of Michigan, developed contrasting models of vote choices. The Columbia model focused on *sociological* processes: how people's social environments and relationships influenced their votes. The Michigan model placed more emphasis on *psychological* variables: how people thought about the parties, candidates, and issues and how these factors influenced their votes. The models had more in common than these descriptions suggest, but the differences were real, and they inspired very different research strategies.

The "Columbia model" emphasized the influence of social groups and relationships on voting decisions. Paul Lazarsfeld and his colleagues conducted a pathbreaking study of Erie County, Ohio, during the 1940 presidential campaign.[7] Remarkably, as part of the study, they interviewed almost 600 respondents *seven times* from May through November, in order to trace changing opinions. (Most surveys interview respondents only once or, at most, twice.) They learned, first, that very few people—about 12 percent—changed their voting intentions from one candidate to the other at any time in the campaign, and about one-third of those changed back by election day. Thus, the campaign did not win many converts, although it apparently did get many people to "pay attention" and eventually to vote. Many more voters moved from "don't know" to a candidate (28 percent) or from a candidate to "don't know" and then back to the same candidate (11 percent). Thus, most voters did change preferences at some point in the campaign.[8]

The direction of these changes was fairly predictable, at least in retrospect. People usually ended up voting as most people of their social class, religion, and place of residence (urban or rural) did. Upper-class rural Protestants were very likely to vote Republican, and lower-class urban Catholics to vote Democratic. The Columbia scholars attributed these patterns to how people's closest relationships—with family and friends, coworkers, fellow churchgoers, and so on—affected their political views. The intensive interview format allowed the scholars to trace, to some extent, how these influences actually worked. Some people tended to be "opinion leaders"—highly interested in politics, usually with a distinctly partisan outlook that colored their reactions to events. By discussing politics with opinion leaders in the same social setting, for example, Aunt Mary or Steve at the mill, other people tended to adopt the same partisan line. Of course, some social settings were more diverse than others, and some people received mixed or opposing signals, or "cross-pressures," that might lead them to delay voting decisions or to skip voting entirely. But most people in the end turned in the direction of most of their social cohort.

To illustrate the power of social influences, the Columbia scholars combined their three key social variables (class, religion, and urban/rural residence) into a seven-point *index of political predisposition* (IPP). The IPP was a very strong predictor of people's votes, as you can see in Figure 8.1. Lazarsfeld and his associates summed up this way: "A person thinks, politically, as he is, socially. Social characteristics determine political preferences."[9]

No one completely believed this statement, not even Lazarsfeld. First, it said little about the *processes* of social *persuasion* that Lazarsfeld was especially interested in. (As a later work put the point, uncertain voters "turn to their social environment for guidance, and that environment tends to support the party that is 'right' for them also.")[10] Second, the Columbia model could not really explain how the political preferences of social groups might vary over time or in different places. Ironically, the IPP tended to direct attention away from the rich dynamics of opinion leadership—the heart of the Columbia theory—and toward the results of one election in one county. The index could not explain fluctuations between elections, much less longer-term trends such as the defection of blacks from the Republican to the Democratic Party after 1930. Thus, critics could say that the model neither explained nor predicted very well.

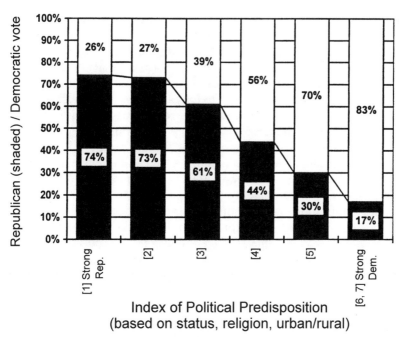

Index of Political Predisposition (based on status, religion, urban/rural)

FIGURE 8.1 Index of Political Predisposition and Presidential Vote, 1940 (Erie County, Ohio). SOURCE: Paul Felix Lazarsfeld, *The People's Choice* (New York: Columbia University Press, 1968), p. 26. Copyright 1968 by Columbia University Press. Reprinted with permission of the publisher.

NOTE: To calculate people's "index of political predisposition" (IPP), first each respondent's socioeconomic status was rated on a four-point scale from 1 for the highest to 4 for the lowest. Then two points were added for Catholics (versus Protestants) and one point was added for urban (versus rural) dwellers. Thus, the IPP rated from 1 to 7, with higher scorers more likely to vote Democratic.

The Michigan school sidestepped these problems by combining a powerful predictive model that arguably explained little completely or persuasively and an unwieldy causal model—the "funnel of causality"—that claimed to explain just about everything. (The first comprehensive statement of the Michigan school, *The American Voter*, was over 500 pages long.)[11] The predictive model emphasized three variables, the most important among them being *party identification*. Party identification (usually called "party ID" for short) is the *attitude* of considering oneself a Republican, Democrat, or whatever—party attachment—as opposed to being an official party member or even voting for the party's candidates. Ever since 1952, the Survey Research Center's National Election Studies (NES) have measured party identification by asking, "Generally speaking, do you usually think of yourself as a Republican, a Democrat, an Independent, or what?" Follow-up questions pin down Republicans and Democrats as "strong" or "weak" and classify independents as leaning toward one party, the other, or neither. Self-identified Democrats and Republicans, as you would expect, are very likely to vote for candidates of their favored party. Moreover, people's party identification is relatively stable over time, compared to their stated issue positions (more on this point soon). In fact, in the 1992 NES, about 70 percent of people identified with or leaned toward the same party that their parents did.[12] One could almost say, outdoing Lazarsfeld, that most people's votes are determined at birth (or at whatever age they internalize their parents' political views).

Party identification predicts individuals' votes better than social characteristics do—but it cannot predict or explain differences between elections. To overcome this weakness, the Michigan model also considers people's *issue* opinions and their images of the *candidates*. Of course, strong partisans tend to like their own party's candidates and to support (or think they support) similar positions on the issues.[13] Still, issues and candidates do matter, even for strong partisans, and especially for independents or weaker partisans. In 1980, 35 percent of "weak Democrats" voted for the Republican challenger, Ronald Reagan, whereas only 5 percent of "weak Republicans" voted for the Democratic incumbent, Jimmy Carter; independents favored Reagan by more than two to one.[14] Here, broad unhappiness with Carter probably accounted for much of the difference.

A model based on party ID, candidates, and issues can easily be applied to any presidential election, making better vote predictions across more places and times than the Columbia model. (Figure 8.2 shows some results from a party-candidate-issue model for the 1992 presidential election.) However, it seems to *explain* little beyond the obvious. People tend to vote for people they like, with positions they like, from the party they like—and party matters most. These facts are important, and maybe even reassuring ("issues" do seem to matter), but they do not seem to explain political change any better than the Columbia model does.

To give their analysis explanatory power, the Michigan scholars initially proposed their complex "funnel of causality," which incorporated just about every imaginable variable (see Figure 8.3). The funnel began, at the wide end, with the social sources of political cleavages, such as the conflict between North and South. These sources were often rooted in events older than the respondents and did not directly influence people's political beliefs. Yet they profoundly influenced the basic values and group loyalties that people formed in childhood and generally held all their lives. These early-formed attitudes in turn influenced people's party ID; party ID influenced people's views of the issues and the candidates—the factors nearest the "tip

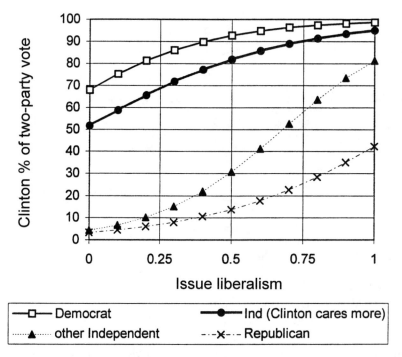

FIGURE 8.2   Party, Candidates, and Issues in the 1992 Presidential Election

of the funnel," where people actually decided how to vote. Major events, election-year economic and social conditions, media coverage, campaign activities, and the opinions of friends (among other things) could also affect people's partisanship and views of the candidates and issues. Just about everything fit into the model—although, in practice, it was almost impossible to juggle all the pieces at once. Few, if any, scholars ever tried to "test" the funnel theory as a whole. Instead, many studies investigated how party ID, issue opinions, and candidate ratings influenced each other and voting decisions. Scholars recognized that how party ID changed over time might matter even more. But it would take many years of data collection to gain much leverage on that question.

Arguably, the Columbia and Michigan schools did not really disagree on much. What really set the Columbia school apart was its interest in how social relationships—with family, friends, coworkers, and other acquaintances—influenced people's attitudes. Lazarsfeld and his colleagues explored social influences by asking many people, in a limited geographic area, detailed questions about their conversations with other people. (This tradition is carried on, for instance, in the research of Robert Huckfeldt

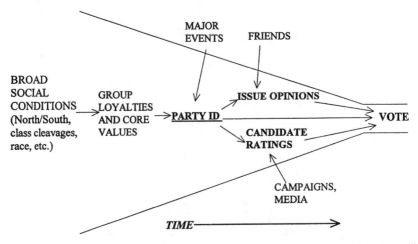

FIGURE 8.3   A Sketch of the "Funnel of Causality." SOURCE: Based on Russell J. Dalton, *Citizen Politics in Western Democracies*, 1st ed. (Chatham, NJ: Chatham House Publishers, 1988), p. 178.

NOTE: Many possible relationships are not shown.

and John Sprague.)[15] The Michigan scholars preferred to conduct *national* surveys that gathered valuable data about how people all around the country thought about politics but revealed less about the social processes that influenced people's thinking.

What did all this voter research imply for democratic competence? There is no simple answer. At first glance, the Columbia model seems to offer the bleaker view: People apparently cast their votes by following, lemminglike, the people around them. However, as Walter Lippmann noted, of course people tend to rely on the judgments of people around them: "Complete independence in the universe is simply unthinkable."[16] Moreover, people in similar settings often have the same interests at stake in an election, so voting alike—however they manage to do it—may evince good sense, not blind followership. (We hope to have convinced you in earlier chapters that social judgments and dynamics are not always bad.) The Michigan model allowed for great individuality. Its voters could form their party identifications, opinion stances, and candidate evaluations through highly sophisticated processes. But these voters could just as well be mindless machines, parroting their parents' party affiliations, their friends' opinions, and their newspapers' candidate endorsements. Although no one said that "the American voter" was mindless, the anecdotes suggested that the voter might not be thinking very hard.

Rational Ignorance, Ideological Innocence, and Nonattitudes

The suspicion that voters might not think very hard was buttressed by Anthony Downs's account in *An Economic Theory of Democracy* (1957) of "rational ignorance." Downs offers a rough-and-ready cost-benefit analysis of how prospective voters (and political parties) ought to behave. For citizens, Downs notes, the tangible benefits of voting are tiny, because each citizen has almost no chance of affecting the election outcome.[17] Against these small benefits, citizens must weigh not only the immediate costs of voting (such as the time entailed) but also the costs of gathering enough information to decide *how* to vote. *Even if* votes mattered a great deal, voters would want just enough information to decide which candidate would probably "pay off" best for them. Since prospective voters could generally afford to be dead wrong, no rational voter would seek out information on candidates and issues. It might sound like good citizenship, but it is a bad investment. The idea of rational ignorance was not new: Tocqueville, for one, had anticipated it in his observation that "the people never can find time or means" to evaluate candidates accurately.[18] But with Downs's elegant formalization, rational ignorance became the skeleton at the democratic banquet.

As we have already seen, many citizens had mastered rational ignorance of politics without any help from Downs. Perhaps people did not need much "quiz-show knowledge" in order to vote wisely, but surely they needed to know something. Political *ideology*—liberalism, conservatism, and so forth—could plausibly be the thread connecting people's issue stands, party ID, candidate evaluations, and votes. A simple model of U.S. ideology places liberals on the left and conservatives on the right. Liberals tend to support (among other things) government spending on social problems, gun control laws, and abortion rights; conservatives tend to oppose these. Conservatives tend to be more supportive of military spending, capital punishment, other policies seen as tough on crime, and prayer in the schools than liberals are. There is no logical reason that these issue positions *must* go together; indeed, many people stake out what they regard as more philosophically consistent positions that straddle "left" and "right."[19] Nevertheless, if a politician is described as, say, "ultraliberal" or "right-wing," any politically knowledgeable observer can make good guesses about the politician's views on many issues. To anticipate language we will use later in the chapter, ideology is one simplifying *heuristic*, or shortcut, that can help people to make good judgments based on limited information. Journalists routinely characterize politicians in terms of this left-right continuum. Do most Americans also rely on this ideological perspective?

In *The American Voter*, the Michigan scholars concluded that very few Americans used ideology to judge political parties and candidates. Respondents in the 1952 National Election Study were asked to list things that they liked and disliked about the parties and presidential candidates. The researchers used these "open-ended" responses to assign people to *levels of conceptualization*, or what we might call levels of political sophistication (see Table 8.3).[20] According to the analysts, ideology mattered to only 11.5 percent of the respondents; of those, only 2.5 percent were "ideologues" who used abstract concepts such as liberalism to evaluate the parties and candidates; and the remaining 9 percent, dubbed "near ideologues," used abstract concepts, but in vague or inaccurate ways. The largest group, 42 percent, appealed to tangible group benefits (e.g., "the Democrats are for the common man"). Of the rest, 24 percent appealed to the "nature of the times": for instance, they credited or blamed President Eisenhower, who was seeking re-election, for the state of the national economy; the remaining 22.5 percent of the population could offer no issue content at all. Critics pointed out that judging Eisenhower on his economic performance or attentiveness to group interests might be at least as sensible as trying to judge his (notoriously obscure) ideology. Still, the failure of the vast majority even to mention ideological principles raised doubts about their grasp of political issues—at least in the terms that political leaders and journalists grasp these issues.

Philip Converse, building upon his collaboration in *The American Voter*, brilliantly argued that "ideological innocence" was widespread among the American public—and, even more disturbing, that most people had hardly any real opinions on many political issues. In addition, Converse's 1964 article, "The Nature of Belief Systems in Mass Publics,"[21] introduced the concept of ideological *constraint,* or the degree of consistency among a person's beliefs. The "ultraliberal" and "right-wing" politicians we described a few pages ago evince high constraint: Their beliefs across a wide range of issues are highly predictable. Converse argued that mass (i.e., most people's) public opinion showed very little constraint: Many people seem unaware of what issues "go together." Mass belief systems tended to be disorganized and tended *not* to depend on "abstract, 'ideological' principles." People more often built their political beliefs—such as they were—around charismatic leaders, family life, and other concrete objects.

To illustrate this disregard for ideology, Converse closely analyzed in-depth interviews in which respondents were asked, "What do the terms liberal and conservative mean to you?"—and 37 percent of the respondents could not name any difference between "liberal" and "conservative" and, beyond that, only about one-half gave answers that Converse judged even roughly correct. Only 17 percent demonstrated a "broad understanding" of the terms, by what Converse considered quite generous criteria. Subse-

TABLE 8.3   Levels of Conceptualization, 1956

Category	Examples (excerpts)	Proportion of Sample
Ideology	"I think [the Democrats] are . . . a more liberal party, and I think of the Republicans as being more conservative and interested in big business" (p. 229).	11.5
Group benefits	"I've just always before been a Democrat. . . . I just don't believe [the Republicans] are for the common people" (p. 238).	42.0
Nature of the times	"[My husband's] stocks are up. They go up when the Republicans are in" (p. 243).	24.0
No issue content	"I'm a Democrat. *(Is there anything you like about the Democratic Party?)* I don't know" (p. 247). "Parties are all about the same to me. . . . I really don't care which man is best or otherwise" (p. 249).	22.5

SOURCE: Adapted from A. Campbell, P. Converse, W. E. Miller, and D. E. Stokes, *The American Voter,* unabridged ed. (New York: John Wiley, 1960).

quent analysts have enjoyed quoting examples of unsophisticated responses to the question noted above—and these are far from the weakest answers:

> Not too much really. For some reason conservative gets identified with the South—identified with drabby looking clothes vs. more something I would wear, drabby clothes, too, but it is just a different type.
> Oh, conservative. Liberal and conservative. Liberal and conservative. [. . .] I wouldn't know. [. . .] Liberal . . . liberal . . . liberal . . . liberal. And conservative. Well, if a person is liberal with their money they squander their money? Does it fall into that same category?[22]

Some analysts have argued that citizens may not use a liberal-conservative continuum to structure their own beliefs but nonetheless have some understanding of what these terms mean for political leaders. For instance, two-thirds of the 1988 NES respondents were able to respond that they have something in mind when they hear that someone's political views are liberal or conservative.[23] Over one-half (54 percent) of respondents were able to locate both presidential candidates (George Bush and Michael Dukakis) on a seven-point ideology scale and to locate Dukakis to the left of Bush. (It is hard to say whether 54 percent is a "good" figure, but at least it is better than 2.5 percent!) We noted earlier that many citizens may not spontaneously remember the names of political leaders or other political facts but can easily be reminded of these facts. Likewise, it appears that many citizens do not spontaneously use the "liberal" and "conservative" categories often used by political elites, but nonetheless, they are able to understand political debates that use these terms.

But might people have highly organized, constrained belief systems without being able to explain them in terms of "liberal" and "conservative"? Logically, people might—but Converse presented two lines of evidence that most people did not. First, he compared the opinions of an "elite" group of congressional candidates and a mass sample from the 1958 NES survey. Converse reasoned that where elite opinions were highly constrained—that is, candidates' views on one issue predicted their views on another—*coherent* mass opinion ought to have the same degree of constraint. Mass public opinion failed this test: On most pairs of issues, the elite sample saw much stronger relationships between issues than the mass public. This result implied that most people's issue opinions were not well anchored in broader belief systems. If these opinions depended neither on factual knowledge nor on belief systems, perhaps they were no more than whims that people might change at the slightest pretext. Worse, perhaps people made up these "opinions" on the spot when asked, in which case they could hardly be called opinions at all.

Converse pointed to evidence that people's policy opinions—if they merited that name—were in fact remarkably unstable. Converse examined an NES "panel" in which a group of potential voters were asked the same questions (among many others) in 1956, 1958, and 1960. He found that on *each issue,* so many people's responses changed from one survey to the next that many respondents seemed to be answering at random. Especially discouraging was the pattern of change over time. For instance, on one question about job guarantees, about 40 percent of respondents changed their basic response (support, opposition, or "not sure") from 1956 to 1958. Suppose that most of these people had really changed their political opinions in this time. Even more people would change their views from 1958 to 1960 (and perhaps some people would return to their 1956 position). Overall, we should find that from 1956 to 1960, considerably more than 40 percent of respondents changed their position on job guarantees. But in fact, only about 42 percent did. It looked as if many, even most, of the people who changed *answers* over time might not really have changed *opinions.*

Converse suggested a simple explanation: A small number of people—around 20 percent—answered the question identically each time, while the vast majority answered pretty much *at random.* This "black and white" model of sages and fools did not fit the data perfectly (although for some questions it came very close) and could not be literally true. Nevertheless, Converse was convinced that many, indeed most, respondents were answering the questions essentially at random. How could this be? Opinion polls revealed a wide range of public opinion on various questions, from 50-50 splits to near unanimity. Obviously, people weren't simply "flipping coins" in their heads—if they were, every question would come out close to 50-50. Converse suggested that various questions evoked varying *probabilities* of "yes" or "no" responses. Some statements were easier to agree with than others (although Converse had little to say about *why* this was true). In effect, respondents might flip coins on one question; on another, they might roll two dice, and answer "yes" only if they rolled a seven or snake eyes (which happens about 20 percent of the time). What they did *not* do was to consult their considered opinions, because they had none: Most people had never seriously considered these issues. As Converse summed up his argument: People's policy attitudes were in fact largely *nonattitudes.*[24]

The proposition of "nonattitudes" posed a challenge not only to democratic competence, but to public opinion analysis itself. If people had no real opinions, why attempt to study them? And how could government be accountable to public opinion if public opinion did not exist? Today, many, if not most, analysts find Converse's emphasis on nonattitudes overdrawn. They see more stability and coherence of various sorts in public responses across issues and over time. Nonetheless, Converse's 1964 essay (which we have only skimmed through here) remains persuasive and compelling on many points. Any account of people's political opinions must reckon with Converse—and with the Downsian logic of "rational ignorance" that helps us make sense of Converse.

Responses to Converse: Lane and Key

In the short run, critics of Converse took two broad lines. One critique, advanced by Robert Lane, was that people had fairly coherent political belief systems, although these systems often did not match the ideological categories favored by political experts. The second critique, developed by V. O. Key Jr., was that people could (at least) vote rationally, even if their belief systems were not very elaborate. Let us consider each critique in turn.

Lane approached the question of political ideology very differently from Converse, conceptually and methodologically. In his 1962 book *Political Ideology*, Lane used in-depth interviews to explore people's political beliefs in detail. He found, among much else, that his respondents differed systematically in their ideas of fair play, the rights that they acknowledged or most valued, their attitudes toward authority, and their beliefs about the distribution of material goods. Lane acknowledged that people's political ideas were, in his terms, more "morselized" than "conceptualized": Instead of having a single abstract theory of political events, his subjects had "several conflicting theories with vague referents."[25] That is, people had pieces, or "morsels," of a political theory but had rarely given much thought to how the pieces fit together. Nonetheless, Lane argued that Converse's work was misleading: Just because the public did not use abstract principles to organize its political ideas, we should not conclude that the public has no political ideas.

Lane called his in-depth investigation of people's political attitudes "contextual analysis," because it sought to explore people's political ideology in the context of their own thinking, not that of political elites. Other analysts have taken similar approaches. Jennifer Hochschild's *What's Fair?* focuses on citizens' attitudes toward fairness in political life.[26] Hochschild argues, based on her own extensive interviews, that citizens tend to use different principles of fairness in different "domains" of life. Most of her respondents insisted on strict equality in the "socializing" and political domains, but not in the economic domain (in Lane's terms, the distribution of goods). This pattern—liberal in two domains, conservative in the third—was "relatively simple, flexible, [and] generalizable." Hochschild's conclusions bear directly on the theme of "democratic elitism":

> Perhaps it is time for academics, journalists, and policy-makers to stop trying to place all issues and all people along a single liberal-conservative dimension if most people do not use such a dimension. Why should we not stop expecting citizens to conform to elite standards of ideological consistency, and start expecting elites to change in response to ordinary citizens' patterns of belief?[27]

According to critics, possibly Lane and others in his tradition have "not so much discovered the ordinary person's ideology as [they have] contributed to its momentary creation."[28] When people are quizzed about their political thinking, they think more. The resulting answers may not reflect how people "really think about politics" when no social scientist happens to be quizzing them. As for Lane's insistence that citizens do have political ideas, Converse nowhere claims otherwise. Rather, Converse argues that most people do not have well-defined policy preferences and apparently are not guided by abstract political ideologies. The work in the contextual tradition rarely challenges either of these arguments per se. Instead, it probes underlying political dispositions, or "core values," that seem logically to imply various policy preferences, although people may not have recognized these policy implications—or may not have resolved conflicts among their own core values and beliefs.

V. O. Key Jr., who agreed with much of Converse's analysis, emphasizes two more optimistic points: that sometimes mass opinion was coherent and that people generally voted rationally even if their political ideas were fuzzy. Key conceded in 1961 that "For most Americans issues of politics are not of central concern.... The average American manages to get along very well without a burdensome equipment of sophisticated political attitudes.... The issues of any kind that attract the attention of large proportions of the people are few."[29] But, he adds, "From time to time questions arise that command general attention and set off wide discussion, which eventually crystallizes an opinion not readily explicable as an unthinking reaction."[30] Here Key foreshadows a major theme of this chapter: that an "issue public"—comprising those citizens who are (as he elsewhere puts it) "alert, attentive, interested, and informed" about a given issue[31]—can grow as the issue becomes more prominent.

With respect to voting, Key plainly felt that not only Converse and the Michigan school, but political science in general, were giving voters too little credit. In his last book, *The Responsible Electorate,* Key announced that he would make a "perverse and unorthodox" argument:

> Voters are not fools.... In the large the electorate behaves about as rationally and responsibly as we should expect, given the clarity of the alternatives presented to it and the character of the information available to it.... [The data reveal] an electorate moved by concern about central and relevant questions of public policy, of governmental performance, and of executive personality.[32]

Key's news here was not all good, since the quality of the information might vary widely. Key argued that the 1960 presidential election offered particularly "fluffy and foggy" information. The candidates, Richard Nixon and John Kennedy, had short and unimpressive public records. "Their broad objectives often sounded similar. When they differed, often they differed about matters both remote and complex."[33] Under these circumstances, voters were liable to fall back on group loyalties and party identification. More generally, Key warned, "The voice of the people is but an echo.... If the people can choose only from among rascals, they are certain to choose a rascal." And if "fed a steady diet of buncombe [bunk], the people may come to expect and to respond with highest predictability to buncombe."[34] As he might have written today: "Garbage in, garbage out."

Do voters behave "about as rationally and responsibly as we should expect"—and is that good enough? Unsurprisingly, social scientists have often returned to these questions, as we will later in the chapter.

The Changing American Voter?

In the 1970s, a number of analysts—notably Gerald Pomper in "From Confusion to Clarity" and Norman Nie, Sidney Verba, and John Petrocik in *The Changing American Voter*—argued that many of Converse and his colleagues' findings were time bound. Politics had changed since the late 1950s, and voters had changed also.[35] These observers pointed to evidence such as the following:

- *Ideological awareness:* Converse had found very few "ideo-logues"—people who used ideological terms to distinguish between candidates or parties—back in 1956. Nie and his associates created their own measure of ideological awareness, based on summary codings of responses instead of the original transcripts used by Converse. Their measure, which was more generous than Converse's, allowed them quickly to examine data for several years. They found a fairly steady increase in the use of ideological terms from 1956 through 1972. In fact, when they used their measure over that time period, the proportion of ideologues more than doubled, rising from 12 percent to 31 percent.[36]
- *Issue awareness:* Similarly, Pomper found a sharp increase in people's ability to distinguish between the parties on political issues, especially civil rights.
- *Attitude consistency (constraint):* Nie's group found a startling increase in the consistency (constraint) of mass policy attitudes. Using Converse's measure, mass constraint abruptly doubled between 1960 and 1964; then it tapered off somewhat, but remained distinctly greater in subsequent years through 1973.
- *Judging candidates on the issues:* Nie and his colleagues also found that when people evaluated candidates, their references to issues increased sharply (reaching 77 percent in 1964, compared to 49 percent in 1952, and then leveling off around 70 percent), while their references to party ties in evaluating candidates fell considerably after 1960 (most sharply in 1972).

What did it all mean? According to these analysts, it meant a new electorate: more ideologically aware, more attuned to political issues, less willing to follow a party line. The 1964 presidential election had offered a sharp ideological contrast between Lyndon Johnson, who later authored the War on Poverty, and strident conservative Barry Goldwater. The entire decade had seen social turmoil, headed by the controversies of civil rights and Vietnam (another Johnson legacy). Apparently these events had changed the way people thought about politics.

Part of this analysis surely was true: the Eisenhower campaigns of 1952 and 1956 had shied away from ideological controversy, whereas the 1964 election—and the two following it—were sharply politicized. It was reassuring that the public noticed the difference, but this did not necessarily prove that the *voters* had changed. (The safest conclusion, especially as of the mid-1970s, was simply that the Eisenhower elections had been unusually bland. The electorate had perhaps been fed not "buncombe," but oatmeal.) Disturbingly, however "politically attuned" people were, they were no more likely to vote. In fact, voter turnout generally *declined* from 1960 on through the next thirty years.[37]

But what of the evidence that people's policy opinions were more consistent? It was criticized, and defended, in a flurry of articles and replies. (One of these bore the ironic subtitle, "Doing Research Is Like Watching a Tennis Match.")[38] Between 1960 and 1964, the wording and format of the policy questions changed drastically. The apparent increase in consistency happened at the same time. Coincidence? The critics thought not. They conducted new surveys testing the two sets of questions and found that the new questions themselves evoked greater "consistency." Nie and his colleagues defended their conclusions by examining other questions and later years. In the end, few critics were convinced. The prevailing opinion was summed up in witticisms on Michael Margolis and Norman Nie and associates' work in the titles of later research: "From Confusion to Confusion" and *The Unchanging American Voter*.[39]

More recently, Warren E. Miller, a coauthor of *The American Voter*, and J. Merrill Shanks revisited and refined the "Michigan model" in their 1996 book *The New American Voter*.[40] *The New American Voter*—perhaps contrary to its name—describes a great deal of continuity in electoral politics. Party identification is still the foremost predictor of candidate choice (although politics have become more complicated in the South, which until recent years was solidly Democratic). One dramatic change is the new (or renewed) salience of religious belief: among religiously committed Evangelical Protestants mobilizing on behalf of conservative political causes and among nonreligious and "other"-religion (not Jewish or Christian) voters reacting against this conservative movement. This new religious cleavage has largely superseded the Protestant-Catholic cleavage described by Lazarsfeld and colleagues.

The New American Voter finds that the Democratic Party has lost ground, nationwide, both to Republicans and to independent voters. This trend does not reflect voters "deserting" the Democratic Party, per se. Rather, it is the result of generational replacement: Voters who were part of the Democratic "New Deal coalition" of the 1930s and 1940s are dying, and new voters are less likely to form Democratic allegiances. The continuing decline in voter turnout also hinges on generational replacement. Citizens of the New Deal generation, whether Democratic or Republican, were much more likely to vote—apparently because most believed in the "civic duty" of voting—than the generations now coming of age. Thus, the "New American Voter" in some ways is overshadowed by the "New American Nonvoter."

The increase in self-identified "independents"—from about 23 percent in the 1952 NES survey to almost 39 percent forty years later—has itself been debated. Sometimes the trend is characterized as "partisan decline." As such, it troubles many analysts who see party conflict as the touchstone of vibrant representative democracy. If almost 40 percent of the electorate cannot be bothered to choose between the two major parties, then how can political leaders be held accountable? Happily, this particular concern seems misplaced. Over two-thirds of nominal independents, when asked, say that they "lean" toward either the Republican or the Democratic Party. It turns out that these leaning independents are very similar to "weak" partisans in their political behavior: Although they do not want to be called Democrats or Republicans, they vote like party identifiers.[41] In the 1992 NES, only about 12 percent of respondents categorized themselves as non-leaning independents—up from 6 percent in 1952, but still a small number. In contrast, as Russell Dalton and Martin Wattenberg have noted, 1992 was also the year when Ross Perot catapulted into national prominence, briefly led in presidential polls, and won 19 percent of the vote. "If ever there was a solid demonstration of the independence of American voters, the Perot phenomenon would be it."[42] Dalton and Wattenberg add that a growing proportion (about one-third) of the electorate professes a neutral view of both parties. This trend toward independence, whatever its political implications, cannot be written off altogether. Many analysts see in it a transition from "party-centered" to "candidate-centered" campaigns (of which we say more in Chapter 12).

Latent Opinions: Postmaterialism, Egalitarianism, and Other Core Values

Many analysts felt that Converse's argument defied common sense. Who were these people with no policy opinions at all? Surely, somehow, Converse's search for these opinions must be looking in the wrong place or in the wrong way. Beginning in the mid-1970s, a new group of scholars argued that they had solved the mystery of the missing beliefs.[43] People had latent opinions, concealed within the pattern of their survey responses. These latent opinions were their underlying beliefs about basic issues, such as the government role in promoting economic equality, that individual survey questions about policy could not measure well directly. In criminology, "latent fingerprints" are invisible until investigators apply special powder. In survey analysis, latent opinions are invisible until investigators apply special techniques that reveal the underlying pattern.

Why were latent opinions hidden? These analysts blamed measurement error: the failure of survey responses to measure accurately people's underlying beliefs (latent opinion). No one doubted that measurement error was real. Robert Putnam, Robert Leonardi, and Raffaella Nanetti depicted respondents as pondering: "What does this question really mean? How can

I convey my honest opinion to this researcher, using this slightly bizarre scheme of his?"[44] Even a person with real, thoughtful, and stable opinions might not answer a survey question identically every time it was asked. According to some researchers, Converse's evidence for nonattitudes indicated something quite different: The respondents had real, highly stable attitudes that the survey questions did not measure very well. Applying different statistical models than Converse had used, these researchers arrived at nearly opposite results from the same data and from other data sets like it.

Converse himself was not convinced. In response to one such analysis that showed high stability in latent opinion, he insisted that the model—whatever its merits—obscured the evidence of widespread confusion and random responses: "To my eye, the authors obliterate these signs of confusion analytically and then turn around to proclaim proudly that no such confusion exists, at least not 'really.' . . . [But] I cannot forget how the data looked before the authors began to process them."[45]

Converse was not just being stubborn. As later studies demonstrated, there is no objective way of measuring "true" stability in three-wave panels, such as the NES panels used by Converse and his critics—and even much longer panels did not settle all the questions.[46]

Ronald Inglehart, in testing his theory of a "postmaterialist culture shift," suggested a different way of demonstrating the reality of latent attitudes. (Postmaterialism is probably not the most "important" latent attitude, but Inglehart's approach to measuring it is especially useful for our discussion.) Inglehart's theory built on psychologist Abraham Maslow's idea of a needs hierarchy. Basic survival needs were at the base of Maslow's "ladder"; then came the needs for social "belonging" and self-expression, with intellectual and aesthetic needs at the top. In any culture, as people's material needs were met, Inglehart reasoned, the higher "postmaterialist" needs would become more important to them.

Inglehart argued that in the United States and Western Europe, the general increase of prosperity over most of the twentieth century had profoundly altered the balance between materialist and postmaterialist values. Each new generation tended to be less concerned about materialist values such as prosperity and security. Postmaterialist values—such as more say in government, a less impersonal society, and freedom of speech—gradually increased in importance. (Inglehart did not argue that younger people were necessarily antimaterialistic or even unmaterialistic. Prosperity allowed them to have more material goods and emphasize postmaterialist values more than the generation of the Great Depression.) Of course, in difficult economic times, material values would seem more important than in boom years. But because people's early experiences shape many of their enduring values, people born in (say) the 1950s would always, on average, be more postmaterialistic than their elders.

Inglehart saw the distinction between materialists and postmaterialists as a new dimension of political conflict, having little to do with the traditional debate between liberals on the "left" and conservatives on the "right." But how could he measure postmaterialism? The direct approach—"Do you consider yourself a postmaterialist?"—obviously would not work very well ("A what?"). Asking, say, "How important do you think self-expression is?" would be almost as confusing. Other questions ("Do you think some things are more important than material goods?") would probably get very one-sided responses, missing most of the underlying differences that Inglehart hoped to get at. No one question would do what Inglehart wanted, so he created a set of questions on national priorities and combined responses to these questions to create an index of (post)materialism. (See Box 8.1.) Here was a straightforward effort to use a group of questions to get at "latent opinions" that a single question would not tap as well. Using multiple questions to measure an underlying variable is a staple of psychology (intelligence tests work in just this way), but Inglehart's use of them to address Converse's argument was new. For instance, Inglehart was able to show that people's postmaterialism scores were more stable over time than their answers to policy questions—implying that this latent opinion, at least, was real and measurable.

In one important study,[47] Inglehart examined West European citizens' responses to these national priority questions, asked repeatedly between 1970

Box 8.1   A Four-Item Index of Postmaterialism

Here is Inglehart's "four-item index" as it has been used in the National Election Studies since 1972:

> For a nation, it is not always possible to obtain everything one might wish. On this card, several different goals are listed.
>
> 1. Maintaining order in the nation.
> 2. Giving the people more say in important political decisions.
> 3. Fighting rising prices.
> 4. Protecting freedom of speech.
>
> If you had to choose among them, which one would seem most desirable to you? Which one would be your second choice?

Choices 1 and 3 are "materialist"; 2 and 4 are "postmaterialist." People who chose one materialist and one postmaterialist goal can be classified as "mixed."

SOURCE: Ronald Inglehart, *Culture Shift in Advanced Industrial Society* (Princeton: Princeton University Press, 1990), pp. 74–75.)

and 1984. (Thus, where Converse had traced individual people's responses over a few surveys, Inglehart studied many surveys, with different respondents, over time.) To see generational effects on postmaterialism, Inglehart divided the respondents into age "cohorts" by their decade of birth. He found that in almost every case, the cohorts were neatly ordered: Younger respondents' national priorities were more postmaterialistic. Also, the cohorts tended to move in parallel groups over time. As inflation rose or fell, so generally did materialism, regardless of age group. Although older respondents were more materialistic than younger ones, respondents did not appear to become more materialistic as they aged.

These results posed a problem for Converse's "black and white" model. If, as the black and white model suggested, only 20 percent of respondents had true opinions, then groups should not differ by more than a fraction of 20 percent. For instance, consider two groups, A and B. In both groups, 80 percent of respondents have no true opinion and divide evenly (40-40) between materialism and postmaterialism. In Group A, among the 20 percent with true opinions, three-fourths are materialists and the rest are postmaterialists (i.e., these 20 percent split 15-5). In Group B, the people with true opinions split the opposite way: only one-fourth of the 20 percent, or 5 percent of the whole group, are materialists. Overall, in Group A, 55 percent are materialists; in Group B, 45 percent are materialists. Thus, the huge difference between three-fourths and one-fourth boils down to only a 10 percent difference overall. But Inglehart found much larger overall differences than this. Take West Germany in 1987: in the 15–24 age cohort, postmaterialists outnumbered materialists by 35 percent to 9 percent (the other respondents were "mixed"), whereas among those 65–74 years old, there were 13 percent postmaterialists and 28 percent materialists.[48] This difference of 22 percent in the number of postmaterialists was pretty much impossible if only 20 percent (or even 30 percent) of respondents were giving meaningful answers. Such differences, also found in other data on opinion distribution and opinion trends, should not occur if survey responses are random or meaningless.

An impressive body of public opinion research (some of it predating Inglehart) similarly uses multiple questions to measure underlying core values and the extent to which these values inform people's political opinions. (Recall our discussion of values and opinions in Chapter 2; unfortunately, there is no very neat definition of a "core" value.) An early investigation found that authoritarianism, or the propensity to defer to political and social authorities, influenced a wide array of political and social attitudes.[49] The literature on authoritarianism easily could inspire a chapter of its own.

One very important core value in the public opinion literature is egalitarianism, which we have already touched on in Chapter 7. Egalitarianism is, roughly, the belief that society or government should strive for equality among citizens. This definition raises many questions (Does equality mean equal rights? Equal chances? Equal wealth? How far should "striving" for equality go?), and there is no agreement on the best way of defining and measuring egalitarianism. National Election Studies since 1984 have used a six-item index. Respondents are asked whether (and how strongly) they agree or disagree with statements such as these: "Our society should do whatever is necessary to make sure that everyone has an equal opportunity to succeed"; "The country would be better off if we worried less about how equal people are." By design, these questions are not, themselves, concrete policy questions. They are intended to tap an underlying value that may influence people's policy views. By various measures (and various names), egalitarianism is strongly related to people's responses on a wide range of policy issues.

Another perennial core value is economic individualism. Closely related to the idea of the American Dream described in Chapter 7, individualism is the belief that hard work and self-reliance are good in themselves and generally "pay off" in material rewards. As Benjamin Franklin simply put it, "Be industrious and frugal, and you will be rich," or, as he went on to hedge, at least you will "stand the best chance" this way.[50] The 1986 National Election Study measured individualism with statements such as these: "Any person who is willing to work hard has a good chance at succeeding" (individualists tend to agree) and "Most people who do not get ahead in life probably work as hard as people who do" (individualists tend to disagree). Often, individualism is construed as the opposite of egalitarianism—and, indeed, supporting equality of outcome is at odds with believing that the hardest workers will and should get ahead. However, one can strongly support equality of opportunity while being fervently individualist. By the same token, since both these values pertain to ideals of fairness, someone who believes that "life just isn't fair" may be neither egalitarian nor individualistic. Like egalitarianism, individualism apparently influences people's views on many policy issues.

We cannot consider all the possible "core values" in much detail, but three points are worth underscoring. First, scholars generally agree that these values should be measured with multiple questions. Second, scholars often find statistical evidence that core values do exist and that they influence people's reported policy beliefs. Even when the "horizontal constraint" among policy questions is very weak, often the "vertical constraint" between core values and the same policy questions is greater. This result implies that people's policy opinions are better structured than Converse's analysis would suggest. Third, no one can say persuasively just what "the" core values are—and there is always room for disagreement about what their content is, how they are formed, whether and how they can change, and generally what they mean.[51]

If we accept that people have latent opinions on "postmaterialism" and other core values, the question remains: So what? Inglehart argues that people generally have "affective orientations" that are "logically relevant to" public policy issues. However, he says, most people have not taken the time and effort to determine their "logical" policy positions.[52] But Robert Luskin asks how different this is from saying that most people simply do not have policy opinions. Not very, Luskin argues: Measurement error on policy questions "is largely the product of non- or minimal cognition."[53] That is, however people feel, they do not think very much about policy issues, so their survey responses on "policy" are not worth much. Even if people's latent opinions on postmaterialism and other values can be inferred from policy questions, this exercise does not prove that they really have policy opinions.

Can we at least infer what people's policy opinions would be, based on their latent opinions, or core values? Often, it is not at all clear how latent opinions translate into concrete policy stances. We can say such things as this: "When people rate themselves on a seven-point scale of whether government should guarantee jobs, egalitarians score X points higher on average than non-egalitarians." But in real life, policy is not made by picking positions on seven-point scales. Asking more specific policy questions does not necessarily solve the problem: How can we tell whether people know enough to reason correctly from their core values to "logical" policy positions? By the same token, it is not clear how changes in latent opinion could or should influence policy. Does, say, a five-point increase in public postmaterialism tell policymakers how they should change the welfare system or handle the latest international crisis? Even a "spineless politician" who wants to follow public opinion could be genuinely confused about where public opinion is headed. Nevertheless, as the next chapter explores in detail, policymakers do seem to respond to trends in public opinion. We should be wary of concluding that public opinion on policy questions is meaningless, if the actions of politicians testify to the contrary.

One final comment on postmaterialism shows how it can be hard to derive policy preferences from core values. Namely, the definition of postmaterialism seems to dodge the hard choices that, many believe, lie at the center of political debate. People who give higher national priority to "protecting freedom of speech" than "fight[ing] rising prices" are—by the logic of Maslow's ladder—not really offering to sacrifice prosperity for liberty. They are simply indicating that to some extent they take prosperity for granted, so no sacrifice is necessary. To find out what people actually value most, we must know what they are willing to give up or to risk. Politically, values matter most when political decisions pit one value against another, and people must wrestle with (or try to ignore) the trade-offs. Any analysis of public opinion that does not address real-world trade-offs risks being ignored as politically irrelevant. Still, one reason to study core values such as postmaterialism, egalitarianism, individualism, and authoritarianism is precisely to see how people respond when their values come into conflict.

Dimensional Typologies of Public Opinion

Research into "core values" implies that a single left-right dimension cannot capture the true structure of people's political beliefs. Various researchers have taken up the challenge of identifying the dimensions that *do* structure people's beliefs. This problem is not quite the same, or not necessarily the same, as identifying "core values." Core values—if they are worthy of the name—presumably affect people's attitudes and behaviors in a wide range of settings; they are akin to personality traits. Political belief dimensions are probably rooted in core values, but they have more explicit political content than core values.

In *The American Ethos,* McClosky and Zaller[54] identify two dimensions of domestic policy beliefs (previously sketched in Chapter 7): *capitalist* values and *democratic* values (see Table 8.4). Although capitalist and democratic values sometimes come into conflict, they are not simply opposites. People can be high or low in "capitalist values" such as support for private enterprise and opposition to government intervention. Separately, people can be high or low in "democratic values" such as defense of free speech, strong protections of civil liberties, and government action to prevent discrimination against minorities. Thus, McClosky and Zaller conclude, there are not two basic political types—liberal and conservative—but rather four, as sketched in the table below. Much "left-right" debate pits the welfare state liberals against the strong conservatives, or democratic values *versus* capitalist values. However, McClosky and Zaller's "nineteenth-century liberals" (who might be called libertarians)[55] strongly favor both capitalist and democratic values, both free markets and individual liberties. Of course, most Americans strongly favor *some* capitalist and democratic values: Capitalism and democracy are the dominant strands of American political thought.[56] For this reason, people who are relatively unsupportive of both capitalist and democratic values are called "antiregime"—although McClosky and Zaller note that they are "often derided as 'rednecks,' 'authoritarians,' 'yahoos,' or 'extremists.'"[57]

Eugene Wittkopf[58] derives his own two-dimensional account of *foreign policy* attitudes. Rejecting the conventional division between "internationalists" and "isolationists," Wittkopf argues that there are two distinct "faces" of internationalism. People may support or oppose cooperative internationalism, the willingness to work with other countries. Separately, they may support or oppose militant internationalism, the willingness to risk military involvement abroad. Militant internationalism and coopera-

TABLE 8.4 McClosky and Zaller's Ideological Framework

	Capitalist Values	
Democratic Values	*Low*	*High*
High	Welfare state liberals	Nineteenth-century liberals
Low	Antiregime pattern	Strong conservative

SOURCE: Adapted from Herbert McClosky and John Zaller, *The American Ethos: Public Attitudes Toward Capitalism and Democracy* (Cambridge: Harvard University Press, 1984), p. 248.

tive internationalism may sound like opposites, but they are not. Some people are relatively willing to cooperate extensively with some countries *and* to risk war with others. Making this distinction allows Wittkopf to move beyond the traditional "hawk-dove" dichotomy, just as McClosky and Zaller reject the conventional "left-right" split. Wittkopf's own four-way categorization appears in Table 8.5.

One pitfall of such typologies is that they tacitly assume that everybody fits one of the categories. People who are genuinely indifferent to the issues posed (or who happen to be "middle of the road") are forced into a category anyway. Another pitfall is that the typologies can direct us away from issues on which most people agree. Still, the categories are not meaningless. In both cases, people in the various categories disagree distinctly on many issues and tend to have different demographic profiles.

James Stimson has shown that education and political information have a powerful effect on the strength of these dimensional relationships. Stimson used a special technique to determine, more or less objectively, how people's beliefs could be grouped into dimensions or "factors." Examining 1972 NES data, Stimson found that better-educated, better-informed respondents tended to have fewer major belief dimensions than other respondents. For the top one-fourth in education and political information, self-assessed ideology combined with opinions on jobs, busing, minority policy, health insurance, the Vietnam War, and inflation in a single strong left-right dimension. (The

TABLE 8.5 Wittkopf's "Internationalism" Framework

	Militant Internationalism	
Cooperative Internationalism	*Oppose*	*Support*
Support	Accommodationists	Internationalists
Oppose	Isolationists	Hardliners

SOURCE: Based on Eugene R. Wittkopf, *Faces of Internationalism: Public Opinion and American Foreign Policy* (Durham, NC: Duke University Press, 1990), figure 2.1, p. 26.

dimension was "strong" in the sense that knowing a person's views on one of these issues would enable you to make a much better prediction about their views on all the rest. In other words, for this group, opinions on these issues were highly constrained.) Three social issues (marijuana, the role of women, and rights of the accused) formed a second dimension. For the bottom one-fourth, more but weaker dimensions emerged: There was little relationship between, for example, opinions on busing and on inflation, and self-assessed ideology did not match any of the dimensions very closely. Thus, the relative political "experts" had a few simple ideas that they applied everywhere, not a great number of complex ideas that they combined in profound ways.[59] This result fit well with Converse's argument that some people's opinions were highly constrained and other people's were not.

Stimson's finding casts a darker light upon much of the statistical evidence that core values or political dimensions drive people's policy views. Much of this evidence is actually consistent with a more complicated version of Converse's "black and white" model: that some citizens very effectively make the connections between their underlying beliefs and policy questions, but many uninformed citizens do not. What are the consequences, for public opinion as a whole, if some citizens manage to make sense of politics and some do not? Do majority values somehow manage to emerge clearly in survey and election results? Or do confusion and ineptitude reign?

Collective Deliberation: The Rational Public?

It is useful to understand how people's beliefs differ systematically among various dimensions, as in the typologies described above. However, if we are asking whether government policy is—or should be—responsive to *overall* public preferences, then typologies are somewhat beside the point. The more urgent question is whether the public as a whole (or majorities of the public) distinctly agrees on specific political positions that could guide policy. Opinion surveys are the most prominent way of trying to identify public policy preferences, although certainly not the only way (see especially Chapter 3, as well as the discussion of "deliberative opinion polls" in Chapter 7). But are citizens competent to guide policy? And do opinion surveys reveal which policies citizens would support if they participated directly in politics?

Benjamin Page and Robert Shapiro strongly affirm that citizens can and should steer policy—and, implicitly, that surveys are useful to identify public preferences. They argue that "the American public, as a collective body, does seem to have a coherent set of policy preferences that fit with people's basic values and that respond to changing realities and changing information. Lacking a supply of philosopher kings or a reliable means of identifying them, it is not easy to find a better source of guidance on what a government should do than the preferences of its citizenry."[60]

Page and Shapiro's first crucial finding draws, like Inglehart's argument, on the *aggregate* opinion of many people, expressed in many surveys over time. Page and Shapiro find that aggregate public opinion is generally stable. That is, if a question about policy preferences is asked repeatedly over several years' time, overall opinion is unlikely to bounce around sharply and unpredictably. This result would not surprise Converse—in fact, if most individuals are always responding randomly, overall opinion should *always* be nearly stable. (For instance, if people answer a question by flipping a coin, we could not predict an individual's answer even if we knew how that person had answered the same question last week. But we *can* predict that the overall split will be about 50-50.)

However, Page and Shapiro's trend data do not show a bunch of people simply flipping coins, or even rolling dice. They find that public opinion sometimes "moves," and that these moves seem to happen for identifiable, and usually sensible, reasons. For instance, during the Cold War, when people expressed greater or lesser fear of the Soviet Union, they were apparently responding to new information about Soviet power and intentions. (Sometimes the new information may have been wrong, but that was not the public's fault.) Moreover, extending Inglehart's "cohort" analysis, Page and Shapiro observe that various demographic groups usually respond similarly—as "parallel publics"—to changing circumstances. This parallel movement suggests that new information is being interpreted by members of these groups in the same way (on average), using common standards of judgment. Much of this new information is transmitted by the mass media, but some of it amounts to people's personal experience of a changing society. For instance, the spread of "feminist" attitudes can be seen as a response to decreasing birth rates and increasing numbers of working women—as well as, perhaps, encouraging these trends. Page and Shapiro argue that survey trends reveal a *rational public* that responds to new evidence in reasonable ways.[61]

Figures 8.4 through 8.7 illustrate the rational public at work. Figure 8.4, which bears on the role of women, shows the largest opinion change that Page and Shapiro found—about a 70-percentage-point increase in public support for allowing a married woman to work if she has a husband to support her. It may be hard nowadays to imagine this as a burning policy issue, but in the economic depression days of the 1930s, Illinois and Massachusetts considered laws that would ban most married women from working.[62] Judging from the polls, such laws would have been fairly popular! The enormous change in opinion from 1936 to 1996 can readily be explained by changes in the lives and roles of women. We will have more to say about public attitudes toward working women in Chapter 10.

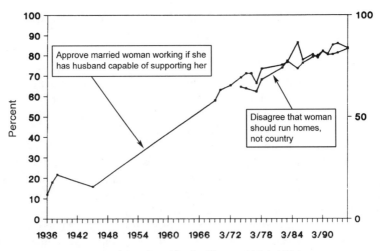

FIGURE 8.4   Women Working Outside the Home, 1936–1996

QUESTION (Gallup, NORC-General Social Survey): "Do you approve or disapprove of a married woman earning money in business or industry if she has a husband capable of supporting her?" or "Do you approve of . . . ." Survey dates: (Gallup)L 6/37, 10/38, 9/69, 6/70, 9/75; (NORC) 3/72–3/96. QUESTION (NORC-General Social Survey): "Do you agree or disagree with this statement: Women should take care of running their homes and leave running the country up to men?" Survey date: 3/74–3/96.

Figure 8.5 addresses whether the rational public is also a democratic public—specifically, whether it supports minority rights and free speech, which we proposed at the beginning of the chapter as an important criterion of democratic competence. The figure documents great changes in public views on the rights and liberties of ascriptive or political groups (Socialists, atheists, Communists, militarists, racists, homosexuals) that have at various times been considered threatening to society or deviant. Over time, the public has become more "tolerant" of these groups. (For simplicity, we illustrate just one issue—who should be allowed to teach in a college or university—but similar trends can be seen for many other issues, and a more complete discussion appears in Chapter 10.)

Figure 8.5 also evinces another aspect of public competence emphasized by Page and Shapiro: The public makes *clear distinctions among issues.* For instance, the public has consistently been more tolerant of Socialists than of Communists. This distinction makes sense, given that the U.S. Communist Party supported the Soviet Union and was generally seen as under Soviet control, while the Socialist Party was perceived as an independent political force. Likewise, although most Americans consider homosexuality immoral, many more support allowing homosexuals to teach in college than would allow militarists or racists to do so, and the gap appears to be

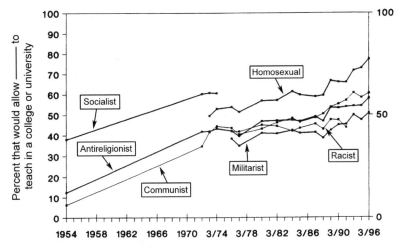

FIGURE 8.5   Civil Liberties College Teachers, 1954–1996

QUESTION (Joint NORC-Gallup, NORC-GSS): "There are always some people whose ideas are considered bad or dangerous by other people. ("Atheist" or "Anti-Religionist") For instance, somebody who is against all churches and religion. . . . Should such a person be allowed to teach in a college or university, or not?" ("Socialist") "Or consider a person who favored government ownership of all railroads and all big industries . . . ." ("Racist") "Or consider a person who believes that Blacks are genetically inferior . . . ." ("Communist") "Now I would like to ask you some questions about a man who admits he is a Communist. . . . Suppose he is teaching in college. Should he be fired, or not?" ("Militarist") "Consider a person who advocates doing away with elections and letting the military run the country. . . . Should such a person be allowed to teach in a college or university, or not?" ("Homosexual") "And what about a man who admits he is a homosexual? . . . Should such a person be allowed to teach in a college or university, or not?" Survey dates: (NORC-Gallup) 6/54; (NORC-GSS) 3/72–3/96.

widening. It should be noted that public permissiveness toward these groups is far from 100 percent (although tolerance of the relatively innocuous Socialists would probably be closer to unanimous today, if survey researchers were curious enough to ask).

Figure 8.6 traces an issue often on the public agenda—crime and criminal punishment. It shows what looks like an explainable public response to rising crime rates (and corresponding news reports) in the 1960s. Public support for capital punishment rose, as did support for less lenient treatment of criminals by the courts. The earlier *drop* in support for capital punishment, almost forgotten today, was associated with concerns that some capital defendants would not get fair trials. In the 1950s and early 1960s, when people generally felt safe on dark city streets and in their homes, these concerns weighed more heavily than today, with widespread fear of crime.

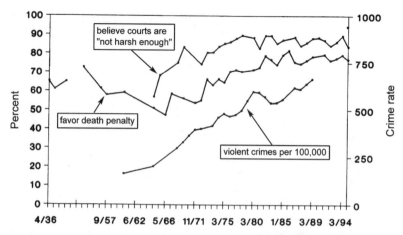

FIGURE 8.6   Capital Punishment and Courts' Treatment of Criminals, 1936–1996

QUESTION (Gallup, NORC-General Social Survey): "Are you in favor of the death penalty for persons convicted of murder?" Variant question in 1936 and 1937: ". . . death penalty for murder?" Survey dates (Gallup): 4/36, 11/36, 11/37, 11/53, 3–4/56, 8–9/57, 3/60, 1/65, 5/66, 6/67, 1/69, 10–11/71, 11/72, 4/76, 3/78, 1/81, 1/85, 11/85, 1/86, 9/88 ("Do you favor or oppose the death penalty for persons convicted of . . . murder?"); (NORC-GSS): 3/72, 3/73. QUESTION (NORC-GSS): "Do you favor or oppose the death penalty for persons convicted of murder?" Survey dates: 3/74–3/96. QUESTION (Gallup, NORC-GSS, *Los Angeles Times*): "In general, do you think the courts in this area deal too harshly or not harshly enough with criminals?" Survey dates: (Gallup) 4/65, 8–9/65, 2/68, 1/69, 12/72, 6/89 (". . . in your area . . . "); (NORC-GSS): 3/72–3/96; (*LAT*) 1/81. The violent crime figures are rates per 100,000 inhabitants. See Benjamin I. Page and Robert Y. Shapiro, *The Rational Public* (Chicago: University of Chicago Press, 1992), pp. 90–94.

Figure 8.7 is an example of the movement of "parallel publics" in a period of great political change. The figure shows parallel opinion changes by region in support for increased defense spending. (Note that the South is consistently most supportive.) The low level of support in 1973 could be seen as a national reaction to the costly, unsuccessful, and intensely controversial U.S. involvement in the Vietnam War. The "spike" in 1980 occurred after the Iran hostage crisis and the Soviet invasion of Afghanistan. This was a time of widespread and plausible concern about the country's military capability, concern fed by political rhetoric that expressed hostility toward the Soviet Union and criticism of the Carter administration. The subsequent reversal of opinion was a response to three factors: an easing of political rhetoric, the fact of an actual increase in defense spending (which had already begun under President Carter), and the advent of the 1981–1982 recession, in which the public gave lower priority to defense spending—preferring fewer "guns" and more "butter," so to speak.

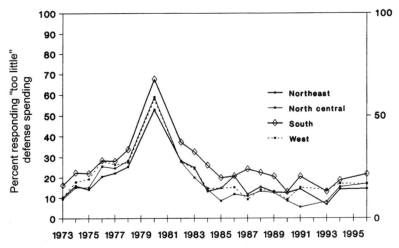

FIGURE 8.7   Defense Spending, 1973–1996: Opinion by Region

QUESTION (NORC-General Social Survey): "We are faced with many problems in this country, none of which can be solved easily or inexpensively. I'm going to name some of these problems, and for each one I'd like you to tell me whether you think we're spending too much money on it, too little money, or about the right amount. . . . Are we spending too much, too little, or about the right amount on . . . the military, armaments, and national defense?" Survey dates (NORC-GSS): 3/73–3/96.

Crucially, the striking opinion changes of Figures 8.4 through 8.7 are possible only if large numbers of people have, in some sense, meaningful opinions. Aggregate opinions change when many people are exposed to new information, pay attention to this information, and change their opinions (i.e., their survey responses) as a result. As the "parallel publics" trends show, these changes are generally similar across smaller subgroups, showing just how pervasive exposure to new information can be, at least in the modern United States.

Other major studies have established the importance, and buttressed the reasonableness, of trends in American public opinion. The research of James Stimson and colleagues on "public mood," elaborated upon in Chapter 9, indicates that general public policy preferences tend not only to influence national policy but also to respond to changes in national policy.[63] William Mayer presents evidence that various opinion trends are in large part influenced and explained by objective changes in conditions.[64] These works contain some distinct differences of interpretation—for instance, Mayer argues that Page and Shapiro overstate the degree of stability in public opinion, and that Stimson's idea of a single "public mood" is too simple. Still, all these studies can be read as buttressing the notion of a rational public.

How should we explain public opinion trends, given the evidence of widespread inattentiveness to politics? Some real, but modest, changes in aggregate opinion (about 10 percentage points or less) could be caused by a large change among a relatively small "attentive" public. Some analysts (including Converse in 1964) describe "issue publics" that closely follow a particular issue and are well-informed about it. Even in cases where issue publics (or a more general attentive public) account for observed opinion change on a policy issue, we can still refer to a "rational public." This view proposes an informal division of labor in which the attentive public responds to new information "on behalf of" the public as a whole. Converse himself asserted in a 1996 article that "there is no reason whatever why the lessons of these opinion time series and the earlier portraits of electorate heterogeneity cannot both be true."[65] This heterogeneity—some citizens attentive and well-informed, most not—is also emphasized by John Zaller, whose analysis we will describe below. From this standpoint, public "volatility" seems relatively unimportant. Paradoxically, if much of the public is oblivious to new information, then the attentive few will account for most observed changes in public opinion. Even though policy responses are not very well-informed on average, aggregate *changes* in policy views are (relatively) well-informed.

Certainly, issue publics or small attentive publics cannot explain all the results gathered by Shapiro and Page. In our earlier discussion of Inglehart, we noted that large subgroup differences would be impossible if just a small minority of people were giving real responses. Likewise, large opinion changes (of 10 points or more) are impossible unless a fairly large proportion of the public is involved. We cannot say what proportion of citizens might be considered part of the "defense issue public"; the percentage is probably fairly small. Nevertheless, between 1978 and 1980, and again between 1980 and 1982, public support for defense spending changed by about 30 percent, indicating that a large proportion of the public was attentive to new information about defense-related issues. "Issue publics," or attentive publics, can actually grow larger or smaller as the political context changes.

In short, as we have described, Page and Shapiro see a *rational public* that responds to new information in reasonable ways. They conclude that the public's "collective policy preferences" are intelligible and important. In other words, analysts can tell coherent stories about "what Americans really think" about the issues[66] because Americans really *do* think about the issues, or at least (in the aggregate), they answer polls as if they do. And if we are serious about democracy, public opinion as measured in polls should be taken seriously.

If most people know very little about political issues, how do their aggregate or collective responses manage to make sense? Page and Shapiro argue that people participate (to varying degrees) in a process of *collective delib-eration*. Policymaking elites and expert analysts often provide much of the substance of this collective debate. However, they do not supply the results. In the end, the public makes "a multitude of individual decisions about who and what is right."[67] For better or worse, sometimes a prevailing pub-lic decision emerges that goes sharply against most "expert" opinion. Page has argued that Zoë Baird's 1993 nomination as attorney general provides a classic example.[68] Baird had failed to pay social security taxes for her full-time babysitter. Many congressional leaders and political pundits initially argued that Baird had made a trivial mistake that should not prevent her from being confirmed. Many Americans begged to differ, on talk shows and in the polls—and Baird's nomination was withdrawn.

Even if public opinion influences policy (as will be seen in the next chap-ter), collective deliberation is no democratic panacea—especially if political elites can control the terms of the debate. In Page and Shapiro's own words, "Government responsiveness to the public would constitute a hollow vic-tory, for example, if public opinion were itself manipulated by elites or in-terest groups in such a way that policy followed the mistaken wishes of a deceived public."[69] Many people may be sufficiently attentive and "in-formed" to react to such manipulation, though not nearly knowledgeable enough to resist it. Here Page and Shapiro hearken back to Key's warning that "the voice of the people is but an echo"—although the case of Zöe Baird suggests that maybe it is not always *just* an echo.

As we did with core values, we must ask how much policy guidance the survey results analyzed by Page and Shapiro can provide. Page and Shapiro discuss at some length how people might respond to a question about building MX missiles. Some people might generally favor building a large number, although their precise answer might vary from day to day. Others might generally favor building a small number or none at all. All these re-sponses would add up to an "average long-term most-preferred policy" of, say, fifty missiles being built—an average that would probably be stable over time, unless new information changed people's opinions.[70] Although no survey ever asked people how *many* MX missiles they wanted to build, Page and Shapiro argue that the available survey data do show collective stability. "If meaningful public opinion existed on such an issue, with its technical complexity, low levels of information, high uncertainty, and fre-quent 'don't know' responses, then it very likely exists on simpler and more salient issues closer to everyday experience."[71]

But what exactly does "meaningful public opinion" *mean*? If people with almost no knowledge about a weapons system consistently support (on av-erage) building 50 missiles, or 120 missiles, or 3.14 missiles, the collective stability may be meaningful and remarkable. But is it a "long-term collec-tive preference"?[72] Even if it is, would policymakers be wise to enact this preference as policy? Surely at some point, where an issue lies outside the knowledge and experience of respondents, the survey results become "garbage in, garbage out." But where is the point? How should we decide which poll results are worth taking seriously and how seriously to take them?

This quandary is not limited to esoteric matters of defense policy, nor do large issue publics appear to resolve it. A pair of 1997 surveys indicated that public support for a U.S. constitutional amendment requiring a balanced budget—a proposal widely discussed for several years—varied by 37 percentage points, depending on the question wording.[73] If the balanced budget issue has not evoked a sufficiently large and informed "issue public" to prevent this sort of paradoxical result, it is hard to imagine many issues that would. Survey results like these have some meaning, but they do not seem to state any clear public mandate. What, then, does "meaningful opinion" mean? We return to this issue (but do not settle it) below.

Making Do: "Gut Rationality," Heuristics, and Political Judgments

Whereas Page and Shapiro investigate what they call "collective deliberation," Popkin's *The Reasoning Voter* offers one effort to make sense of voters' individual deliberations. Popkin draws on the insights of the Columbia school, the "information shortcuts" noted by Downs, and findings from cognitive psychology to make the case for *gut rationality* in presidential voting. He argues that people can and do make decent voting decisions without having to conduct systematic research into presidential candidates.

> People learn about specific government programs as a by-product of ordinary activities. . . . They obtain economic information from their activities as consumers, from their workplace, and from their friends. They also obtain all sorts of information from the media. Thus they do not need to know which party controls Congress, or the names of their senators, in order to know something about the state of the economy or proposed cuts in Social Security or the controversies over abortion.[74]

Similarly, and sensibly, voters use "campaign competence as a proxy for competence in elected office—as an indication of the political skills needed to handle the issues and problems confronting the government." And voters "use evaluations of personal character as a substitute for information about past demonstrations of political character."[75] If certain candidates have made a hash of their campaign or their personal life, maybe they should not be trusted to steer the national government into the future. Because it is hard to pin down candidates on the issues and because presidents often cannot enact their policy preferences anyway, basing votes on "personalities instead of issues" makes more sense than policy experts may want to admit. In fact, research indicates that well-informed people are at least as likely as less-informed respondents to weigh personalities more heavily than issues.[76] Thus, voters use shortcuts, or *heuristics*, in gathering and analyzing information, so that they can make good votes without much hard (or impossible!) work.

Although Popkin's analysis is limited to voting, other researchers have found that people employ heuristics in making all kinds of political judgments—such as positions on policy views.[77] Different people use different heuristics, depending on their political sophistication and their cognitive styles. Some heuristics are group based and follow the logic of attitudinal consistency we discussed in Chapter 4. A person may "reason" as follows: "Blacks like affirmative action, and I like (dislike) blacks, so I like (dislike) affirmative action." "Republicans favor lower taxes on capital gains, and I am a Democrat, so I oppose them." Similar heuristics can be based on individuals: "Ralph Nader endorsed this referendum, and I respect Nader, so I will vote for it."[78] Other heuristics engage simple values: For instance, Sniderman and colleagues argue that people evaluate some social policies by asking whether the likely beneficiaries are deserving (a "dessert heuristic"). For some people, although (as we have seen) not very many, ideological beliefs such as liberalism or conservatism serve as powerful heuristics. Heuristics, by definition, do not require very much thought, but this does not mean that they are merely "emotional," "irrational," or arbitrary. On the contrary, heuristics may be very reasonable, in the sense that they enable people to reason and act effectively without very much knowledge or effort.

One especially powerful heuristic for voting decisions is *retrospective voting*, or voting on the basis of incumbent performance (rather than issue positions or other criteria). In the preceding chapter, we quoted Lippmann's view that the essence of democratic governance is "to support the Ins when things are going well; to support the Outs when they seem to be going badly." Many studies indicate that voters do weigh incumbent performance, as well as economic conditions (whether incumbents are strictly responsible for these conditions or not), very heavily in determining their presidential votes.[79] A broad and impressive body of research on *on-line tallies* posits that people judge candidates by keeping an internal count of "pros" and "cons"—but not necessarily recalling the content of these likes or dislikes![80] Thus, heuristics can take a dizzying array of forms—and, just as there is no overarching and widely accepted "theory of core values," there is no single "theory of political heuristics."

Several studies show that heuristics do not resolve all the problems of limited political information. Delli Carpini and Keeter find that the presidential votes of politically knowledgeable respondents are powerfully predicted by their ideology and issue positions. For the least knowledgeable respondents, however, issue positions have little predictive power, and ideology has hardly any at all.[81] This result implies, of course, that uninformed voters do not use issues and ideology to decide their votes. But it also implies something more disturbing: that, despite whatever heuristics these voters use, they are more likely than informed voters to vote *contrary to* their stated preferences. Unfortunately, not all such heuristic failures "wash out" at the aggregate level. Larry Bartels, studying presidential elections from 1972 through 1992, estimates that incumbent presidents win about 5 percent more of the vote—and Democratic candidates about 2 percent more—than they would if all voters were fully informed.[82] In individual elections (and perhaps especially in congressional elections), voters' lack of information could lead to even more dramatic distortions.

The policy opinions expressed in opinion surveys may also be crucially distorted by many respondents' lack of information. As a dramatic example, Scott Althaus examines responses to a 1992 NES question on whether married women should be required to notify their husbands before having an abortion. Overall, almost two-thirds of respondents supported spousal notification requirements. However, the respondents with the most factual knowledge were roughly evenly divided on this requirement, whereas those with the least knowledge favored it by about 4 to 1. This gap apparently cannot be explained by other social, economic, or political differences. It appears that the most knowledgeable respondents are better able to think out the arguments on both sides of this issue, leading more of them to oppose spousal notification requirements—and revealing much more controversy than the raw results would indicate. Althaus finds many other (albeit less extreme) gaps between informed and uninformed respondents.[83] Clearly, heuristics do not necessarily allow people to vote or to respond to survey questions as if they were fully informed. However, analysts are far from a consensus on how well heuristics work in general.

Some analysts emphasize not heuristics, but *schemas*. Schemas are "mental prototypes, images, metaphors, 'scripts,' or categories that provide a frame of reference against which experience is compared and interpreted."[84] In some ways, schemas create expectations just as stereotypes do (see Chapter 4). Schemas will also make particular concerns, rather than others, appear relevant. According to schema theory, people interpret new information in terms of their existing schemas. Unlike heuristics, schemas are not really reasoning shortcuts. Rather, schemas "tell" people *how* to reason about the matter at hand.

For instance, when Iraq invaded Kuwait in the summer of 1990, many people used a schema inspired by the Munich Pact of 1938. After Nazi Germany invaded Czechoslovakia in 1938, Great Britain and France attempted to appease Adolf Hitler by ceding some territory to Germany without Czechoslovakia's consent. The "appeasement schema" (or "Munich schema") holds that such conciliatory responses to aggression only encourage further aggression—such as Germany's invasion of Poland in 1939. President Bush invoked the appeasement schema when he publicly compared Iraqi president Saddam Hussein to Adolf Hitler. Other observers relied on the "Vietnam schema," in which the use of force to punish a much weaker opponent leads to a military quagmire with heavy casualties. A stream of public commentaries related the Gulf crisis to either the appeasement or the Vietnam schema, illuminating some aspects of the crisis while obscuring others. The appeasement schema evoked considerations about what territory Iraq might attempt to seize next; it implied that stopping Iraqi aggression now would be simpler and less costly than trying to do so later. By contrast, the Vietnam schema encouraged people to consider the possibility of a long-term military involvement, the risk of heavy American casualties, and the chance that military action would not achieve U.S. policy goals.

Similarly, various people draw on different schemas in thinking about welfare programs. Some people tend to think of hardworking parents temporarily down on their luck who deserve help to get back on their feet again. Others think of lazy or spoiled women who would rather live on the dole than work to support themselves and their children. Again, countless public commentaries invoke one schema or the other, often at great length. Many thoughtful and detailed discussions of welfare are heavily influenced by one of these schemas. Logically, these schemas are not mutually exclusive; neither are the appeasement and Vietnam schemas. However, when schemas point in opposite directions, people often favor one at the expense of the other. (We can understand this tendency as an effort to reduce cognitive dissonance or affective inconsistency, as described in Chapter 4.)

A weakness of schema theory is that we generally cannot predict very well which schema a person will apply to new information. Sometimes, to be sure, we can make some predictions. For instance, someone who lived through World War II should be more likely to rely on the appeasement schema than someone who did not—although other events could lead someone to a similarly jaded view of appeasement. This ambiguity points to another weakness of schema theory, one it shares with many other psychological theories. Since we cannot "see" schemas directly, it is hard to pin down what they are or how they influence people's thinking in a way that would convince a skeptic. Still, many political psychologists find schema theory a useful way of understanding why many political debates seem to restate a few arguments over and over. These debates often hinge not on "new ideas" but on efforts to persuade people to apply one widely held schema instead of another. In the short run, schemas themselves are generally stable and largely impervious to rational argument. It may be much easier to convince people that, for example, the Vietnam schema applies to the Gulf crisis than to persuade them of a new and unfamiliar way of thinking about such crises.

The New Synthesis

John Zaller (in collaboration with Stanley Feldman) has offered an influential new "theory of the survey response" that wrestles with the issues raised by Converse, Inglehart, Page and Shapiro, and other scholars.[85] Zaller flatly agrees with Converse that people do not have predetermined "true" (crystallized) attitudes on many, if any, survey questions. Yet he also agrees with Inglehart that people do have predispositions (values, interests, and ideological views) that have important implications for the issues treated in political surveys. And he implicitly agrees with Page and Shapiro that public opinion as reported in polls, in the aggregate, is generally stable and responds sensibly to new information (to the extent that this information is received)—although he does not believe that public opinion should be as influential in policymaking as Page and Shapiro would like. Zaller relates all these familiar views to a theoretical framework different from anything we have seen so far in this chapter, although it has deep roots in political psychology.

If people do not have established opinions on, say, defense spending, how do they answer survey questions about it? Zaller argues that they make up these responses on the spot, based on whatever relevant *consideration* first comes to mind. (A consideration is simply "any reason that might induce [someone] to decide a political issue one way or the other.")[86] However, for considerations to "come to mind," they have to be in the mind first! Zaller proposes a three-step "receive-accept-sample" (RAS) model that pivots on *political awareness.*

1. People who pay closer attention to politics—who are more politically aware and knowledgeable—are more likely to *receive* new political messages that can serve as considerations.[87] When President Bill Clinton argued in 1993 that a new national health care program was needed to protect the uninsured, some people "got the message," whereas others never tuned in. (Political messages often do not come from politicians. Many "messages" about AIDS, for instance, come from TV news stories that may not mention politicians or even specific policy issues. Other political messages come from talk and variety shows, TV situation comedies, rap music, advertisements of various kinds, and many other sources.)
2. Politically aware respondents are also more likely to *accept* messages that suit their predispositions—and to reject messages that do

not. Thus, knowledgeable liberals were more likely to "buy" President Clinton's argument about the uninsured than knowledgeable conservatives were. Conversely, knowledgeable conservatives were more likely to accept the opposing argument that Clinton's proposal would create a wasteful, oppressive bureaucracy. However, most people accepted some considerations on both sides. Bear in mind that not all considerations are arguments (or depend on ideology). For instance, a person might simply figure, "Clinton supports this plan, and I like/hate him, so that's a reason to support/oppose it."

3. Come survey time, people *sample* from among whatever considerations they have received, pro or con, that are "accessible" and seem relevant to the question. In the case of a yes-or-no question, it is almost as if people throw all these considerations into a hat, then pull one out at random to decide how to answer. (For more complicated questions, it is as if people "average" the considerations.) Of course, neither Zaller nor anyone else thinks that we can really count up all of someone's considerations. Considerations (like many concepts in social science) seem "real" but cannot be counted or measured very precisely. Here, Zaller's argument sounds like the idea of "on-line tallies" mentioned earlier, but there is a crucial difference: his discussion of what goes into the hat, that is, which considerations are accessible.

Accessibility depends on several things. One is political knowledge. Liking or hating Clinton does not help you answer a question on health care reform unless you know (or think you can guess) whether Clinton supports the reform. Another important influence is how recently the consideration has been called to mind. Survey designers can actually manipulate (deliberately or accidentally) which considerations are called to mind by the way in which they *frame* their questions. Indeed, a growing body of research focuses on frames as a crucial element in understanding how people respond to survey questions.[88] In the terms of schema theory, we can think of frames as cues in the question text that encourage people to apply one schema or another and thus to use particular considerations when they answer.

As an example of how "frames" can work, consider the question "Do you support the health care proposal now before Congress?" Rewording it—"Do you support Bill Clinton's health care proposal, now before Congress?"—would encourage people to "sample" their view of Clinton. Alternatively, changing "Bill Clinton's" to "President Clinton's" or even "the president's" might bring to some people's mind the consideration that "presidents deserve the benefit of the doubt" and thus evoke more support. (You might argue that these wordings are not just changes in "frame" but actually add *information* to the original question, which did not mention Clinton. That is quite true. Frames can be thought of as a kind of information, and there is no way to supply information—even "balanced" information—without influencing a question's frame.) By altering the wording and order of *earlier* questions in the survey, designers could profoundly influence what people are thinking about when they answer a question on health care reform. These question-wording and "context" effects have long troubled survey analysts, in part because they seem to complicate the task of finding "true public opinion." Zaller argues, however, that these effects amount to important evidence about the nature of public opinion. His elegant theory of these effects, rooted in the idea of "considerations," is a major advance.

Now we can see how Zaller can agree with all the authors mentioned above. If people are pulling their survey answers out of a hat, it is pointless to ask what answer is their "real attitude." However, based on their awareness and their predispositions, some people will be much more likely to offer, say, a "postmaterialist" opinion than others. (We might think of someone's "real attitude" as the average answer that person would give if asked a question repeatedly—although even this average would be affected by nuisance factors such as question order.) Also, based on people's predispositions and awareness, we can predict to some extent how they will respond to new information (political messages). Most important for Page and Shapiro's argument, we can predict that the public as a whole *will* respond to new messages, although some people will either ignore or reject them.[89] If most major sources of political information agree that the United States needs a military buildup, public opinion will probably move in that direction, as it did in 1980—in what Zaller calls a "mainstream effect." Also, we can expect that if there are no new and strong messages, public opinion will be fairly stable. This view is compatible with a fairly rational public, although some parts of the public are more rational than others. However, Key's caveat (echoed by Page and Shapiro) still applies: If the public is systematically fed bunk, it will probably respond to it.

Although Zaller's model seems compatible with Page and Shapiro's argument, he has a strikingly different view of democratic competence. Where Page and Shapiro emphasize the "good news" about stability and change in public opinion, Zaller underscores the bad news: "Many citizens . . . are blown about by whatever current of information manages to develop the greatest intensity. . . . Most of the rest [i.e., the politically aware] respond mechanically on the basis of partisan cues," tending to rely upon elites that share their predispositions.[90] This view leads Zaller to the next question: "If, as I have implied, only specialists are competent to conduct political debate, why bring the public into it at all?" Why not just leave government to the experts? Zaller answers: Because "government, in the absence of checks, invariably goes astray and becomes overbearing or worse. . . . It is the collective ability of citizens in a democracy to pressure leaders in useful directions and, when necessary, to remove the leaders, more than the collective wisdom of the people, that seems to me critical."[91] Thus, Zaller's view is similar to Lippmann's—the public's role is to choose between the Ins and the Outs—although "pressur[ing] leaders" may allow for a somewhat larger role. Although the public cannot *conduct* political debate, at least it can tell when its leaders go astray.

Even so, Zaller resembles Page and Shapiro more in his concerns than he is different in his conclusions. None of these authors sees the public as inherently capricious, rash, authoritarian, or otherwise dangerous. They worry more that elite debate might become one-sided: In Zaller's closing words, "The real problem is guaranteeing the existence of . . . [a] vigorous competition among opposing ideas."[92] As long as elite debate thrives and is accessible to the public, Zaller reasons, the public will be able to support the side that matches its own prevailing predispositions. Page is less optimistic: He worries that no matter what policy experts are saying and no matter what the public believes, nothing can force the major political parties to adopt public preferences.[93] Either way, clearly it is possible for the government to go against public predispositions. The next chapter investigates policy responsiveness to public opinion in great detail.

Conclusion

This chapter began by citing three standards for considered public opinion or democratic competence. What have we concluded about these three standards? First, the public does not have much knowledge, at any one moment, about a wide range of political issues or related facts. However, what citizens do know, and what they learn about issues when they become salient and important, appears to be adequate for many purposes—or at least such a case can be made. But "adequacy" is a subjective judgment, and even those who have argued that the public is "rational" or reasonable or sensible would agree that political life would be better for citizens and the nation if people learned more about political issues.

Second, although individual citizens may not have the opportunity and information to engage fully in deliberation on political issues, research on *aggregate* public opinion and voting decisions finds these to be largely explainable, understandable, and even sensible. The trends and patterns that we see can be described in terms of collective deliberation, conducted by a thoughtful public that weighs new information and experiences against its previous values. However, the quality of this deliberation is only as good as the information presented to the public—and skeptics doubt that it is even that good. Moreover, the results of deliberation, as measured by public opinion polls, can be frustratingly enigmatic, if not downright contradictory. Some observers hope that deliberative polls, such as the National Issues Convention described in Chapter 7, may evoke clearer evidence about citizens' considered policy preferences. Others argue, more cautiously, that survey questions on an issue should incorporate all the important frames that prevail in the debate on that issue in order to give a rounded perspective on the public's thinking.[94]

Third, we have seen data in this chapter and elsewhere in this book (see also Chapter 10) that evince growing respect among the American public for democratic norms such as minority rights and freedom of speech. To be sure, some Americans reject these norms, and there is always debate about how far these norms should be extended. Still, we find little support for the notion that the American public is fundamentally undemocratic and therefore that its influence on policy should be minimized.

We are inclined to conclude on an optimistic note, but at the same time, we want to honor our own warnings against trimming our facts to suit our values. At the very least, we believe that democratic competence is possible and that government policy can be reasonably guided by public preferences. However, we cannot guarantee that public opinion will always be wise or good. Perhaps we can only insist that it is wiser and better than many critics might lead you to believe.

Notes

1. Party primaries open to the public now play a large role in candidate selection for most offices. Still, for many reasons, these do not guarantee that citizens will be satisfied with the choice of candidates.

2. In Albert H. Cantril, ed., *Polling on the Issues: Twenty-One Perspectives on the Role of Opinion Polls in the Making of Public Policy* (Cabin John, MD: Seven Locks Press, 1980), p. 170.

3. Walter Lippmann, *Essays in the Public Philosophy* (Boston: Little, Brown and Co., 1955), p. 20.

4. To some extent, Lippmann and Gallup may be talking past each other. Most of the polling data mentioned by Gallup did not exist when Lippmann wrote in 1955. Lippmann's "prevailing public opinion" may differ profoundly from what Gallup found in the survey results. It is doubtful, however, that Lippmann would be much impressed by Gallup's survey data.

5. A thorough survey of the evidence appears in Michael X. Delli Carpini and Scott Keeter, *What Americans Know About Politics and Why It Matters* (New Haven: Yale University Press, 1996), especially chaps. 2 and 3. Stephen Earl Bennett and colleagues find similar results for public knowledge of foreign policy in several nations, although Germans stand out as the most knowledgeable (Stephen Earl Bennett, Richard S. Flickinger, John R. Baker, Staci L. Rhine, and Linda L. M. Bennett, "Citizens' Knowledge of Foreign Affairs," *Harvard International Journal of Press/Politics* 1 [1996]:10–29).

6. Some Americans surely confused Nicaragua with the neighboring country of El Salvador, where the United States backed the *government* against the Marxist rebels there.

7. Paul F. Lazarsfeld, Bernard R. Berelson, and Hazel Gaudet, *The People's Choice* (New York: Duell, Sloan, and Pierce, 1944).

8. Ibid., pp. 65–66.

9. Ibid., p. 27.

10. Bernard R. Berelson, Paul F. Lazarsfeld, and William N. McPhee, *Voting: A Study of Opinion Formation in a Presidential Campaign* (Chicago: University of Chicago Press, 1954), p. 293. This book describes the 1948 "Elmira (NY) study."

11. Angus Campbell, Philip E. Converse, Warren E. Miller, and Donald E. Stokes, *The American Voter*, unabridged ed. (New York: John Wiley, 1960; Chicago: University of Chicago Press, 1976).

12. Of course, some people may misremember which party their parents supported. Also, "relatively stable" does not mean "fixed in stone": Often people's party ID does change—slowly or quickly—over time. The transmission of partisanship and how partisanship can change over time is examined by M. Kent Jennings and Richard G. Niemi in *Generations and Politics* (Princeton: Princeton University Press, 1981) and *The Political Character of Adolescence* (Princeton: Princeton University Press, 1974).

13. See the discussion of projection effects in Chapter 6.

14. These figures—which exclude votes for independent candidate John Anderson—come from the 1980 National Election Study. Here we combine all self-described independents, including those who said that they leaned toward one or the other party.

15. Robert Huckfeldt and John Sprague, *Citizens, Politics, and Social Communication: Information and Influence in an Election Campaign* (New York: Cambridge University Press, 1995).

16. Walter Lippmann, *Public Opinion* (1922; New York: Free Press, 1965), p. 143.

17. In fact, the likelihood was so small that to explain why so many people vote anyway, Downs argued—somewhat murkily—that they consider voting a form of "insurance" against the collapse of democracy (p. 268). However, if it is unlikely that one person's vote could determine an election, it is nearly unimaginable that it could save democracy! Probably the best explanation is that many people believe they have a civic duty to vote and therefore gain an *intangible* benefit from voting.

18. Alexis de Tocqueville, *Democracy in America* (New York: HarperPerennial, 1988), vol. 1, chap. 5 (at p. 198).

19. For instance, the U.S. Catholic bishops oppose both abortion rights and capital punishment, in what is sometimes called a "consistent pro-life" or "seamless web of life" ethic. Interestingly, people who favor abortion rights while opposing capital punishment (liberals) or vice versa (conservatives) often criticize their counterparts' inconsistency but see no inconsistency in their own views. Actually, philosophically consistent arguments can be made for any of these positions.

20. This chapter touches on several measures of political sophistication, but in limited detail. The best overview is still Robert C. Luskin, "Measuring Political Sophistication," *American Journal of Political Science* 31 (1987):856–899.

21. Philip E. Converse, "The Nature of Belief Systems in Mass Publics," in David E. Apter, ed., *Ideology and Discontent* (NY: Free Press, 1964), pp. 206–261.

22. Cited in W. Russell Neuman, *The Paradox of Mass Politics: Knowledge and Opinion in the American Electorate* (Cambridge: Harvard University Press, 1986), pp. 19–20.

23. Richard Herrera, "Understanding the Language of Politics: A Study of Elites and Masses," *Political Science Quarterly* 111 (Winter 1996–1997):619–637. Notice that Converse obtained a similar result (37 percent were not able to name any difference between liberal and conservative, meaning that 63 percent were— although Converse rejected some of these answers as obviously incorrect).

24. See Philip E. Converse, "Attitudes and Non-Attitudes: Continuation of a Dialogue," in Edward R. Tufte, ed., *The Quantitative Analysis of Social Problems* (Boston: Addison-Wesley, 1970), pp. 168–189. This paper was originally presented in 1963.

25. Robert E. Lane, *Political Ideology: Why the American Common Man Believes What He Does* (New York: Free Press, 1962), p. 353. For Lane's critique of Converse, see Robert E. Lane, *Political Thinking and Consciousness: The Private Life of the Political Mind* (Chicago: Markham Publishing Company, 1969).

26. Jennifer L. Hochschild, *What's Fair?: American Beliefs About Distributive Justice* (Cambridge: Harvard University Press, 1981). Other works with similar approaches include Karl A. Lamb, *As Orange Goes: Twelve California Families and the Future of American Politics* (New York: W. W. Norton, 1974); Kathlyn Taylor Gaubatz, *Crime in the Public Mind* (Ann Arbor: University of Michigan Press, 1995).

27. Hochschild, *What's Fair?* p. 237.

28. Donald R. Kinder and David O. Sears, "Public Opinion and Political Action," in Gardner Lindzey and Elliot Aronson, eds., *Handbook of Social Psychology, vol. 2: Special Fields and Applications* (New York: Random House, 1985), p. 669.

29. V. O. Key Jr., *Public Opinion and American Democracy* (New York: Alfred A. Knopf, 1961), pp. 47, 49, 270.

30. Ibid., p. 270.

31. Ibid., p. 428.

32. V. O. Key Jr., with the assistance of Milton C. Cummings Jr., *The Responsible Electorate: Rationality in Presidential Voting, 1936–1960* (New York: Vintage Books, 1968), pp. 7–8. Notice that "public policy, 1/4 governmental performance, and 1/4 executive personality" all find a place in the work of the Michigan school.

33. Ibid., p. 113.

34. Ibid., pp. 2–3, 7.

35. Gerald M. Pomper, "From Confusion to Clarity: Issues and American Voters, 1956–1968," *American Political Science Review* 66 (1972):415–428; Norman H. Nie, Sidney Verba, and John R. Petrocik, *The Changing American Voter* (1976; Cambridge: Harvard University Press, enlarged edition, 1979). Earlier articles had noted that voters in 1964 seemed more responsive to candidates' ideological cues: see Pomper, "From Confusion to Clarity," p. 416, nn. 16, 17.

36. Nie, Verba, and Petrocik, *Changing American Voter*, p. 115. These are the figures for people who used ideological terms for *either* parties or candidates. However, another group of researchers applied the original Converse criteria (as closely as they could manage) to the 1968 transcripts. They found that the proportions of ideologues and near-ideologues in 1968 were both roughly double the 1956 figures. See Philip Converse, "Public Opinion and Voting Behavior," in Fred A. Greenstein and

Nelson Polsby, eds., *The Handbook of Political Science* (Reading, MA: Addison-Wesley, 1975).

37. A good discussion of these trends is Steven J. Rosenstone and John Mark Hansen, *Mobilization, Participation, and Democracy in America* (New York: Macmillan, 1993), pp. 57–60. According to National Election Survey estimates, presidential turnout reached an all-time high in 1960; midterm turnout, in 1966. The extension of suffrage to 18–20-year-olds in 1972 intensifies the trend but did not create it. Black turnout in the South increased sharply during the 1960s (from about 15 percent in 1956 to about 70 percent in 1968); whites and blacks have followed similar trends since then.

38. Norman H. Nie and James N. Rabjohn, "Revisiting Mass Belief Systems Revisited: Or, Doing Research Is Like Watching a Tennis Match," *American Journal of Political Science* 23 (February 1979):139–175.

39. Eric R.A.N. Smith, *The Unchanging American Voter* (Berkeley: University of California Press, 1989); Michael Margolis, "From Confusion to Confusion: Issues and the American Voter, 1956–1972," *American Political Science Review* 71 (March 1977):31–43.

40. Warren E. Miller and J. Merrill Shanks, *The New American Voter* (Cambridge: Harvard University Press, 1996).

41. The fullest development of this line of argument is Bruce Keith et al., *The Myth of the Independent Voter* (Berkeley: University of California Press, 1992).

42. Russell J. Dalton and Martin P. Wattenberg, "The Not So Simple Act of Voting," in Ada W. Finifter, ed., *Political Science: The State of the Discipline II* (Washington, DC: American Political Science Association, 1983).

43. A few of the crucial contributions were: Christopher H. Achen, "Mass Political Attitudes and the Survey Response," *American Political Science Review* 69 (1975):1218–1231; Robert Erikson, "The SRC Panel Data and Mass Political Attitudes," *British Journal of Political Science* 9 (1979):89–114; Charles M. Judd and Michael A. Milburn, "The Structure of Attitude Systems in the General Public: Comparisons of a Structural Equation Model," *American Sociological Review* 45 (1980):627–643; Ronald Inglehart, "Aggregate Stability and Individual-Level Flux in Mass Belief Systems: The Level of Analysis Paradox," *American Political Science Review* 79 (1985):97–116. An analysis of latent attitudes in foreign policy is Jon Hurwitz and Mark Peffley, "How Are Foreign Policy Attitudes Structured? A Hierarchical Model," *American Political Science Review* 81 (1987):1099–1119.

44. Robert D. Putnam, Robert Leonardi, and Raffaella Y. Nanetti, "Attitude Stability Among Italian Elites," *American Journal of Political Science* 23 (August 1979):471.

45. Philip E. Converse, "Comment: Rejoinder to Judd and Milburn," *American Sociological Review* 45 (1980):646.

46. Christopher H. Achen, "Toward Theories of Data: The State of Political Methodology," in Finifter, ed., *Political Science*.

47. The discussion here refers to Inglehart's influential 1985 article, cited above. The argument is developed and the evidence extended in Ronald Inglehart, *Culture Shift in Advanced Industrial Society* (Princeton: Princeton University Press, 1990) and Paul R. Abramson and Ronald Inglehart, *Value Change in Global Perspective* (Ann Arbor: University of Michigan Press, 1995). A critique of the latter book—especially

the four-item index and the importance of "formative economic security"—appears in James A. Davis, "Review Essay," *Public Opinion Quarterly* 60 (1996):322–331; see also Abramson and Inglehart, "Formative Security, Education, and Postmaterialism: A Response to Davis," *Public Opinion Quarterly* 60 (1996):450–455.

48. Inglehart, *Culture Shift*, p. 93.

49. T. W. Adorno, Else Frenkel-Brunswik, Daniel J. Levinson, and R. Nevitt Sanford, *The Authoritarian Personality* (New York: Harper and Row, 1950).

50. Letter of August 9, 1768, cited in the *Columbia Dictionary of Quotations* (New York: Columbia University Press, 1995).

51. For instance, some of the measures of "authoritarian/conservative" thinking in the 1972 National Election Study closely resemble measures of "(non-) egalitarian" thinking in the 1984 and later NES surveys. Authoritarianism, as defined in the text, should not simply be the opposite of egalitarianism. In fact, many argue that the former Soviet Union promoted both authoritarian values (submission to authority) and egalitarian ones (material equality).

52. Inglehart, "Aggregate Stability," p. 101.

53. Robert C. Luskin, "Measuring Political Sophistication," *American Journal of Political Science* 31 (1987):873.

54. Herbert McClosky and John Zaller, *The American Ethos: Public Attitudes Toward Capitalism and Democracy* (Cambridge: Harvard University Press, 1984).

55. Many libertarians, however, would oppose most government efforts to prevent discrimination.

56. Recall Hochschild's argument that most people are committed to equality in the socializing and political domains, but not in the economic domain. In McClosky and Zaller's terms, she might say that most people are high on democratic values—at least those pertaining to equality—but also fairly high on capitalist values.

57. McClosky and Zaller, *American Ethos*, p. 247.

58. Eugene R. Wittkopf, *Faces of Internationalism: Public Opinion and American Foreign Policy* (Durham and London: Duke University Press, 1990).

59. James A. Stimson, "Belief Systems: Constraint, Complexity, and the 1972 Election," *American Journal of Political Science* 20 (August 1975):393–417. Delli Carpini and Keeter find similar results in their analysis of 1988 NES data *(What Americans Know About Politics*, p. 237).

60. Benjamin I. Page and Robert Y. Shapiro, "The Rational Public and Democracy," in George E. Marcus and Russell L. Hanson, eds., *Reconsidering the Democratic Public* (University Park, PA: Penn State University Press, 1993), p. 61.

61. Benjamin I. Page and Robert Y. Shapiro, *The Rational Public: Fifty Years of Trends in Americans' Policy Preferences* (Chicago: University of Chicago Press, 1992). We emphasize here, as we will again, that "information" is not necessarily factual.

62. See the 1939 Gallup surveys cited in Page and Shapiro, *Rational Public*, p. 100.

63. See James A. Stimson, *Public Opinion in America: Moods, Cycles, and Swings* (Boulder: Westview Press, 1991) and the works discussed in Chapter 9.

64. William G. Mayer, *The Changing American Mind* (Ann Arbor: University of Michigan Press, 1992).

65. Philip E. Converse, "The Advent of Polling and Political Representation," *PS: Political Science and Politics* 29 (December 1996):649–657. Russell Neuman's *The Paradox of Mass Politics*, cited earlier, extensively discusses variation in attentive-

ness to politics. An interesting discussion of issue publics in the context of elite accountability is David J. Elkins, *Manipulation and Consent: How Voters and Leaders Manage Complexity* (Vancouver, British Columbia: UBC Press, 1993).

66. Barry Sussman, former director of polling for the *Washington Post*, wrote a book called *What Americans Really Think—and Why Our Politicians Pay No Attention* (New York: Pantheon Books, 1988). Of course, the title only makes sense if Americans really do think something.

67. Page and Shapiro, *Rational Public*, p. 365.

68. Benjamin I. Page, *Who Deliberates? Mass Media in Modern Democracy* (Chicago: University of Chicago Press, 1996), chap. 4.

69. Page and Shapiro, "Educating and Manipulating the Public," in Michael Margolis and Gary A. Mauser, eds., *Manipulating Public Opinion: Essays on Public Opinion as a Dependent Variable* (Pacific Grove, CA: Brooks/Cole, 1989), 294. Benjamin Ginsberg argues that mass opinion in the Western democracies has been tamed and harnessed to increase the power of the state. See Ginsberg, *The Captive Public: How Mass Opinion Promotes State Power* (New York: Basic Books, 1986).

70. Page and Shapiro, *Rational Public*, pp. 17–23; this phrase appears on p. 21.

71. Ibid., p. 23.

72. Ibid., p. 20.

73. The first survey, conducted by the *New York Times* and CBS News in January 1997, asked, "Do you think requiring the Federal Government to balance the budget is the kind of issue you would like to change the Constitution for, or isn't balancing the budget that kind of issue?" In the response, 39 percent said that it was that kind of issue, and 49 percent that it was not. A survey conducted by CBS News two weeks later asked, "Would you favor or oppose a balanced budget amendment to the Constitution that would require the Federal Government to balance its budget by the year 2002?" In favor were 76 percent, against only 17 percent opposed. Except for the mention of the year 2002, there is no tangible policy difference between the two questions; no major event between the surveys can explain the seeming contradiction. Apparently, in responding to the first question, people focused on the seriousness of changing the Constitution; in responding to the second, people focused on the desirability of a balanced budget. Here is an example of a "framing effect" such as is described later in the text. See David E. Rosenbaum, "Deficit: Public Enemy No. 1, It's Not," *New York Times*, February 16, 1997, section 4.

74. Samuel Popkin, *The Reasoning Voter* (Chicago: University of Chicago Press, 1991), p. 213.

75. Ibid.

76. David P. Glass, "Evaluating Presidential Candidates: Who Focuses on Their Personal Attributes," *Public Opinion Quarterly* 49 (1985):517–534; Ester R. Fuchs and Robert Y. Shapiro, "Government Performance as a Basis for Machine Support," *Urban Affairs Quarterly* 18 (1983):537–550.

77. A major collection of studies on this theme is Paul M. Sniderman, Richard A. Brody, and Philip E. Tetlock, *Reasoning and Choice: Explorations in Political Psychology* (New York: Cambridge University Press, 1991). A useful overview of the heuristics literature is Jeffery J. Mondak, "Cognitive Heuristics, Heuristic Processing, and Efficiency in Political Decision Making," *Research in Micropolitics* 4 (1993):117–142.

78. See Arthur Lupia, "Short Cuts Versus Encyclopedias: Information and Voting Behavior in California Insurance Reform Elections," *American Political Science Review* 88 (Spring 1994):63–76.

79. Morris P. Fiorina, *Retrospective Voting in American National Elections* (New Haven: Yale University Press, 1981), makes the case most extensively at an individual level. *The New American Voter* gives prominent place to retrospective voting in its revision of the Michigan model. Michael B. McKuen, Robert Erikson, and James Stimson have argued that future economic prospects matter more than "retrospective" evaluations in "Peasants or Bankers? The American Electorate and the U.S. Economy," *American Political Science Review* 86 (1992):597–611.

80. Rich discussions of the on-line tally theory and related models can be found in Milton Lodge and Kathleen M. McGraw, eds., *Political Judgment: Structure and Process* (Ann Arbor: University of Michigan Press, 1995).

81. Delli Carpini and Keeter, *What Americans Know About Politics*, pp. 256–257.

82. Larry M. Bartels, "Uninformed Votes: Information Effects in Presidential Elections," *American Journal of Political Science* 40 (February 1996):194–230. Here Bartels uses only demographic characteristics, not political attitudes, to predict vote choice. Although this choice is limiting, it spares him from the objection that information may also affect people's political views, as argued by Althaus later in this chapter.

83. Scott L. Althaus, "Information Effects in Collective Policy Preferences," *American Political Science Review* (in press).

84. James DeNardo, *The Amateur Strategist: Intuitive Deterrence Theories and the Politics of the Nuclear Arms Race* (New York: Cambridge University Press, 1995), p. 181. A useful overview of schema theory is David O. Sears, Letitia Anne Peplau, Jonathan L. Freedman, and Shelley E. Taylor, *Social Psychology*, 6th ed. (Englewood Cliffs, NJ: Prentice Hall, 1988), pp. 101–115.

85. John R. Zaller, *The Nature and Origins of Mass Opinion* (New York: Cambridge University Press, 1992); John Zaller and Stanley Feldman, "A Simple Theory of the Survey Response: Answering Questions Versus Revealing Preferences," *American Journal of Political Science* 36 (1992):579–616.

86. Zaller, *Nature and Origins*, p. 40.

87. What we call "political messages," Zaller usually calls "information"—but he emphasizes that he does *not* mean neutral facts. Notice, however, that there is no neat distinction between "political" and "nonpolitical" messages.

88. See Donald R. Kinder and Lynn M. Sanders, *Divided by Color: Racial Politics and Democratic Ideals* (Chicago: University of Chicago Press, 1996), chap. 7.

89. These messages can affect public opinion in two ways. They can add new considerations or they can change the way that people "sample" among their existing considerations, by priming or framing (see the further discussion in Chapter 11).

90. Zaller, *Nature and Origins*, p. 311; see also p. 328.

91. Ibid., pp. 331–332.

92. Ibid., p. 332.

93. See Page, *Who Deliberates?*

94. See Kinder and Sanders, *Divided by Color*, chap. 7, especially p. 195.

Chapter Nine

Public Opinion and Policymaking

COAUTHORED WITH LAWRENCE R. JACOBS

Unless mass views have some place in the shaping of policy, all the talk about democracy is nonsense. As [Harold] Lasswell has said, the "open interplay of opinion and policy is the distinguishing mark of popular rule."

—V. O. Key Jr., *Public Opinion and American Democracy*

V. O. Key Jr. firmly emphasizes what we observed in the first chapter: When we talk about democracy we must talk about public opinion.[1] By definition, in a democracy (from the Greek word *demos*), the people are supposed to rule. This expectation pervades American history; it is an important symbolic hope—if not a realistic aspiration—from the Declaration of Independence to the Constitution to reminders by Abraham Lincoln and others who have emphasized government "by the people" as well as "for the people."

The influence of public opinion on government is a central normative question (concerning the way things *should be*) as well as an empirical question (concerning the way things *are*) about democracy and politics. How much influence the public *should* have is a philosophical question that requires, as we saw in Chapter 8, that we evaluate the basic competence of the mass public. One major challenge to any aspirations for democracy is the possibility that V. O. Key Jr. himself feared: "that democratic government only amounts to a hoax, a ritual whose performance serves only to delude the people and thereby to convert them into willing subjects of the powers that be."[2]

How much effect the public actually has on government policymaking is, in fact, a question we can try to answer. Specifically, we can point to evidence that boldly shows that public opinion affects what government does to some more than minimally important degree. This may surprise some readers who are skeptical, or even cynical, about what happens in politics. Others may be puzzled that we even consider the question; from American history or social studies classes in high school, they may have learned that "of course, public opinion affects public policy in the United States." But we do not accept these assumptions without evidence that government does or does not respond to public opinion. Furthermore, if we find support for the assertion that government policies do in some noticeable way respond to public opinion, whether we would want to call this government responsiveness "democratic" is another question. We will return to this question at the end of the chapter.

Public Opinion Only Constrains Policy?

In considering the causal impact of public opinion on policy, it is useful to consider three possibilities: Public opinion constrains public policy; public opinion exerts strong pressure to direct or redirect government policy; public opinion is ignored in government policymaking.

In Chapter 1, we observed how public opinion can ultimately at least *constrain* policymaking. (Attentive readers will note that we use "constrain" here in a context different from the term "ideological constraint" in Chapter 8.) This occurred in the case of foreign policy issues such as aid to the contras in Nicaragua after a long period in which public opinion was ignored when the issue was not particularly salient and important. By "salient," we mean widely visible to the public, particularly in the mass media, or felt directly by people and their families and friends, as a poor economy might be. The issue of support for the contras in Nicaragua increased in visibility and prominence in the media as it was divulged that funds secretly obtained from the sale of arms to Iran were used to supply aid to the contra rebels, whom the United States was supporting against the leftist Nicaraguan government. This was the "Iran-Contra Affair," the event that catapulted U.S. marine Oliver North into the public eye as the allegedly heroic "fall guy" for the Reagan administration.[3]

To take another case, in the Gulf War period from late 1990 to 1991, President George Bush had the public's backing in his decision first to help defend Saudi Arabia against Iraq and then to lead a multinational, though largely American, attack against the Iraqis in Kuwait and Iraq. Similarly, in 1964–1965, Lyndon Johnson went to war in Vietnam initially with substantial public support. Much later, as we will discuss later in this chapter, the

United States decreased its level of participation in the war after public opposition gathered momentum. Another case in point occurred when the United States supported the admission of the People's Republic of China (then commonly referred to as "Communist China" or "Red China") to the United Nations in 1971 only after public support very gradually—reflecting a long-standing reluctance—increased for this controversial decision.

On the domestic policy front, too, we can readily cite cases of government policies responding to public opinion. The Supreme Court initially legalized abortion in the United States (the well-known *Roe v. Wade* decision in 1973) after a ten-year period of declining public opposition to the legalization of abortion. The historically important Civil Rights Act of 1964 and Voting Rights Act of 1965 passed after public opinion became increasingly supportive of desegregation and of liberalizing "civil rights" policies broadly. Capital punishment was ruled unconstitutional in the early 1970s, following increasing public opposition to it from the 1950s on, as is shown in Figure 8.6 in Chapter 8. But then in the 1970s, public opinion moved decisively in the opposite direction, and a subsequent ruling by the Supreme Court made capital punishment legal once more.[4] Ironically, in these cases of abortion and capital punishment, the government institutions changing these policies were the courts. In the end, the Supreme Court, which is supposed to be more insulated from shifts in public opinion than the other branches of government, which are held directly accountable to the electorate, made the final decision.

In focusing the discussion on the public's constraining influence, it is ambiguous whether the word "constrain" gives too little credit to the power of public opinion. In the examples just cited, the public was often an important *driving force* that attempted to end racial inequities, fight crime, and either send American troops abroad or bring them home. These are, in part, subjective judgments: One person's "constraining effect" is another's "powerful effect." We will let the cases and data speak for themselves, so that the reader may judge. The authors of this chapter would argue that public opinion is more than a constraint, since the force of public opinion can be used to push policies through. Clearly, to take some later examples, public support was critical to the passage in 1996 of welfare reform (which the public had long wanted in some form);[5] to increasing the minimum wage that same year; and to enacting at the same time some modest incremental health care reforms and regulations (the requirement that "preexisting conditions" be covered by insurance policies and that health insurance be "portable" as people change from one job to another). The public's second thoughts about enacting major health care reform, evoked by sharp congressional and organized group opposition, helped stop dead in its tracks the Clinton administration health care reform plan in 1994 (the plan was voted down in committee, never making it even to floor debate in Congress).

In sharp contrast to these cases, we can also point out noteworthy instances in which the government has not done what public opinion (as revealed by opinion polls) has ostensibly wanted. This clearly happened in the case of aid to the contras for a significant period of time. There were also widespread public perceptions from 1970 to 1996 that "too much" was spent on foreign aid, and also on the space program, but there was not any responsive government reaction to this. But foreign aid, as a single general and amorphous policy, and the space program have not been among the most urgent and salient issues in the mass media and thus are not high on the public's radar screen.

There have been some well known and widely debated examples of the failure of government to respond to what have been clear public preferences as reported in national opinion surveys. These include support for allowing some form of prayer in schools, as well as support for more stringent gun control laws (short of actually banning the possession of rifles or even handguns), although we have seen the enactment of restrictions on the sale of assault weapons and the requirement of a waiting period before a gun sale is permitted (the Brady Bill, named after President Reagan's press secretary, who was shot during an assassination attempt on the president). In the cases of both school prayer and gun control, however, questions have been raised about how responding to public opinion would lead to conflicts with the Constitution concerning the "separation of church and state" and the "right to bear arms." On gun control, political pressure from lobbies of gun owners (mainly the National Rifle Association) and gun and ammunition manufacturers have come into play—occurring so extensively that it has been widely criticized.

President Clinton's decision to invade Haiti during the 1994–1995 period clearly went against public opinion and against the preferences of most members of Congress in both parties. Nor did Clinton's decision to work vigorously for the passage of the North American Free Trade Agreement (NAFTA) initially have clear public support.

Clearly, the public's wishes are not always followed. This apparent lack of responsiveness, however, may not mean a decision is, in the end, "undemocratic." We will return later to the question of what is "democratic" and what is not.

Theories

The problem in drawing general conclusions about the responsiveness of policymaking to public opinion is that we can point to different examples supporting different conclusions. The way political scientists attempt to resolve this is to consider *theories* about what to expect in American politics and to look as sweepingly as possible at what the available evidence shows.

Theoretically, there is good reason to expect a noticeable pattern of responsiveness of policymaking to public opinion. Specifically, we can identify *political processes* at work that should contribute to responsiveness. First and foremost, the reason to expect some minimum—and observable—responsiveness in the United States has to do with periodic elections of government officials, when voters have the chance to voice their approval or disapproval of the actions of these leaders. Because elected leaders know that they (or, if they are not running for reelection, their party's candidate) will be held accountable at election time, they have reason to *anticipate* public opinion, so their attention to such opinion is not reserved only for election campaigns. Studies have tried to confirm in different ways that policy responsiveness increases as elections near.[6] We can also point again to the passage in the wake of the 1996 election of a modest health care reform bill, an increase in the minimum wage, and welfare reform. At election time, leaders ignore public opinion at their own peril; at other times, they know that they or their party may have to answer for their past acts at the next election.

Another possible reason to expect policy responsiveness is that voters elect leaders who are simply like themselves in enough ways that the leaders happen to *share* the opinions of the those who elect them. The leaders share the wants and values of the public.[7] This might also occur if leaders were chosen simply by random lottery among voters, which is an idea that has been given some consideration historically.[8] It is not clear, however, how similar political leaders actually are, individually or as a group, to ordinary citizens. These leaders self-select to be very active in politics, and they are clearly of upper status in terms of education, income, and occupation (disproportionately lawyers, today). For a long time, women and members of minority groups rarely held important public offices. It is more likely that other processes and pressures occur that lead to responsiveness.

In addition to electoral pressure, there may be social pressure to comply with the public's wishes. There may be a feeling among elected representatives that they should represent those who have elected them. These representatives may feel that they are obligated to do what their constituents or voters have delegated them to do. In fact, representative who adopt this as a style of representation have been called "delegates." Other leaders—elected or appointed—feel that they have been chosen to act as their own consciences dictate, to do what they think is best for the public. There is no reason to expect these "trustees," as they have been called, to respond more to the demands voiced by the public than to other types of information related to policy decisions.[9] It is possible that the style of representation that leaders use may vary by issue or at different times. The term "political" or "politico" has been used to describe representatives who adopt varying styles for political or other reasons.

The critical question that we have to address here is how the public's preferences are determined by policymakers and then brought into, or *linked* to, the policymaking process. It has become popular in recent years to talk about how opinion polls and, in the 1990s, how "focus groups" have become increasingly important as ways candidates and political leaders learn about public opinion (though the latter have long been used, but less visibly; see the earlier discussion in Chapter 3).[10] In fact, with information about public opinion so widely available, we would have reason to expect more responsiveness in the 1990s and in the future than ever before. But politicians and government officials of the past as well as the present have long had other sources of information about public opinion available to them: constituency mail; various informants who report what they observe, including staffs, advisers, and even friends and acquaintances; information from political party leaders and others in the party; reports, editorials, and commentaries in the mass media; and the opinions and information conveyed by organized groups.

Political scientists have long thought that interest groups play a major, if not a critical, role in processes by which public opinion influences, or fails to influence, policymaking. Groups have the capacity to (as political scientists say) "aggregate and articulate"—that is, to find out about and widely communicate—opinions found among the public. A powerful theory was offered by political scientists to show how interest groups helped represent public opinion in politics and thereby facilitate democracy. This theory of "democratic pluralism," or "pluralism," essentially maintained that over time and across all issues that arise, we can expect public opinion to be fully represented. This would occur through existing groups and by new groups that would be formed as new issues arose or as segments of the public who felt unrepresented began organizing them.[11] Later, we will examine how political parties, as organized groups, might also provide this linkage between the public and government through processes of selecting candidates and by developing policy stances that are supported by party members and party loyalists in the electorate.

Some readers may be suspicious about the role of "special interests" and "lobbyists" in American politics. Not surprisingly, a number of critics of democratic pluralism have presented counterarguments to any expectations that organized groups act democratically. In short, these critics argue that in the case of seemingly open group processes, there have still been ample opportunities for nondemocratic influences to occur; that is, there are influences at work on policymakers that prevent the public from getting what it wants or getting what is in its best interest.

For one thing, according to these critics, not all opinions have groups to represent them. And in particular, it is not so easy for groups to organize and become effective at communicating the opinions of previously unrepresented interests into the political process. Further, the groups that are likely to form and remain influential are those that are small, have substantial wealth or other resources, and have much to gain, which motivates them to organize and act.[12] If there are no groups to pick up the banner of unrepresented opinions as they emerge from a dormant, inactive, or "latent" stage,[13] this clearly has devastating consequences for a pluralist or group-based form of democracy. If those who were well-off financially and in other ways from the start were also the most likely to organize their interests, then the "heavenly chorus" of public opinion would clearly have an upper-class bias.[14]

In contrast to democratic pluralism and the above criticisms of it, other theorists have argued that policymaking is dominated by powerful elites— individuals or small groups (such as business leaders, military leaders, and specific political leaders who have connections to each other)—who dominate all areas of policymaking, nationally and locally. These individuals and groups have been given various political labels such as "the power elite."[15]

Another theory has maintained that American democracy was thwarted by particular powerful groups that exerted political control not over all areas of public policymaking but rather over the narrow, but important, policy areas that were of special interest to them. Thus, different groups controlled specific areas of policymaking, especially in different states and localities. For example, farmers controlled farm policy in their states, if not nationally; power and utility companies influenced how states and localities regulated their enterprises; and the like. As a result of this dominance by different private centers of power, it is rare for public opinion to be very influential.[16]

One way elites or special interests dominate and thwart public opinion is by keeping issues off the visible political agenda. As a result, the public is not aware of what is happening and thus does not mobilize against these groups or elites.[17] Clearly here, the role of the mass media in making issues widely visible is very important (see Chapter 11). It has even been claimed that policymaking is dominated by the influences of business and industry or the need for government or "the state" to act in business's interest in order to strengthen both the nation and state by enhancing economic growth.[18] Other arguments emphasize the blatant dominance of money in interest group activity and in political campaigns, which further reduces the influence of ordinary people, who, even collectively, may have fewer financial resources to contribute.

Overall, then, there are different types of political processes at work that have different consequences for the public's influence on government. Electoral accountability, how political leaders see their roles, and group-based democratic pressures can lead the public to have substantial influence on policymaking. In direct conflict with this are other processes that can sharply limit the public's ability to constrain or drive what government does.

Evidence

But what is the reality here? As we will see, there is considerable evidence that although the public does not always rule, it is often able to move—or maintain—government policies in desired directions.

Thanks to the expansion of survey research and the recently increasing number of studies that have focused directly on the opinion-policy relationship, students of public opinion are now in a much better position than in the past to examine these matters. But the general issues and expectations have not changed, especially with respect to whether public opinion is a constraint or a director of policymaking. V. O. Key Jr. wrote in 1961:

> The anxieties of students about their inability to gauge the effects of opinion rest on an implicit assumption that public opinion is, or in some way ought to be, positively directive of government action. Our analyses suggest that the relationships between government and public opinion must be pictured in varied ways, none of which requires solution of the problem of the precise measurement of the weights of opinion in the governing process. Mass opinion may set general limits, themselves subject to change over time, within which government may act. In some instances opinion may be permissive but not directive of specific action. In others opinion may be, if not directive, virtually determinative of particular acts.[19]

To examine these effects of public opinion we need to consider a variety of research strategies. To start, how do we *broadly* compare public opinion and government policies to get a sense of the results of democratic procedures in action? This is the simplest and most fundamental question, but it is one that it took political scientists a long time to analyze directly in a social-scientific fashion. Some of the earliest empirical studies of this, which were the first to be widely cited in public opinion textbooks, had to do with representation in Congress. These studies of constituency representation, as we will see later on, examined the votes cast by legislators on proposed laws; they did not directly compare public opinion with government policies that were ultimately fully enacted.

Students might quickly—and quite correctly—think that a simple way to study the effect of public opinion on policy in a democracy would be to compare *majority* public opinion with subsequent government policy, given that we have majoritarian rules and we make simple favor-or-oppose decisions on policies in our Madisonian or constitutional tradition. The simplest question to ask is this: How often does majority opinion get what it wants from government? One way to try to answer this directly would be to count how frequently national government policies have corresponded with *prior* public opinion. We say "prior" opinion since we are interested in the responsiveness of government to prior public demands (or lack thereof). To keep matters simple, by "public opinion" here, we again mean majority opinion that we could measure through responses to questions in opinion polls that ask explicitly about identifiable government policies.

Although this would appear to be a relatively simple research task, it has actually been more difficult than expected. Modern scientific opinion polling began in the United States in 1935, but many of the polls that became available to researchers were not designed with this type of study in mind. That is, the surveys did not ask many questions that were worded in ways that would enable researchers to study the effect of majority opinion on a wide range of government policies. It took thirty years or more for enough public opinion data to become available. At that point, a handful of researchers—most notably Donald Devine, Robert Weissberg, and Alan Monroe[20]—developed appropriate strategies for using these data to examine government responsiveness to public opinion. These were the first and broadest studies of aggregate national opinion.

Monroe's study was the largest one to compare majority opinion and policy in the United States. His research design compared public support for proposed changes in policy with subsequent policies themselves. For example, if in response to a survey question, 51 percent or more of survey respondents opposed our establishing diplomatic relations with Cuba and the government did not establish such relations up to four years later, this would be a case in which government policy was consistent or "congruent" with public opinion. In this case, too, we would have majority support for existing policy, or the "status quo," in Monroe's terms. If majority opinion had favored the establishment of diplomatic relations and the government had subsequently complied, this would be a case of congruence with a "change" in policy. Table 9.1 summarizes Monroe's results for a large number of policy issues. Clearly, the 64-percent level of consistent cases is striking for 222 cases of majority support for particular policies. It is far more than 50 percent of the time, which would be expected through chance alone.

TABLE 9.1   Public Preference and Policy Outcome for All Nonspending Cases

	Preference	
Outcome	*Status Quo*	*Change*
Status quo	56 (76%)	61 (41%)
Change	18 (24%)	87 (59%)
Total	74 (100%)	148 (100%)

NOTE: Consistent = 64%; N = 222

SOURCE: A. D. Monroe, "Consistency Between Public Preferences and National Policy Decisions," *American Politics Quarterly* 7, p. 9. Copyright 1979 by Sage Publications. Reprinted by permission of Sage Publications.

Monroe, however, cautioned against concluding too quickly that there is a cause-and-effect relationship between public opinion and policy. The data clearly pointed in that direction, but this was still incomplete evidence. Adopting a similar method for comparing majority opinion and policy, other researchers found less evidence of this sort for responsiveness, particularly in other countries.[21] Additional studies using different research methods and other data were clearly needed to confirm or challenge Monroe's finding. Examining such other studies, we find further evidence of the impact of public opinion on policymaking in the United States.

Taking a different approach, Benjamin Page and Robert Shapiro undertook a project somewhat larger in scope than Monroe's.[22] One part of their study used a method similar to Monroe's and confirmed a comparable level of "majoritarian" opinion-policy congruence. But they were much more interested in finding out how often *changes in policy* occurred after *changes in public opinion.* Specifically, they wanted to see how frequently they found cases in which a change in opinion from one time point to another was followed by a corresponding or parallel change in government policy. In this case, they ignored whether the level of support for a policy was a majority or not; they examined only the *direction* of opinion change and the direction of policy change. For example, if support for increasing spending on health care increased (by more than survey sampling error) from 1980 to 1982 and government spending increased (in real dollars, adjusting for inflation) from 1980 to 1983, then this was considered a case of "covariational congruence" between policy change and opinion change. Had spending decreased from 1980 to 1983, this would have been classified as an instance of noncongruence. To put it simply, the idea was to count how often public opinion and policy changed in the same direction.

In their analysis of 231 instances of changes in policy preferences and changes of policy, Page and Shapiro found that policies one year later moved in the same direction as opinion 66 percent of the time. These results are shown in Table 9.2. Note that the 66-percent figure depended on their excluding 120 cases of "no change in policy," which included, according to the authors, a great many cases in which policy (the "status quo" in Monroe's term) was already maximally congruent with opinion; cases in which congruent policy changes occurred more than one year after public opinion changed; and cases in which even with some noticeable opinion change, there was still only small minority support for a policy change, so that a change in policy could not yet plausibly be expected to occur.

Table 9.3 shows further that these data clearly pick up the responsiveness of policy to the degree of change in public opinion: Larger opinion changes made corresponding policy changes more likely, with congruent policy change (53 percent) not much more likely than chance (50 percent) for a

TABLE 9.2   Congruence Between Opinion and Policy, 1935–1979

	Total Cases		Cases with Policy Change	
	%	N	%	N
Congruent change in opinion and policy	43	(153)	66	(153)
Noncongruent change in policy	22	(78)	34	(78)
No change in policy	33	(120)		
Uncertain	2	(6)		
Total	100	(357)	100	(231)

NOTE: Each case is an instance in which public policy preferences changed significantly, according to repeated administration of identical survey items.

SOURCE: Benjamin I. Page and Robert Y. Shapiro, 1983, table 1, p. 178.

TABLE 9.3   Frequency of Congruence for Opinion Changes of Different Sizes

Size of Opinion Change in Percentage Points	Direction of Policy Change					
	Congruent		Noncongruent		Total	
	%	N	%	N	%	N
6–7	53	(25)	47	(22)	21	(47)
8–9	64	(32)	36	(18)	22	(50)
10–14	62	(40)	38	(25)	29	(65)
15–19	69	(22)	31	(10)	14	(32)
20–29	86	(18)	14	(3)	9	(21)
30+	100	(10)	0	(0)	4	(10)
Total	65	(147)	35	(78)	100	(225)

NOTE: Gamma = –.29.

SOURCE: Benjamin I. Page and Robert Y. Shapiro, 1983, table 3, p. 180.

6–7 percentage point change, and a near certainty (86 percent or more) with opinion changes of 20 percentage points or more. Similarly, Monroe had found congruent policy changes more likely when there was larger majority support.[23] Page and Shapiro (as well as Monroe) also show that congruence was more likely for the most salient issues. Thus, this kind of "covariational" (over time) congruence occurred in ways consistent with theories about when we would expect changes in policy to correspond to changes in opinion. This kind of issue-by-issue correspondence between

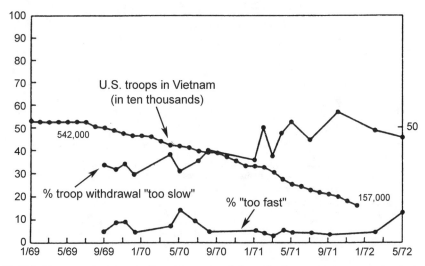

FIGURE 9.1a   Opinion-Policy: Troop Withdrawals from Vietnam, 1969–1972.
SOURCE: Robert Y. Shapiro and Benjamin I. Page, "Foreign Policy and Public Opinion," in David A. Deese, ed., *The New Politics of American Foreign Policy* (New York: St. Martin's Press, 1994), figure 10-8a, p. 232. Copyright 1993 by St. Martin's Press, Inc. Reproduced by permission of St. Martin's Press, Inc.

Response in the figure is to the following: QUESTION: (Harris): (Version A) "In general, do you feel the pace at which the president is withdrawing troops from Vietnam is too fast, too slow, or about right?" Survey dates: 10/69, 12/69. (Version B) adds "Nixon." Survey date: 8/70. (Version C) omits "from Vietnam." Survey date 10/69. (Version D) adds "U.S." Survey date: 4/70. (Version E) puts "slow" first. Survey date: 1/71. (Version G) substitutes "think." Survey dates: 5/70, 7/70. (Version H) adds "Nixon" and "slow" first. Survey dates: 3/71, 4/71. (Version I) omits "in general," puts "slow" first. Survey date: 10/71. (Version J) long prologue on RN plan, substitutes "more rapid rate," "slower rate," "satisfactory." Survey date: 10/71. (Version K) "Do you feel the pace of withdrawal of U.S. troops from . . . ? Survey dates: 2/72, 5/72. Source for U.S. troop data: SS-2 Unclassified Statistics on Southeast Asia, Comptroller, Office of the Secretary of Defense, Table 6. Reported in Raphael Littauer and Norman Uphoff, eds., *The Air War in Indochina* (Boston: Beacon Press, 1972), pp. 265–272, table 6.

public opinion and policy has been confirmed by other types of research that we will turn to next.

There have been "time series" studies comparing trends in public opinion and public policy on particular issues. Figures 9.1a and 9.1b and Figure 9.2 show these trends for cases of U.S. troop withdrawal in Vietnam and changes in defense spending. In Figures 9.1a and 9.1b, the rate of troop withdrawal from Vietnam was sensitive to public attitudes toward the war in general and toward the rate of troop withdrawal in particular, as shown by the parallel and relatively synchronized opinion and policy trend lines.

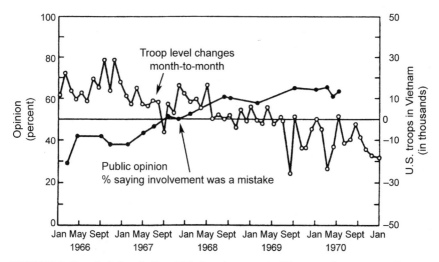

FIGURE 9.1b Opinion-Policy: U.S. Involvement in Vietnam. SOURCE: Robert Y. Shapiro and Benjamin I. Page, "Foreign Policy and Public Opinion," in David A. Deese, ed., *The New Politics of American Foreign Policy* (New York: St. Martin's Press, 1994), figure 10-8b, p. 233. Copyright 1993 by St. Martin's Press, Inc. Reproduced by permission of St. Martin's Press, Inc.

Response in the figure is to the following: QUESTION: (Gallup): "In view of the developments since we entered the fighting in Vietnam, do you think the U.S. made a mistake sending troops to fight in Vietnam?" Survey dates: 8/65, 3/66, 5/66, 9/66, 11/66, 2/67, 5/67, 7/67, 10/67, 12/67, 2/68, 3/68, 4/68, 8/68, 10/68, 2/69, 9/69, 1/70, 3/70, 4/70, 5/70, 1/71, 5/71.

Figure 9.2 shows an even more impressive correlation (which is well documented and analyzed by other researchers as well) between the level of U.S. defense spending and public support for increasing such spending.[24] The most immediate interpretation of this graph is that the public helped give defense spending a big boost in the early 1980s, then reversed the process; this hardly appears to be a passive role for public opinion.

These time-trend analyses are arguably the best quantitative method for evaluating whether there is a possible cause-and-effect type of correlation between opinion and policy. But good time series data like those shown in Figures 9.1a, 9.1b, and 9.2 have not been widely available, so that other data typically from only one or two time points were analyzed in the case of the majoritarian (Monroe) and covariational congruence (Page and Shapiro) studies described above.

Another common statistical method that has been used to compare public opinion and indicators of policymaking or related behavior is shown in

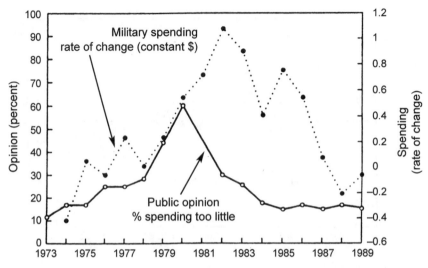

FIGURE 9.2   Opinion-Policy Relationship: Defense Spending. SOURCE: Robert Y. Shapiro and Benjamin I. Page, "Foreign Policy and Public Opinion," in David A. Deese, ed., *The New Politics of American Foreign Policy* (New York: St. Martin's Press, 1994), figure 10-7, p. 231. Copyright 1993 by St. Martin's Press, Inc. Reproduced by permission of St. Martin's Press, Inc.

Response in the figure is to the following: QUESTION: (NORC-GSS): "Are we spending too much, too little, or about the right amount on ... the military, armaments, and national defense?" Defense spending data were obtained from *The Budget of the United States* and were deflated.

Figure 9.3 and described further in Box 9.1. This is a method that can be used for comparing data for different geographic units such as legislative districts or states or even different countries at the same point in time. These are "cross-sectional" data, in contrast to time series data. (Similarly, when we study data from a single public opinion survey, we are comparing the responses of different people representing a "cross-section" of the American public at a single time point.) In time series analysis of the relationship between public opinion and policy, we compare the same unit—the country as a whole, in the case of Figures 9.1a, 9.1b, and 9.2—at several time points to see how policy changes and opinion changes are related.

In contrast, Figure 9.3 is an illustration of cross-sectional data analysis. For purposes of explaining this method clearly, Figure 9.3 presents hypothetical data. Here, we can examine any variation in policymaking activity by comparing one congressional district with a certain level of constituency support for a policy to another district with a different level of public support, to see if congressional representatives' voting records differ in ways consistent with responsiveness. That is, if constituency opinion is more sup-

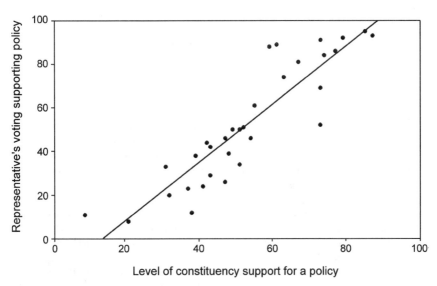

FIGURE 9.3   Relationship Between District Opinion and Congressional Voting

portive of a policy in District A than District B and if representatives were responsive, we would expect District A's representative to be more supportive of the policy than District B's. This is in fact the case we present in Figure 9.3. If such differences were widely prevalent, then we would see the upward sloping pattern of districts also shown in Figure 9.3. We see that the more supportive public opinion is in a congressional district, the more supportive the voting record of the representative in Congress. Using this comparative method, for which there are ways of calculating statistical correlations, we can study public opinion and policymaking across states, counties, cities, regions, or even countries. If we find no upward or downward slope (that is, if a flat line fits the data better than any other), then policymaking would be unrelated to opinion; if the slope were downward ("negative," not "positive"), we would see that policymaking is consistently the opposite of what citizens in the units want (see Box 9.1).

The reason for presenting the illustration in Figure 9.3 is that the first classic study of representation of pubic opinion used this method to study representation in Congress. In addition, this method has been used extensively to study the effect of public opinion on policymaking by state governments in the United States.

The case of representation in Congress does not allow us to examine the actual enactment of policies per se but rather to observe a political mechanism or process that "links" public opinion and policy. The pathbreaking Warren Miller and Donald Stokes study of 1963, "Constituency Representation in

Box 9.1   "Scatter Plot" and Statistical Correlation

In this chapter, we cite studies that examined the relationship between public opinion and policy by explicitly or implicitly drawing on "scatter plots" and statistical correlations of the sort shown in the graphs that follow. In these scatter plots, each point on the graph represents a unit such as a congressional district, a state, or a policy issue. In our first example, each point represents data plotted for congressional districts. The horizontal axis (X-axis) is the level of public or constituent support in a district for some policy such as economic welfare or civil rights; the vertical axis (Y-axis) is a congressional representative's roll-call voting record or score supporting the corresponding policy in question.

Graph A shows a "positive correlation," in which the points cluster close to a line sloping upward representing a positive correlation; that is, in districts in which there is a high level of public support for a policy, the district's congressional representative has a more supportive voting score than representatives in districts where there is less public support for the policy. Graph B shows a "negative correlation," in which the points cluster close to a line sloping downward. Graph C shows the case of "no correlation," in which the points do not cluster around either an upward or a downward sloping line but where a horizontal line fits best. In this case, districts with high levels of public support for a policy do not tend to have congressional representatives who disproportionately favor or oppose the policy.

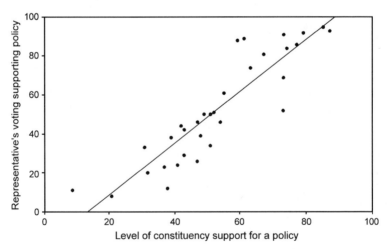

A. Positive Relationship Between District Opinion and Congressional Voting
  NOTE: Hypothetical data.

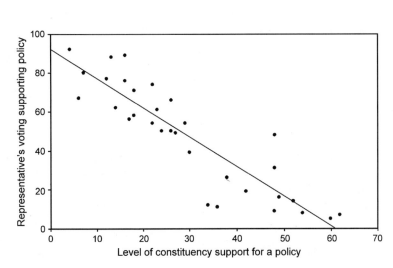

B. Negative Relationship Between District Opinion and Congressional Voting
NOTE: Hypothetical data.

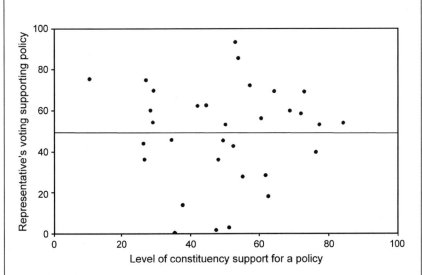

C. No Relationship Between District Opinion and Congressional Voting
NOTE: Hypothetical data.

Congress," used this correlational method to examine both the relationship between public opinion and roll-call voting in Congress and also the processes and linkages by which public opinion was perceived and consequently influenced voting by individual legislators.[25] Miller and Stokes found modest correlations of the sort (though not so well-defined) shown in the scatter plot in Figure 9.3. It was clearly the case that the votes cast by legislators were more supportive of a policy when a greater proportion of the public in their districts favored that policy. Miller and Stokes found a greater correlation (which would be shown by a steeper line and by the points on the scatter plot falling closer to the line) for the highly salient civil rights issues of the 1950s than for economic issues. The correlation was least for foreign policy (a less steep line, with points falling further away from it), which was less salient than civil rights and economic issues at the time. This kind of domestic–foreign policy distinction has long been debated. The difference between foreign and domestic policies is largely in their relative salience and complexity and in the speed with which important events affect both mass and elite opinion and the main policymakers involved. The White House is expected to act first in the case of many foreign policy and most national security issues, with Congress weighing in subsequently, so that the linkages between district level public opinion and the behavior of individual members of Congress may be weaker on foreign policy than domestic issues.

Later studies of constituency representation using the Miller and Stokes methodology found similar and stronger patterns of constituency representation. Interestingly, this did not necessarily indicate an increase in responsiveness but, rather, less measurement error than in Miller and Stokes's original data. The cause of measurement error was not only the small sample sizes (numbers of respondents) from the selected congressional districts but the fact that the sampling method used did not guarantee representative samples within each district.[26]

The method of statistical correlation illustrated in Figure 9.3 has also been used in interesting and informative ways to study specific policies across U.S. states. In a wide range of studies, noticeable correlations between state policies and various indicators of state-level public opinion have been reported. In such studies, good measures of public opinion have been hard to come by, since there have been few national surveys with samples large enough to even approximate state-level public opinion. Some innovative studies provide good illustrations. Using some large Gallup poll samples from the mid-1930s, Robert Erikson in 1976 cleverly showed a relationship between state public opinion and policy in the cases of the enactment of *child labor laws* (some states had them and others did not, until national legislation settled the issue) and of *allowing women to serve on juries* (some states did not allow this, despite the fact that women by then had the right to vote).[27]

On a more visible contemporary issue, Figure 9.4 shows Matthew Wetstein's findings for the issue of abortion in 1988, for which states have had some discretion with respect to the restrictiveness of regulations.[28] This and Wetstein's other analyses, as well as a similarly apt study by Malcolm Goggin and Christopher Wlezien,[29] showed that public opinion had some effect on states' policies concerning abortion. The correlation shown is no more than modest, which has been fairly typical for studies of the opinion-policy connection at the state level. The points for each state cluster around an expected downward sloping line, representing a negative correlation, since a high level of support for permitting legal abortions is associated with a state having fewer procedural restrictions on abortions. One reason for the weakness of the relationship may be the result of error in measuring state-level public opinion (due to small and not ideally representative samples, as in the Miller and Stokes study, as well as errors due to survey question wording). But it is also quite possible that states are limited in their responsiveness, issue by issue, to public opinion. State-level policies may not be particularly salient (though abortion may be atypical in this regard), and often the issues involved may not be perceived and associated with state government action alone, compared to national issues such as abortion that have been widely covered in the press. State policymaking may be affected heavily by organized groups and other influences described earlier.

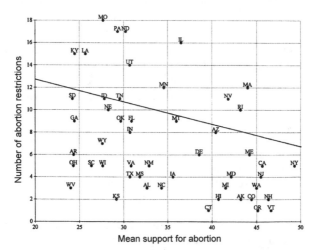

FIGURE 9.4   Abortion Policy Restrictions and Support for Abortion in the States, 1988. SOURCE: M. E. Weinstein, *Abortion Rates in the United States: The Influence of Opinion and Policy* (Albany: State University of New York Press, 1996), figure 10, p. 89.

Responsiveness to Specific Issues Versus Public Mood or Ideology

One question that these studies of specific issues raise is whether policymakers respond to public opinion issue by issue or whether they respond to a more general sense of public sentiment. In terms of the behavioral process at work by which political leaders learn about and respond to public opinion, we need to ask whether they do so one issue at a time or whether they try to get a more general sense of the "mood" of the public. Responsiveness to specific issues is very plausible for the most salient issues, about which policymakers are likely to receive some clear indications of the public stance. But for other policy questions or for a range of issues toward which opinions represent broad liberal to moderate to conservative moods, policymakers are less likely to be concerned with opinions on each issue separately. A general sense of liberalism or conservatism may be sufficient.

The appeal of focusing on the public mood is that this is what leaders may be more likely to sense if they do not have other detailed information about public opinion on specific issues. Some political leaders may not think or perceive that the public has identifiable and specific attitudes and opinions on many—or even any—issues. Both political leaders and citizens may use ideology as a shortcut in making judgments about issues and about where others stand on them (see the discussion in Chapter 8; but as we will see below, political leaders are more likely now than in the past to have information about particular attitudes and opinions based on polls and other information and analyses). Just as journalists and political leaders themselves typically talk about political issues, so Democrats define liberal stances and Republicans describe conservative positions on economic and social issues.

Recent studies of the effect of the "public mood" in comparing both state and national public opinion and policymaking bear out yet another observation by V. O. Key Jr. on how broad public mood and government action matter most:

> Parallelism between action and opinion tends not to be precise in matters of detail; it prevails rather with respect to broad purpose. And in the correlation of purpose and action time lags may occur between the crystallization of a sense of mass purpose and its fulfillment in public action. Yet in the long run majority purpose and public action tend to be brought into harmony.[30]

The studies of the public mood or liberal-conservative ideology have shown clear and pronounced effects of public opinion on policymaking. These studies have examined the effect of liberal-conservative mood on state policymaking and on trends in national policymaking. They have used innovative and persuasive measures of the degree of the public's ideological liberalism or conservatism.

Figure 9.5, taken from Robert Erikson, Gerald Wright, and John McIver's 1993 study, *Statehouse Democracy*,[31] shows a strong correlation between states' opinions and policy liberalism. State-level opinion was measured by combining responses to a question about self-identified liberalism (survey respondents were asked whether they consider themselves "liberal," "conservative," or "moderate") from many years of the CBS News/*New York Times* polls. The overall responses for individual states were compared with different policies and a combined policy measure. The systematic variations that are apparent in state-level opinions and policies are suggestive, indeed, of how the "devolution" of welfare and other policies from the national government in Washington to the states in the 1990s may play out, as even greater reliance occurs on the states that have been expected to act as policy innovators and as "laboratories" for policy experimentation.[32]

Although the *Statehouse Democracy* results are impressive, in some ways more striking and important is the 1995 study by James Stimson, Michael MacKuen, and Robert Erikson on dynamic representation at the national level.[33] Using a measure developed earlier by Stimson of public mood that combined numerous issue-specific opinion trends over time (thus showing that there has been an identifiable public mood),[34] "Dynamic Representation" shows how liberal mood and policymaking by different national institutions and actors track each other over time in a way indicating long-term policy responsiveness to opinion. These basic trends are shown in Figure 9.6. Different institutions have different political dynamics, with

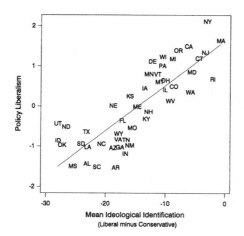

FIGURE 9.5   State Policy and Public Opinion. SOURCE: R. S. Erikson, G. C. Wright, and J. P. McIver, *Statehouse Democracy: Public Opinion and Policy in the American States* (New York: Cambridge University Press, 1993), figure 4.2, p. 79.

Public Opinion over Time: Domestic Policy Mood, 1956-1993

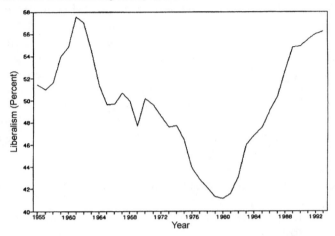

Indicators of Public Policy Change in Four Parts of American Government (Three Year Moving Averages)

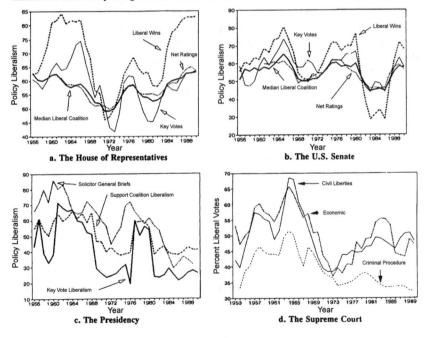

FIGURE 9.6 Public Mood (Liberalism) and Public Policy Change. SOURCE: J. A. Stimson, M. B. MacKuen, and R. S. Erikson, "Dynamic Representation," *American Political Science Review* 89:549, 551.

trends in policymaking by the House of Representatives looking most like trends in the public opinion. You might pause for a moment and think about why this would be the expected result. Similar cyclical patterns in all institutions provide significant support for responsiveness being substantially connected to policymakers' sensitivity to a general public mood.[35] There was increasing opinion and policy liberalism into the 1960s, declining liberalism into the early 1980s, followed by some increasing liberalism. This responsiveness to general ideological shifts does not, of course, preclude responsiveness to salient policies on an issue-by-issue basis, since not all opinion trends track in complete synchronization with the public's overall ideological mood.[36] In the mid-1990s, for example (not shown in Figure 9.6), welfare reform can be interpreted as a response to a conservative shift in opinion since 1992,[37] but the passage of the minimum wage increase and incremental health care reform can be associated with liberal opinions on these particular issues. The point here is that policy is not completely explained by liberal or conservative mood.

Having reviewed the evidence, what do we conclude overall about the relationship between public opinion and policy? On balance, though it is hardly a social scientific law that government policies consistently (policy by policy) reflect public opinion, government policymaking in the United States has reflected ideological shifts in public opinion and also, noticeably, "what the people want in those instances where the public cares enough about an issue to make its wishes known."[38]

A Further Look at Linkages: Parties, Polling, and In-Depth Case Studies

The sections above describe striking patterns of correlations between public opinion and policies. But this evidence is in most respects still circumstantial, since the *cause and effect linkage processes* are not fully traced, although some have been mentioned. In particular, in social science language, the analysis has focused on only opinion and policy variables. Certainly, we need to look at other variables that could affect both public opinion and policy to avoid attributing an influence to public opinion when some other causal influence may actually be at work. In addition the relationships that are based on cross-sectional data, in contrast to time series evidence, do not allow us to observe which moved first—opinion or policy. This leaves the direction of any causal effect in doubt. That is, the correlation between opinion and policy could represent the effect of *policy* on *opinion*, a situation in which the public ratifies or just goes along with government-enacted policies. To be persuaded that opinion is affecting policy requires evidence concerning processes that solidly link public opinion to subsequent policy decisions.

TABLE 9.4   Convention Delegates to the 1996 Party Conventions: How They Compare on Issues

	Democratic Delegates (%)	Democratic Voters (%)	Republican Voters (%)	Republican Delegates (%)
Scope of government				
Government should do more to:				
Solve the nation's problems	76	53	20	4
Regulate the environment and safety practices of business	60	66	37	4
Promote traditional values	27	41	44	56
Social Issues				
Abortion should be permitted in all cases	61	30	22	11
Favor a nationwide ban on assault weapons	91	80	62	34
Necessary to have laws to protect racial minorities	88	62	39	30
Affirmative action programs should be continued	81	59	28	9
Organized prayer should be permitted in public schools	20	66	69	57
International				
Trade restrictions necessary to protect domestic industries	54	65	56	31
Children of illegal immigrants should be allowed to attend public school	79	63	46	26

SOURCE: *New York Times*, August 26, 1996, p. A12.

If we take electoral motivation as the critical driving force that pressures political leaders to respond to public opinion, one point of consensus can be found in the research on the opinion-policy linkage: Political parties, as we alluded to earlier, can play a major part in this process. A number of different studies have shown how party activists, leaders, and government officials convey or magnify the preferences of their fellow partisans among the mass public. There is evidence of this in the policy stances of political party delegations to the national conventions for presidential elections and also in the party platforms adopted at these conventions.[39] We also find this in Congress and in American state legislatures, as well as in evidence for Western Europe.[40]

In particular, we can trace processes by which delegates to party conventions in the United States tend to represent the opinions of party identifiers in the electorate. We also find that party platforms tend to represent the preferences of the mass public. Table 9.4 and Figures 9.7a-e present data for the 1996 Republican and Democratic convention delegates. When we compare across issues—that is, each case plotted in Figures 9.7a-e is an issue, with party voters' opinions on the horizontal axis and party delegates' opinions on

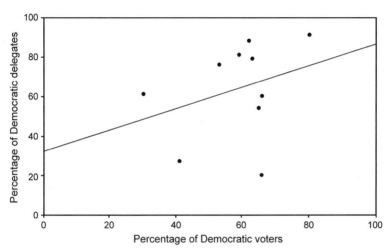

FIGURE 9.7a   Relationship Between Democratic Voters and Democratic Delegates on Issues

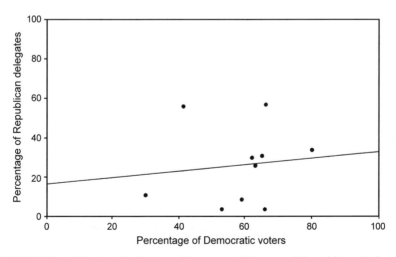

FIGURE 9.7b   Relationship Between Democratic Voters and Republican Delegates on Issues

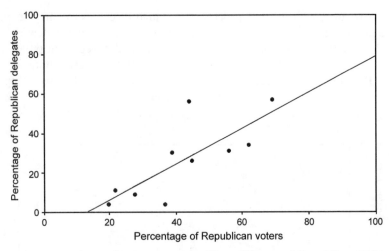

FIGURE 9.7c   Relationship Between Republican Voters and Republican Delegates on Issues

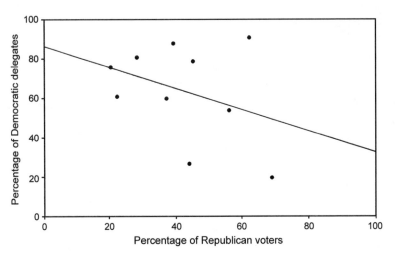

FIGURE 9.7d   Relationship Between Republican Voters and Democratic Delegates on Issues

the vertical axis—we find that voters' opinions are more strongly correlated (positively) with the opinions of their own party's delegates than with those of the other party. The opinions of each parties' delegations are negatively correlated (downward sloping line) with those of the other party. Therefore, the party delegates magnify existing opinion differences in the electorate, in a sense representing them by overrepresenting them.

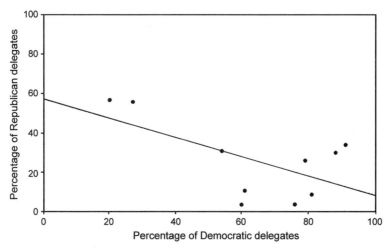

FIGURE 9.7e   Relationship Between Democratic Delegates and Republican Delegates on Issues

As part of this linkage process or as part of a separate process by which American political parties attempt to appeal to the broad electorate and not just to their own partisans, parties attempt to appeal to public opinion through their platforms or through the promises their presidential candidate makes and attempts to keep. They do this by following through on the preferences of their partisans on some issues or by moving to the overall center of public opinion.[41]

Table 9.5 presents Alan Monroe's data showing how both parties across the issues he examined tended to adopt party platform pledges that were consistent with majority opinion; this occurred 64 percent of the time for Republican pledges and 74 percent of the time for Democratic Party positions. Although this shows that both parties appear to be sensitive to public opinion, perceptive readers will note that we cannot tell directly from these data whether the Republican and Democratic platform pledges are more responsive to Republican and Democratic Party identifiers, respectively, within the public.

The data in Tables 9.4 and 9.5 and Figures 9.7a-e concerning the behavior of political parties and their activist delegates also fit in well with another development. As parties have remained weak in the electorate, there is the possibility that the frequency of opinion-policy congruence has declined since the 1980s (though, as we will consider below, there are other processes linking public opinion to policymaking that may have become stronger but may not have offset the declining role of parties).

Emphasizing the role of political parties in this way is useful, but politics involves complex processes in which a variety of other influences are at

TABLE 9.5   Majority Opinion and Party Pledges

Party Pledges	Percentage of Majority Opinion Favors		Percentage Consistent
	Change	Status Quo	
Republican			
Change	65	39	64
Status quo	35	61	
Total	100	100	
N	94	44	
Democratic			
Change	79	41	74
Status quo	21	59	
Total	100	100	
N	117	46	

SOURCE: From Alan D. Monroe, "American Party Platforms and Public Opinion," *American Journal of Political Science,* 27 (February 1983), table 5, p. 32. Reprinted by permission of the University of Wisconsin Press.

work at the same time. Additional evidence and analysis are required in order to strengthen any conclusions we wish to make about cause and effect. Even if parties provide an important linkage, there may be other political mechanisms at work. We must look further for other processes that can connect the public to policymakers and policymaking.

Additional evidence and insight comes from historical and in-depth *case study research*. This type of research takes longer to do, requiring archival, interview, and secondary analyses as well as other ways of gathering information that directly allow researchers to track how policymakers learn about and respond to public opinion. The case studies that have been done have helped complement and supplement the wide range of research that has already been described and that has made a strong circumstantial case for a significant effect of public opinion on policymaking in the United States. These include, for example, Lawrence Jacobs's 1993 study of health care policy in Britain (the establishment of its National Health Service after the war) and the United States (the passage of Medicare in 1965).[42] In particular, Jacobs uncovered what has been called a "recoil effect" (see Box 9.2), by which political leaders wound up responding to public opinion despite their original intentions to track public opinion for the purpose of manipulating it.

Among the other case studies that have been done, foreign policy issues—the area of policymaking in which presidents and their administrations may feel less compelled than in domestic policy to follow public opinion—have provided important illustrations of policy responsiveness.

Box 9.2 "Recoil Effect"

This chapter discusses next how American presidents have used opinion polls and other information about public opinion in regular and institutionalized ways, constituting what might be called a "public opinion apparatus." The opinion polling that presidential administrations do is actually part of political campaign and party activity and spending; this is not paid for by the American government.

Lawrence Jacobs studied this increasing attention to public opinion in Great Britain as well as the United States.[1] He traced the history of how public opinion analysis became institutionalized and, in particular, how this attention to public opinion has appeared to backfire or "recoil" in a way that has sometimes led to more democratic policymaking than was actually intended. Jacobs found that this occurred in the establishment of Britain's National Health Service after World War II and in the passage of Medicare in 1965 in the United States. These changes in health care policy were notably responsive to particular values and attitudes of the British and American people.

The way the process of tracking public opinion began in Britain is quite telling. According to Jacobs's research:

> During the war government officials created the first administrative structures to track public opinion systematically. The purpose of building an intelligence gathering capacity was to "provide . . . [an] effective link between the people of the country and the government . . . convey[ing] the thoughts, opinions, and feelings of the public . . . [so that they were] constantly in the minds of administrators." In particular, the Ministry of Information produced two distinct types of data on public opinion: a qualitative survey conducted by the ministry's Home Intelligence Division and a statistical report by its Social Survey Division. Over the course of the war, the focus of intelligence gathering shifted from assessing the effectiveness of government publicity efforts and measuring general "morale" to studying public preferences toward particular government policies, especially as they related to postwar reconstruction.[2]

The creation of the British National Health Service was part of this postwar reconstruction. Further, for the executive branches of the British and later the U.S. government,

> the public opinion apparatus equipped government officials with two capabilities, the ability to *manipulate and to respond* to public opinion. The aspect of the apparatus that was developed first and most extensively was the capacity to conduct public relations campaigns aimed at shaping popular preferences. The second capacity involved gathering intelligence on public opinion; in particular, polling became a central aspect of

(continues)

Box 9.2   *(continued)*

government efforts to gain a regular and reliable grip on public opinion. The development of these two capacities was tied to the struggle for political power and institutional position; the apparatus became integrated into the policymaking process when executive branch officials recognized that it presented opportunities to offset advantages possessed by others, the legislature as well as nongovernmental groups and individuals.

The evolution of the public opinion apparatus had a profound effect on policymakers' perspective toward the public; (and quoting the phrase used by Marjorie Ogilvy-Webb,[3] an authority on public administration in Britain during the period discussed) its *"recoil effect* is greater than its blast."* In striving to have an outward effect on public opinion, the creation of this apparatus has an inward effect; it educated government officials to be aware of and sensitive to public opinion. Thus, while the apparatus originated as an attempt to manipulate popular preferences through public relations campaigns, its development over time increased senior government officials' interest in tracking and responding to public popular preferences. This new outlook among politicians and civil servants involved a shift from a preoccupation with secrecy and seclusion to a recognition of public opinion as an important factor in administrative decision making. (emphasis ours)[4]

---

1. Lawrence R. Jacobs, "The Recoil Effect: Public Opinion and Policy Making in the United States and Britain," *Comparative Politics* 24 (1992):199–217; Lawrence R. Jacobs, *The Health of Nations: Public Opinion and the Making of American and British Health Policy* (Ithaca: Cornell University Press, 1993).

2. Jacobs, "The Recoil Effect," p. 205.

3. Marjorie Ogilvy-Webb, *The Government Explains: A Study of the Information Services: A Report of the Royal Institute of Public Administration* (London: George Allen and Unwin, 1965), p. 196.

4. Jacobs, "The Recoil Effect," p. 200.

Studies of specific foreign policy issues and processes have confirmed that public opinion has mattered in identifiable ways in U.S.-Chinese relations, such as in the admission of China to the United Nations, as we noted earlier;[43] in U.S. policymaking toward the contras in Nicaragua, as we have also discussed;[44] and in foreign policymaking during the Reagan-Bush years, in which one author observed that it was imprudent for policymakers to ignore public opinion.[45]

Further, although specific case studies have been informative, including those of the issues highlighted at the beginning of the chapter,[46] more systematic evidence has come from efforts that synthesize in-depth research in order to unravel historical and current trends in the causal relationship between public opinion and policy. This strategy requires, first, finding trends over time in the extent to which policymakers seek out (or otherwise get information on) public opinion; and, next, determining how political leaders respond to or are otherwise affected by this information. Jacobs did this in the case of health care policy and Thomas Graham did the same for nuclear arms control from the beginning of the Cold War to the 1980s, a period in which he found that more attention was paid to public opinion than political leaders would admit.[47] Philip Powlick found that there has been an increase in serious and responsive attention to public opinion in the State Department.[48] This represented a change in what Bernard Cohen had found earlier: Officials in the State Department had explicitly seen their role as one of shaping public opinion, not responding to it.[49] However, the most recent trend that Powlick found appeared to move back in that direction for the Reagan and Clinton administrations, which tended to place more institutional emphasis in foreign policymaking as leading rather than following public opinion.

Other historical research that has focused on finding out how presidents and others *directly* used information about public opinion has revealed that there is a *reciprocal* relationship between public opinion and policymaking. There is evidence that the government has attempted to lead as well as respond to public opinion. This is consistent with the many correlational studies cited earlier, since most of them had not ruled out that there was also an effect of policy on opinion. These effects need not be mutually exclusive. Clearly, it is necessary to track these relationships and processes over time, in order to see if particular trends or tendencies have been more likely at some times than others.

In this spirit, using archival and other primary sources, some recent research examined the increasing "institutionalization" of public opinion analysis by American presidents, which refers to the establishment and continuation of what can be called a "public opinion apparatus" in each presidential administration. One objective of this work was to see what impact this routine public opinion analysis had on the overall opinion-policy relationship. The opinion-policy process that has evolved is one in which presidents have increasingly, since Kennedy, assembled and analyzed their own information on public opinion. Indeed, political leaders are now far more likely than in the past to have this information, based simply on the widespread availability of polls and analyses of public opinion. Although presidents and politicians had long used unscientific methods to estimate where the public stood on issues, and scientifically gathered public opinion data had found their way into the White House beginning with Roosevelt, only since Kennedy has the entire process been routinized by each president.

The evidence indicates that the driving force for this has been elections, as once in office, presidents strive to be reelected. In the 1960s, presidents started to use their own pollsters and public opinion consultants or staff, with private polls being paid for by the political parties or other non-governmental sources.[50]

Table 9.6 summarizes the extensiveness of private polling by the White House from Kennedy to Nixon. The most important data are the numbers of polls done by Johnson and Nixon during their first terms in office (when they were governing and not also campaigning for reelection), which shows that this polling activity became substantial. It continued to be extensive for later presidents. Our best estimate at this writing is that as of 1996, President Bill Clinton's polling and public opinion analysis is the most extensive of any president. The result of this institutionalization of public opinion analysis is that the White House has become increasingly better positioned than in the past to respond to, or to attempt to lead or manipulate, public opinion.[51]

With respect to the choices faced by presidents Kennedy, Johnson, and Nixon to lead or to follow public opinion, research has found evidence that has shown the following: government responsiveness to public opinion; cases of opinion leadership; and cases of presidents working against public opinion for particular reasons. As might be expected, responsiveness occurred on salient issues, especially those that clearly had potential electoral consequences.[52]

Although Kennedy was the first president to run for office using the services of a publicly known pollster and political consultant—Louis Harris—polling and analysis of public opinion did not become a regular part of White House operations until the Johnson and Nixon administrations. Johnson had available to him information obtained by pollster Oliver

TABLE 9.6 The Number and Distribution of Private Polls During the Kennedy, Johnson, and Nixon Presidencies

	Kennedy	Johnson	Nixon
Total number of private polls	93 (1958–1963)	130 (1963–1968)	233 (1969–1972)
Number of polls during presidential election periods	77 (1958–1960)	48 (Fall 1963– 1964, and 1968)	153 (1972)
Number of polls during governing period	16 (1961–1963)	82 (1965–1967)	80 (1969–1971)

SOURCE: L. R. Jacobs and R. Y. Shapiro, "The Rise of Presidential Polling: The Nixon White House in Historical Perspective," *Public Opinion Quarterly* 59 (1995), table 1, p. 167. Data derived from archival records in the presidential archives of John Kennedy, Lyndon Johnson, and Richard Nixon.

Quayle, and Nixon (privately and through the Republican Party) commissioned full polls devoted to the president's need for particular information. During the Johnson administration, the 1964 election provided an important juncture in how the president used information on public opinion. Concerned about being reelected, Johnson at first tended to respond to the public's wishes, emphasizing the popular desire to pursue disarmament and peace, in sharp contrast to the widely perceived positions of his Republican opponent, Barry Goldwater. Based on his polling reports, Johnson made sure to distinguish himself regarding the use of U.S. military force, including the use of nuclear weapons in Vietnam. But Johnson, like Kennedy before him, attempted to lead rather than respond to the public on the issue of foreign aid. Johnson's apparent strategy of responding to public opinion was particularly pronounced on domestic issues as well. Johnson continued this responsive behavior even after it became clear he would easily defeat Goldwater. He did so for the purpose of solidifying his public support for the purposes of leading the public on his racial and social policy agenda in his new full term as president.[53]

Beginning after the election in 1965, Johnson chose to lead, not follow, the public. His domestic proposals, especially the War on Poverty, had not been demanded by the public, but the public came to support this effort. In the case of foreign policy, the Vietnam War became an issue of extreme contention, and here Johnson had no intention of letting the public influence his actions. There was a clear break in this opinion-policy relationship between 1964 and 1965–1966, with responsiveness declining and leadership increasing from the first to the second period, with Vietnam being the dominant issue in foreign policy. In the end, however, after 1965–1966, the failure to respond to what Johnson knew to be public opinion on particular aspects of the Vietnam War had increasingly adverse effects on his presidency.[54]

The Nixon administration greatly expanded the institutional organization and sophistication of White House–directed polling and public opinion analysis. Despite his claims that political leaders should not be influenced by polls, Nixon and his advisers used polling data to avoid taking unpopular positions and to enhance their ability to lead the public on policies that they wanted to pursue, especially in the area of foreign policy, in which Nixon clearly wanted to leave his historical mark. The archival evidence shows that in struggling with how to deal with the Vietnam War, Nixon responded to public opinion in a manner that explains the relationship between the trends in public opinion and the withdrawal of troops shown in Figure 9.1.[55] Clearly, the Vietnam War was regarded as a most crucial election issue in 1972, even as Nixon maintained a substantial and steady lead over his Democratic opponent, George McGovern, in preelection polls.

The research further shows that the Nixon administration was persistent in tracking public opinion on a wide range of policy and political concerns (especially approval of the president).[56] An important case of both opinion responsiveness and leadership in foreign policy concerned the admission of Communist China to the United Nations, paving the way for the formal recognition of China by the United States. Based on publicly reported and other information about public opinion, Nixon and his advisers could detect the softening of the public's hostility toward Communist China in 1971, making it more receptive to efforts to lead it further in a less belligerent direction. The result was Nixon's trip to China and China's admission to the U.N., which Nixon and his administration did not finalize until there was further public support for it in opinion polls.[57] At the same time, Nixon raised the visibility of this issue in a way that enhanced his and his party's electoral appeal. We find evidence here and in the cases discussed above for presidential responsiveness to public opinion that can be directly associated with actual or anticipated electoral advantages, during a period in U.S. history in which Cold War foreign policies could become major election-year issues.

Is Government Responsiveness to Public Opinion *Democratic?*

Overall, the evidence we have discussed shows that government in the United States is more than minimally responsive to public opinion. The apparent effect of public opinion is more than just a constraint of last resort that is effective only because political leaders and their parties have to face elections. But based on this, do we want to claim that we have largely democratic policymaking in the United States? As we noted in Chapter 7, it is not only democratic governments that pay attention to public opinion. Indeed, as V. O. Key Jr. stated in the very first sentence of his classic *Public Opinion and American Democracy*, "Governments must concern themselves with the opinions of their citizens, if only to provide a basis for repression of disaffection."[58] At this extreme, opinion may then be repressed or forcibly reshaped, so that it comes into line with what a government has done and will do. In this case, the agreement between public opinion and policy that appears can hardly be pronounced "democratic" responsiveness.

But short of this extreme case, which we would expect to find in authoritarian governments, to make judgments about democracy we need to consider both *what* has influenced public opinion and *the quality* of the opinion that has resulted. The quality of the policies that are enacted also matter to the extent that "democracy" involves holding up certain norms and values. Many of us would be reluctant to call "democratic" those policies that violate what we have cherished as fundamental civil liberties and rights (see Chapters 8 and 10). Thus, the lack of government responsiveness on the issue of prayer in public schools and other proposals that might violate constitutional protections may still be interpreted as democratic— that is, consistent with liberal-democratic norms that have been established and supported for all time, even though they might be opposed by the public at a given moment.

As we saw in Chapter 8, the public itself is not omniscient; individuals do not walk around with all the information they need to make judgments about issues that arise and to decide what government should do about it. They depend on information from others, and when it comes to national issues, the public is heavily dependent on political leaders, other elites, organized groups, and others; the positions and ideas and other information these sources have to offer are conveyed to the public through the mass media. The mass media themselves, too, can have some independent impact on public opinion based on what news outlets—depending on the decisions made by reporters, editors, publishers, and others—choose to report about, including the sources they select for news stories and any personal opinions that reporters or editors themselves offer.

What matters here is the quality of the information that is provided and whether the process involved is one that we would call political leadership or education, as opposed to manipulation or deception. Leadership and education are processes that could fit in well with a responsiveness to public opinion that is worthy of being called democracy. If, in one case, the public is influenced by accurate facts and persuasive stances that do not distort reality, so that the public is able to pursue its interests, we would find this very different from a case in which public opinion is influenced by incomplete information, distortions, or outright falsehoods from self-serving elites or other interests, so that the public did not have the best available information to pursue its interests. In the latter case, the quality of public opinion would be problematic and the responsiveness of government to this opinion would not be "democratic."

Clearly, making judgments of this sort is not easy and can be politically charged as well. What is true or false is sometimes not easy to determine. The same holds especially for judging whether information provides a "biased" presentation of reality (what would "unbiased" presentations look like?). But in order to make judgments about whether a policy decision is democratic, we have to wrestle with these questions. Some cases are easier to draw conclusions about than others.

For example, what some now call an infamous case of policy responsiveness involving political manipulation that defied democracy occurred when President Lyndon Johnson marshaled support for escalating U.S. involvement in Vietnam. Johnson initially rallied public support to expand American military involvement in Vietnam by misrepresenting alleged attacks on two ships, the *Maddox* and the *Turner Joy*, off the coast of North Vietnam in 1964. Public support rose for increased military action in Vietnam, and the Johnson administration responded by going to war. Other cases, again subject to further debate, might include observations about how prior to the U.S. entry into World War II, the Roosevelt administrations essentially goaded the Germans to attack American ships that engaged in naval reconnaissance for the British;[59] or how the Bush administration misrepresented American options prior to the start of all-out fighting in the Gulf War against Iraq.[60] Although the validity of these examples may be a subject for debate, it is no accident that they are foreign policy issues: It has been argued that there is danger to democracy in foreign policymaking because the public has fewer competing sources of information available to it (that is, the source is overwhelmingly the government) than in other areas.[61]

Standing in contrast, though also not beyond further debate, is the case of the passage of an increase in the minimum wage in 1996. This had overwhelming public support and might be hailed as a triumph for democracy. For one thing, this was a case in which the public could make an independent judgment that the prior minimum wage of $4.25 per hour was not an adequate living wage for an individual or family. Political leaders and others could echo this through the press. Opponents might claim—and did claim—that the public was being misled and that raising the minimum wage would adversely affect small business and low-end employment. But a good case can be made that these trade-offs were widely acknowledged (the fact that it took so long to pass an increase in the minimum wage is an indication of this), and in the end, the public made value judgments based on the trade-offs and decided that raising the wage would lead to a better outcome for the nation overall.

If we take a more controversial issue, opponents of welfare reform legislation in 1996 might readily claim that the public was misinformed: that Aid to Families with Dependent Children (AFDC) spending was not enormous; that fraud was less rampant than portrayed in the media; and that reforms would in fact have clear adverse effects, so that any government responsiveness to widespread support for reform was hardly democratic. However, to the extent that the public had simply made value trade-offs and concluded—perhaps correctly—that there is substantial uncertainty regarding how to deal with welfare (especially given limited resources), the passage of welfare reform could be considered democratic.

To take this even further, since the quality of public opinion is so central to reaching such normative conclusions about the opinion-policy relationship, we should also not dismiss policymakers' failure to respond to public opinion as undemocratic. There can be cases in which policymakers feel they must make policy decisions that do not have public support (when acting as the "trustees" we described earlier), because they feel (and they think there is evidence that) the public has been misled or manipulated or has not yet become fully informed about a policy at issue. Ideally, such policy decisions should be delayed until the public is more fully engaged in them, but even when this delay does not occur, persuading the public after the fact of the merit of a policy need not be dismissed as undemocratic, that is, only as long as deceit or manipulation has not occurred.

Conclusion

We have covered a lot of new ground in this chapter. Thanks to the expansion of public opinion research, there is much more evidence than ever before to tell us about the relationship between public opinion and policymaking and the workings of democracy. We have offered answers about the basic degree of correspondence or correlation between what the public has wanted and what the government has done. To make judgments about calling this "democracy at work" has required that we interrogate the evidence further in ways that are not simple and straightforward. This may be yet another frustration for students of public opinion.

But in everyday life, we now see a more direct and dynamic role than ever before of public opinion in politics and policymaking. We see this in the reporting of opinion polls and in the continual appeals to public opinion (often referred to as "going public")—including all types of political advertising—that are made through the mass media by presidents, members of Congress, political parties, organized groups, and others interested and active in the political process.[62] Some see this as a bad development that detracts from institutional consultations and deliberations among political leaders and experts who may be best able to formulate effective policies. Others see this as bad because it gives the public itself a false sense that what government does is democratic, even as the public is then manipulated in ways that do not necessarily serve the public's interests. Short of regulating public discourse, political leaders will have to adjust to this more visible role for the public (although the "recoil effect" cited earlier may lead elites unknowingly to respond to public opinion in their attempts to control it!).

Here, as in other areas of research, there is still some uncertainty in the findings and evidence we have reported, as well as in what to make of them, concerning how much actual public control of policymaking there is. Further archival research and interviews with former policymakers and government officials (when they are free to reflect honestly) should help decrease the uncertainty, along with further tracking of trends in public opinion and policymaking. Whether we conclude that the public only loosely constrains policymaking or that the public at times forcefully pushes the government to act in different ways, there is evidence that government policies are responsive to public opinion in the United States.

Whether there is "enough" or "too much" responsiveness and whether we should call this responsiveness to public opinion "democratic" depends on the quality of public opinion and the information received and on the independent capabilities of policymakers. Even with the optimism that can be found in the assessment of the public's competence in Chapter 8, it is still of great importance to try to improve the public's level of attention to politics and its level of knowledge about policy issues, so that the citizenry can constrain and influence its leaders in ways that can ultimately improve government policies and American democracy.

Notes

1. V. O. Key Jr., *Public Opinion and American Democracy* (New York: Alfred A. Knopf, 1961). See also Harold D. Lasswell, *Democracy Through Public Opinion* (Menasha, WI: Banta, 1941).

2. Key, *Public Opinion and American Democracy*, p. 7; see also Benjamin Ginsberg, *The Captive Public: How Mass Opinion Promotes State Power* (New York: Basic Books, 1986). For related discussion about mass opinion and government, see Susan Herbst, *Numbered Voices: How Opinion Polling Has Shaped American Politics* (Chicago: University of Chicago Press, 1992), and James A. Morone, *The Democratic Wish: Popular Participation and the Limits of American Government* (New York: Basic Books, 1990).

3. See Amy Fried, *Muffled Echoes: Oliver North and the Politics of Public Opinion* (New York: Columbia University Press, 1997).

4. On some of these issues and other related research, see Paul Burstein, *Discrimination, Jobs, and Politics: The Struggle for Equal Employment Opportunity in the United States Since the New Deal* (Chicago: University of Chicago Press, 1985); Benjamin I. Page and Robert Y. Shapiro, "Effects of Public Opinion on Policy," *American Political Science Review* 77 (1983):175–190; and Benjamin I. Page and Robert Y. Shapiro, *The Rational Public: Fifty Years of Trends in Americans' Policy Preferences* (Chicago: University of Chicago Press, 1992).

5. R. Kent Weaver, Robert Y. Shapiro, and Lawrence R. Jacobs, "The Polls—Trends: Welfare," *Public Opinion Quarterly* 59 (1995):606–627.

6. See James H. Kuklinski, "Representation and Elections: A Policy Analysis," *American Political Science Review* 72 (1978):165–177; and Edward R. Tufte, *Political Control of the Economy* (Princeton: Princeton University Press, 1978).

7. On the "sharing model," see Robert S. Erikson and Kent L. Tedin, *American Public Opinion*, 5th ed. (Boston: Allyn and Bacon, 1995), pp. 18–19, 281–286.

8. See James S. Fishkin, *The Voice of the People: Public Opinion and Democracy* (New Haven: Yale University Press, 1995).

9. See John C. Wahlke, Heinx Eulau, William Buchanan, and Leroy C. Ferguson, *The Legislative System* (New York: Wiley, 1962).

10. See Michael X. Delli Carpini and Bruce Williams, "The Method Is the Message: Focus Groups as a Means of Social, Psychological, and Political Inquiry," in Michael X. Delli Carpini, Leonie Huddy, and Robert Y. Shapiro, eds., *Research in*

Micropolitics, vol. 4, *New Directions in Political Psychology* (Greenwich, CT: JAI Press, 1994).

11. See David B. Truman, *The Governmental Process: Political Interests and Public Opinion,* 2d ed. (New York: Alfred A. Knopf, 1971); and Robert A. Dahl, *Who Governs: Democracy and Power in an American City* (New Haven: Yale University Press, 1961).

12. See Mancur Olson, *The Logic of Collective Action: Public Goods and the Theory of Groups* (Cambridge: Harvard University Press, 1965).

13. On "latent opinion" or latent interests, see Truman, *The Governmental Process,* and Key, *Public Opinion and American Democracy.*

14. See E. E. Schattschneider, *The Semi-Sovereign People* (Hinsdale, IL: Dryden Press, 1960); and Kay Lehman Schlozman and John T. Tierney, *Organized Interests and American Democracy* (New York: Harper and Row, 1986).

15. See C. Wright Mills, *The Power Elite* (New York: Oxford University Press, 1956); Floyd Hunter, *Community Power Structure* (Chapel Hill: University of North Carolina Press, 1953).

16. See Grant McConnell, *Private Power and American Democracy* (New York: Random House, 1966).

17. See Schattschneider, *The Semi-Sovereign People;* and Peter Bachrach and Morton S. Baratz, "Two Faces of Power," *American Political Science Review* 56 (1962):947–952, and "Decisions and Nondecisions: An Analytical Framework," *American Political Science Review* 57 (1963):632–642.

18. For example, see Charles E. Lindblom, *Politics and Markets: The World's Political-Economic Systems* (New York: Basic Books, 1977).

19. Key, *Public Opinion and American Democracy,* p. 97.

20. Donald J. Devine, *The Attentive Public: Polyarchical Democracy* (Chicago: Rand McNally and Company, 1970); Robert Weissberg, *Public Opinion and Popular Government,* (Englewood Cliffs, NJ: Prentice-Hall, 1976); Alan D. Monroe, "American Party Platforms and Public Opinion," *American Journal of Political Science* 27 (1983):27–42.

21. Compare Devine, *Attentive Public;* Weissberg, *Public Opinion and Popular Government;* Joel E. Brooks, "Democratic Frustration in the Anglo-American Polities: A Quantification of Inconsistency Between Mass Public Opinion and Public Policy," *Western Political Science Quarterly* 38 (1985):250–261, and "The Opinion-Policy Nexus in France: Do Institutions and Ideology Make a Difference?" *Journal of Politics* 49 (1987):465–480.

22. Benjamin I. Page and Robert Y. Shapiro, "Effects of Public Opinion on Policy," *American Political Science Review* 77 (1983):175–190; Robert Y. Shapiro, *The Dynamics of Public Opinion and Public Policy,* Ph.D. diss., University of Chicago, 1982.

23. See also Thomas W. Graham, "Public Opinion and U.S. Foreign Policy Decision Making," in David A. Deese, ed., *The New Politics of American Foreign Policy* (New York: St. Martin's Press, 1994).

24. See Thomas Hartley and Bruce Russett, "Public Opinion and the Common Defense: Who Governs Military Spending in the United States?" *American Political Science Review* 86 (1992):905–915; Christopher Wlezien, "The Public as Thermostat: Dynamics of Preferences for Spending," *American Journal of Political Science*

39 (1995):981–1000, and "Dynamics of Representation: The Case of U.S. Spending on Defence," *British Journal of Political Science* 26 (1996):81–103; Charles W. Ostrom Jr. and Robin F. Marra, "U.S. Defense Spending and the Soviet Estimate," *American Political Science Review* 80 (1986):819–841; Larry M. Bartels, "Constituency Opinion and Congressional Policy Making: The Reagan Defense Buildup," *American Political Science Review* 85 (1991):457–474.

25. Warren E. Miller and Donald E. Stokes, "Constituency Influence in Congress," *American Political Science Review* 57 (1963):45–56.

26. See Robert S. Erikson, "Constituency Opinion and Congressional Behavior: A Reexamination of the Miller-Stokes Data," *American Journal of Political Science* 22 (1978):511–535; Benjamin I. Page, Robert Y. Shapiro, Paul W. Gronke, and Robert M. Rosenberg, 1984. "Constituency, Party, and Representation in Congress," *Public Opinion Quarterly* 48 (1984):741–756.

27. Robert S. Erikson, "The Relationship Between Public Opinion and State Policy: A New Look Based on Some Forgotten Data," *American Journal of Political Science* 20 (1976):25–36.

28. Matthew E. Wetstein, *Abortion Rates in the United States: The Influence of Opinion and Policy* (Albany: State University of New York Press, 1996).

29. Malcolm L. Goggin and Christopher Wlezien, "Abortion Opinion and Policy in the American States," in Malcolm Goggin, ed., *Understanding the New Politics of Abortion* (Newbury Park, CA: Sage Publications, 1993).

30. Key, *Public Opinion and American Democracy*, p. 553.

31. Robert S. Erikson, Gerald C. Wright, and John P. McIver, *Statehouse Democracy: Public Opinion and Policy in the American States* (New York: Cambridge University Press, 1993).

32. David Osborne, *Laboratories of Democracy: A New Brand of Governors Creates Models for National Growth* (Cambridge: Harvard Business School, 1988).

33. James A. Stimson, Michael B. MacKuen, and Robert S. Erikson, "Dynamic Representation," *American Political Science Review* 89 (1995):543–565.

34. James A. Stimson, *Public Opinion in America: Moods, Cycles, and Swings* (Boulder: Westview Press, 1991).

35. For a review of studies of the responsiveness to public opinion by different institutions and levels of government, see Robert Y. Shapiro and Lawrence R. Jacobs, "The Relationship Between Public Opinion and Public Policy: A Review," in Samuel Long, ed., *Political Behavior Annual,* vol. 2 (Boulder: Westview Press, 1989).

36. See Page and Shapiro, *Rational Public.*

37. See Weaver, Shapiro, and Jacobs, "Poll Trends: Welfare."

38. Paul Burstein, "The Sociology of Democratic Politics and Government," in Ralph H. Turner and James F. Short, eds., *Annual Review of Sociology,* vol. 7 (Palo Alto, CA: Annual Reviews, 1981), p. 295.

39. Alan D. Monroe, "American Party Platforms and Public Opinion," *American Journal of Political Science* 27 (1983):27–42.

40. See Erikson, Wright, and McIver, *Statehouse Democracy*; Page et al., "Constituency, Party, and Representation in Congress"; Russell J. Dalton, *Citizen Politics: Public Opinion and Political Parties in Advanced Western Democracies* (Chatham, NJ: Chatham House Publishers, 1996).

41. See Anthony Downs, *An Economic Theory of Democracy* (New York: Harper and Row, 1957); Benjamin I. Page, *Choices and Echoes in Presidential Elections: Rational Man and Electoral Democracy* (Chicago: University of Chicago Press, 1978); Gerald M. Pomper with Susan S. Lederman, *Elections in America: Control and Influence in Democratic Politics*, 2d ed. (New York: Dodd, Mead, 1980); Kelly D. Patterson, *Political Parties and the Maintenance of Liberal Democracy* (New York: Columbia University Press, 1996); Jeff Fishel, *Presidents and Promises: From Campaign Pledge to Presidential Performance* (Washington, DC: Congressional Quarterly Press, 1985).

42. Lawrence R. Jacobs, *The Health of Nations: Public Opinion and the Making of American and British Health Policy* (Ithaca: Cornell University Press, 1993).

43. Compare Leonard A. Kusnitz, *Public Opinion and Foreign Policy: America's China Policy, 1949–1979* (Westport, CT: Greenwood Press, 1984).

44. See Richard Sobel, ed., *Public Opinion in U.S. Foreign Policy: The Controversy over Contra Aid* (Lanham, MD: Rowman and Littlefield, 1993).

45. See Ronald H. Hinckley, *People, Polls, and Policymakers: American Public Opinion and National Security* (New York: Lexington Books, 1992).

46. On employment and civil rights, see Paul Burstein, *Discrimination, Jobs, and Politics: The Struggle for Equal Employment Opportunity in the United States Since the New Deal* (Chicago: University of Chicago Press, 1985).

47. Jacobs, *Health of Nations*; Thomas W. Graham, *The Politics of Failure: Strategic Nuclear Arms Control, Public Opinion, and Domestic Politics in the United States, 1945–1985*, Ph.D. diss., Massachusetts Institute of Technology, 1989, and "Public Opinion and U.S. Foreign Policy Decision Making," in David A. Deese, ed., *New Politics of American Foreign Policy*.

48. Philip J. Powlick, "The Attitudinal Bases of Responsiveness to Public Opinion Among American Foreign Policy Officials," *Journal of Conflict Resolution* 35 (1991):611–641, and "Public Opinion in the Foreign Policy Process: An Attitudinal and Institutional Comparison of the Reagan and Clinton Administrations," paper presented at the Annual Meeting of the American Political Science Association, Chicago, 1995.

49. Bernard C. Cohen, *The Public's Impact of Foreign Policy* (Boston: Little, Brown, 1973).

50. Some of the history of this is described in Lawrence R. Jacobs and Robert Y. Shapiro, "The Rise of Presidential Polling: The Nixon White House in Historical Perspective," *Public Opinion Quarterly* 59:163–165; Diane J. Heith, *Polling for Policy: Public Opinion and Presidential Leadership*, Ph.D. diss., Brown University, 1997; Robert Eisinger, "Presidential Polling in the 1950s and Beyond," paper presented at the Annual Meeting of the American Political Science Association, New York City, 1994.

51. See John G. Geer, *From Tea Leaves to Opinion Polls: A Theory of Democratic Leadership* (New York: Columbia University Press, 1996).

52. See Lawrence R. Jacobs and Robert Y. Shapiro, "Public Decisions, Private Polls: John F. Kennedy's Presidency," paper presented at the Annual Meeting of the Midwest Political Science Association, Chicago, 1992; "The Public Presidency, Private Polls, and Policymaking: Lyndon Johnson," paper presented at the Annual Meeting of the American Political Science Association, Washington, DC, 1993;

"Issues, Candidate Image, and Priming: The Use of Private Polls in Kennedy's 1960 Presidential Campaign," *American Political Science Review* 88 (1994):527–540; "Lyndon Johnson, Vietnam, and Public Opinion: Rethinking Realists' Theory of Leadership," paper presented at the Annual Meeting of the Midwest Political Science Association, Chicago, 1994; and especially the major theoretical analysis in John G. Geer, *From Tea Leaves to Opinion Polls: A Theory of Democratic Leadership* (New York: Columbia University Press, 1996).

53. Lawrence R. Jacobs and Robert Y. Shapiro, "The Public Presidency, Private Polls, and Policymaking: Lyndon Johnson," paper presented at the Annual Meeting of the American Political Science Association, Washington, DC, 1993.

54. Jacobs and Shapiro, "The Public Presidency, Private Polls, and Policymaking: Lyndon Johnson," and "Lyndon Johnson, Vietnam, and Public Opinion: Rethinking Realists' Theory of Leadership."

55. For a detailed account of this, see Andrew Z. Katz, "Public Opinion and Foreign Policy: The Nixon Administration and the Pursuit of Peace with Honor in Vietnam," *Presidential Studies Quarterly* 27 (1997):496–513.

56. Lawrence R. Jacobs and Robert Y. Shapiro, "The Rise of Presidential Polling," and "Presidential Manipulation of Polls and Public Opinion: The Nixon Administration and the Pollsters," *Political Science Quarterly* 110 (1995–96): 519–538.

57. See Page and Shapiro, *Rational Public*, pp. 242–251; compare Kusnitz, *Public Opinion and Foreign Policy*.

58. Key, *Public Opinion and American Democracy*, p. 3.

59. On these and other ostensible cases of manipulation of public opinion, see Page and Shapiro, *Rational Public*, chap. 9.

60. On political communication during the Gulf War, see the essays in W. Lance Bennett and David L. Paletz, eds., *Taken by Storm: The Media, Public Opinion, and U.S. Foreign Policy in the Gulf War* (Chicago: University of Chicago Press, 1994), and Benjamin I. Page, *Who Deliberates? Mass Media in Modern Democracy* (Chicago: University of Chicago Press, 1996).

61. See Page and Shapiro, *Rational Public*, chaps. 5, 6, 9.

62. In the case of presidents, see Samuel Kernell, *Going Public: New Strategies of Presidential Leadership,* 3d ed. (Washington, DC: Congressional Quarterly Press, 1997).

Chapter Ten

The Content of Our Attitudes: Public Opinion in the Contemporary United States

JILL A. EDY

Today, modern opinion polling technologies are available to scholars, political leaders, journalists, market researchers, and a host of others. Public opinion, as measured by such polls, is monitored continuously. "Instant" polls measure public opinion within hours of major events such as the outbreak of the Gulf War, the announcement of a verdict in O. J. Simpson's trial, or the conclusion of a presidential debate. Tracking polls, taken during political campaigns, attempt to ascertain public attitudes about a political candidate as they change over the course of the campaign. Marketing studies explore consumer attitudes and behavior, documenting lifestyle changes as well as providing business with valuable information about what the public wants, or thinks it wants. Scholarly studies of public opinion attempt to develop theories to explain consistency and change in public opinion as well as to discern the effects of public opinion on other social processes.

In this chapter, we will consider some recent public opinion trends relevant to the theories we have discussed in earlier chapters. First, we will look at how some important American social norms have changed over the past thirty years or more. Next, we will turn our attention to the concept of considered public opinion as it is expressed in public tolerance for diversity. Finally, we will consider the way people feel about their government and the public's own beliefs about the linkages that connect citizen opinion to state policy.

In order to assess public opinion, we turn to survey research. Thus, we should keep in mind the limitations of surveys, both as a methodology and as a means of conceptualizing public opinion. Many of these imperfections have special implications for measuring public opinion about social norms and public policy. We also need to keep in mind what we have learned about people's limitations and the ways those limits affect opinion formation.

The content of current public opinion is in large part determined by pollsters themselves. This is not to say that all polls are biased. However, it is ultimately the pollsters who decide what to ask the public about. Pollsters determine which of hundreds, even thousands, of public issues are worth ascertaining public opinion on. Their choices may be influenced by many things. They may conduct a survey to gauge public opinion on an issue that has received a great deal of media attention. Polling agencies associated with news organizations may survey citizens in order to ascertain public opinion about an issue about which they plan to produce a story. In 1997, ABC News conducted a poll on teenage drug use and communication between teens and parents about drugs and presented the results as part of a weeklong series about teens and drugs. Polling firms that work for political candidates may be searching for issues to highlight during the campaign because their candidate takes the more popular stand on them. In other words, polls are not always conducted to determine what the public wants so that the democratic government can respond.

Most of the data we report in this chapter was produced by the National Opinion Research Center's (NORC) General Social Survey (GSS). The GSS is a random sample survey of U.S. adults that has been administered nearly annually since 1972. It contains questions about a large number of social issues and frequently repeats the same questions year after year so that an analysis of trends in public opinion is possible. Where we use GSS data, the percentages reported for each year are based on a sample of at least 800 cases; sometimes, as many as 1,500 people responded to the question. The data on public attitudes about government come from the National Election Studies (NES), surveys taken every even-numbered year since the late 1950s. The NES surveys also use large random samples and repeat the same questions in order to measure trends as accurately as possible. Many researchers consider these sources to be some of the best available for determining long-term trends in public opinion.

Public Opinion and Social Norms

In Chapters 5 and 6, we explained that social norms and perceived social norms can have important impacts on the opinions that people express. Norms are a product of public opinion, but at the same time, they constrain public opinion. They affect our social interactions on an interpersonal level and the public policy enacted by political elites.

The relationship among social norms, public opinion, and public policy is complex. Norms may remain constant for long periods of time, or they may change dramatically. People may accept and internalize norms, or they may merely comply with these social directives. Sometimes, changing social norms seem to be the source of changes in public policy, but other times, changes in public policy seem to lead to changes in norms. Further, since norms are not always consistent with each other, social issues may involve powerful but conflicting values. In this section, we will describe some social norms that have remained constant and others that have been transformed over the last several decades. We will explore how these norms have affected public opinion expression, support for public policies, and individual behavior.

Norms About Race

Norms can and do change. Despite the extraordinary gap between the opinions of white and black Americans on many important issues (see Chapter 7), public opinion about the status of African-Americans in our society appears to have changed dramatically over the last forty years. At the turn of the century, segregation in public places was the norm. Children of different races attended different schools, men of different races were assigned to different units in the military, and families of different races lived in different neighborhoods. Many African-Americans were denied their right to participate in the political system. Socializing between races was rare and nonnormative.

Beginning in the 1950s, a series of dramatic court decisions and even more dramatic public protests seem to have caused the public to rethink its norm of segregation. Howard Schuman, Charlotte Steeh, and Lawrence Bobo found that in 1942, only 32 percent of the public favored racially integrated schools. By 1956, the number had risen to 50 percent. By 1982, 90 percent of the public approved of African-Americans and whites attending school together.[1] Figure 10.1 breaks down support for racial desegregation by region and education. There was an enormous increase in support for school desegregation following the Supreme Court's 1954 ruling in *Brown v. Board of Education of Topeka* that schools could not be racially segregated by law. The pattern of increasing support is an example of what Page and Shapiro call "parallel publics"[2] (see Chapter 8). In this case, the parallel is somewhat weak because the most educated respondents rapidly approach the 100 percent level and cannot move further.

In Chapter 4, we noted that it is often the case that attitudes and behavior do not match. We noted in Chapter 5 that public compliance with a

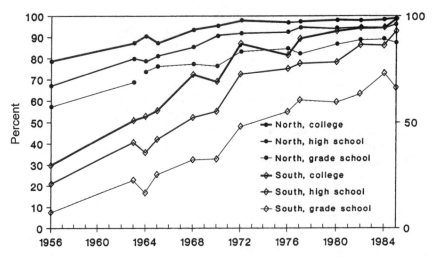

FIGURE 10.1   Racial Desegregation: Responses by Education and Region, 1956–1985. SOURCE: Benjamin I. Page and Robert Y. Shapiro, *The Rational Public* (Chicago: University of Chicago Press, 1992). Original from Schuman et al., 1985.

norm does not necessarily indicate private acceptance of that norm. Although most people show strong support for racial integration in general, more specific attitudes toward mechanisms that might be used to reach the goal of an integrated society are not as favorable. In the case of school desegregation, public support seems to be wider than it is deep. Figure 10.2 shows public attitudes toward school integration and the chief mechanism that has so far been used to achieve it—busing. The figure shows that most Americans would not object to sending their children to schools that were also attended by a few children of another race. However, as the proportion of children of a different race in a school grows, parents become more likely to object to sending their children there. Although more parents object to sending their children to a school in which the children would be a minority, support (at least in the abstract) for such a plan remains above 50 percent.

In spite of their apparent support for the idea of racial integration in schools, the vast majority of Americans apparently disapprove of the main public policy that is meant to achieve it. Although support has increased recently, at no time does more than 37 percent of the public favor busing. The increase in support may be due to internalization of the norm or to changes in the policy. In the early 1970s, busing programs and their problems frequently made the news. More recently, new busing initiatives have been less common and have received less media coverage. Many of those that remain in place are now less troubled.

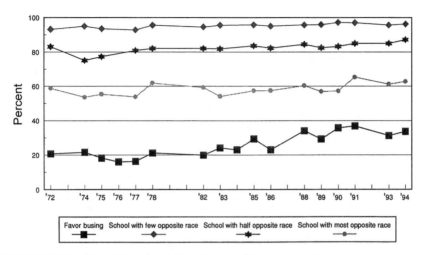

FIGURE 10.2   School Desegregation: Degree of Integration, Busing.

(NORC-GSS) QUESTION: In general, do you favor or oppose the busing of (Negro/ Black/African-American) and white school children from one school district to another?

Would you yourself have any objection to sending your children to a school where a few of the children are (Whites/[Negroes/Blacks/African-Americans])?

If No or Don't Know to A: Would you yourself have any objection to sending your children to a school where half of the children are [Whites/(Negroes/Blacks/African-Americans]?

If No or Don't Know to B: Would you yourself have any objection to sending your children to a school where more than half of the children are (Whites/[Negroes/Blacks/African-Americans])?

In general, people seem to support the idea of racial integration, but they are far less supportive of the specific behavioral changes necessary to achieve it. Of course, it is possible that parents object to busing for other reasons. The tradition of the neighborhood school may be a more important value for them than racial integration is. However, as we noted in Chapter 6, people often give survey researchers answers they believe are more socially desirable, especially where there is a clear social norm. As racist attitudes have become less socially acceptable, respondents may be motivated to give the "right" answer to questions that ask them about their attitudes but respond more candidly to questions that ask about their willingness to change their behavior. Figure 10.2 thus suggests a certain ambivalence about desegregating schools. This result is similar to those we discussed in Chapter 7 with regard to affirmative action and public assistance.

When we consider ways in which the new norm of racial integration has affected social life in the United States, a somewhat different picture emerges. Support for specific kinds of social integration has slowly increased over the years, although as we might expect, actual reports of interracial social interaction lag far behind. Figure 10.3 depicts public attitudes

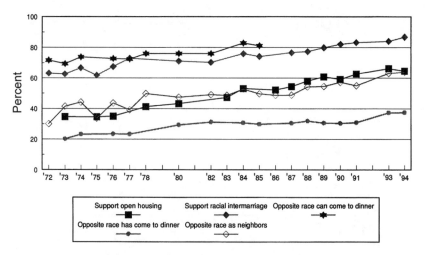

FIGURE 10.3   Attitudes Toward Social Integration

(NORC-GSS) QUESTION: Suppose there is a community-wide vote on the general housing issue. There are two possible laws to vote on. One law says that a homeowner can decide for himself whom to sell his house to, even if he prefers not to sell to (Negroes/Blacks/African-Americans). The second law says that a homeowner cannot refuse to sell to someone because of their race or color. Which law would you vote for?

(NORC-GSS) QUESTION: Do you think there should be laws against marriages between (Negroes/Blacks/African-Americans) and whites?

(NORC-GSS) QUESTION: How strongly would you object if a member of your family wanted to bring a (Negro/Black) friend home to dinner? Would you object strongly, mildly, or not at all?

(NORC-GSS) QUESTION: During the last few years, has anyone in your family brought a friend who was a (Negro/Black/African-American) home for dinner?

(NORC-GSS) QUESTION: Are there any (Negroes/Blacks/African-Americans) living in this neighborhood now?

toward various kinds of social integration. It shows that support for racial intermarriage[3] and open housing has increased slowly but relatively steadily. More people report living in racially mixed neighborhoods as well.

Of course, the trouble with the measures of public opinion contained in Figure 10.3 are the problems of all attempts to measure opinion where a norm is involved. Are people reporting what they really think, or are they reporting what they believe the interviewer wants to hear? We cannot be sure.

Despite these difficulties, we can draw some conclusions about the ways in which norms involving race have changed over the last few decades. First, it seems clear that a new norm of racial integration has taken hold and that people understand this norm to have broad implications for social interaction. That is, they favor integration in housing as well as in schools, and they support interracial marriage as well. Further, support for this norm has increased over time. It remains unclear whether the new norm exacts compliance or acceptance from most Americans. We have seen both here and in Chapter 7 that although they support the idea of integration, many Americans do not support policy changes that would promote integration as an outcome.

Norms About Gender

As we noted in Chapter 8, norms about women's role in society have also changed dramatically since the World War II era. In the 1930s, most Americans believed that women should not work if they had husbands to support them. Today, the vast majority say they approve of married women working. However, once again, we find elements of an older norm that suggest that a woman's primary duty is to her home and her family. Figure 10.4 reveals that the presence of children can drastically change the level of

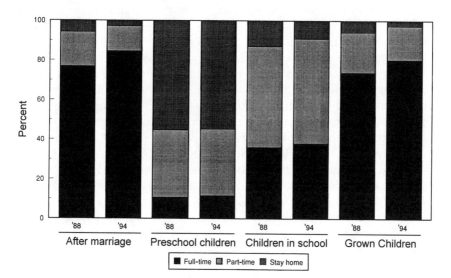

FIGURE 10.4   Support for Women Working Outside the Home

(NORC-GSS) QUESTION: Do you think that women should work outside the home full-time, part-time, or not at all under these circumstances:

Please circle one answer on each line.

A. After marrying and before there are children.
B. When there is a child under school age.
C. After the youngest child starts school.
D. After the children leave home.

support for working women. Although well over 75 percent of respondents favor women working after marriage, once children enter the picture, support for working women drops precipitously. Over 50 percent of respondents believe that a woman with pre-school-age children should be a full-time mother. Support for women working outside the home increases as children grow up and require less care. Once the children leave home, public support for working women nears the levels for married women without children.

Figure 10.4 also shows that in the six years between surveys, support for women working when children are not present in the house has grown but that the low levels of support for working mothers of young children have remained almost constant. Thus, although real social changes such as women going to work can lead to support for a new norm, elements of the old norm remain. Most Americans clearly believe that mothers of young children ideally should take care of them full-time, though the survey does not ask respondents to address the hard choices that face low-income families and single mothers. It is noteworthy that a certain preconception on the part of the researchers is revealed in these questions as well: The survey does not contain a comparable battery of questions about men's roles in child care. The attitudes held by the survey researchers may be affecting the way we perceive the norm.

When it comes to women's roles in the political system, more evidence of changing norms can be found. However, once again, there are ambiguities suggestive of norms in transition. As Figure 10.5 shows, public support for women in politics has increased steadily. The scales used for each question have been transformed so that a rising trend indicates increasing support for women participating in the political sphere. In 1972, 74 percent of Americans said they would vote for a qualified female presidential candidate. By 1994, 92.5 percent said they would. Similarly, in 1974, 54 percent of respondents disagreed with the statement "Women are not suited for politics." In 1994, 78.6 percent disagreed.

However, a closer examination of the trend lines suggests some ambivalence about the political activities of women. Although 92.5 percent of respondents in 1994 say they would vote for a female presidential candidate, 21.3 percent of them say that women are unsuited for politics, and 13.4 percent say that women should take care of the home, not the country. If these measures are accurate, at least some respondents who claim they would vote for a woman for president also believe that women are unsuited for politics. The gap between willingness to vote for a woman for president and belief that women are suited for politics averages over 21 percentage points during the years of the GSS survey, although the gap has narrowed in recent years. The reason for the gap is difficult to fathom. However, it seems likely that conflicting norms play a role. Perhaps asking about

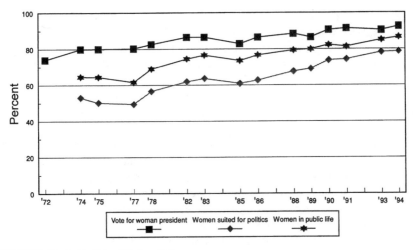

FIGURE 10.5   Political Role of Women

(NORC-GSS) QUESTION: If your party nominated a woman for president, would you vote for her if she were qualified for the job?

(NORC-GSS) QUESTION: Tell me if you agree or disagree with this statement: Most men are better suited emotionally for politics than are most women.

(NORC-GSS) QUESTION: Do you agree or disagree with this statement? Women should take care of running their homes and leave running the country up to men.

women's right to run for public office encourages respondents to consider norms of political equality whereas asking about women's suitability for public office does not. Whatever the exact reason, the trends suggest some uncertainty about women's role in public life.

Like the norms involving racial integration and equality, norms about gender and men's and women's social roles have implications for both interpersonal interaction and public policy. At the interpersonal level, expectations about the relative obligations of men and women in the home and the workplace and about the role of each partner in relationships will be affected by social norms. Laws regarding issues such as divorce, day care, abortion, and aid to the poor will be affected by the same norms as the struggle to define women's place in society continues.

Legislating Morality

There is an old adage that says: "You can't legislate morality." In fact, the government, often with the support of public opinion, does so all the time. Americans have experimented with outlawing liquor, legalizing gambling, and requiring warning labels on cigarette packages, compact disks, and television programs, among other things. Our opinions about what should be considered immoral activity have changed over the years as well.

The use of drugs, both legal and illegal, is a regular feature of American public debate. Today, America's experiment with Prohibition, which made the consumption and sale of alcoholic beverages illegal, is considered an abject failure. Even though modern public opinion polls were not available in the 1920s when the Prohibition laws were debated and enacted, it is important to recognize that the constitutional amendment that banned alcohol could not have passed without a great deal of public support. In more recent times, Americans have come to favor laws that make cigarette smoking increasingly difficult. Laws limit the age at which people can buy cigarettes and the places where cigarettes can be smoked. Structural changes have been proposed that would increase the amount of regulatory power the government has over cigarette manufacturing by classifying cigarettes as a drug. In the 1940s, when nearly half of all adult Americans were smokers, such policies would have been unthinkable.

In addition to considering bans on the sale or use of some substances that are currently legally available, the nation also sometimes considers legalizing the possession and consumption of some drugs that are currently illicit. The most common debate revolves around legalizing the sale and use of marijuana. Figure 10.6 displays the trends in public opinion on this issue. As you can see, the GSS surveys have found consistently low levels of support for legalization. At no time does support for the idea rise much above 30 percent. However, the pattern of the curve does seem to reflect some of the changes our society has experienced over the past two decades. After reaching a peak in 1978, support for legalization plunges during the years of the Reagan administration and the so-called drug wars. Political scientists Page and Shapiro suggest that this may be because the public came to associate drugs with violent crimes in cities.[4] After the election of Bill Clinton, a president who claimed he had tried marijuana but had not inhaled, support for legalization seems to be on the rise again.

Another type of "sin" that is regulated to some extent by public policy but nevertheless remains legally available to adults is pornography. This issue can be thought of in terms of gender or in terms of sex, but it can also be described as a kind of semi-illicit activity. Attitudes about pornography may be the product of two competing norms—one a social norm about morality, the other a democratic norm about free speech. Figure 10.7 depicts the ways in which the American public has balanced these two competing ideals. At no time does more than 11 percent of the public believe that pornographic material should be unrestricted, and the percentage of people who wish to see pornography banned has remained relatively constant. The percentage of people who would prefer to see some restrictions

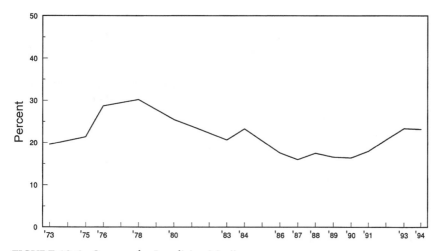

FIGURE 10.6   Support for Legalizing Marijuana

(NORC-GSS) QUESTION: Do you think the use of marijuana should be made legal or not?

Legal   Illegal if under 18   Illegal

FIGURE 10.7   Legality of Pornography

(NORC-GSS) QUESTION: Which of these statements comes closest to your feelings about pornography laws?

There should be laws against the distribution of pornography whatever the age.
There should be laws against the distribution of pornography to persons under 18.
There should be no laws forbidding the distribution of pornography.

but less than a total ban has grown slowly and steadily, most of its increase coming at the expense of support for unrestricted pornography.

However, these measures of public attitudes about pornography suffer from a problem: The definition of what constitutes pornography may very well have changed since 1973. The public may be more "broad-minded" today than it was in the past, so material that is now labeled pornographic may be more extreme in its content than material that was labeled pornographic in the early 1970s. In his historical examination of various campaigns to ban sexually explicit material, Dennis Chong demonstrates that sometimes material once considered offensive later came to be seen as acceptable, even tame.[5] Changes in social context may be masking changes in public opinion.

Norms About Sex

According to the conventional wisdom, the United States underwent a sexual revolution in the 1960s and 1970s. Changing attitudes about sex, new technology to prevent pregnancy, and effective treatments for sexually transmitted diseases are said to have transformed norms about sexual behavior. Both laws and attitudes about abortion changed during this period. The same is true of the laws and public opinion about access to birth control and family-planning information.

Figure 10.8 depicts changing public attitudes about premarital sex. Note that the data in this figure come from a period after the revolution was supposedly over. Clearly, public opinion becomes gradually more favorable to premarital sex. In 1972, 27.7 percent of GSS respondents said that sex before marriage was "not wrong at all." By 1994, the proportion had climbed to 43.5 percent.

The same pattern does not hold true for teenage sexual behavior. In 1986, 67.1 percent of the GSS respondents said they believed it was "always wrong" for teenagers between the ages of fourteen and sixteen to have sex. By 1994, that figure had climbed to 70 percent. However, public opinion does seem to consistently favor sex education for teens in school throughout the period covered by the GSS. The survey consistently finds that over 75 percent of Americans favor sex education, and the percentage has slowly climbed. By 1994, 88 percent of the sample reported being in favor of sex education. About half of those surveyed by the GSS believe that birth control should be made available to fourteen- to sixteen-year-olds with or without their parents' consent. Although most people do not seem to approve of teenagers having sex, they do seem to favor policies that will make teenagers aware of the consequences of sexual activity and encourage teens to take responsibility for those consequences. The norms for teenagers, however, have not changed in the way that the norms for adults have.

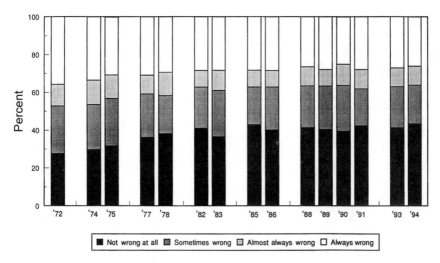

FIGURE 10.8   Opinions on Premarital Sex

(NORC-GSS) QUESTION: There's been a lot of discussion about the way morals and attitudes about sex are changing in this country. If a man and woman have sex relations before marriage, do you think it is always wrong, almost always wrong, wrong only sometimes, or not wrong at all?

Some would argue that an important part of the sexual revolution has been renewed debate over the issue of abortion. Others might argue that this renewed discussion has more to do with issues of gender than with issues of sex. Regardless, public opinion about abortion has changed significantly since the mid-1960s. Figure 10.9 depicts the changes in public opinion between 1962 and 1996. Support for legalized abortion has grown since the 1960s, but it is interesting to note that the circumstances surrounding the abortion make a big difference in the level of support. Nearly 90 percent favor permitting abortions if the pregnant woman's life is in danger. Less than 45 percent favor abortion on demand. The figure clearly shows that norms about sexuality and its consequences have changed. It also demonstrates that at least on some issues, the public is capable of making very fine distinctions.[6]

Norms About the Environment[7]

Another area in which social context, and perhaps social norms, may be changing is public opinion about the environment. Over the years, public perceptions of the environment and public opinion about the environment have been revolutionized. At the turn of the century, as the frontier of the American West closed, public debate about the environment focused on the

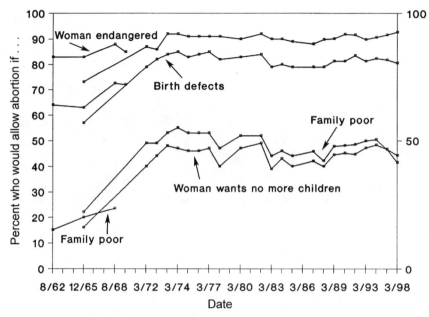

FIGURE 10.9   Abortion, 1962–1998

QUESTION (NORC, NORC-General Social Surveys, CBS News/*New York Times*): "Please tell me whether or not *you* think it should be possible for a pregnant woman to obtain a legal abortion . . . If there is a strong chance of serious defect in the baby? . . . If she is married and does not want any more children? . . . If the woman's own health is seriously endangered by the pregnancy? . . . If the family has a very low income and cannot afford any more children?" Survey dates (NORC): 12/65, 12/72; (NORC-GSS): 3/72–3/96; (CBS/*NYT*): 1/98, with special thanks to Dr. Kathleen Frankovic, CBS News, for providing these data. QUESTION (Gallup): "Do you think abortion operations should or should not be legal in the following cases: . . . when the child may be born deformed? . . . where the parents simply have all the children they want although there would be no major health or financial problems involved in having another child? . . . where the health of the mother is in danger? . . . where the family does not have enough money to support another child?" Survey dates: 8/62, 12/65, 5/68 and 12/68 (averaged), 9/69.

preservation of wild places and creatures. Following the publication of Rachel Carson's *Silent Spring* in 1962, public perceptions of the environment were transformed. People began to realize that not only were scenic wonders and wildlife endangered by human expansion but they themselves were placed at risk by environmental hazards like pollution.

Public concern about the environment has grown markedly since the 1960s. Although there is evidence of what Anthony Downs calls an "issue-attention cycle,"[8] a semiregular pattern of increases and declines in attention, the increases seem to outweigh the declines such that the overall level of concern today remains higher than it was thirty years ago. Figure 10.10

FIGURE 10.10   Support for Preserving the Environment

(NORC-GSS) QUESTION: We are faced with many problems in this country, none of which can be solved easily or inexpensively. I'm going to name some of these problems, and for each one I'd like you to tell me whether you think we're spending too much money on it, too little money, or about the right amount. Are we spending too much money, too little money, or about the right amount on . . . improving and protecting the environment?

(CAMBRIDGE) QUESTION: We must sacrifice economic growth in order to preserve and protect the environment/We must be prepared to sacrifice environmental quality for economic growth.

(CAMBRIDGE) QUESTION: Which of these two statements is closer to your opinion?

There is no relationship between economic growth and the quality of the environment— indeed, we can have more and more goods and services and also a clean world.

We cannot have both economic growth and a high level of environmental quality.

depicts some of the evidence of the public's increasing concern about the environment. Riley E. Dunlap concludes from data like these that the environment is a consensual issue. Large majorities usually voice pro-environmental positions, whereas only small minorities express anti-environmental views.[9]

Despite the increased regard for the environment that people seem to express, there is less evidence that people actually behave in pro-environmental ways. Very few people seem to judge candidates primarily on their environmental policies, perhaps because they assume that candidates share in the widespread consensus about environmental protection.[10] Further, although most people claim they are pro-environment, individual consumption patterns suggest that many do not put their beliefs into practice. One example of this is Americans' current demand for large sport-utility vehicles, which consume much more gas than smaller passenger cars.

Some have argued that the creation of an ecologically sustainable society will require a transformation of the norms and beliefs that currently govern American life. They argue that American norms such as materialism, consumerism, individualism, and faith in progress are not compatible with environmental sustainability.[11] Indeed, some studies show that support for these kinds of values are associated with less concern for environmental protection.[12] However, as Figure 10.10 above shows, many Americans believe that a healthy economy and a healthy environment are not incompatible. This suggests that most Americans do not perceive a trade-off between the two.

Dunlap and Kent D. Van Liere argue that support for current social norms, often called the "dominant social paradigm," and pro-environmental attitudes are dissonant cognitions (see Chapter 4). For now, people hold incompatible values, but these researchers believe that over time, members of the public will become aware of the dissonance and seek to alleviate it. At the social level, dissonance is expressed as public debate over competing values and beliefs. This has resulted in the construction of what Dunlap and Van Liere call a "new environmental paradigm" to challenge the dominant social paradigm. Will the new paradigm conquer the old? Dunlap and Van Liere believe that the success of the new, pro-environment norms will depend upon "the degree to which they work": "If we are in fact entering an era of ecological limits in which the societal impacts of environmental pollution, resource scarcity, etc., become more pronounced, the resultant experiences will provide increasing pressure for revision of our [dominant social paradigm] toward a more ecologically sustainable world."[13] However, the authors point out that social institutions and practices tend to sustain existing norms. The norms may change, but the process will almost certainly be gradual, as it has been in other cases.

Current measures of public opinion on issues that invoke these kinds of social values, or norms, offer us only tantalizing clues about what public opinion may be and how opinion may be changing. The fact that respondents may feel social pressure to answer a survey's questions in ways that comply with social norms may mask truths about real social behavior and real opinions on issues. These lies, however, are also informative because they can help researchers understand the social norms that govern our public behavior. The size of the gap between opinions and behavior may help us to perceive the gap between compliance and acceptance.

Measuring public opinion over the long term is also difficult because social context and public opinion are both changing at the same time. Public expectations about what is "normal" or "normative" in fashion, social interaction, or public policy are constantly in flux. Events that might have shocked television audiences in 1960, such as an interracial kiss, might go unnoticed in 1990. An "event" such as the television character "Ellen" revealing that she is gay might be a newsworthy event in 1997 but unremarkable by 2010. A federal program for supporting elderly Americans, unheard of in the 1930s, by 1990 has become an entitlement. These changes in context can hide dramatic changes in public opinion. Despite these and other measurement problems, understanding changes in the norms that govern public behavior is crucial.

Public Opinion and Political Tolerance

In Chapters 7 and 8, we argued that considered public opinion should take into account the rights of minorities and the legitimate expression of unpopular ideas. This important democratic norm is frequently described as *tolerance*. Tolerance is one's "forbearance with reference to views, opinions, or actions with which one is not oneself fully in sympathy."[14] At a psychological level, tolerance is a function of one's own likes and dislikes. At a social level, tolerance is frequently defined in terms of respecting the civil rights of groups, especially minority groups, that are or have been targets of public distaste. Like any other attitude, tolerance has cognitive, affective, and behavioral components.

The study of public opinion about civil rights, civil liberties, and prejudices is both substantively and theoretically important. Tolerance is a part of our identity as Americans. We tell stories of the Pilgrim fathers and of generations of immigrants who came to America to escape persecution in their homelands. Fundamental elements of the American political system such as the right to free speech and the separation of church and state institutionalize a norm of tolerance for divergent points of view. However, Americans do not necessarily live up to their ideals of tolerance. Racial, religious, political, and sexual discrimination on both personal and institutional levels have been a regular feature of the American scene. Some scholars have argued that this intolerance damages the vitality of our democracy;[15] others argue that a certain level of consensus is necessary to maintain a viable political system.[16]

In addition to forming an important part of our political culture, political tolerance and intolerance, like other social norms, can have important impacts on public policy. Laws regarding equal opportunity in housing or access to banking, prayer in public schools, and affirmative action can be affected by the public's tolerance of diverse religions, races, and genders. But beyond its impact on the legal structures of our nation, social tolerance can affect our everyday lives. Very early studies demonstrated that the opinions of those around us have an impact on what we think and do.[17] If the attitudes of those around us are more tolerant, the community we live in is likely to be more diverse, and, some argue, our democracy may be more vibrant.[18]

The study of political tolerance is also theoretically interesting for public opinion scholars. Since the social scientific study of tolerance began in the 1950s, scholars have worked to develop theories that attempt to explain why the targets and levels of public intolerance change over time.

The earliest major study of political tolerance was the work of Samuel Stouffer.[19] In the 1950s, during the height of the McCarthy era and the Cold War, Stouffer became interested in studying Americans' attitudes toward various kinds of political dissent. In general, he wanted to know how strongly Americans supported civil liberties, such as freedom of speech, thought to be so much a part of American political culture. Stouffer focused on tolerance for leftist groups such as Communists and atheists, then under attack by many political elites. What he found was disturbing. A generous majority of people were willing to infringe on the rights of people who were Communists. They were prepared to allow the government to tap the phones or even revoke the citizenship of American Communists. They felt that such people should not be permitted to teach in schools (or even to work as clerks in stores) and that Communist-authored books should be removed from library shelves.

However, Stouffer was confident that changes in American society would promote and enforce norms of political tolerance. He theorized that increases in education and in geographic mobility would make people more aware and tolerant of diversity. Changes in the ways children were raised would also help, for the more authoritarian modes of prior eras were giving way to practices that emphasized independent thinking and respect for others. The new mass medium of television, Stouffer believed, also held promise because it brought diverse vicarious experiences into American homes.

In the early 1970s, a large-scale replication of Stouffer's study was performed. The researchers found a marked increase in tolerance for the demonized groups of the 1950s. Even more positive, their evidence suggested that tolerance was a generalized characteristic. That is, tolerance for one group seemed to be a good indicator of tolerance for other groups. If people were tolerant of antiwar protesters, they also tended to be tolerant of homosexuals. The researchers concluded that the level of political tolerance in America had increased from the 1950s to the 1970s.[20] It appeared that Stouffer's prediction was right.

In fact, the change in public opinion known as the "Stouffer shift" was one of the most dramatic transformations of public opinion ever documented. Table 10.1 compares Stouffer's findings[21] with those of Clyde Nunn, Harry Crockett, and J. Allen Williams.[22] As you can see, researchers found that the percentage of people who were willing to permit various nonconformist groups' expressions of their views increased substantially between 1954 and 1972. People were more willing to let nonconformists

TABLE 10.1   The "Stouffer Shift": Percent of People Tolerant of Nonconformists

	1954	1972	% Change
Admitted Communists			
Speak	27	52	+25
Teach	6	32	+26
Work as clerk	25	53	+28
Socialists			
Speak	60	77	+17
Teach	33	56	+23
Library	52	68	+16
Atheists			
Speak	37	65	+28
Teach	12	40	+28
Library	35	61	+26

speak in public, teach in universities, work as clerks, and make their writings available in public libraries.

Stouffer's work inspired continued study of political tolerance, and the work has evolved along two main branches. One focus of study has been the exploration of psychological and other personal characteristics that make an individual more or less tolerant of others. The central research question is: "What makes people tolerant?" The second area of study has attempted to document changes in the degree and kind of political tolerance present in American political culture. It asks: "Are people more tolerant or less tolerant now than they have been in the past?" Let us look at each question in turn.

Personal Characteristics and Political Tolerance

In the wake of Stouffer's findings that Americans were relatively intolerant and his hopeful prediction that this might soon change, scholars began to explore the sources of political tolerance. Several personal characteristics and habits of mind turned out to be important predictors of tolerant attitudes, as were certain kinds of social attainment.

One reason Stouffer believed that Americans would become more tolerant of diversity as time went on was their increasing levels of education. Scholars have consistently found, as Stouffer himself did, that higher levels of educational attainment are positively associated with tolerance, although some have questioned the validity of this relationship.[23] There might be a variety of reasons education leads to tolerance. Education socializes people to understand and accept the norms of the society in which they live,[24] so the more educated Americans become, the more likely they should be to embrace American ideals of political tolerance. Education might also help people more realistically assess the threat posed by divergent behavior and points of view. Lawrence Bobo and Frederick Licari believe that the mechanism increasing tolerance in better educated people may be the increased cognitive sophistication that comes with more years of formal schooling.[25] Skeptics, however, argue that what education really does is teach people the "right" answers to questions about civil liberties. That is, people merely comply with the norms rather than accepting them (see Chapter 5).

The relationship between cognition and tolerance is complex. Using depth-interview data, Dennis Chong confirmed that education affected the way people thought about civil liberties issues. Faced with such questions, people tended to weigh two primary considerations: the norm, or legal principle, and the group involved. People with more education tended to think first about the principle and then about the group. People with less education tended to think about the group first and the principle second.[26] If people tend to give "top of the head" responses to survey questions,[27] this may explain why those with more education appear to be more tolerant.

James Kuklinski and his colleagues discovered that the more people thought about an issue that invoked norms of tolerance, the less tolerant they became. This was true even when the group they were asked about was a group they liked. It seems that people do, in fact, tend to respond to questions involving tolerance by consulting their emotions rather than by thinking the issues through.[28] If people perceive that a question involves general principles of tolerance, their gut reaction is to be tolerant, although if people pay more attention to the group than the norm, their dislike for the group can sometimes overwhelm their commitment to the norm.[29] As they begin to think more about the question, the potential consequences of permitting the activity and other important values that may conflict with the norm of tolerance become salient.[30]

Stouffer also turned out to be right about the impact of increasing urbanism and migration on political tolerance.[31] Subsequent studies have confirmed that people who live in large cities are more tolerant than those who live in small towns. People who have moved to a new community are more tolerant than people who stay in the same community, regardless of the size of the town to which they move.[32] However, G. Edward Stephan and Douglas McMullen argue that urbanism has its greatest impact on young people. The strongest relation between city size and tolerance for "sexual nonconformity" was the size of the community the respondent had lived in at age sixteen.[33]

Several researchers have also demonstrated that those espousing a liberal political ideology are generally more tolerant than conservatives. Although many initially thought that this finding was a result of measurement tools that asked respondents to tolerate groups on the left rather than groups on the right, later measurements that included both left-wing and right-wing groups confirmed the finding.[34] Similarly, people who have dogmatic personalities[35] or are psychologically insecure[36] seem to be more intolerant than those who are less dogmatic and more secure.

Another important factor contributing to political tolerance is perceived threat. When people believe that a group poses a genuine danger to public order or other important civic values, they are less likely to tolerate its activities than if the group is perceived as nonthreatening or ineffectual. This argument first became prominent in the work of John Sullivan, James Pierson, and George Marcus.[37] Subsequent studies have provided a good deal of evidence that perceived threat has a strong impact on political tolerance.[38] It is also possible that a behavior may be tolerated if it seems innocuous or rare but become unacceptable if it becomes more commonplace or threatening. For example, James Gibson found that states in which public opinion was more tolerant of civil disobedience in general were actually more likely to enact laws restricting campus protest during the late 1960s and early 1970s. The more tolerant climate had helped make the demonstrations possible, but when they became threatening to civic order, public opinion became less tolerant.[39]

Although they sometimes enacted intolerant policies, community leaders tended to be more tolerant than the general public, according to Stouffer's findings.[40] A number of scholars took this finding, together with the discovery that the public was quite intolerant, as support for what is known as the *elitist theory of democracy*. You will recall that Lippmann argued in favor of elite democracy because he believed that the public would never be sufficiently informed to govern itself wisely (see Chapter 7). Evidence of public intolerance also seemed to some a good reason to leave policymaking in the hands of the few.

The elitist theory of democracy posited that it was not strictly necessary for the public to be tolerant as long as elites were. Several safeguards of the American political system could prevent an intolerant public from trampling on the rights of political, racial, religious, and gender minorities. The leaders who actually made public policy were more tolerant than the masses, rights were protected by constitutional safeguards, and the court system that determined the constitutionality of public policy was relatively unaccountable to the intolerant public. However, more recently, some scholars have rejected the elitist theory of democracy, arguing that public tolerance really does matter (see Box 10.1).

Although it is not precisely a personality characteristic, we should note that Stouffer's initial prediction that younger generations would be more tolerant than previous generations[41] has also been generally upheld by later research.[42] People who were born later tend to be more tolerant than those born earlier, so over time, the public has become more tolerant. For

Box 10.1 Democratic Elitism

In response to Samuel Stouffer's findings in the 1950s that the American public was in fact quite intolerant of the political views of others, some scholars advanced the argument that public intolerance was offset by the more tolerant views of political leaders. The antidemocratic implications of this view soon became obvious. Ironically, it meant that if average people did not participate in democratic institutions, their rights and freedoms would be better protected than they would be if everyone participated actively. The more tolerant leaders would protect the civil liberties of the intolerant masses who stayed at home. From this perspective, encouraging public participation in governance (in other words, democracy) was risky and ill-advised.

In the decades that followed, several scholars began to demonstrate that, as usual, things were not that simple. In the early 1990s, for example, Paul Sniderman and colleagues showed that elites are not uniform in their commitment to civil liberties. In a comparison between Canadian political elites of various political parties and the Canadian public at large, they demonstrated that with regard to "the politics of liberty," elite opinion on civil rights is sufficiently divided that the average level of tolerance within some parties is lower than that of the general public, even though the average level of tolerance among elites as a whole is consistently greater than that of the public. When they turn to the "politics of order"—issues that require the respondent to balance competing desires for freedom and order—the results are even more striking. In some cases, the public is more tolerant than the elites, and the elites continue to be quite divided on these issues. When questions concern not just potential disorder but possible overthrow of the government, the masses are almost always more tolerant than the elites, and the elites are again widely dispersed in their views.

The figure shown here stylistically diagrams how elites as a whole can be more tolerant than the public even though the leaders of some political organizations are less tolerant than the mass public. Sniderman and his colleagues point out that the bimodal distribution of elite opinion is likely to change depending on the issue. Nevertheless, note that the mean level of tolerance of elites will always be greater than that of the public.

Sniderman and associates conclude that it is not enough to rest assured that elites, not the general public, make policy decisions. Which elites are in power and what kinds of issues are addressed make major differences in the level and type of commitment to civil liberties as expressed in public policy.

James Gibson goes further and argues that the intolerance of the general public has direct consequences for political freedom in the United States. His research shows that people who hold intolerant attitudes perceive themselves to be more politically constrained than those who have more tolerant opinions. Environment seems to make a difference as well. Those who live in less

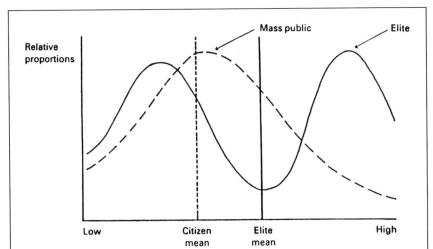

A Stylized Comparison of Elite and Mass Means and Modes: Commitment to Civil Liberties. SOURCE: Paul M. Sniderman et al., "The Fallacy of Democratic Elitism: Elite Competition and Commitment to Civil Liberties," *British Journal of Political Science* 21 (1991), figure 1, p. 368.

tolerant communities with homogeneous peer groups and less tolerant spouses also perceive less political freedom than those who live in more tolerant atmospheres. Drawing on Elisabeth Noelle-Neumann's concept of a spiral of silence, Gibson argues that these intolerant climates and attitudes breed a culture of conformity that robs democracy of its vitality. No matter how tolerant leaders are, the intolerance of the general public matters because it is average citizens whom the nonconformist confronts day-to-day.

It seems clear from the work of these scholars that public intolerance does indeed matter and may be detrimental to effective democracy.

SOURCES: Samuel C. Stouffer, *Communism, Conformity, and Civil Liberties* (New York: Doubleday, 1955); Paul M. Sniderman et al., "The Fallacy of Democratic Elitism: Elite Competition and Commitment to Civil Liberties," *British Journal of Political Science* 21 (1991):349–370; James L. Gibson, "The Political Consequences of Intolerance: Cultural Conformity and Political Freedom," *American Political Science Review* 86 (1992):338–356; Elisabeth Noelle-Neumann, *The Spiral of Silence: Public Opinion—Our Social Skin* (Chicago: University of Chicago Press, 1984).

example, people born in 1945 seem to be more tolerant than those born in 1935, so as time passes and the older generations with it, the public as a whole becomes more tolerant. This generational effect is not simply because the average level of education has risen with each succeeding generation. Generation seems to have an effect all its own. However, as we will see, it may not always be the case that newer generations are *more* tolerant than the old.

Social Trends in Political Tolerance

Following the apparently dramatic transformation of public opinion about the activities of nonconformists between the mid-1950s and the early 1970s, the National Opinion Research Center began regularly asking a battery of questions designed to measure political tolerance on its General Social Survey. The questions originally solicited respondents' opinions about three different activities (speaking in public, teaching in a college, and authoring a book in the public library) as performed by three different groups (Communists, atheists, and homosexuals).

However, all of the groups originally selected by the GSS could be considered "left wing." They are groups that are more likely to be tolerated or even supported by liberals than by conservatives. Reflecting the criticism of Sullivan, Pierson, Marcus,[43] and others, the GSS added two new groups to the battery in 1976: militarists (those who would prefer to see the nation's governance handled by the armed forces) and racists. These groups were more likely to be supported or tolerated by those with conservative political views. The new measures, researchers hoped, would do a better job of measuring the overall level of public tolerance for nonconformity. They also hoped that the addition of right-wing groups to the battery would provide them with better ways to measure the relative levels of tolerance of liberals and conservatives.

Figure 8.5 in Chapter 8 displays the trends in public tolerance for several nonconformist groups teaching in the public schools. Figure 10.11 in this chapter shows the trends for allowing these same groups to speak in public. Although the figures suggest that the American public has grown more tolerant since 1972, the dramatic increases in tolerance recorded between 1954 and 1972 did not continue in later years. For example, the average increase in public tolerance for Communists exercising their civil liberties was 5.5 percent per year between 1954 and 1972. The average annual increase between 1972 and 1994 was less than 1 percent. The level of tolerance for racists speaking, teaching, or writing has remained virtually unchanged for the entire period.

Another strange anomaly about public tolerance had been documented back in 1960. James Prothro and Charles Grigg found that even when peo-

FIGURE 10.11   Tolerance for Nonconformist Public Speech

(NORC-GSS) QUESTION: There are always some people whose ideas are considered bad or dangerous by other people. For instance, somebody who is against all churches and religion. If such a person wanted to make a speech in your (city/town/community), should he be allowed to speak or not? . . . Now I should like to ask you some questions about a man who admits he is a communist. Suppose this admitted communist wanted to make a speech in your community. Should he be allowed to speak or not? . . . And what about a man who admits he is a homosexual? Suppose this admitted homosexual wanted to make a speech in your community. Should he be allowed to speak or not? . . . Or consider a person who believes that blacks are genetically inferior. If such a person wanted to make a speech in your community, claiming that blacks are inferior, should he be allowed to speak or not? . . . Consider a person who advocates doing away with elections and letting the military run the country. If such a person wanted to make a speech in your community, should he be allowed to speak or not?

ple said they supported norms of tolerance, their support broke down when they were asked to apply their principles to specific cases. For example, over 93 percent of those they surveyed agreed with the following statement: "People in the minority should be free to try to win majority support for their opinions." But in the same survey, 58 percent of respondents agreed with the statement, "A Communist should not be allowed to run for mayor of this city."[44] Other researchers confirmed Prothro and Grigg's results, including McClosky and Zaller, whose findings we discussed in Chapter 7.

This evidence for public tolerance becomes even weaker when we remember that people frequently respond to poll questions insincerely when their true attitudes run counter to perceived social norms (see Chapter 6). Measures that ask about general support for norms such as the right to speak, assemble, or worship might seriously overestimate citizens' willingness to tolerate diversity. John Mueller even argued that perhaps poll questions about generic support for civil liberties measured nothing at all, that people's attitudes about civil liberties had no content: "A survey in an Orwellian world could be expected to find principles like 'slavery is freedom' as emptily and mechanically accepted."[45]

Another difficulty with measuring political tolerance was discussed in Chapter 4. People do not always behave in accordance with their attitudes, whether those attitudes are tolerant or intolerant.

A different problem with measuring trends in political tolerance was raised by John Sullivan and his associates. In 1979, they introduced the idea that by replicating Stouffer's study, later researchers had not really measured tolerance. In the 1950s, Communists were among the most feared and hated groups in American society. The actions of the House Un-American Activities Committee and Senator Joseph McCarthy and the ongoing Cold War made domestic communism a very salient issue for the American public. By the 1970s, the threat of domestic communism probably did not seem as great, and the actions of the Communist hunters of the 1950s had been strongly criticized by civil libertarians. Thus, Sullivan and colleagues argued, measuring tolerance for leftist groups was not the same as measuring the general level of political tolerance in the society.

Sullivan and his collaborators argued that the only way to measure tolerance consistently over time was to let respondents name their own most disliked groups and ask how tolerant they would be of actions by those groups. That way, if Communists were demonized at one point in time but racists came to be the most disliked group later on, the researchers could take account of those changes. Their argument was based on the idea that tolerance implied putting up with something that one neither liked nor approved of. If one were indifferent or actually approved of the belief or practice or group, then there was no need for tolerance. They called this a *content-controlled* measure of tolerance.

Sullivan and his associates conducted such a study. They found that when respondents named their own most disliked group, the overall level of political tolerance in society had not changed since the 1950s. They argued that the only real change had been in the targets of intolerance. In the 1950s, public intolerance had one primary target: domestic Communists. By the 1970s, there were many targets of public intolerance, and their very diffuseness protected them from the kinds of persecution that suspected Communists had suffered twenty years earlier. But that did not mean that the public was, in general, any more tolerant than it had been before. Sullivan and his associates called this phenomenon *pluralistic intolerance*.

This debate between the "Stouffer approach" and the "content-controlled approach" is ongoing. We need not resolve it, for both perspectives can be useful. When we consider issues of civil rights and civil liberties, a content-controlled approach seems more appropriate since we are concerned with people's willingness to tolerate the opinions, characteristics, and lifestyles they dislike the most. However, for many issues involving important race, class, religious, and gender groups, tolerance for a particular group is the key issue, and here the Stouffer approach seems most appropriate. The two are not indivisible. Several researchers have found evidence that tolerance may be a generalized attitude: Those who are willing to grant civil liberties to one group seem prepared to grant them to all groups. However, there does seem to be merit in measuring tolerance both for specific, historically disadvantaged groups and for civil liberties in general.

Several scholars have tried to explain the slowdown in the expansion of tolerant public attitudes. James Davis's analysis of the GSS data suggests that the reason for this slower rate of increase is that during the 1970s, for the first time, young adults were less tolerant of free speech than their elders. Thus, Stouffer's theory that the nation would continue to grow more tolerant as new generations came of age seemed in need of modification. Davis also suggests that the unique historical events of the Vietnam era may have concealed "what would have been a plateau as the secular trend toward tolerance hit a ceiling in the 1960s." During the 1970s, his analysis demonstrates, anti–free speech factors in the nation as a whole affected every generation, and the young most of all. This trend also contributed to the slowdown. The years of the Stouffer shift had seen "strong intracohort increase in tolerance," whereas the 1970s "saw weak intracohort declines."[46]

Davis does not believe that the news is all bad. He observes, "Even in a period where 'reactionary' forces dominated, Free Speech did not decline, [and c]ohort replacement should provide a positive force for the next few years."[47] Indeed, support for civil liberties apparently continues to expand, though at a slower rate. Other scholars, however, have not been so sanguine about these trends. As Sullivan, Pierson, and Marcus might point out, these measures do not even capture Americans' intolerance of groups that they themselves specify as disliked.

Recently, some scholars have called the "content-controlled" approach into question.[48] These scholars argue that asking respondents about their willingness to tolerate the activities of their most disliked group underestimates political tolerance. Some people dislike far fewer groups than others, which means that they are more tolerant. For example, two people may name Nazis as their most disliked group. Each may be unwilling to permit a Nazi to teach in a college, speak in public, or author books in the public library. Sullivan and his associates would say that these two people are equally tolerant (or intolerant). However, one respondent may name only Nazis as a disliked group to which freedom of speech should be denied. The other may wish to deny such civil liberties to Nazis, atheists, Communists, and several other groups as well. Clearly, these two respondents are not equally tolerant. Some studies address this problem by asking respondents to name the three groups they most dislike in order to better distinguish individual levels of tolerance, but the essence of the problem remains.

Scholars like Dennis Chong go further, arguing that in order to truly assess public tolerance, we must consider changing social norms.[49] People may do more than tolerate; they may come to accept. That is, they may become used to new social ideas and norms. It seems inappropriate to insist that such acclimation does not constitute tolerance. For example, the norm of racial equality has become particularly salient in the last few decades. According to Chong:

> Two forms of adjustment are taking place. On the one hand, some individuals have modified their attitudes in light of changes in the social norms. . . . On the other hand, a new generation of Americans has grown up and been socialized in a radically transformed political environment which no longer promotes and legitimates old-fashioned racist appeals. . . . Whites are not "putting up with" Blacks increasingly; rather, Whites now see Blacks differently than they used to, in a manner more benign than was true in the past.[50]

It would be strange indeed to argue that a society that comes to accept and respect diversity is less "tolerant" than one that merely "puts up with" groups and ideas.

Is Tolerance a Social Good?

The debate over what tolerance really is and how to measure it raises another important issue. Is tolerance a good thing in and of itself? Many of us, without thinking too much about it, would say yes. Our cultural values, as we have seen, support a social norm of tolerance. But take a moment to think it through and the issue becomes more complex. As we pointed out in Chapter 7, there must be some level of consensus in a social system or it will collapse. How can we be tolerant of all viewpoints and still maintain enough consensus for our democracy to work?

Further, should we tolerate all viewpoints, even the intolerant ones? If someone wants a public forum to make racist statements, should they have it? Box 10.2 describes such a case. In 1977, the American Nazi Party sued the Village of Skokie, Illinois, for the right to hold a rally on the steps of the village hall.

What sorts of behavior should be tolerated, and what goes too far? Should we be tolerant of parents whose religious beliefs make them unwilling to obtain medical treatment for their children, even when the children are seriously ill? Should we be tolerant of Native American religious practices that involve ingesting hallucinogenic drugs like peyote? Should we be tolerant of same-sex marriages?

Box 10.2 The Nazis in Skokie

Just outside of the city of Chicago lies the village of Skokie. It is a middle-class town of small bungalows and green lawns. In 1977, the leader of the National Socialist Party of America (often referred to as the American Nazi Party) announced that his group intended to hold a white power rally on the steps of the village hall. At that time, almost half of the town's population was Jewish, and many in the community were Holocaust survivors.

Local leaders, in consultation with several rabbis, decided to grant the Nazis a permit to demonstrate and at the same time to draw as little attention to the demonstration as possible. They hoped that if the village raised a minimum of fuss, the Nazis would come and go quietly and their demonstration would be ignored by the villagers. The decision seemed both expedient and tolerant. However, it outraged the survivor community.

Holocaust survivors felt that by allowing the Nazis to hold a rally, the village government had abdicated its responsibility to protect survivors from the threat of violence and persecution they believed Nazism represented. The intense reaction of Holocaust survivors to the local government's plans to permit the rally caused the Village Board of Trustees to reverse its decision. Instead of granting a permit, the trustees obtained an injunction against the Nazis and enacted several city ordinances that were designed to prevent the rally. The Nazis sued.

For nearly a year, the litigation made its way through the state and federal court system. The state supreme court of Illinois lifted the injunction against the demonstration, and the U.S. district court overturned the city ordinances that were meant to prevent it. The village government complied with the courts' decisions and issued the Nazis a permit to hold their rally. Four days later, it issued a second permit to the Jewish Federation of Metropolitan Chicago to hold a counterdemonstration on the same day that the Nazis held their rally. Three days before the demonstrations were scheduled, the Nazis announced that they were canceling their march.

Although the Nazis never marched in Skokie, the controversy caused many thoughtful Americans to consider what the limits of public tolerance might be. After the persecution of American Communist and Socialist sympathizers during the 1950s and in earlier eras, it seemed to many that the United States had an obligation as a liberal democratic state to tolerate political views its citizens found noxious. However, many argued that the Nazis had abused the tolerance institutionally required by the American system of government. Although the purpose of First Amendment rights to speak and assemble were designed to encourage public debate from which the truth might emerge, the Nazis' threat to demonstrate in Skokie seemed blatantly provocative, designed primarily to traumatize Jewish residents and only secondarily, if at all, to enhance public discourse.

(continues)

Box 10.2   *(continued)*

But where should we draw the line? The courts have ruled that there is no First Amendment right to incite violence, but they have also ruled that public agencies may not limit speech on the grounds that violence might result. Further, citizen debate is often most effectively stirred by dramatic public protest, as in the confrontations staged by civil rights and antiwar activists during the 1960s and early 1970s. The courts' compromise has been to demand that laws affecting freedom of speech be "content neutral"; that is, they must apply equally to everyone who wishes to speak or publish regardless of viewpoint. But should we tolerate advocates of viewpoints that would curtail or eliminate some of the freedoms we now enjoy or that would abolish those freedoms for certain groups? Should we tolerate the public expression of political viewpoints that are hurtful or threatening to individuals or groups? Does our democratic code require us to entertain any idea, no matter how horrendous? If we should draw a line, where should we draw it? And how?

At some level, any kind of social norm represents a form of intolerance. It implies that some beliefs or behaviors are accepted but others are unacceptable. We are intolerant of teenage pregnancy, cocaine use, and communism in this society. Expressing disapproval of these things conforms to social norms, but it is also intolerant of alternative viewpoints and behaviors.

Further, social institutions are frequently created in order to promote these social norms. Thus, the structure of the society often expresses intolerance of some groups and practices. For example, Sunday closing laws were on the books in many cities and states for many years during a time when most Americans attended church weekly. The laws benefited workers who wanted their Sundays free for worship because they required businesses (even retail businesses, like grocery stores) to be closed on Sundays. However, those who practiced religions that worshiped on another day of the week, such as Saturday, were systematically disadvantaged because they were forced to close for two days each week in order to observe their day of worship.

Ultimately, practicing tolerance means walking a fine line. Americans appear to support and cherish civil liberties, at least in the abstract. Opinion surveys suggest widespread approval for tolerance of diversity in race, class, gender, and religion. However, no society is, or should be, value free, and other important values often conflict with the ideal of tolerance.

Faith in Government

Another element that would seem to be crucial to an effective democracy is a healthy level of mutual respect between political leaders and citizens. In

Chapter 9, we discussed some of the linkages that connect public opinion to public policy. We also described some of the ways that political leaders have tried to manipulate public opinion. You will recall from Chapter 1 that some scholars believe public opinion to be solely the creation of political elites. An important debate among public opinion scholars involves the extent to which public policy responds to public opinion.

The public, for its part, seems to be increasingly unconvinced that the government it elects responds to its wishes. Public cynicism has been on the rise since the 1960s, and faith in government has declined precipitously. The National Election Studies collect data in federal election years and frequently include questions asking people how they feel about their government. Figure 10.12 reveals some of their findings. Beginning in the late 1960s, people's feelings of efficacy (their belief that they can affect what government does)

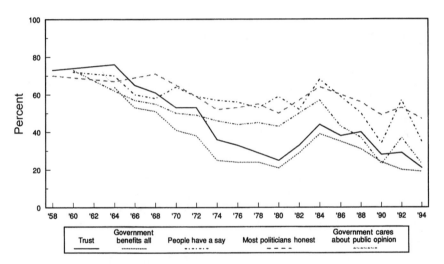

FIGURE 10.12   Public Trust in Government

(NATIONAL ELECTION STUDIES) QUESTION: Would you say the government is pretty much run by a few big interests looking out for themselves or that it is run for the benefit of all the people?

(NATIONAL ELECTION STUDIES) QUESTION: Do you think that quite a few of the people running the government are (1958–1972: a little) crooked, not very many are, or do you think hardly any of them are crooked (1958–1972: at all)?

(NATIONAL ELECTION STUDIES) QUESTION: How much of the time do you think you can trust the government in Washington to do what is right—just about always, most of the time, or only some of the time?

(NATIONAL ELECTION STUDIES) QUESTION: People like me don't have any say about what the government does.

(NATIONAL ELECTION STUDIES) QUESTION: I don't think public officials care much what people like me think.

and trust in the government have dropped drastically. A minor recovery at the outset of Reagan's second term has not offset continuing losses. Further, the decline in efficacy and trust extends beyond government to other public institutions such as business, science, religion, and the media.

Of course, a certain amount of public skepticism about government can be a good thing. Indeed, American democracy owes its structure in part to its founders' skepticism about government. Without some critical thinking on the part of the public, the specter of tyranny may not be far away. But many scholars believe that healthy skepticism has given way to mordant cynicism. Richard Stivers usefully contrasts cynicism with idealism, noting that each can be damaging to democratic government. Idealism is oblivious to the workings of power. Cynicism sees nothing beyond the workings of power.[51] Skeptics recognize that politicians sometimes do the right thing for the wrong reasons. For cynics, the fact that a politician's motives may be impure is all-important.

What has prompted this deteriorating faith in public institutions? Some have blamed it on the disillusionment created by Americans' experience of the war in Vietnam and the Watergate scandal. These events do seem to mark the beginning of steep declines in public trust. Later upturns such as the one marking the Reagan presidency and a brief increase following the Persian Gulf War have not been maintained.[52] Others have cited the media's increasingly negative coverage of politics as a source of public cynicism about government.[53] Kathleen Hall Jamieson and Joseph Capella found that public cynicism seems to be triggered by more than one aspect of media coverage. Coverage that focuses on the strategic aspects of policymaking and campaigning seems to encourage people to be cynical about politics.[54] This may be because such coverage focuses on the personal aspirations of politicians more than on the social outcomes of policies. Public debate that is strongly negative and does not balance critiques of a policy with more positive alternatives also seems to awaken public cynicism.[55]

Other scholars believe that structural changes in government are to blame for public distrust. William Schneider argues that a phenomenon he refers to as the professionalization of politics has been a key source of the problem. He notes that even after World War II, many state legislators were amateurs and many state legislatures met only infrequently. The citizen-politicians were close to the voters but relied on bureaucrats and the states' governors for expertise in policymaking. State legislatures in the 1950s had a turnover rate of almost 40 percent. But beginning in the 1960s, there was a move to professionalize legislatures. Today, most state legislatures are in session for much of the year. The legislators have large staffs, and almost 20 percent of lawmakers consider the legislature a career.[56]

At the same time that the state legislators became professionals, the national political parties declined in importance. The result was an "every-man-for-himself" ethic. Legislators became as interested, perhaps more interested, in getting themselves reelected as they were in solving the state's or the nation's problems. Schneider explains:

> There's only one problem [with professionalized legislatures]. The voters hate it. They hate the idea that people go into the legislature as a career. And they hate the fact that state legislatures are becoming more and more like Congress— full-time professional bodies where members have become independent entre- preneurs requiring elaborate fund-raising activities to mount extensive cam- paigns. . . . Congress is the most professional legislature in the country, but it still cannot govern. . . . Members of Congress are professionals at getting and staying elected. But the very things that a career legislator must do to stay elected make it more difficult for the collective body to solve problems.[57]

Rather than focusing on solving national problems through taking risks and making compromises, professional legislators often concentrate on raising money and providing services to constituents. This may explain why many voters love their member of Congress but hate Congress itself. A 1990 poll found that 41 percent of Americans agree that "congressmen spend more time thinking of their own political futures than they do in passing wise legislation."[58]

How can a democratic government with such low levels of public sup- port survive? Seymour Martin Lipset and William Schneider discovered an odd and interesting answer to the question: People do not seem to believe that there is anything fundamentally wrong with democracy itself. Instead, they are cynical about their leaders. They have faith in the system, but not in the people running it. They also found evidence of an "impersonal im- pact" (see Chapter 6) phenomenon that they labeled the *confidence gap*: "'My own life is fine,' people told poll takers, 'and I am confident about my personal future. But there is something wrong "out there." The people in charge of things aren't doing their jobs, and the future of the country is in doubt.'"[59] The result, according to Lipset and Schneider, is not a crisis of le- gitimacy but a backlash against the people in power. Schneider notes that in the 1990 congressional elections, for example, incumbents of both parties lost support. It was not the case that one party's incumbents were thrown out of office to make way for another party's newcomers. Instead, incum- bents of both parties were thrown out about equally.

Although most scholars seem to agree that the lack of public faith in gov- ernment does not constitute a crisis of legitimacy, public cynicism has had important political fallout. Politicians of all types have, in recent elections, tried to portray themselves as "outsiders" who are not part of the "mess in Washington." Even 1996 presidential candidate Robert Dole, who had served in the U.S. Senate for decades, claimed to be an outsider. Another expression of the public's lack of faith in the current electoral system has been the recent success of laws that impose term limits on legislators (see Box 10.3).

Box 10.3   Political Cynicism and Support for Term Limits

One apparent outcome of declining public trust in the political system is the movement to enact term limits. In many states, voters have acted to restrict the number of times their representatives can be elected to public office. Evidence suggests that public support for term limits is not related to dissatisfaction with legislative performance. Instead, voters support these measures if they are cynical about the political process and, to some extent, when it is in their self-interest to do so. One study showed that in Florida, where the state legislature had been controlled by Democrats for some time, Republicans were more likely to support term limits, a case of political self-interest. However, the best explanation for public support for term limits in this case was cynicism.[1]

Many see term limits as strange, since voters have always had the power to "throw the bums out" by voting for another candidate to replace them. William Schneider, however, argues that the reason voters see term limits as a sensible approach is that they dislike not their own legislator but the legislature itself.[2] Perhaps this is an instance of a third-person effect (see Chapter 6). Citizens wish to protect themselves from the poor decisions of other citizens.

Nevertheless, term limits may not produce the outcomes the public seems to hope for, nor will they necessarily rejuvenate public trust in government. As Schneider points out: "The voters have always had the ability to reject incumbents who are not doing their jobs. Now they want to give up the ability to keep incumbents who are doing a good job."[3]

Term limits reduce the expertise of the legislature relative to that of a bureaucracy, such as the Federal Communications Commission or the Social Security Administration, agencies whose workers remain in their jobs despite turnover in the legislature. This may give more power to these agencies, which both advise lawmakers about what policies should be created and ultimately enforce the laws that are passed. Bureaucrats are not elected, so they are unlikely to be responsive to public opinion. Term limits mean that legislators eventually become "lame ducks"—elected officials who cannot run again. Such lame ducks have no real incentive to be responsive to the public's wishes

---

If citizens' lack of faith in the people who govern has not so far done damage to their faith in the principles of democracy, is public cynicism something we need to worry about? Many scholars say yes. Jeffrey Goldfarb argues that public cynicism is detrimental to civic discourse about many important issues:

> Cynicism in our world is a form of legitimation through disbelief. There exists an odd but by now common practice. Leaders use rhetoric which neither they nor their constituents believe, but which leaders and followers nonetheless use to justify their actions. . . . Cynicism dominates the assumptions of our political and cultural life. We not only do not recognize the cynicism; we confuse it with democratic deliberation and political wisdom.[60]

because the voters cannot reward them with another term in office. Thus, the legislature may become less likely to act in accordance with public opinion rather than more accountably. Another problem with term limits has to do with the piecemeal way in which these limits have been enacted. Legislatures, at both state and national levels, are organized according to a seniority system. The longer a legislator has been in office, the more power that person has in the legislature. Seniority gives legislators access to leadership positions and the power to achieve goals that benefit the constituencies that elected them. Legislators with less seniority, regardless of their intentions, may not be capable of producing such results for the voters back home. As a result, states that do not enact term limits have more legislative clout at the federal level than states that do, for voters who return their legislator to office over and over again can reap tangible benefits.

Term limits do solve a systemic problem that concerns scholars and citizens alike. Many legislative elections are not very competitive. The advantages of being an incumbent legislator are enormous: Because they are already in public office and their names are already known to some of their constituents, incumbents find it easier to raise campaign funds and capture media attention. For many challengers, these advantages are impossible to overcome, and the result is that incumbent legislators are returned to office almost automatically in many cases. Term limits require that "open" elections be held periodically. The incumbent must step down, and the new challengers face each other for the open seat. Such elections may be more competitive. What remains to be seen is whether the cure is worse than the illness.

---

1. Jeffrey A. Karp, "Explaining Public Support for Legislative Term Limits," *Public Opinion Quarterly* 59 (1995):373–391.

2. William Schneider, "'Off with Their Heads': The Confidence Gap and the Revolt Against Professionalism in American Politics," in Gary Marks and Larry Diamond, eds., *Reexamining Democracy: Essays in Honor of Seymour Martin Lipset* (Newbury Park, CA: Sage Publications, 1992), pp. 315–331.

3. Ibid., p. 324.

Jean Bethke Elshtain argues that we are caught in what she calls a "spiral of delegitimation." She explains:

Over time, the "culture of mistrust" grows, aided . . . by public scandals; by an ever more litigious and suspicious society; by a determination to "get mine" no matter what may happen to the other guy; and by salacious snooping into the private lives of public figures, which further fuels cynicism about how untrustworthy our leaders are even as we delight in their downfall.[61]

Elshtain worries that the malaise goes deeper than political discourse and the relationships between leaders in Washington and the folks back home. She believes that public cynicism has an impact on the way we interact in our own communities and with our neighbors. It is the combination of a "rhetoric of individualism" and a "culture of cynicism" that has moved us from "Oh, I hope he is not hurt! What would his children do without him?" to "I hope he isn't hurt. He might sue." Elshtain describes this cynical community:

> In America today, fearful people rush to arm themselves, believing safety to be a matter of aggressive self-help. Angry people want all the politicians to be kicked out of office, but they believe new ones will be no better. Anxious people fear that their neighbors' children may get some unfair advantage over their own. . . . Careless people ignore their children and then blast the teachers and social workers who must tend to the mess they have made, screaming all the while that folks ought to "mind their own business."[62]

There appears to be no simple cure for public cynicism. Deal making and compromise, essential components of our political system since its founding, are now dismissed as self-serving political ploys used by professional politicians to advance their personal goals. The public, now with access to more information than ever before, has become more disillusioned than ever before about the leaders who represent them. The human fallibility of many leaders has become plain for all to see. The question remains: In the absence of flawless philosopher-kings, how much imperfection will the public tolerate?

Conclusion

In this chapter, we have reviewed some of the long-term trends that have interested public opinion researchers from some of the theoretical perspectives we have outlined in this book. The fit between theory and data is sometimes imprecise. However, in order to understand public opinion, it is not enough to simply describe the trends we see. We must delve deeper and attempt to understand the cultural, social, and psychological forces that generate changes in public opinion. We must be able to connect the changes in public opinion to the social outcomes they produce.

The tools that we use to measure public opinion are imprecise. Surveys are subject to a variety of measurement errors, many of which we discussed in Chapter 3. Equally important, they may suffer from more subtle problems over the long term. Changes in social norms and in social contexts may affect people's responses to survey questions in ways that the surveys themselves cannot measure. As social norms change, what was once acceptable may become unacceptable, and vice versa. We observed that trends in public opinion about pornography have been very minor, for example. These small apparent changes in public opinion may have masked major real changes because the content of the material itself may have changed dramatically. Measured changes in public tolerance for nonconformity have also been affected by changes in social context as the apparent Communist threat waxed and waned.

However, sometimes theory can help us to interpret otherwise confusing data. For example, the concept of a norm and the theories that come to us from social psychology can help us to understand why respondents sometimes lie to researchers about their "real" opinions. Theories such as cognitive dissonance can explain why it is that some people's opinions do not seem to go together. Theories about the public's lack of knowledge and the reasons for it offer alternative explanations for the same phenomenon. Theories about the role of the media, about the structure of government, and about the connections between public opinion and public policy may help us to understand why public faith in government is declining.

The relationship between theory and data is interdependent. Theories are developed based upon the research techniques and measurement instruments that exist or can be devised. Theories cannot be supported or refuted in the absence of data. Data cannot be effectively interpreted in the absence of theory. The drive to produce better ways of measuring public opinion and better theories to interpret it go hand in hand.

Notes

1. Howard Schuman, Charlotte Steeh, and Lawrence Bobo, *Racial Attitudes in America* (Cambridge: Harvard University Press, 1985).

2. Benjamin I. Page and Robert Y. Shapiro, *The Rational Public: Fifty Years of Trends in Americans' Policy Preferences* (Chicago: University of Chicago Press, 1992).

3. Note that the scale for this question has been transformed. The trend line depicts the percentage of respondents who said they opposed laws forbidding interracial marriage.

4. Page and Shapiro, *Rational Public*, p. 114.

5. Dennis Chong, "Tolerance and Social Adjustment to New Norms and Practices," *Political Behavior* 16 (1994):21–53.

6. Page and Shapiro, *Rational Public*.

7. The author would like to thank James Shanahan for his helpful contributions to this section.

8. Anthony Downs, "Up and Down with Ecology: The 'Issue-Attention Cycle,'" *Public Interest* 28 (1972):38–50.

9. Riley E. Dunlap, "Public Opinion and Environmental Policy," in J. P. Lester, ed., *Environmental Politics and Policy* (Durham, NC: Duke University Press, 1989).

10. Ibid.

11. See, for example, Bente Lis Christensen and Jorgen Stig Norgard, "Social Values and the Limits to Growth," *Technological Forecasting and Social Change* 9 (1976):411–423; Thomas Devaney Harblin, "Mine or Garden? Values and the Environment—Probable Sources of Change in the Next Hundred Years," *Zygon* 12

(June 1977):134–150; Donald W. Whisenhunt, *The Environment and the American Experience* (Port Washington, NY: Kennikat Press, 1974).

12. For example, see Riley E. Dunlap and Kent D. Van Liere, "Commitment to the Dominant Social Paradigm and Concern for Environmental Quality," *Social Science Quarterly* 65 (December 1984):1013–1028.

13. Ibid.

14. *Webster's New International Dictionary* (Springfield, MA: G. and C. Merriam Company, 1935), p. 2661.

15. James L. Gibson, "The Political Consequences of Intolerance: Cultural Conformity and Political Freedom," *American Political Science Review* 86 (1992): 338–356.

16. See Chapter 7.

17. Bernard R. Berelson, Paul M. Lazarsfeld, and William N. McPhee, *Voting: A Study of Opinion Formation in a Presidential Campaign* (Chicago: University of Chicago Press, 1954).

18. James L. Gibson, "Political Consequences of Intolerance."

19. Samuel C. Stouffer, *Communism, Conformity, and Civil Liberties* (New York: Doubleday, 1955).

20. Clyde A. Nunn, Harry J. Crockett, and J. Allen Williams, *Tolerance for Nonconformity* (San Francisco: Jossey-Bass, 1978).

21. Stouffer, *Communism, Conformity, and Civil Liberties*.

22. Nunn, Crockett, and Williams, *Tolerance for Nonconformity*.

23. For a good discussion of this debate, see Lawrence Bobo and Frederick C. Licari, "Education and Political Tolerance," *Public Opinion Quarterly*, 53 (1989): 287–289.

24. Benjamin Ginsberg, *The Captive Public* (New York: Basic Books, 1986).

25. Bobo and Licari, "Education and Political Tolerance."

26. Dennis Chong, "How People Think, Reason, and Feel About Rights and Liberties," *American Journal of Political Science* 37 (1993):867–899.

27. John Zaller, *The Nature and Origins of Mass Opinion* (Cambridge, England: Cambridge University Press, 1992).

28. James H. Kuklinski et al., "The Cognitive and Affective Bases of Political Tolerance Judgments," *American Journal of Political Science* 35 (1991):1–27.

29. Chong, "How People Think, Reason, and Feel."

30. Kuklinski et al., "Political Tolerance Judgments."

31. Stouffer, *Communism, Conformity, and Civil Liberties*, pp. 109–130.

32. Thomas C. Wilson, "Urbanism, Migration and Tolerance: A Reassessment," *American Sociological Review* 56 (1991):117–123.

33. G. Edward Stephan and Douglas R. McMullen, "Tolerance of Sexual Nonconformity: City Size as a Situational and Early Learning Determinant," *American Sociological Review*, 47 (1982):411–415.

34. John L. Sullivan et al., "The Sources of Political Tolerance: A Multivariate Analysis," *American Political Science Review* 75 (1981):92–106; Paul M. Sniderman et al., "Principled Tolerance and the American Mass Public," *British Journal of Political Science* 19 (1989):25–45.

35. John L. Sullivan et al., "Why Politicians Are More Tolerant: Selective Recruitment and Socialization Among Political Elites in Britain, Israel, New Zealand and the United States," *British Journal of Political Science* 23 (1993):51–76.

36. Sullivan et al., "Sources of Political Tolerance."

37. John L. Sullivan, James Pierson, and George E. Marcus, "An Alternative Conceptualization of Political Tolerance: Illusory Increases 1950s–1970s," *American Political Science Review* 73 (1979):781–794.

38. Sullivan et al., "Sources of Political Tolerance"; Donald Philip Green and Lisa Michele Waxman, "Direct Threat and Political Tolerance: An Experimental Analysis of the Tolerance of Blacks Toward Racists," *Public Opinion Quarterly* 51 (1987):149–165; James L. Gibson, "The Policy Consequences of Political Intolerance: Political Repression During the Vietnam War Era," *Journal of Politics* 51 (1989):13–35.

39. Gibson, "Policy Consequences of Political Intolerance."

40. Stouffer, *Communism, Conformity, and Civil Liberties.*

41. Ibid.

42. See, for example, Thomas C. Wilson, "Trends in Tolerance Toward Rightist and Leftist Groups, 1976–1988, *Public Opinion Quarterly* 58 (1994):539–556; James A. Davis, "Communism and Cohorts Continued: American Tolerance in 1954 and 1972–1987," *GSS Social Change Report No. 30* (Chicago: NORC, 1988). [online] Available: www.icpsr.umich.edu/GSS/report/s-report/soc30.htm.

43. Sullivan, Pierson, and Marcus, "Alternative Conceptualization of Political Tolerance."

44. James W. Prothro and Charles M. Grigg, "Fundamental Principles of Democracy: Bases of Agreement and Disagreement," *Journal of Politics* 22 (1960): 282–285.

45. John Mueller, "Trends in Political Tolerance," *Public Opinion Quarterly* 52 (1988):21.

46. Davis, "Communism and Cohorts Continued."

47. Ibid.

48. Sniderman et al., "Principled Tolerance."

49. Dennis Chong, "Tolerance and Social Adjustment to New Norms and Practices," *Political Behavior* 16 (1994):21–53.

50. Ibid., p. 40.

51. Richard Stivers, *The Culture of Cynicism: American Morality in Decline* (Cambridge, MA: Blackwell Publishers, 1994).

52. William Schneider, "'Off with Their Heads': The Confidence Gap and the Revolt Against Professionalism in American Politics," in Gary Marks and Larry Diamond, eds., *Reexamining Democracy: Essays in Honor of Seymour Martin Lipset* (Newbury Park, CA: Sage Publications, 1992), pp. 315–331.

53. See, for example, Thomas E. Patterson, *Out of Order* (New York: A. Knopf, 1993); Stephen Ansolabehere and Shanto Iyengar, *Going Negative: How Attack Ads Shrink and Polarize the Electorate* (New York: Free Press, 1995); Kathleen Hall Jamieson and Joseph N. Cappella, "News Frames, Political Cynicism, and Media Cynicism," *Annals of the American Academy of Political and Social Science,* 546 (July 1996):71–84.

54. Jamieson and Cappella, "News Frames, Political Cynicism, and Media Cynicism."

55. Ibid.

56. Schneider, "'Off with Their Heads.'"

57. Ibid., pp. 322–323.

58. Herb Asher and Mike Barr, "Popular Support for Congress and Its Members," in Thomas E. Mann and Norman J. Ornstein, ed., *Congress, the Press, and the Public* (Washington, DC: American Enterprise Institute, 1994), pp. 15–44.

59. Schneider, "'Off with Their Heads.'"

60. Jeffrey C. Goldfarb, *The Cynical Society: The Culture of Politics and the Politics of Culture in American Life* (Chicago: University of Chicago Press, 1991), pp. 1–2.

61. Jean Bethke Elshtain, *Democracy on Trial* (New York: Basic Books, 1995), p. 25.

62. Ibid., p. 20.

Chapter Eleven

Communicating with
the Public

In Chapter 1, we looked at many ways of defining public opinion, based on what the term means to different people in different contexts. We have established that public opinion is *not* a static, immobile object that holds a constant shape and mass over time. Rather, it is a highly dynamic, fluid process that reflects how people think, interact with one another, and deal with the bodies politic into which they have organized themselves.

We have seen how at the individual or personal level, citizens constantly change and reassess their attitudes and opinions, the better to fit new knowledge and experience. At the macro, or mass, societal level, politically salient events occur that transform political coalitions, the nature of issues, and the appropriateness of given policy options. And at the level of group interaction and networking, the everyday give and take of political talk at the dinner table, at the workplace, and over the phone or the Internet reshapes what we think of one another and about politics. At each of these levels, the development and generation of public opinion requires active communication processes to be at work. Recall from Chapter 6 how mass and interpersonal communication interplay to promote such phenomena as the spiral of silence and third-person effects from media. We have also learned that when people do learn new things or change attitudes or behaviors as a result of what they see or hear from others, complex psychological processes are involved, some involving highly logical steps, some based more on whims of the moment.

This chapter begins by examining how our thinking about the role of communication in the public opinion process has progressed. We will emphasize the interplay of mass media and public opinion, where most of the gains in our knowledge have taken place over recent decades. We will also, however, demonstrate the obvious but sometimes overlooked importance of interpersonal communication in the mix.

Communication, Mass Media, and Public Opinion: Early Development and Perspectives

Communication serves many functions to keep our diverse society working well enough to maintain basic equilibrium. The sociologist Harold Lasswell defined three key functions of communication for societies, each of which also has clear ramifications for public opinion.[1] The first is *surveillance*, or keeping one another abreast of what is taking place in the world, especially events that may be threatening to the common good. Print and electronic news media have become a ritualized force to which we entrust much of this responsibility. A second function, *correlation*, serves to keep us in touch with what others are thinking about what is going on, how events are being interpreted, and the opinions of others toward various topics. Lasswell saw this correlation among views and building of consensus as a social "glue" necessary to getting things done in a community or society. Such a correlating function helps develop democratic consensuses out of conflict situations, a central tenet of modern democratic theory raised in Chapter 7. A third function is *transmission*, or the passing of the norms and morals of the culture to others entering the social system, most obviously the young. Formal education fills much of this role for the society as a whole. Other more informal communication channels often help transmit norms within groups, initiating new members into the rituals that keep organizations together over time.

Lasswell was thinking as much or more about interpersonal as mass communication channels in defining these three functions. Other scholars have added specific additional functions for modern mass media—entertainment being one, economic enhancement another.[2] The modern advertising-marketing multiplex driven by media enterprises has been claimed as necessary for keeping our present consumer-based economy operating.

Historically, we see a distinct change in thinking about the social purposes of communication as mass media developed in the late nineteenth century and on into the twentieth. It became popular—and sometimes convenient—for social critics and scholars to blame the new media technologies for a host of other changes occurring about the same time, many of them viewed as threatening. Much of that concern was likely grounded in fear of the unknown—of novel, mysterious, and seemingly unrestricted technologies that might be challenging and changing not only the political but the social and cultural worlds of the time.

Not coincidentally, this was also the era in which mass society theories of public opinion began to emerge.[3] Western industrialized societies were viewed as moving away from clusters of closely knit communities with close personal linkages toward becoming more transient, urbanized, and impersonal. The basic economically driven movement of people from rural communities and farms to centralized factory-driven cities was a key component here. This was seen as leading to breakdowns in community structure and personal relationships, with individuals becoming more anonymous and isolated. Such isolation, it was feared, could result in publics that acted as more of a "mass" of less socially tied and responsible citizens. Such masses, lacking closer social ties, could be more amenable to various forms of propaganda and demagoguery. The new media of the era were thus even more feared as a catalyst that could sway these masses. At this time, communication about politics per se was rapidly moving away from a largely interpersonal pursuit—buttressed by printed materials available to the relatively well-educated and affluent few. It was becoming a more institutionalized system, involving more free-flowing information from a variety of sources to huge audiences.

The development of higher-speed printing technologies in the early and mid-1800s made inexpensive daily newspapers available to millions of urban dwellers, giving them up-to-date local and telegraph-fed national news and commentary. The technology also greatly reduced the cost of and increased the availability and visual appeal of magazines, books, pamphlets, catalogs, and other print items. Motion pictures became a mainstream entertainment medium in the early 1900s, with such popular fare as D. W. Griffith's *Birth of a Nation* showing the potential political and social clout of film. By midcentury, radio blossomed into a mature technology capable of reaching into every U.S. home, providing a diverse mix of popular to more sophisticated entertainment, commentary, and news, including "live" coverage of war, disasters, political speeches, and elections.

Television entered the scene on a grand scale in the 1950s and within a decade, became the dominant mass medium for entertainment as well as a medium heavily depended on for national and international news. By the 1980s, telecommunication via satellite had greatly expanded television's content capabilities to include dozens of cable-cast and direct satellite channels covering a much wider range of interests. The same satellite capabilities, attended by rapid innovation in the computer industry, allowed greatly enhanced personal interactive communications in the 1990s, relying on Internet capabilities and far more sophisticated telephone systems that were soon to be linked with television. E-mail and World Wide Web sites have emerged as significant communication channels, bridging mass communication with interpersonal communication, blurring many distinctions between the two concepts.

Each of these developments caused a certain amount of awe at its potential for opinion-shaping power. Concerns rose about the impact of each new communication technology on public opinion and often about its influence on the cultural and moral fabric—and social behavior—as well. Political debate was thought to be cheapened by many nineteenth-century newspapers' penchant for sensationalism, called "yellow journalism" (meaning in part unfair, biased coverage), and often crude, close-to-libelous attacks on public officials. *Birth of a Nation* displayed a popular motion picture's ability arguably to misrepresent the post–Civil War South in a way blatantly unfair to black citizens. Radio's ability to provide live access in the homes of its audiences to the words of political leaders—champions and demagogues alike—caused considerable concern. Moreover, the propagandistic value of radio as an international medium via shortwave broadcasting was quickly discovered by many countries. This perhaps peaked during the World War II and the subsequent Cold War battles for the airwaves among the Voice of America, the British Broadcasting Corporation, and Radio Moscow. The onset of television appeared to some to take the more persuasive and perhaps more odious elements of all of the above channels and drop them into the laps of citizens in their living rooms. Many critics see the relatively unrestricted accessibility of the Internet as aiding political radicalism and pornography and as a threat to individual privacy.

In sum, each of these new technologies in its own way fueled concerns that it had the power to sway public opinion unduly, to influence or propagandize large groups of people to believe or act in ways somehow unhealthy for themselves and their society. Taking these media as a group and coupling them with the concurrent large-scale economic, political, and social changes taking place in the United States and elsewhere, it is not surprising that legitimate questions have been raised by social observers about their influence. Others have vehemently attacked media at various times, having found a convenient scapegoat for war, economic depression, the social upheavals fermented by industrialization, and related ills.

But how much have these new media really mattered? How much of a difference did they make in how public opinion is developed and shaped? In truth, we will probably never really know what their consequences were in previous decades. Nevertheless, we can hazard some well-educated guesses and, at the least, frame the questions in ways that will help us more successfully figure out the influence of communication media in our present environment and what we should make of that. Perhaps in its most simplistic—if not too simplistic—terms, the ongoing debate is between (a) scholars, social critics, and policymakers concerned that mass media have an edge over the publics or audiences they reach, unduly influencing them, and (b) those who argue that these publics can resist such influences and indeed use media in largely beneficial ways.

Before turning to the evidence on either side of that debate, we should carry the thread from previous chapters a bit further and say more about who decides what kinds of information media carry with respect to public opinion and who decides what that information is. Recall that Chapter 9 discussed how elites try to influence more general publics directly on political issues, with interpersonal opinion leadership being a key concept. Here, we will first consider how elites—and others—try to use mass media as agents of influence and then, from the point of view of the public, consider the evidence concerning how successful such manipulation may be.

Who Decides What the Media Present?

A critical question is how issues, events, and, indeed, personalities, come into media view in the first place. It is worth recalling here Lippmann's point that at their best, the media give us representations, pictures of an outside world we do not directly see or experience (see Figure 11.1).[4] Someone is preparing those pictures or stories for us—of events, of issues, of personalities—that we

FIGURE 11.1   The media give us representations of the world beyond our experience. SOURCE: © Tom Tomorrow. *Greetings from This Modern World* (New York: St. Martin's Press, 1992).

will likely never encounter "live" on our own. *Who* prepares those pictures, with what biases, and with what intents is a critical question.

In its most basic form, the evidence shows that for most major public issues, most of the public begins to pay them more heed after they have been reported in newspapers and on television.[5] How much the public is interested in events and issues is for the most part proportional to how much news coverage the issues get. But journalists seldom report on issues or events unless they see some compelling public interest or need to be served by doing so. Even in reporting the most trivial or sensational stories, reporters are driven by an assumption that audiences will want to know about it and will "buy" the story by reading or watching it. Hence, the news agenda may be set in large part by the press's expectations of what audiences want or need. It becomes not quite so surprising that audiences eventually place those topics higher on their own agendas. There are likely instances in which the news media discover stories about events that are already priorities on the public agenda. More localized community or grassroots issues come to mind here—concern generated by neighbors about a landfill problem may be presented to a city council hearing or lead to organized protest, attracting news media attention. In fact, this is becoming a more common tactic used by citizens to gain attention for issues that occupy them.

It is also commonplace for organized interest groups—including corporations and government agencies and other elites—to try to influence the press and by that the public agenda.[6] A cursory scan of mainstream daily newspapers or news broadcasts suggests that most of the information presented in them originates from governmental organizations, lobbying groups, corporations, and other institutions with their own agendas and influence strategies. These can include efforts by, say, federal health agencies to inform citizens of how to protect themselves from a new disease outbreak or attempts by a tobacco company to put the best possible light on the risks involved in cigarette smoking. An environmental group holds a press conference on what it regards as a major threat by Congress to watershed protection; a U.S. senator alerts a *New York Times* reporter of the possibility that his election opponent has a campaign slush fund. Although we count on the press to sort out the merits of these episodes, report on them as appropriate, and assemble them into the day's news agenda, it seems undeniable that the news that is produced is in part a function of the agendas of others.

Much of the U.S. public relations industry is built around encouraging the press to give more play to a company, personage, issue, or event. Anecdotal evidence suggests that political candidates can significantly influence news play during campaigns and that incumbents can be highly successful at it. Research shows that presidents in particular can use the power of

their office to sway the news agenda,[7] more likely when they are more popular with the public and the press.[8] Officeholders and other individuals
who are regarded by the media as public spokespersons typically have a
major influence simply in the access they have to the media and journalists,
who often seek their opinions and reactions to events. Such elites are also
able to *frame* or develop the context of media presentations and stories,
which can lead reporters to emphasize certain aspects of an event or issue
at the expense of others.[9] Such framing, as explained by Robert Entman,
can exaggerate particular aspects of political problems, leading to suggested solutions to those problems that may be slanted toward particular
political biases or moral judgments. Entman offers the global example of
the Cold War between the United States and the Soviet Union, which dominated most news accounts of world events from the 1950s through the
1980s. Civil wars in developing countries, for example, tended to be reported in U.S. news media more in the context of whether a possibly
"Communist" or Soviet-leaning faction was involved and how that had
happened, rather than on issues and causes perhaps more germane to the
country in question.

Another example would be whether a story about decreased Medicare
support for the elderly is framed more in terms of its impact on the health
of the elderly, on spiraling health care costs that affect the quality of health
care in the U.S. overall, or on the contribution of Medicare costs to the federal spending deficit. Depending upon which frame is chosen and by whom,
the line of argument for solutions and the moral issues involved can be
quite different. Part of this process includes attempts by elite spokespersons
to "spin" stories, or emphasize angles of issues that will put themselves or
their viewpoints in the most favorable light.

As Clarice Olien, George Donohue, and Phillip Tichenor remind us, these
and other influences on the news media render them far from being independent, autonomous, "objective" observers.[10] The press can be viewed as a
socially controlled institution in the same sense that executive government
agencies, the courts, schools, and higher education are. All respond to and
are constrained by other societal forces, notably including one another, and
the public.

At the core of most approaches to how communication and public opinion relate is the notion of public *issues* that people agree or disagree about.
Inherent in the concept of an issue is *conflict*, the grist not only of public
opinion (see Chapter 7) but of everyday news coverage as well. A series of
studies by Olien, Donohue, and Tichenor on the role of the press in community conflict and public opinion have suggested that news media may
too often report conflict in ways that satisfy established, powerful political
and social groups.[11] This may be at the expense of the less potent, and perhaps of the public trust.

The First Amendment protections accorded the press imply that it serves something of a "watchdog" role, alerting the community at large to potentially conflicting intrusions. Olien and associates challenge this and argue that in too many cases, the news media act more as a "guard dog," favoring more powerful and influential community interests. This does not imply that the press favors individuals or organizations when they behave inappropriately, which could be more of a "lap dog" role. Rather, the news establishment is seen as having developed power relationships with other community institutions and focuses more on maintaining those relationships and on exploiting conflicts that work toward that end. Olien and associates suggest that such reporting emphasizes conflict between individuals within power structures rather than opposition to the power structure itself. More ritualistic controversies, such as election campaigns, are played up, as opposed to threats to the political system. Olien and colleagues offer the example of the 1972 presidential election, in which "ritualistic" coverage of McGovern versus Nixon on traditional candidate and campaign topics displaced coverage of the system-threatening Watergate affair until after the election.

More critical observers such as Edward Herman and Noam Chomsky view most contemporary media as being conservatively bound up in the marketplace of commerce rather than in the marketplace of ideas, reluctant to examine problems and issues that could push the economic or political status quo too far off-center.[12]

The Effects of Mass Media on Public Opinion

Do these efforts at influence and manipulation through the media work? Is public opinion affected? A succinct answer might be a rephrasing of Harold Lasswell:[13] Some of the messages on some of the media have some effects on some audiences some of the time. Here we will consider four broad categories of possible effects on (1) the public agenda for issues; (2) how informed the public is about issues; (3) public opinions, attitudes, and behaviors; and (4) public values and norms.

The Media and the Public Agenda

A major and often underestimated force in public opinion dynamics is how and why people choose to direct their attention to one issue at the expense of another, to spend more time and effort thinking about one problem than another. Awareness of and attention to issues precedes the shaping of opinion positions about them. Our attention spans, as well as the scope of issues we can deal with at any one time, are limited. Some of us may find ourselves giving much attention to gender discrimination, and others to U.S. involvement in international conflicts; some may be concerned over animal rights, and still others over global environmental issues. But few if any of us can give equal attention to all of those and others; rather, we "agendize" and prioritize our concerns. And the news media appear subtly and consistently to influence the agenda of issues we have opinions about. As succinctly put by political scientist Bernard Cohen, "The press may not be successful much of the time in telling people what to think, but it is stunningly successful in telling its readers what to think about."[14] A multitude of studies have validated this *agenda-setting* function of the news media. The more play and emphasis newspapers or television news give to particular events or issues, the more likely are audiences of those media to regard them as more salient, more important. Recall the status-conferring ability of the media discussed previously: The mechanism may be quite the same, but here it is spread across the larger workings of the entire news-dissemination process.

Early work on agenda setting in the 1970s, primarily by communication scholars Maxwell McCombs and Donald Shaw of the University of North Carolina, found direct links between the ranking of issues as treated in the news media and the ranking of importance given to those issues by the public in opinion polls (Table 11.1).[15] When citizens were asked which issue or issues they regarded as most important, the order of those issues corresponded quite well with the degree of news play they had received. How audiences of specific news media ranked Vietnam War issues or the economy or race issues was presaged by how much news coverage those issues had received. News coverage in these studies is typically measured by content analysis of newspapers, magazines, and television news. Individual topics are rated according to how much coverage they get in terms of space in print media or time in broadcast news. Account is also taken of the prominence of coverage given a topic, for example, by how much front-page coverage it

TABLE 11.1   Correlations of Voter Emphasis on Issues with Media Coverage

	Major Items	*Minor Items*
Newsweek	.30	.53
Time	.30	.78
New York Times	.96	.97
Raleigh Times	.80	.73
Raleigh News and Observer	.91	.93
Durham Sun	.82	.96
Durham Morning Herald	.94	.93
NBC News	.89	.91
CBS News	.63	.81

SOURCE: Based on Maxwell E. McCombs and Donald Shaw, "The Agenda-Setting Function of the Mass Media," *Public Opinion Quarterly* 36 (1972), table 4, p. 183.

received in a newspaper or how close to the beginning of a newscast it was in the case of television.

Some of the research has carefully traced the time order of this relationship, a critical point in demonstrating that the news helps form audience agendas, rather than the other way around. For the most part, issues appear to be first emphasized in the news agenda, which then leads to their being ranked more highly by the public, rather than vice versa. Laboratory experiments involving television newscasts across a number of topics have borne this out.[16] Governmental policymakers may also be influenced by news agendas, independently of their influence on citizens.[17] Recalling the discussion of third-person effects in Chapter 6, we can speculate on whether public officials and policymakers may be prompted to act in anticipation of the impact they *think* news will have on the public. The implications of this become problematic if policymakers think the news media have a greater effect on the public than is actually the case and make decisions based on that assumption.[18]

If news media influence which issues people think about, how does the news provide cues to prompt or focus that thinking about any one issue? Some clues to this can be found in Iyengar and Kinder's use of the concept of *priming*.[19] When faced with an often bewildering array of complex information about an issue, citizens need to choose which facets of it they will consider as most relevant. The news helps them do that, Iyengar and Kinder hypothesize, by priming, or drawing greater attention to some aspects of an issue at the expense of others.

This psychological phenomenon may become most relevant when linked to a soon-to-happen decision or behavior. I may be primed to choose one movie over another at the video shop by happening to see a display ad emphasizing that a favorite actor is in it. Or if I am driving to the polls to vote in a major election, I may be swayed by hearing an effective radio spot linking a political candidate to a cause I believe in, especially if it is in a lesser contest involving candidates I know little about. An important point about priming phenomena is that they are usually short-lived, almost inevitably replaced by the next attracting stimulus that grabs our attention (see Box 11.1).

However, in some contexts, including political ones, they may prove somewhat longer term. Jon Krosnick found, for example, that President George Bush was more likely to be assessed on the basis of his handling of the Persian Gulf War following the massive press coverage of it than on his handling of the rather unchanged domestic economy and other foreign affairs issues.[20] These latter issues had been paramount in citizen judgments of Bush prior to the war. One might argue they returned to greater importance as the 1992 election neared, contributing to Bush's defeat.

This power of the press to shape the public agenda has its limits. It is not quite clear how much the news media may determine citizens' agendas

Box 11.1 Priming Time for Television?

Shanto Iyengar and Donald Kinder ran a series of experiments examining what role "priming" played in the way people make judgments about the performance of the president. Different groups of subjects were shown different television newscasts, each emphasizing a particular national issue. One newscast dealt primarily with national defense, another with inflation, another with energy, and so forth. The subjects were then asked to rate the president on several attributes, including his performance in each of the issue areas that had been experimentally manipulated.

The subjects put more weight on the particular issue to which they had been exposed when they made their judgments of the president: Those who had seen the national defense newscasts rated the president based more on how good a job they thought he was doing on national defense; those who had seen the inflation news judged him more on the inflation issue, and so on. Also bearing out the priming hypothesis was the finding that the various newscasts had no influence on how the subjects rated the president's overall character, a judgment presumably based on a much wider array of personal and performance traits less touched by one issue or another.

Importance of Unemployment as a Function of Vividness of TV News Presentation: Experiment 6

Story	Measure of Importance	Presentation		Difference: Vivid Presentation Minus Pallid Presentation
		Pallid	Vivid	
Chicago's West Side	Composite ratings	95	84	–11[c]
	Percentage naming	83	64	–19[a]
CETA cuts	Composite ratings	87	88	01
	Percentage naming	62	83	21[b]

[a] $p < .18$
[b] $p < .12$
[c] $p < .05$

SOURCE: Shanto Iyengar and Donald R. Kinder, *News That Matters: Television and American Opinion* (Chicago: University of Chicago Press, 1987), table 4.2, p. 38.

without their knowledge or consent, versus how much citizens purposively use the media to help them prioritize the complex aggregations of issues they confront on a daily basis. In many cases, individuals are clearly quite aware that they rely on media for a sense of what is important in the world, and in fact, they may occasionally rebel if they think they are not getting what they need. Poll questions asking whether respondents think the media are giving "too much attention" to some events—the 1995 O. J. Simpson murder trial is a case in point—often draw substantial numbers of affirmative replies. Moreover, there is evidence that more vivid, dramatic, and emotionally driven news coverage does little to enhance the agenda-setting effect on citizens.[21]

Maxwell McCombs and Tamara Bell reported that citizens with a higher need for political orientation—those who are politically interested but less knowledgeable—had agendas more closely matching those of news media, presumably because they were more actively seeking such input.[22] Despite a wide range of studies exploring other aspects of agenda setting, firm conclusions as to the conditions under which it is likely to be greater or weaker are few. Some research indicates that interpersonal discussion of issues diminishes agenda setting,[23] but other findings conclude that the more involved citizens are with particular issues, the greater the media agenda setting.[24] Individuals may be more disposed to such media influence when it reinforces their own interests or experience.

The Media and an Informed Public

How people become informed as citizens and how well informed they become are two critical aspects of public opinion dynamics. The level of information and knowledge underlying public thought, discussion, and debate obviously constrains the quality of the process, drawing from Lasswell's surveillance function of communication in society. These are also consequences of communication that until quite recently, have been uncritically "assumed to happen" rather than having been studied as an active process. It is ironic that the most obvious effect of interpersonal and mass-mediated communication—the gain of information or knowledge—has been examined less than the more debatable communication effects of attitude and behavioral change.

We know in the most rudimentary way that citizens gain information about public issues from one other and from institutions such as schools, governmental and political organizations, and mass media. From studies of election campaigns in recent times, we assume that these campaigns are an important educational tool for voters in the sense that they learn not only about candidates and their positions but also about issues of the day. We also assume that major news events very quickly inform the public about issues of consequence, whether involving war, natural disasters, violent protest, assassinations, major medical discoveries, or economic booms or busts. We can also assume that in cases involving political persuasion or change, at least *something* in the form of information is conveyed. But we still have little understanding of how information gets transferred, from what sources, through which channels, and to which audiences or publics.

Media as Information Sources.   Certain myths about how people gather information in today's multimedia environment have been called into serious question, however. One is that television is *the* main and most effective purveyor of political and other kinds of information. Several studies summarized by John Robinson and Mark Levy argue to the contrary.[25] For one thing, research indicates that television news viewers did not gain any more information about current events than users of other media; in fact, in some cases television news viewers were less well-informed. In terms of *understanding or comprehension* of news, television viewers ranked a poor third behind newspaper and magazine readers. Moreover, the extent to which people discussed the news more often with others was as good a predictor of news comprehension than use of any mass media source.

In the end, most people use a variety of news sources for different purposes, and it makes little sense to regard any one medium as the most predominant. There has been some concern, however, that among the minority who use only one source, television news is most likely to be the one chosen. That, coupled with significant declines in newspaper readership—especially among the young—could signal the emergence of a less news-conscious public.[26] Nonetheless, recent years have also seen increases in at least the quantity of television news content and the growth of Internet news sources and other electronic channels. However, a 1994 follow-up analysis by Robinson and Levy of people's news sources and what they knew about current events showed little change from their study of the previous decade: Television news produced the least learning.[27] Debate continues over the quality of news, especially the increasing trend in the 1990s toward sensationalizing news, including a renewed focus on lurid personal incidents in the lives of public figures (see Figure 11.2).

The twin questions "How much do people know about current events?" and "How much should they know?" have forever plagued observers of public opinion. We simply do not have a very good handle on either question. With respect to the first question, opinion polls and surveys by and large have not provided a useful overview of either the quantity or quality of civic knowledge citizens hold, likely in part because scholars and even most critics are reluctant to overly proscribe answers to the second question. There is probably agreement in these times that we do not need more knowledge of the deepest personal revelations of public figures or of campaign-constructed pseudo-events or outright falsehoods; accurate, reflective knowledge of germane elements of political issues and values of the day would be welcome. Nevertheless, how far do we go in arguing against knowing the character attributes of our leaders and in favoring perhaps minute dollars-and-sense detail of health care cost coverage?

Indications of possible decline in public familiarity with traditional political knowledge or civic "facts" by Delli Carpini and Keeter are noted in Chapters 1 and 8.[28] One caution here is that knowledge of civic facts should

FIGURE 11.2   Princess Diana's life and death were avidly followed by the media. (Photo courtesy of Associated Press/Elvis Barukcic)

not be considered the only or even the optimal indicator of being politically informed. For instance, the complexity or depth of knowledge and the ability to use it in discussion and decisionmaking are also factors to consider; unfortunately, these are also more difficult to assess across the population.[29]

Media and Knowledge Gaps.   We have confirmed, however, that the learning of politically relevant information occurs unequally across society: Some people have greater access to information; but even among those with quite equal access, learning may differ substantially. The pioneering campaign studies of the 1940s and 1950s established that voters selectively attended to political information, with the more interested citizens being more exposed to it and presumably becoming more informed as a result. Logically, politically attentive, active, and involved people were more motivated to get more information, and did so. Studies since then have found that characteristics of the social system—especially social class and education levels in particular—may affect the *rate* at which citizens acquire information. This has led to the development of the *knowledge gap* hypothesis:

As the rate of information flow into a social system increases, groups with higher socioeconomic status acquire the information at a faster rate than lower-status groups, widening the knowledge gap between them.[30]

Several studies have supported this tendency across a wide range of content areas, including politically relevant ones. The mechanics of the process are not yet quite clear, but a key factor is that the status variable of *education* is a major player. People with more education appear to acquire information at an accelerated rate for a number of reasons—because they have greater access to it, greater skill in processing it, more motivation to seek it out, or greater use for it, or some combination of those factors.[31]

This hypothesis has subtle but significant consequences for the flow and distribution of knowledge across society and, in turn, for public opinion processes. We have often previously assumed that increasing the flow of information in a democracy would help promote more equal levels of awareness and knowledge across the system, reducing differences between "information rich" and "information poor" segments of society. Mass media have been an integral part of this thinking, leading to childhood television programs such as *Sesame Street* and massive public education efforts aimed at voter participation, public safety, disease prevention, and the like. Presumably, such public efforts could help reduce information disparities brought on by circumstances of social class and lack of education. However, the knowledge-gap hypothesis predicts the exact opposite—that the more information that gets put "out there," the information rich get richer and the poor get poorer.

Media and Public Knowledge and Public Opinion

Recent research also shows that the more someone already knows about political affairs, the more likely that person is to learn about current news events.[32] The best predictor of people's having learned about a range of topics in the news—from abortion debates to primary elections to celebrity trials—was how much they already knew about politics, despite the specific ways in which they used news media. The conclusion here is that there is a "general news audience," consisting of citizens who are more politically astute, who use news media more, and who gain more information from that use. John Zaller extends this line of thinking into the realm of political persuasion.[33] He presents evidence that these same politically aware heavier news media users are more adept at resisting arguments that go against their own partisan positions or values. Presumably, they have a greater storehouse of contextual information from which to draw material for successful counterarguments. Zaller also adds to the picture the interesting concept of *considerations*, or tentative reasons or justifications for taking one side or the other on issues, which people largely draw from communication sources, as explained in Chapter 8. There is also evidence that television viewers in general may have their opinions swayed by what they see and hear on television news programs (see Box 11.2).[34]

Equally important here is how mass media may frame facts or issues for public presentation and the impact that may have on audiences. Another series of experiments by Iyengar demonstrates the potential for framing effects.[35] Television news has often been criticized for too much emphasis on stories that are "episodic," or event-based, without providing adequate context or explanation—the garden variety "murder-and-mayhem" syndrome of much local news coverage being one example. However, more "thematic" stories that develop issues and show more complex relationships across events or policies may be more broadly informative, but news producers—and viewers as well—may shun them as deadly dull talking-

---

Box 11.2   Can Television News Sway Opinions?

Benjamin Page, Robert Shapiro, and Glenn Dempsey traced changes in opinion poll answers to numerous public policy issues between 1969 and 1983. They particularly looked for changes in answers to the same question asked in polls a few months apart in order to find out whether the public support for specific policy options had shifted over a fairly short time. They then analyzed television news coverage of these issues over the same short time periods and noted the extent to which statements presented on the news about those issues had been supportive.

It is also important that they noted the *source* of each statement, that is, whether it was made by a news reporter or commentator, by the president or administration members, other officeholders, policy experts, interest groups, and so forth. They then statistically traced how well such statements about issues predicted changes in public opinion on the same issues. All in all, the televised news statements strongly predicted changes in public response to specific poll items. The more "pro" statements made on television about a policy option, the more likely public response was to swing to a more "pro" stance on that option. But it made a difference *who* made the statement. If the statement had been made by a television commentator or by an "expert" on the particular topic, the public swing was more pronounced than if the viewpoint had been voiced by a politician or interest group member. It is likely that commentators or experts are viewed as less biased and therefore more credible sources. There is also a possibility that television commentators could be reflecting consensus opinions being formulated by elite groups—including other journalists—compounding their impact on the public, but this is a more speculative conclusion.

SOURCE: Benjamin I. Page, Robert Y. Shapiro, and Glenn R. Dempsey, "What Moves Public Opinion?" *American Political Science Review* 81 (1987):23–43.

heads video. Do these two different ways affect how audiences respond to and interpret them? Iyengar's studies suggest they do.

He showed audiences newscasts depicting six issues—crime, international terrorism, poverty, unemployment, racial inequality, and the 1980s Iran-Contra scandal. Different audience groups received different treatments of each—some saw episodic versions about particular issues, others viewed thematic ones. Audience members were then asked in various ways where responsibility for the problems depicted in the stories should lie. In other words, individuals were asked to form political judgments about the causes of these problems, just after having seen the stories. In most but not all cases, audiences who saw the episodic versions of the stories tended to attribute responsibility more to the individuals involved in them, whereas groups seeing the thematic stories placed more responsibility on societal or policy-related causes (see Figure 11.3).

This was particularly true for stories dealing with poverty. When the issue was framed by stories depicting the plight of poor people—examples of coping by the homeless, for example—audiences were more likely to hold the poor responsible for their situations. But when the stories centered on the economics of the rise of poverty and cuts in federal programs, audiences were more apt to blame societal conditions. When the news subject was unemployment, however, the type of frame did not matter: Audiences laid the cause to economic conditions whether the frame was episodic or thematic. Mixed results were found across the other subject areas, depending to some extent on specific story content; nonetheless, episodic frames were tied more often than not to attribution of responsibility to individuals.

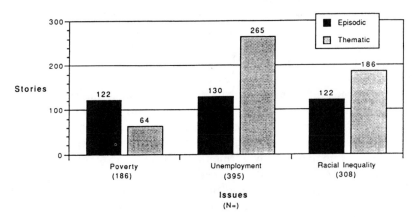

FIGURE 11.3   Episodic and Thematic Coverage of Poverty, Unemployment, and Racial Inequality, 1981–1986. SOURCE: S. Iyengar, *Is Anyone Responsible? How Television Frames Political Issues* (Chicago: University of Chicago Press, 1991), figure 5.1, p. 47.

Iyengar argues that implications from this include—in the case of poverty, for example—more willingness by television news viewers to fault individual shortcomings than societal conditions or policies for problems. Like Zaller, Iyengar relates this to *accessibility bias* in the way in which we recall information from memory, arguing that the more often such stories are viewed on television, the more likely information and conclusions drawn from that information will be more accessible in our memory systems and more easily recalled when prompted. Although the body of evidence for such media effects on our cognitions is interesting and useful, we need to keep in mind the focus on television news here, remembering that it is but one unit in the mix of information sources people use.

Newspapers and magazines, for example, likely deal far more with thematic frames and may well counter television effects, providing a better-balanced information diet to the public. Somewhat overlooked in the above controversy is the simple fact that audiences carry out their own framing exercises as they observe and communicate, putting information into the perspective of their own cognitive experience.[36]

Media Effects on Change in Public Opinions, Attitudes, and Behaviors

Studies of what people learn from media and how they process such information are surprisingly recent, having come about only since the 1970s or so. Earlier research on media effects focused on the somewhat more propagandistically driven questions about whether media were directly impacting changes in our opinions, attitudes, and behaviors. From the early 1900s through the 1940s, many thought the media to be quite powerful in directly affecting citizen views and behaviors. An analogy was drawn between the media and a hypodermic needle, with the media "injecting" members of an increasingly atomized mass public with whatever thoughts and opinions the media manipulators wanted inscribed. Fanciful, yes, but the hypodermic model made the point that media did have previously unheard of *direct* access to individuals—in their homes, providing information unfiltered and uncensored by other human interaction or dialogue. Likely adding to the speculative fear was the seeming ease with which the Nazi political party gained leadership in Germany during the 1930s, with extensive and sophisticated use of radio, film, and print media.

Anecdotal evidence of powerful media effects in the United States was fanned by such events as Orson Welles's 1938 radio broadcast of "The War of the Worlds," a fictional invasion from Mars that reportedly scared countless listeners (see Box 11.3). U.S. involvement in World War II led to heavy investment in wartime propaganda, some of which was thought to succeed in the highly stressed and focused wartime culture.

However, when scholars later reexamined these and other supposedly strong media effects, the evidence became much less clear, and other important mitigating factors became apparent.[37] This was also the era in which survey research entered the picture, as did other more sophisticated social science tools, including content analysis, focus groups, and field experiments (see Chapter 3). These techniques allowed a more valid and accurate depiction of potential communication influences and of public opinion per se. Despite several notable efforts, scholars of that era came up short of finding a significant effect for mass communication on public views and actions.

A Revised View: Media's Limited Power.   Two of these studies, led by Paul Lazarsfeld and his colleagues at Columbia University during the 1940s, pioneered the use of scientific surveys to improve understanding of electoral behavior and have already been noted in Chapter 8.[38] Recall that Lazarsfeld was expecting something of a rational, information-based model for voting decisions, in which people would weigh information they received from the candidates and news media, then make their final electoral decisions as the November election day neared. He proposed that mass media would serve such important functions as converting undecided and wavering voters to particular candidates, reinforcing voters who had already firmly decided, and activating people to get out and vote.

Instead, Lazarsfeld discovered that the vast majority of voters knew for whom they would vote all along and that political party affiliation far overwhelmed direct media effects in choosing candidates. Although most voters followed the campaigns in newspapers and magazines and over radio, they attended more to content that supported their own chosen candidates. The small minority of undecided voters appeared among the least knowledgeable citizens and the least attentive to the campaign as well.

In cases where individuals did make up their minds to vote for a candidate during the campaign or decided to switch support from one candidate to another, interpersonal influence seemed to hold more sway. The opinions of a spouse or respected, knowledgeable neighbor appeared more likely to carry weight than campaign news coverage, candidate speeches, or editorials. *Primary reference groups*, consisting of family and close friends, and *secondary* ones (e.g., party, union, church) appeared to far outreach media in terms of influence. This gave rise to the popular *two-step flow* hypothesis of social influence mentioned in Chapter 8, with more politically aware and active *opinion leaders* passing information and perhaps influence from the media to other citizens. This hypothesis struck yet another blow against the power of the media to sway political opinions or behaviors.

The Era of Minimal Media Effects.   All in all, these studies supported what came to be known as a model of "indirect" or "minimal effects" of

Box 11.3   Mars Invades

On October 30, 1938, the night before Halloween, the CBS radio network program *Mercury Theater of the Air* broadcast a "virtual journalism" version of H. G. Wells's classic science-fiction novel *The War of the Worlds*. The novel details an invasion of England by Martians, including the mass destruction of major cities and their inhabitants, with national military forces defenseless in the onslaught. (The novel generated the 1996 movie thriller *Independence Day* and a host of lesser films, television series, and stories.)

To many of the estimated 6 to 12 million listeners of the 1938 radio version, however, the story rang too true and produced episodes of mass panic in several parts of the country. The program, produced by Orson Welles, took the approach of beginning the show as a typical live orchestra program, popular in those days. Then, a "news bulletin" interrupted with the announcement of a "flaming object" falling to the earth in the New Jersey countryside, followed later by more detailed announcements of Martian creatures emerging from the object and others in other locales wreaking havoc and death. The production values of the show were excellent, with top-flight scripting, actors, and special effects.

Thousands of listeners across the country were drawn into the fantasy enough to swamp police and radio station switchboards, call relatives and friends to spread the panic, and flee their homes in areas close to those identified on the program as being under attack. As reality sank in over the next several hours, the network came under sharp attack, issued strong apologies, and the Federal Communications Commission put out guidelines against such mixing of news and fiction. Press stories over the next several days described hundreds of accounts of sheer terror on the part of listeners.

the media on public opinion and behaviors. This view also gained support from several other studies of that time—particularly ones on public information programs aimed at promoting social change on a variety of topics. According to sociologist Joseph Klapper, media influence was slight because when people encounter media messages, they are already armed with strong predispositions—personal beliefs, attitudes, and behaviors—that cause them to *selectively expose* themselves primarily to messages they already agree with.[39] *Selective perception and retention* of messages may also be factors: People were viewed as capable both of easily distorting what they see and hear to match their own biases and of remembering what they find agreeable and forgetting that which they do not.

Thus, the media in effect end up mainly *reinforcing* the existing views of audience members. Voters more exposed to campaign media were less likely to change their minds. Interpersonal interaction was seen as a much stronger—and difficult to counteract—form of influence, more likely to

A pioneering group of broadcast researchers at Princeton University quickly undertook a more formal study of the panic, interviewing people who had been affected and trying to pin down the scope of the event, in an attempt to understand why some people had reacted but others had not.[1] They estimated that perhaps 10 to 20 percent of the listeners had been genuinely frightened by the broadcast, with smaller, undetermined numbers acting out their fear by calling others, trying to escape their communities, or generally becoming panicked. Many of these people had not heard the introduction to the broadcast that set the stage for the imaginary news coverage and either did not hear or ignored later statements indicating that it was a fictionalized account. To some extent, the lesser educated, the more insecure, and those with stronger religious beliefs were more inclined to panic.

In retrospect, we can also emphasize the tenor of the times and the reliance on radio during that era.[2] The United States was just emerging from a turbulent economic depression, and fear of war was building as Germany threatened more of Europe. People had learned to turn to the relatively new medium of radio as a source of credible, updated news, with live reports of major national and global events. Many audience members who may not have been listening that closely or critically at first may have been primed by other events of the times or by their own circumstances to react with fear and panic.

----

1. Hadley Cantril, *The Invasion from Mars: A Study in the Psychology of Panic* (Princeton: Princeton University Press, 1940).

2. Sharon A. Lowery and Melvin L. DeFleur, *Milestones in Mass Communication Research* (New York: Longman, 1988).

----

stimulate change. To the extent that the two-step flow proposition was valid, any media effects would have to be *indirect*, being filtered through opinion leaders to the more general populace.

This view of media effects has a fair amount of common-sense appeal; it was also probably reassuring to hear that media could not easily propagandize citizens into unwanted or bizarre positions or behaviors. Perhaps that is one reason that the view was so readily accepted and indeed persisted as the dominant model of media influence until well into the 1960s—despite some, though not a great deal, of empirical evidence. More recent and critical evaluations of the two-step flow, selective exposure, and other lynchpins of the model have found they do not quite hold up—at least not across enough contexts and time frames to be regarded as healthy scientific generalizations that can be relied on from situation to situation. We will consider some specific reasons for this later in the chapter. For now, it is important to consider these factors: (1) Lazarsfeld's and related studies dispelled the myth of the omnipotence of mass media as a force affecting public opinion—simple audience exposure to a message did not necessarily mean it would have an effect; (2) media were not having much persuasive influence on political—and perhaps social—behavior in elections of the 1940s and may be unlikely to in situations paralleling those of that period; (3) we cannot look at mass media as isolated from other social forces, especially interpersonal conversation and discussion; and (4) in all of the above cases, we are dealing with a media system offering competing messages within the political framework—no one party had significant control over what was presented.

Research on the impact of mass media—and of personal communication, for that matter—on public opinion entered the doldrums throughout the 1950s and 1960s in the United States. This was of course ironic, since on the campaign trail, the new and arguably most exciting political medium to date—television—was being quickly adopted, adapted, and often co-opted by candidates of all shapes and persuasions. Television had grown into preeminence as a political news medium, with extended coverage of nominating conventions, candidate debates, the assassination of President Kennedy, and the "living-room war," Vietnam.

Reconsiderations of Media Effects:
Television and Social Change

The growth of television paralleled an array of changes in U.S. society that had potentially significant consequences for public opinion processes. Social unrest and protests in the 1960s accompanied the rise of the post World War II "baby boom" generational bulge, pushing a proportionally greater number of teens and young adults into the populace than had been witnessed in decades. They were also more educated and more affluent than their predecessors, with a less-constrained, more mobile lifestyle. People in general moved around more, usually toward urban and suburban centers, reducing the pull of traditional family, neighborhood, and community affiliations. Attitudes and behaviors regarding politics became more fluid, witnessed most readily in increasing numbers of undecided voters in election campaigns, in greater fluctuation of voter turnout, and most notably in a significant rise in independent, non-party-affiliated voters and "ticket-splitting" voting for candidates of different parties on the same ballot. By the early 1970s, such volatility made it quite hard to safely predict voting behavior from party affiliation alone or to predict opinions and attitudes across a range of issues. (Ironically, the public perhaps more closely resembled what Lazarsfeld and his colleagues had expected in the 1940s.) Political communication researchers finally began catching up with these trends in the 1970s, and several new perspectives on the relationship between mass media and public opinion emerged.

Videomalaise

Two novel and intriguing approaches to mass media effects were developed at the time that seemed to put much of the blame for more negative communication influences back into the hands of the media—and especially, television. In an effort to link the increased political disaffection and distrust that arose in the 1960s and 1970s directly to television news, political scientist Michael Robinson coined the concept of *videomalaise*. Robinson argued that the roots of videomalaise were in the then heavily watched evening television network news reports of ABC, CBS, and NBC.[40] These programs, he contended, contained reports that were often too interpretive and that placed too much emphasis on negative events and explanations. Robinson analyzed the overall themes of these programs as anti-institutional, claiming that they place too much emphasis on violence and conflict. (Such content analysis and interpretation of news programming is not in of itself novel and has likely been around in various forms since the first attempt by a correspondent to record an observation in a way that someone else objected to.)

Robinson's content analysis was quite rigorous, and a case may be made that the television networks and other news media have placed greater emphasis on overt interpretation of events over the past two or three decades than they did previously. However, the extent to which news and interpretation of events may be more "negative" than the "reality" being depicted in a "real" fashion is a far more subjective call, often open to much legitimate argument. Recall that much of the news being reported at this time was on the Vietnam War and opposition to it, such government scandals as then Vice President Spiro Agnew's resignation under influence-peddling accusations, and, ultimately, President Nixon's resignation over the Watergate issue. These were indeed hard times for government credibility.

In any case, perhaps the more intriguing aspect of Robinson's thesis is his linking the impact of the "negative" television network news to a somewhat passive and overly trusting news audience. Network television news had a largely "inadvertent" audience, according to Robinson, many of whom watched out of habit. Moreover, the nature of television news led audience members from one story to another, despite their level of interest in particular story topics. Viewers less interested in politics thus received a steady diet of disturbing, negative information about political issues they were not familiar enough with to counterassess, leading to doubt and malaise about the system. Furthermore, the high credibility of the evening news anchors was seen as enhancing this effect. Newspapers were judged as less culpable. Regardless of the biases newspaper stories may have displayed, readers of political news more actively chose to read them. In doing so, they were probably more critical of them, not to mention that the more politically interested and astute were more likely to be active readers in the first place.

Robinson offered some intriguing support for this hypothesis from surveys and an experiment, but subsequent studies have largely not supported it. Generally, people who are exposed to more television news, to newspapers, or to other media for political information have been found to be *more* confident in political figures and institutions.[41] Nonetheless, Robinson's proposition had enough intuitive appeal to make one wonder if it *might* apply with the right audience, under the right circumstances, in some present or future setting (see Figure 11.4).

Cultivating the Public

A second and more holistic approach to television's impact on public opinion is known as the *cultivation* perspective, and it proposes far-reaching influences of the medium on virtually all aspects of audience perceptions and attitudes. Developed by George Gerbner and his colleagues at the University of Pennsylvania, the proposition asserts that television has become the "common storyteller of our age," providing our diversified society with consistent and repeated messages and images.[42] This integrated content reaches across all levels of our society, "cultivating" shared views and conceptions of reality among otherwise diverse social groups.

Extensive analyses of television content since 1967 support the notion that television programming across the board does depict somewhat consistent portrayals of American life and values, despite differences in kinds of programs, specialized topic cable networks, and the like. Also supported is the idea that television content often does not square with what is actually going on the "real world" of U.S. social and political life. One example is that both entertainment and news-information programming provide a relatively high dose of crime and violence, much beyond that which proportionately occurs in "actual" American life on a day-to-day basis. (This should not be all that surprising: One function of news is to alert the citizenry to out-of-the-ordinary events, particularly threatening ones like homicide and robbery; we do not typically define "news" as the mundane. Similarly, entertainment in the form of escapist—sometimes violent—drama is as old as theater, with little intent of showing the world as it actually is. However, the extent to which crime and violence dominate public airwaves—to the exclusion of other material—is a highly legitimate concern.)

As with Robinson's videomalaise hypothesis, the evidence on cultivation becomes less firm when attempting to show that this "unreal" array of television content has significant impact on audiences watching it. Unlike

FIGURE 11.4   TV: The Electronic Hearth? Do the negative images of the world portrayed in television news produce videomalaise? Cultivation effects? The evidence is mixed. SOURCE: © Tom Tomorrow. *Greetings from This Modern World,* (New York: St. Martin's Press, 1992).

Robinson, who predicted that television *news* portrayals of politics would influence *attitudes* toward public figures and processes to become more negative, Gerbner predicts a more subtle effect: Heavier exposure to television content *overall* will cultivate *perceptions* or *beliefs* about social reality that are more consistent with the "television view" than with the "real-world" view. With crime, for example, individuals who watch more television would be more inclined to regard crime as more frequent and serious than it is. Some early evidence suggested that this was indeed the case and that heavier viewers of television were more fearful of crime as well. However, subsequent surveys of public opinion about crime have included more exact measures of how people view crime and have controlled for possibly confounding influences of age, gender, social class, and related demographics. These show little evidence that the overall amount of television viewing has any effect on crime perceptions or attitudes, although crime *news* viewing per se may have some influence.[43]

A refinement of the initial cultivation perspective posits that exceptionally heavy viewing of television—several hours per day—may override other social and cultural differences between people. That is, people who share watching great amounts of television may have more closely shared world-views than their demographic and other social differences would suggest. This phenomenon is called *mainstreaming*, and Gerbner and associates have found that people who watch more television, regardless of their demographic makeup, see themselves as somewhat more moderate in their political and social beliefs. Gerbner attributes this to television's attempt to program for the middle ground, balancing countering perspectives and avoiding controversy. The cultivation approach has not been widely applied to other aspects of public opinion, and social scientists continue to debate its rationale and analytic methods.[44] The approach is useful, however, for reminding us of the potential force of television as the currently dominant mass medium in our society and of the possibilities for entertainment and other kinds of programming to influence public opinion.

Moving Toward the Active Audience

Both the videomalaise and cultivation perspectives regard audiences in a more passive light, more subject to being acted upon than acting. Emphasis has turned to the more active aspects of individuals' use of mass media in recent years. Included has been a revised look at what people *do with* media, as opposed to what media *do to* people, as communications researchers Wilbur Schramm, Jack Lyle, and Edwin Parker posed the question.[45] The research findings of the 1940s and 1950s had suggested—although with little evidence—that any power of the media to persuade was effectively counterbalanced by the power of individual audience members to use media toward their own ends, for their own purposes. Individuals may be viewed as using media to perform certain psychological functions for them, including providing support for their already existing beliefs, attitudes, and behaviors. Many studies over the past three decades have put this proposition more to the test.

This view proposes that audiences are far more proactive in their dealings with media, deliberately using them to seek out such rewards or gratifications. These include reinforcement of opinions, learning new information of value, surveillance of the environment, entertainment, excitement or stimulation, companionship, diversion, passing time, and others. The approach became known as the *uses-gratifications* model of communication effects: People purposively use certain media contents to gratify specific needs. Individuals try to choose media content that they expect will do the best job of meeting those needs, based on previous experiences.[46] You may read editorials in the *New York Times*—or in the *Wall Street Journal*—

when you get the chance because you know the views of that newspaper agree with your own on most subjects and reading them will give you the satisfaction of knowing a prestigious source is on your side. You will also likely get more facts and substantiation to buttress your case. Or you may always turn on a certain radio station in the morning because you know it will play music you like to hear then and the station gives you a little—but not too much—surveillance on what is going on in the world through its brief news and weather segments.

Obviously, however, the media chosen do not always provide the rewards people expect them to; moreover, media use may have unintended effects or consequences for the public. You may select MTV or go to a rock music web site expecting some stimulating entertainment, which you have desperate need of after a rough day. But instead, you may catch a short documentary on involvement of musicians in a particular political cause, which may make you aware of that cause for the first time or more sympathetic to it. (Or you may so much resent not getting the entertainment you were hoping for that you will at least temporarily reject that cause.) In a more subtle way, media content can help shape our thinking even when we do get from a message much of what we had intended. It is seldom that we obtain the *exact* gratification or reward we seek without also getting at least a little extra baggage—the particular spin put on a point of view by a newscaster, extraneous information that alters the context of what we expected or wanted, or the putting of information into a larger context that expands our horizons.

The Audience-Media Transaction

Most theories of media influence today generate from a view of audiences being largely active players in choosing what they hear, watch, or read, and responding accordingly. However, we cannot reject the notion that at times people are quite passive or reactive in attending to media—or in everyday conversations, for that matter, simply letting words or images wash over them, leaving themselves more open to influence or manipulation.[47] This juxtaposition of more active versus more passive possibilities for audience involvement with media has led many researchers to look at media effects on public opinion as a more *interactive* or *transactional* process. The nature of the relationship between audiences and media likely changes and shifts across different personal traits, moods, contexts, and situations.[48] Often, as audience members, we may clearly have a stronger hand in deciding what we want and get from a given communication; in other instances, we may come across unexpected messages that may motivate and move us in unexpected—and sometimes unexplained—ways. In still other situations, we may be seeking nothing in particular and get nothing in particular, so not much of consequence happens. Taking a broader political communication context, Robert Huckfeldt and John Sprague have noted the great interdependency between political information seekers and potential suppliers of it:

> The citizen is an information processor, but information is environmentally supplied, and individual choices are embedded within informational settings that systematically vary in time and space. Neither individual choice nor the environment is determinate in creating these informational settings, and hence the acquisition of political information is the end result of a complex interplay between individual choice and environmental supply.[49]

Media Dependency

How much we rely on media for such gratifications and the degree of media influence also depends on other options open to us—for information, social support, diversion, and so forth. Some people are perhaps more "media dependent" than others because of ease of access to such channels, or temperament, or the availability of functional alternatives for information, entertainment, and other rewards.[50] In the larger societal sense, we need to consider how necessary mass communication is to the culture and societal structure we live in. How much individuals depend on media may vary with what is taking place socially and politically in the society at any given time. Sociologists Sandra Ball-Rokeach and Melvin DeFleur have argued that in times of greater conflict and change, media dependency is apt to rise: Media may provide a mechanism for helping cope if such change challenges other more traditional social means for coping with threats to established norms and behaviors.[51]

During the late 1960s, for example, many citizens may have turned more to newspapers and especially television to try to make more sense out of a seeming explosion of social protest and turmoil. The news media were able to not only keep audiences up to date on the latest expressions of discontent but to put something of a perspective on those developments and on the reactions of other citizens to them. (There have been anecdotal suggestions that in times of crisis, it may be somehow reassuring to see those events depicted in the more familiar, institutional framework of one's regular daily newspaper or reported by a familiar voice backed by the ABC or CNN logo.) A related argument is that more immediate kinds of politically relevant information may be more salient to citizens in times of conflict, and they in turn depend on media sources more. If people sense a need to act quickly based on the facts at hand, traditional ideological considerations may be less relevant.[52] At the time of the buildup for the 1992 war in the Persian Gulf, for example, many if not most citizens appeared to be putting more weight on the immediate consequences of Iraq's takeover of Kuwait, particularly in terms of the threat to the oil supply, and on risks to American military forces, than to the ideology of party positions or patriotism.

Media Influences on Norms and Values

Sometimes overlooked are other kinds of normative and value-laden influences that people might seek out from or inadvertently gain from dependence upon mass media. Some of these were captured in a classic essay by Lazarsfeld and Merton.[53] Media may often be capable of *conferring status* on issues, individuals, organizations, and movements. We often regard people who get "in the news" for their allotted fifteen minutes (or however long their fame lasts) as being more prominent than those who do not, of being somehow more deserving. This of course is not lost on public office-holders, who seek out the camera quite readily to maintain visibility and viability in the public eye. Another potential societal influence of media is the *enforcement of social norms*, based upon the ability of news media to reaffirm such norms by publicizing deviations from them. By exposing a corrupt city official, for example, and treating the behavior as "wrong" or deviant, the press in effect upholds the sanctioned norm of honesty among public officials, reinforcing that view for the public. In fact, perhaps the most popular of all news story genres—the crime story—routinely upholds norms of deviance and justice.

Lazarsfeld and Merton posited a third influence they regarded as more subtle and more negative that they called the *narcotizing dysfunction* of mass media. This gives a complex label to the often popular critical view that extended use of media leads to public apathy rather than involvement. The argument goes that too much exposure to information can "narcotize" rather than "energize" the media consumer, leading to mistaking "*knowing* about the problems of the day for *doing* something about them."[54] The extent and significance of this phenomenon remains hotly debated today.

It is also important to regard the ability of mass media to *reinforce* the status quo as a potentially significant effect—one working *against* social change. "Simply" reinforcing as opposed to significantly changing beliefs, attitudes, and behaviors that already exist may not be a trivial effect—or a healthy one—under conditions in which certain kinds of social change may be warranted and desirable. In many civil rights protests of the 1950s in the South, for example, many news media were seen as allies of the segregationists by the protesters because of the lack of news coverage of the movement or overt siding with the opposition. Similar accounts have been given of at least the early national news coverage of the anti–Vietnam War movement.[55]

The Interpersonal Factor

Oddly, most of the recent studies of communication influences on public opinion have left out the role of interpersonal conversation and discussion, the most common grounding for opinion development and change. The everyday transmission of opinions among citizens has rarely been studied, perhaps because of its ubiquity. The popular two-step flow model of the minimal media effects era still provides the jumping-off point for consideration of how personal influence works its likely considerable effects in our social system. However, that model preassumed strong, stable primary group relationships, with influentials in specific areas of expertise using established media more than other people and passing along to "followers" interpretations of media messages. Whatever the appropriateness of that model for earlier times, it is more difficult to apply it to our era of less social and political stability, with its far more diversified and widespread mass media system.

John Robinson made several inroads in redefining the model by suggesting more attention be given to *interaction among* media, opinion leaders, and other citizens, noting that influence is seldom a one-way street.[56] If one person interacts with another, influence is likely to be at least somewhat shared rather than being unidirectional. The "flow" is likely to be at least somewhat "upward" as well as downward. Another issue is whether opinion leaders actually use media more than other citizens. Gabriel Weimann, in an extensive study of influential individuals in the United States, Germany, and Israel, found that although the frequency of their media use was no greater than anyone else's, they tended to use higher "quality" media, specifically print sources in the form of books and magazines on specialized topics.[57] Weimann also found influential people to have political news agendas that were more closely tied to those of news media, indicating that their more qualitative media use had more of an agenda-setting effect on them.

Another view of the relative interplay and impact between mass media and interpersonal discussion in election campaigns comes from Jeffrey Mondak.[58] Taking advantage of the unique opportunity of a Pittsburgh newspaper strike during nearly the entire 1992 postprimary election campaigns, Mondak studied how the loss of newspaper coverage of local races affected citizen discussion and vote decisions. Generally, he found less interpersonal discussion of the upcoming elections (as compared to discussion rates in his "control" city of Cleveland, which had no such strike and similar political characteristics). He concluded in part that news coverage provided material for topic-specific discussions of elections and that without newspapers such discussions were attenuated. However, interpersonal discussions that did occur appeared to exert more influence on vote choices in the absence of newspapers. Mondak draws from these findings an interesting model of media-interpersonal dynamics: Media coverage and personal conversation are *complementary* in terms of citizen exposure to campaign information but *conflict* with one another in terms of influence. That is, news media are necessary to provide election-based topics for discussion, in that sense complementing discussion. But in the case of influencing political decisions, media use and discussion compete, with voters likely to choose one source or the other as a basis for deciding whom to vote for.

In a unique work, William Gamson arrives at a somewhat similar picture but depicts the media as more of a tool that average citizens use occasionally for opinion formation and discussion. Media may be chosen for their availability, ease of access, and suitability for the task at hand.[59] Gamson observed groups of primarily working-class citizens discussing political issues of the day and found that media content, when used, was weighed in with their own personal experiences in forming their conversation points and conclusions. Gamson observed political discussions that were not always the best-informed but that were deliberative, complex, and well-reasoned, though not typically likely to result in overt political activity.

Unanswered questions about influence flow still abound. For example, to what extent is "influence" or persuasive communication flowing here, versus information? How is information translated and altered in everyday discussion rife with gossip, personal agendas, and the like? Given that those most likely to discuss politics are the more politically interested and involved, what about those who may discuss very little with anyone? Could mass media have even more impact on them? These and related issues need more attention for a fuller understanding of communication processes and public opinion.

Few would argue, however, with the sense that public opinion inherently develops out of interconnected, interacting individuals. When people confront a decision or a challenge to their existing views, they seek information and advice from the most available—and the most trusted—sources. Mass media may serve some of these functions some of the time, but social contingencies and interactions are apt to provide a more meaningful context for influence.[60]

More speculatively, many academicians and social critics have decried what they view as a loss in sense of civic community, or "sense of place" in Joshua Meyrowitz's term, and the potential role of television in that.[61] Robert Putnam has named television as a prime culprit in what he sees as a decline in "social capital," or the social networks, discussions of values, and shared participation that move citizens more effectively toward shared objectives.[62] James Carey has traced the entwined historical roots of journalism and public opinion processes throughout U.S. history and persuasively argues that mass media have become more privatized and less of a public space for democratic discussion.[63] He optimistically suggests that the turn in the 1990s to increased political uses of smaller forums such as talk radio, citizen councils, and the Internet are a reaction against the journalism establishment, an effort to reassert emphasis on public discussion and participation in civic life.

Notes

1. Harold Lasswell, "The Structure and Function of Communication in Society," in Lyman Bryson, ed., *The Communication of Ideas* (New York: Harper, 1948), pp. 32–51.

2. Charles Wright, "Functional Analysis and Mass Communication," *Public Opinion Quarterly* 24 (1960):606–620.

3. For example, see Herbert Blumer, "The Mass, the Public and Public Opinion," in Bernard Berelson and Morris Janowitz, eds., *Reader in Public Opinion and Communication* (New York: Free Press, 1960), pp. 43–50.

4. Walter Lippmann, *Public Opinion* (New York: Macmillan Co., 1922).

5. Maxwell E. McCombs and Donald L. Shaw, "The Agenda-Setting Function of the Press," *Public Opinion Quarterly* 36 (1972):176–187.

6. Oscar Gandy, *Beyond Agenda Setting* (Norwood, NJ: Ablex, 1982).

7. Michael B. Grossman and Martha J. Kumar, *Portraying the President: The White House and the News Media* (Baltimore: Johns Hopkins University Press, 1981).

8. Benjamin I. Page, Robert Y. Shapiro, and Gregory R. Dempsey, "What Moves Public Opinion?" *American Political Science Review* 81 (1987):23–43.

9. John R. Zaller, *The Nature and Origins of Mass Opinion* (Cambridge: Cambridge University Press, 1992); Robert M. Entman, "Framing: Toward Clarification of a Fractured Paradigm," *Journal of Communication* 43 (1993):293–300.

10. Clarice N. Olien, George A. Donohue, and Phillip J. Tichenor, "Conflict, Consensus and Public Opinion," in Theodore L. Glasser and Charles T. Salmon, eds., *Public Opinion and the Communication of Consent* (New York: Guilford Press, 1995), pp. 301–323.

11. Ibid.

12. Edward Herman and Noam Chomsky, *Manufacturing Consent: The Political Economy of Mass Media* (New York: Pantheon, 1988).

13. Lasswell, "Structure and Function of Communication in Society."

14. Bernard Cohen, *The Press and Foreign Policy* (Princeton: Princeton University Press, 1963), p. 13.

15. McCombs and Shaw, "Agenda-Setting Function of the Press."

16. Shanto Iyengar and Donald R. Kinder, *News That Matters: Television and American Opinion* (Chicago: University of Chicago Press, 1987).

17. David L. Protess et al., *The Journalism of Outrage: Investigative Reporting and Agenda Building in America* (New York: Guilford Press, 1991).

18. Klaus Schoenbach and Lee B. Becker, "Origins and Consequences of Mediated Public Opinion," in Glasser and Salmon, eds., *Public Opinion and the Communication of Consent*, pp. 301–323.

19. Iyengar and Kinder, *News That Matters*.

20. Jon A. Krosnick, "The Media and the Foundations of Presidential Support: George Bush and the Persian Gulf Conflict," *Journal of Social Issues* 49, 4 (1993):167–182.

21. Iyengar and Kinder, *News That Matters*.

22. Maxwell McCombs and Tamara Bell, "The Agenda-Setting Role of Mass Communication," in Michael B. Salwen and Don W. Stacks, eds., *An Integrated*

Approach to Communication Theory and Research (Mahwah, NJ: Lawrence Erlbaum Associates, 1996), pp. 93–110.

23. Lutz Erbring, Edith Goldenberg, and Arthur H. Miller, "Front-Page News and Real World Cues: A New Look at Agenda-Setting by the Media," *American Journal of Political Science* 24 (1980):16–49.

24. Iyengar and Kinder, *News That Matters.*

25. John P. Robinson and Mark R. Levy, *The Main Source: Learning from Television News* (Beverly Hills, CA: Sage Publications, 1986).

26. Leo Bogart, *Strategy in Advertising*, 3d ed. (Lincolnwood, IL: NTC Business Books, 1996).

27. John P. Robinson and Mark R. Levy, "News Media Use and the Informed Public: A 1990s Update," *Journal of Communication* 46 (1996):129–135.

28. Michael X. Delli Carpini and Scott Keeter, "Measuring Political Knowledge: Putting First Things First," *American Journal of Political Science* 37 (1993): 1179–1206.

29. Jack M. McLeod, Gerald M. Kosicki, and Douglas M. McLeod, "The Expanding Boundaries of Political Communication Effects," in Jennings Bryant and Dolf Zillman, eds., *Media Effects: Advances in Theory and Research* (Hillsdale, NJ: Lawrence Erlbaum, 1994), pp. 123–162.

30. Phillip J. Tichenor, George A. Donohue, and Clarice N. Olien, "Mass Media and the Differential Growth in Knowledge," *Public Opinion Quarterly* 54 (1970): 158–170.

31. K. Viswanath and John R. Finnegan Jr., "The Knowledge Gap: Twenty-Five Years Later," in Bryant R. Burelson, ed., *Communication Yearbook 19* (Thousand Oaks, CA: Sage Publications, 1996), pp. 187–228.

32. Vincent Price and John Zaller, "Who Gets the News: Alternative Measures of News Reception and Their Implications for Research," *Public Opinion Quarterly* 57 (1993):133–164.

33. Zaller, *Nature and Origins of Mass Opinion.*

34. Page, Shapiro, and Dempsey, "What Moves Public Opinion?"

35. Shanto Iyengar, *Is Anyone Responsible: How Television Frames Political Issues* (Chicago: University of Chicago Press, 1993).

36. McLeod, Kosicki, and McLeod, "Expanding Boundaries of Political Communication Effects."

37. Hadley Cantril, Hazel Gaudet, and Herta Hertzog, *The Invasion from Mars* (Princeton: Princeton University Press, 1940); Carl I. Hovland, Arthur A. Lumsdaine, and Fred D. Sheffield, *Experiments in Mass Communication* (Princeton: Princeton University Press, 1949).

38. Paul F. Lazarsfeld, Bernard Berelson, and Hazel Gaudet, *The People's Choice* (New York: Duell, Sloan and Pearce, 1944); Bernard Berelson, Paul. F. Lazarsfeld, and William N. McPhee, *Voting: A Study of Opinion Formation in a Presidential Campaign* (Chicago: Chicago University Press, 1954).

39. Joseph Klapper, *The Effects of Mass Communication* (New York: Free Press, 1960).

40. Michael J. Robinson, "Public Affairs Television and the Growth of Political Malaise: The Case of 'The Selling of the Pentagon,'" *American Political Science Review* 70 (1976):409–431.

41. Garrett J. O'Keefe, "Political Malaise and Reliance on Media," *Journalism Quarterly* 57 (1980):122–128.

42. See, for example, George Gerbner, Larry Gross, Michael Morgan, and Nancy Signorelli, "Living with Television: The Dynamics of the Cultivation Process," in Jennings Bryant and Dolf Zillman, eds., *Perspectives on Media Effects* (Hillsdale, NJ: Lawrence Erlbaum, 1986), pp. 17–40.

43. Paul M. Hirsch, "The 'Scary World' of the Non-Viewer and Other Anomalies—A Reanalysis of Gerbner et al.'s Findings in Cultivation Analysis, Part 1," *Communication Research* 7 (1980):403–456; Anthony Doob and Glenn E. MacDonald, "Television Viewing and the Fear of Victimization: Is the Relationship Causal?" *Journal of Personality and Social Psychology* 37 (1979):170–179; Garrett J. O'Keefe, "Television Exposure, Credibility and Public Views on Crime," in Robert Bostrum, ed., *Communication Yearbook 8* (Newbury Park, CA: Sage Publications, 1984), pp. 513–536.

44. See W. James Potter, "Cultivation Theory and Research: A Conceptual Perspective," *Human Communication Research* 19 (1993):564–601.

45. Wilbur Schramm, Jack Lyle, and Edwin Parker, *Television in the Lives of Our Children* (Palo Alto, CA: Stanford University Press, 1961).

46. Elihu Katz, Jay G. Blumer, and Michael Gurevitch, "Utilization of Mass Media by the Individual," in Jay G. Blumer and Elihu Katz, eds., *The Uses of Mass Communication* (Beverly Hills, CA: Sage Publications, 1974), pp. 9–32.

47. Alan M. Rubin, "The Effect of Locus of Control on Communication Motivation, Anxiety and Satisfaction," *Communication Quarterly* 41 (1993):161–172.

48. Jack M. McLeod and Lee B. Becker, "Testing the Validity of Gratification Measures Through Political Effects Analysis," in Blumer and Katz, eds., *The Uses of Mass Communication*, pp. 137–164.

49. Robert Huckfeldt and John Sprague, *Citizens, Politics, and Social Communication* (New York: Cambridge University Press, 1995), p. 292.

50. Karl E. Rosengren and Sven Windahl, "Mass Media Consumption as a Functional Alternative," in Dennis McQuail, ed., *Sociology of Mass Communication* (Hammondsworth, England: Penguin Books, 1972), pp. 166–194.

51. Sandra J. Ball-Rokeach and Melvin DeFleur, "A Dependency Model of Mass Media Effects," *Communication Research* 3 (1976):3–21.

52. Carl A. Sheingold, "Social Networks and Voting: The Resurrection of a Research Agenda," *American Sociological Review* 38 (1973):712–720.

53. Paul F. Lazarsfeld and Robert K. Merton, "Mass Communication, Popular Taste and Organized Social Action," in Bryson, ed., *Communication of Ideas*, pp. 95–118.

54. Lazarsfeld and Merton, "Mass Communication, Popular Taste and Organized Social Action," p. 106.

55. Todd Gitlin, *The Whole World Is Watching: Mass Media in the Making and Unmaking of the New Left* (Berkeley: University of California Press, 1980).

56. John P. Robinson, "Interpersonal Influence in Election Campaigns: Two-Step Flow Hypotheses," *Public Opinion Quarterly* 40 (1976):304–319.

57. Gabriel Weimann, *The Influentials: People Who Influence People* (Albany: State University of New York Press, 1994).

58. Jeffrey J. Mondak, "Media Exposure and Political Discussion in U.S. Elections," *Journal of Politics* 57 (1995):62–85.

59. William A. Gamson, *Talking Politics* (New York: Cambridge University Press, 1992).

60. Huckfeldt and Sprague, *Citizens, Politics, and Social Communication.*

61. Joshua Meyrowitz, *No Sense of Place* (New York: Oxford University Press, 1985).

62. Robert D. Putnam, "Bowling Alone: America's Declining Social Capital," *Journal of Democracy* 6 (1995):65–78.

63. James W. Carey, "The Press, Public Opinion and Public Discourse," in Glasser and Salmon, eds., *Public Opinion and the Communication of Consent,* pp. 373–402.

Chapter Twelve

Campaigning and Opinion Change

In Chapter 11, we made the case that changing communication styles, formats, and technologies affect public opinion processes. Mass media in particular have significantly altered how we view, think about, and respond to our political world. Now we turn to one specific media-related process—the highly visible and pragmatic issue of *communication campaigns*. We will dwell later in this chapter on the most obvious type of public opinion–directed campaign: promoting candidates in elections for public office. But first we put these campaigns in the broader context of more common kinds of campaigns that influence everything from our purchasing habits to health practices to cultural myths. We will first examine the overall domain of campaigns aimed at creating or altering public opinion and then focus on the central role of campaigns in elections. In both cases, we will discuss the purposes and practice of contemporary campaigns and how well they seem to work. We will also examine an underlying tension between the effects campaigns may have on individual attitudes and behaviors and their less obvious but sometimes more consequential impact upon the society as a whole.

The Campaign Environment

Communication campaigns try to "(1) generate specific outcomes or effects (2) in a relatively large number of individuals, (3) usually within a specified period of time and (4) through an organized set of communication activities."[1] This definition fits a multitude of persuasive situations we are all too familiar with as media consumers today.

That television commercial for, say, a new model of sport-utility vehicle is likely to be just one component of a campaign-generated orchestrated set of communication activities. These may range from commercials to magazine ads, promotional displays at automobile dealers, reviews of the vehicle in auto trade publications and newspapers, and perhaps even the use of the vehicle in a hot new action movie. These components are tied together to push a particular theme that isolates the vehicle from its competition and puts it in the most favorable light possible.

The specific ads and other messages used to promote the vehicle will vary depending on the medium used and the type of audience being aimed at. A commercial slotted for MTV may emphasize virility, power, and economy, whereas an ad for *Outside* magazine may display the model's off-road capabilities in a setting of solitude. In any case, the campaign as a whole publicizes the vehicle to varieties of individuals who may be potential purchasers. The campaign tries to make them aware of the product in a positive way, motivating them to test-drive it, and ultimately to buy it. The time frame of the campaign can be quite important—in case of the sport vehicle the campaign might peak during the heavy spring and early summer auto-buying seasons and end as newer models become available in the fall.

Similarly, the seemingly unending tape spool of public service advertisements we see around the clock on television are simply the most visible sightings of other kinds of extensive campaigns at work. "If you drink, don't drive," Smokey the Bear, McGruff the Crime Dog, and the latest AIDS-prevention commercials are products of long-term public policy initiatives to get people to change certain kinds of behaviors for their own good, for the public good, or for the benefit of the environment (see Figure 12.1). These efforts may promote social change pertinent to health, public safety, or the common societal welfare. Such change may range from making people more aware of a problem and the possible solutions to it to either promoting more positive attitudes about what individuals can do or motivating them to take actions of their own. These "social marketing" programs attempt to use many of the precepts of commercial marketing efforts to promote social change.[2]

The public service ads are, like automotive or any other consumer spots, coordinated to match specific audience characteristics and desired responses. One AIDS-prevention advertisement, for example, may segment gay men as an audience, whereas another—using a very different approach—may focus on heterosexual at-risk high-school students. The campaigns underlying these ads may include press releases and other publicity efforts aimed at news media, organized community, and neighborhood-level preventive efforts and at lobbying for legislation to help remedy the problem—as with antismoking and automobile safety programs, for example.

FIGURE 12.1   McGruff the Crime Dog is the main symbol of an information campaign that attempts to help citizens prevent crime. SOURCE: Registered marks of the National Crime Prevention Council.

Campaign Strategies and Tactics

In both the commercial product and social marketing campaign situations—and as we will shortly see, for political campaigns—the strategies and tactics used are markedly similar. Marketing research is heavily relied on at first to identify potential audiences and to determine their existing ideas and behaviors regarding the product or problem. Then, potential themes and messages are tested with smaller groups of people. The targeted audiences are segmented by their demographics, awareness, and interest in the topic and by their existing behaviors, and appropriate media are then chosen to reach particular audience groups.

Modern polling and statistical analysis techniques are critical here, allowing marketers to fine-tune the audience segments they are aiming for with considerable precision (see Box 12.1). Earlier polling-based conceptualizations of American "lifestyles" have found their way into most major communication and marketing campaigns. Computer-based typologies of individuals can be found not only for purchasing habits but for such

---

Box 12.1   The Genesis of Marketing Profiles: VALS

Most of today's marketing profiles draw from a prototype survey developed at SRI International, a California think tank, in the early 1980s. Working from national population survey data, Arnold Mitchell and his colleagues developed the VALS (values and lifestyle) typology that relates basic values to lifestyles, drives, and needs, later including consumer habits, political leanings, and other social trend data. Essentially, the typology defines four basic need-driven groups of people, broken down into nine different lifestyles:

1. *Need-driven* groups:
   Survivors, about 4 percent of the U.S. population, mainly the aged, fearful, and socially isolated.
   Sustainers, including 7 percent of the population, living on the edge of poverty, rebellious, resentful, and streetwise.
2. *Inner-directed* groups:
   I-am-me, includes 5 percent, young, often students, narcissistic, impulsive, concentrated on own needs.
   Experiential, at 7 percent, also often students, concerned with inner growth, seeking experience, and direction.
3. *Outer-directed* groups:
   Belongers, includes 35 percent of the population, middle-class, family-oriented, conventional, wanting to do the right thing, patriotic.
   Emulators, a younger 9 percent of the population, ambitious, upward-striving, fashionable.
   Achievers, at 22 percent of the population, the more prosperous leaders and builders, successful, hardworking, self-reliant.
4. *Combined inner- and outer-directed* group:
   Integrated, at 2 percent, more psychologically mature and "together," tolerant, flexible, visionary.

SOURCE: Arnold Mitchell, *The Nine American Lifestyles: Who We Are and Where We're Going* (New York: Macmillan, 1983).

---

other behaviors as health practices and potential for various diseases, automobile safety, environmental activities, and, of course, political action, including voting choices. Psychological dispositions toward behavior change, as well as media habits, are often tied into these profiles. Marketers use such catchy terms as Yellowstone Yuppies to profile perhaps fortyish upper-income urbanites with a yen for expensive sport-utility vehicles and outdoor gear, backpacking vacations, gourmet foods, and socially liberal but economically conservative political leanings. Postal zip codes are often used to identify pockets of one such marketing profile or another, allowing links to U.S. census data, direct mail lists, and shopping locations.

Such data are used to focus on chosen market segments to be reached by television and radio, newspapers and magazines, billboards and posters, and direct mail. More interactive tactics may include telephone pitches, talks to civic organizations, special-interest clubs and discussion groups, and, increasingly, E-mail and the Internet. Positive news media coverage of products, services, and promoted behaviors is sought for added reach and legitimacy. Streams of messages, media, and audiences are carefully balanced to interact with one another for maximum effect within the specified time.

Campaigns have become notoriously expensive undertakings over the years, with skyrocketing research and media costs. This has led to greater concern about finding out what worked and what did not in the campaign mix to plan more efficiently for the next round. Commercial-product campaigns have an easier time measuring actual public impact, since the ultimate test is how well a product sold. But even for, say, our new sport-utility model, assessing how "well" or "badly" the campaign itself did can be hard when compared with the actual advantages or shortcomings in the vehicle compared with others. Despite the sophistication of today's marketing strategies, it is still very difficult to promote or sell a genuinely poor product or idea. Two of the most heavily market-researched and cleverly promoted "innovative" products of their times were the Edsel automobile in the mid-1950s and the "new Coke" formula of the late 1980s, both of which proved abject failures.

Evaluating social marketing campaigns is much harder. There is no yardstick such as product sales to rely on, and doing surveys measuring changes in public awareness and attitudes can be a dauntingly expensive—and often slippery—task. Most public-service campaigns operate on small budgets, especially when compared with the hefty amounts spent by industry to promote consumer goods. Many public-service efforts only become possible through the willingness of media outlets—especially television—to donate free time or space. However, the few formal scientific studies carried out on public-service campaign impact suggest that they can build awareness and concern among citizens and, on occasion, prompt behavioral changes.

The same mechanisms that both drive and inhibit media effects discussed in the previous chapter are at work here. Think of a campaign as an orchestrated cluster of communication stimuli capable of prompting learning, persuasion, reinforcement, agenda setting, priming, and other vehicles leading to social influence and change. An overriding inhibition against strong campaign effects in our own society is simply that campaigns are typically competing against one another in the clamor for public attention. The automotive campaign competes against several—perhaps dozens—of similar ones with the same "buy *our* product" goals in mind and with the same persuasive techniques being employed. The AIDS-awareness program competes against a multitude of other health prevention and other social welfare messages; antismoking ads aimed at teens stack up against a background of glitzy cigarette promotions surrounding sports and other events appealing to the young.

How Campaigns Can Succeed

Just as it is difficult for specific campaigns to make their public mark through all the competing clutter, it becomes even harder for programs *not* to jump into the fray for fear of being ignored altogether. How well campaigns "work" depends a great deal on how effectively they are planned, produced, and disseminated to reach their audiences. Reviews of successful campaign strategies and tactics suggest that key factors include:

1. *Using social science models of public opinion and persuasion in their design rather than relying on "gut feel" or conventional wisdoms about social influence.* A prominent heart-disease prevention campaign at Stanford University in the 1980s based its rationale on the social learning theory that behavioral change can be successfully promoted through modeling the actions of others.[3] Incorporating research on source credibility, fear appeals, and audience learning capabilities can go a long way toward designing more effective programs.
2. *Taking into account audiences' existing cognitions, attitudes, and behaviors and their communication patterns and habits.* Knowing what audiences already know, think, and do can save wasted effort, as can knowing what information needs individuals have and the sources they use to satisfy those needs.
3. *Using extensive precampaign research to examine audience perceptions and needs, then pilot-testing possible themes and messages on targeted groups.* Extensive use of audience surveys, focus groups, and copy testing can provide a more reliable image of what the campaign should attempt to change and how it would have the best chance of doing so.
4. *Having clear and realistically spelled-out campaign goals, high-quality professionally produced materials, and a well-planned and orchestrated dissemination strategy.* It may seem obvious that setting goals and following through on them in a professional manner is more likely to produce results, but many campaigns suffer from simple lack of knowledge about how modern media systems operate. In some cases, lack of funding leads to poor quality advertisements and other material. Often, campaign producers do not fully think

through what they really want to accomplish in the way of building awareness or behavioral change, subverting their best intentions.[4]

5. *Using mass media channels early in a campaign to help build awareness and salience of an issue, while noting that interpersonal communication is more effective for stimulating action.* Making people aware of problems and solutions is far easier than prompting changes in their behaviors, especially ones that individuals see as costly or effortful. Recall from the previous chapter the ability of mass media to set agendas and legitimize issues. However, this does not necessarily lead to taking action; more personal, up-close communication can be more successful at doing so.

Societal Consequences of Campaigns

Both commercial and public information campaigns may have other influences on public opinion than their directly intended ones. Ford's latest campaign to sell its newest Explorer may or may not successfully sway buyers away from Nissan Pathfinders, but we can be more certain that the ads promoting both companies' vehicles combined will build public awareness of and perhaps more desirability for such vehicles overall. The societal impacts of even such a seemingly innocuous product can be consequential: increased fossil fuel consumption and air pollution, land erosion from increased off-road traffic, and, as claimed in the late 1990s, increased risk of injury or death to occupants of smaller vehicles involved in accidents with the larger, often more sturdily built sportsters.

Recent arguments to ban tobacco advertising have been based upon the premise that although each cigarette ad promoted an individual manufacturer's brand, the cumulative effect was to increase the appeal of cigarettes and other tobacco products overall, especially to the young. Some social critics have extended this argument to conclude that product campaigns taken as a group inherently drive us toward being a society of consumers, more concerned with shopping and material possessions than other pursuits.[5] More economically oriented commentators hold the same view but praise advertising campaigns as helping to strengthen the market, in part by making consumers aware of new products and services.[6]

In any case, it seems undeniable that commercial campaigns help shape what is apt to be "in" or "out" of our consumer culture. How such consumer opinions may carry over into the political sphere is far less clear. But if, for example, product advertising builds expectations of goods and services that are beyond the capabilities of many individuals to obtain, the consequences may not be trivial.

The same can be said to some extent for public information campaigns. The tremendous growth in preventive health campaigns over the past thirty years, for example, may have strongly contributed to making us a more health aware and responsible society, regardless of any individual gains in fighting cancer, nutritional deficiencies, or substance abuse. The more subtle message of most public health and safety campaigns has been one of citizens taking more individual responsibility for their well-being, moving away from overreliance on governmental and quasi-public agencies.

A moderately successful instance has been the McGruff "Take a Bite out of Crime" campaign, supported by the U.S. Justice Department. The program encourages citizens to take individual and collective action to prevent crime in their neighborhoods rather than relying on police alone to shoulder the task. The McGruff program raises another aspect of campaign impact—the fact that in some cases, it is necessary for a critical mass number of individuals in a community to change individually before campaign objectives can be met. In the case of crime prevention—and traffic safety and a few other instances—enough people have to take the desired action for crime to be significantly curtailed. The collective actions of block watches and neighborhood cooperation with police are needed to reduce criminal activity in a community rather than just to relocate it from a locked home to an unlocked one next door.

Concerns often rise over which "social good" programs should be promoted, since support for one can lead to neglect of another (see Figure 12.2).[7] If more media time is allocated to a crime prevention program, will that take away from an equally salient program promoting proper infant nutrition practices? And who is to set the agenda to decide which issues win out? A related concern has been that the vast majority of public information

FIGURE 12.2　Too many information campaigns may produce confusion rather than change. SOURCE: Gary Brookins, 1997, *Richmond Times-Dispatch*.

campaigns that win media acceptance are uncontroversial: Few responsible citizens would argue for "more" crime, drug use, or cancer. Greater media attention to such black-and-white issues may draw attention away from more controversial problems such as economic welfare benefits, government-sponsored abortion, and drug legalization.[8]

Another criticism of overreliance in particular on governmentally sponsored information campaigns is that they may promote a more "top-down" channeling of information from institutions to the public, putting less emphasis on public discussion of problems and solutions[9] and perhaps lessening public involvement or buy-in to solutions. For example, rather than by being "told" by municipal information program commercials how to cut water use during a drought, more cooperation might be gained by working within neighborhoods to see what kinds of particular solutions might be optimal for particular kinds of users. Notably, the more successful programs such as McGruff and many recent health education efforts take a communitywide approach to soliciting citizen opinions and ideas for options. International development programs involving agricultural productivity and environmental protection have benefited from similar approaches.[10] Of course, these approaches all serve to involve the "public" more intimately in the process of opinion formation and change, leaving the more "elite" institutional sources such as government with a more limited charge of generating and validating research information that then enters into the mix of public debate. Campaign planners and strategists themselves face new responsibilities as more is learned about what kinds of campaign techniques "work" on both individuals and on the society as a whole: Knowing the kinds of impact their programs can have increases the need for these communicators to act ethically and professionally.[11]

Election Campaigns

We turn now to those campaigns that have the most conspicuous consequences for public opinion: those that have as their direct, avowed intent to build or sway opinions and actions—votes—with respect to public figures or issues. Election campaigns are nothing new, going back to the infancy of the country. From George Washington's day on, candidates for all levels of office have proudly trumpeted their own virtues, roundly disparaged their opponents, and put odd twists on the "facts" regarding their positions and records on issues of concern. However, each political era has changed the context and conduct of political campaigns, the formats of which have been in part dependent upon the political and communication structures of their times (see Figure 12.3).

Changes in political campaigns have gone through some dramatic turns during this century because of the technological developments in communi-

FIGURE 12.3   Draft Goldwater for President Rally in Washington, D.C., Armory, August 4, 1963. Rallies like this one serve a variety of functions in political campaigns. (Photo courtesy of the Library of Congress)

cation media noted in the previous chapter. Other causes of change have included shifts in the demographic, economic, and social structure of the country and, over the past few decades, the decline of political party structures and identifications, changes in nomination procedures, campaign finance laws, and the like. The influence of political party membership on voting behavior has declined markedly. By the 1990s, as many or more people now call themselves "independents" as label themselves either Democrats or Republicans.

As with any other type of campaign, political campaigns are shaped by the times and places in which they occur, by the personalities and issues being promoted, and by the public temper of the day. Political campaigns include not only the highly visible national presidential election races but also those for Congress, state executive and legislative branches, and local mayoral and council contests.

An increasing number of political campaigns are based solely on issues—such as those aimed at voters in public referenda decisions. Campaign tactics are also being used more to fuel public support or opposition to legislative and executive action. Witness the rise in direct mail and television ad blitzes concerning gun control legislation, for example, or the watershed of organized health industry opposition to the Clinton administration health care proposals in 1994. Abortion also remains an emotionally charged campaign field.

As with other kinds of campaigns, the financial cost of political campaigns has risen exponentially over recent decades. These campaigns, however, also share certain characteristics that set them apart from commercial or social marketing programs. For one thing, political campaigns usually operate in a more compressed time frame, during which two or more competing campaigns are directly pitted against one another. Rarely do commercial products go head-to-head in campaigns that end on a particular date, and social marketing programs are unlikely to compete openly against one another. But in election campaigns in particular, it is all over on election day, when the targeted audience votes en masse, one way or another.

Election campaigns are also distinctive in that usually the "product" being promoted is a living, breathing candidate, full of human virtues and frailties. Thus, campaigners have to sell the complexities of a human personality to the public, along with ideological and issue-related attributes. Indeed, election campaigns have increasingly emphasized personality and image aspects of candidates, often at the expense of more issue-related appeals.[12] We do not know whether this trend has followed or led any greater public concern with candidate character over issue positions.

How Do Election Campaigns Work?

Political campaign organizations are also transitory, at least as compared to corporate and public interest campaign programs. When the election is over, the losers' organizations rapidly dissipate, whereas the winners turn to the problems of governance. (In recent decades, at least at the presidential level, governance has included careful attention to public opinion through polling and related public relations activities.)[13] This transitoriness of political campaigns, coupled with the intricate complexities of fundraising, staffing, scheduling, polling, and message and media selection, has led to greater use of hired professional campaign managers. These consultants may be involved in several campaigns at once and provide key expertise in such areas as media relations, polling, and, perhaps most often, candidate marketing. Many of the tactics and strategies used have distinct consequences for traditional pluralistic democratic theory.

Consultants can be instrumental in giving candidates the latest in communication technologies and techniques and in developing strategies for pursuing funding from political action groups and votes from particular voting blocks (see Figure 12.4). As with their commercial counterparts, they rely heavily on market segmentation techniques, identifying characteristics of dominant voting segments and playing campaign messages to the needs and

FIGURE 12.4 Today many candidates hire professional staff to run their campaigns. This group managed Bill Clinton's 1992 presidential campaign. (Photo by David Burnett, courtesy of Contact Press, © 1992)

biases of those groups. These professional campaign planners synchronize candidate appearances and speeches, testimonials from notable individuals and organizations, planned press coverage and "staged" events, and timely reactions to the unexpected news events of the day, in as seamless a dress as possible in keeping with central campaign themes and images.

There is a "good news-bad news" twist to all this, from several points of view. For one thing, it is probably good that these techniques may be quite effective at identifying for candidates what voters view as the critical issues of the day and how they would like to see them resolved. It is also a plus that a variety of political viewpoints are identified and tied to different types of people. However, it may become bad news when candidates insincerely pander to voters by espousing views they think will get them elected rather than challenging voters with evidence and logic based upon their own beliefs. It also does not serve enlightened democratic theory when candidates may try to play one voting segment against another, exaggerating the differences between blocs to manipulate votes for themselves.

Much of the above suggests that it is very much an open question as to whether elites, as represented by campaign producers, lead or follow public opinion in the electioneering process. It is an interesting cycle to consider.

To begin with, techniques such as polling give candidates fairly reliable estimates of what various publics want. Doubtless, this influences their decisions about how to campaign and, ultimately, how to govern if elected. In this sense, the public does affect elite leadership. Yet this information also gives candidates an edge in shaping future public opinion by designing persuasive strategies to suit their own needs. Somewhere in the middle is the press, at least to some extent trying to inform the public of what the candidates are up to, not only with respect to where candidates stand but, more recently, concerning how the candidates are trying to influence the public. One argument on the side of elites having the better of this bargain is that the press itself is often viewed as elitist, although of a somewhat different stripe; numerous recent polls documenting a loss of public respect for journalists support this. And it is the politicians and the press that have the polling and other sophisticated information-gathering capacities, not the public.

At their worst, political consultants can resemble the truth-spinning media tricksters that caused Robert Redford's all-too-successful political neophyte character to turn against his altruistic goals in the 1970s movie *The Candidate*. At their best, consultants may give candidates more reliable information about what the concerns of voting publics actually are, while giving voters greater access to the views and personalities of candidates.[14]

Most political campaign enterprises rely heavily on the help of troops of dedicated volunteers. Even small city elections may require a major personnel logistics plan to recruit and train such individuals, coordinate their efforts, keep them informed and motivated, and give them adequate psychological rewards for their work. Much of their work involves the inevitably mundane tasks of checking voter lists, preparing mailings, phone canvassing, and leaflet dropping. These behind-the-scenes jobs are often obscured by the glamour of catchy television ads and by the drama of major news-event coverage. But the day-to-day hustle of countless volunteers reaching out one-on-one with the electorate is often the critical factor in personalizing the campaign and getting out the vote.[15] It is through such activity that the citizenry comes closest to true participation in political campaigns, probably quite effectively. This linkage of the politically committed with one another over long hours and days or weeks and their direct interplay with candidates or their close representatives, most likely has strong effects on staffers and candidates alike and deserves more attention and scrutiny (see Figure 12.5).

Fund-Raising

The raising of money and collateral support to run a campaign can be a time-consuming task, made even more so by the multifold financial pres-

FIGURE 12.5 Campaign volunteers are critical to a candidate's success, but much of their work is very mundane. Here, Eugene McCarthy's campaign staff cleans up after the Democratic National Convention in Chicago in 1968. (Photo © David Douglas Duncan 1968)

sures and regulations that beset contemporary campaigning. Inordinate amounts of most candidates' waking hours are spent pursuing funding, right up to—and sometimes even after—election day. Presidential campaigns offer the advantage of federal funding options throughout the primaries and into the general election; however, candidates who choose to use that support cannot exceed mandated spending limits.

Thus, halfway into the 1996 Republican presidential primaries, Robert Dole found himself in trouble for having come close to having spent his $30-million-plus limit. One reason for his early excess spending was his attempt to match the television advertising blitz of multimillionaire publisher Steve Forbes, who had refused federal funding and was running his campaign on his own fortune, seemingly willing and able at the time to outspend Dole. In 1996 overall, an estimated $2 billion was spent on campaigns for the presidency and Congress, almost double the amount spent in 1992.

The dilemma from the pluralistic electorate point of view is that the emphasis on funding cuts some citizens out of candidate selection procedures, yet it seems unfair to forbid wealthier people from contributing to the candidates or causes of their choice. Heightened concern over campaign financing has led to moderate regulation at federal, state, and, in some cases, local levels. The basic worries are twofold: (1) that candidates will be "bought" by dominant contributors, who will expect favors from those elected; (2) that candidates who spend the most—particularly on media—will attract the most votes, eliminating perhaps more worthy but less affluent candidates.

The first problem continues to be heavily debated at all levels of government and is hardly a new issue, going back to the earliest experiments in democracy. Special-interest groups donate enormous amounts of money to campaigns of all kinds and enthusiastically lobby the elected officials to support this cause or that on their behalf. The power of such industrial trade groups, unions, citizen action panels, and the like is of genuine concern, particularly since the costs of campaigning—and the attendant need for money to meet them—have risen so dramatically. Despite repeated campaign promises year after year to do something about this one particular "mess in Washington" (and in state capitals across the nation), no firm legislation has been enacted since the early 1970s. Even a rash of serious press accusations and investigations concerning President Clinton's arguably aggressive courting of funds during his 1996 campaign in particular drew no immediate remedial legislation. (A main charge against Clinton—solicitation of funding from foreign nationals—was already illegal, and admission of errors in judgment by his campaign staff appears to have mitigated further action.)

Federal campaign finance laws were enacted primarily to limit exceptionally large contributions by single persons or organizations that might bring undue influence to bear on candidates. In brief, the regulations require that all donated money and expenditures need to be carefully documented by campaign managers. Any one person cannot contribute more than $1,000 to any one candidate's campaign, and any one organization cannot contribute more than $5,000. Higher and flexible limits are set on how much a political party can contribute to individual candidates. Parties can do far more in providing other kinds of organizational support, such as in effect campaigning for its own slate of candidates independently of the individual candidate's effort.

The rise of another kind of political organization—political action committees (PACs)—has added more confusion to the funding situation. PACs are made up of special-interest groups ranging from public advocacy groups to corporations to trade organizations to unions. Individual members may contribute freely to the committee, which is then limited in the same way as other organizations in not being able to give more than $5,000 to any one candidate's campaign. However, PACs may spend as much as they choose *on their own* in support of a candidate—by running their own commercials, their own direct mail campaigns, and so forth—as long as those efforts are made independently of the candidate's own efforts. Some PACs focus on single issues—abortion, health care, and gun control are prominent examples—and may lend their support to a range of like-minded candidates across the country.

Obviously, PACs can have substantial influence on what voters see and hear during election campaigns. Some observers have argued that PACs not only may weaken the rights of individual citizens in the campaign process but also those of political parties as well.[16] However, the ability of citizens to band together to promote a specific issue to candidates and voters alike may be seen as a basic right and indeed a virtue. And political parties are able to raise as much as they choose from all sources—including corporations and unions, which cannot contribute directly to candidates. The party funds are directed by law to administrative costs, get-out-the-vote drives, and advertising that promotes voting for the party's candidates in general—but such ads are often de facto candidate promotions. Clinton's strong personal fund-raising efforts in 1996 were in large part aimed at increasing the Democratic Party war chest, which he knew would indirectly but surely strengthen the Clinton-Gore campaign.

Campaign Media

What has made fund-raising more necessary over the past forty years has been the rise of the mass media campaign, with television absorbing the lion's share of the expense. With the cost of television spot advertising running from hundreds of dollars a minute in the smallest market areas to hundreds of thousands of dollars nationally, it is easy to see how Robert Dole could have spent some $25 million before reaching the late winter halfway point in the 1996 Republican primary elections.

Although buying television time is the major cost, other big expenses include hiring professional advertising staffs to produce the material that goes into televised messages. These include developing campaign themes, slogans, and graphic images, which need to blend into posters, as well as direct mail pieces, issue position papers, and the ubiquitous bumper stickers and buttons. Competently done political polling can be another major expense item.

Types of campaign media can be broadly separated into *controlled* and *uncontrolled* media. Controlled media are those that planners pay for and produce themselves, selecting their own themes, messages, target audiences, and schedules. Advertising is the primary format. The main form of uncontrolled media is news coverage, which is cost-free to the candidate and can offer wide and credible exposure. The downside is that the candidate has no direct control over what is reported, when, or to whom.

Controlled Media. Controlled media include commercials and other bought-and-paid-for broadcast and cable time, newspaper advertising, direct mail, World Wide Web pages, billboards, posters, telephone canvassing, and the like. Speeches and other public appearances by or for candidates generally fall into the controlled category as well, although news media will often use portions of them, edited to their own liking. As in any campaign, controlled messages are carefully designed to influence particular kinds of audiences, and media channels are chosen to maximize impact on those audiences.

Brochures and other print pieces are useful for providing more detailed information on policy positions, past voting records, and other specifics. Often these can be tailored for direct mailing to certain zip code addresses with particular demographic or lifestyle characteristics. Residents of a neighborhood with a high proportion of retirees, for example, may be mailed highlights of a candidate's assurances about continued Social Security benefits. A heavily Hispanic area, by contrast, may be targeted with mailings in Spanish emphasizing the candidate's commitment to affirmative action standards.

Radio typically provides another vehicle for careful voter-bloc targeting. The diversity of radio stations across musical tastes, talk show politics, and other formats delivers to advertisers distinct listener types to whom campaigners can appeal. Newspaper ads reach a broader, more mainstream audience that is more inclined to be politically active and informed and more apt to vote. Internet web sites are quickly emerging, but they primarily serve already committed political junkies.

Television commercials remain clearly the dominant form of controlled political media, and they include an interesting mix of advantages and disadvantages for candidates. A decided and obvious advantage of televised political commercials is their reach. No other medium can bring to a given message millions of viewers nationally or even tens of thousands statewide or locally, often in a single showing. Not only are these spots seen in the viewers' own homes, but they are difficult to avoid as well. It is difficult for audiences to tune out ads selectively that they might disagree with or be uninterested in. Further, commercials are squeezed into programs in an increasingly cluttered environment, with spots of less than half a minute becoming the norm. This makes it more difficult for any type of ad to stand out on its own.

Political commercials can be aimed at some audience segments by carefully choosing the types of programs during which they appear. However, the match is not always a close one, given the diverse audiences television draws. Also, those who watch television more heavily are among the more politically disenfranchised, and some efficiency may be wasted by aiming candidate spots at them. These disadvantages are related to the biggest one of all: the extremely high expense of airing ads during programs that draw the largest and most desirable audiences. Costs of hundreds of thousands of dollars per minute for national spots are not uncommon, and even locally shown spots can run into the thousands of dollars per showing.

The commercials' ability to convey moving sight and sound visually dramatizes not only a candidate's personal attributes but political issues and themes as well.[17] The ten- to sixty-second television spot format offers a wide array of creative possibilities, ranging from focus on candidate leadership characteristics to "toughness" on crime or foreign policy to snippets of policy positions put into human, emotive terms. The mix of creative elements varies heavily with the type of candidate, the nature of the opposition, and the voter groups and concerns being addressed. Political newcomers may push their personal strengths and seek popular endorsements early in a race, whereas well-known incumbents emphasize their records in office. More telegenic contenders may show more visuals of themselves in action, with others focusing on less personal visual imagery.

Comparative ads contrast one candidate's attributes with the opposition's, often exaggerating differences in policy positions or voting records. The fairness of these has sometimes been called into question, and some news media have run "AdWatch"-type news briefs to refute the claims of more biased ads. A trend toward more *negative* or *attack* ads on television seems to have emerged during the late 1980s, in which candidates attack their opponents on personal or policy points rather than promoting their own virtues (see Box 12.2).

Candidates have also taken advantage of the "unfiltered" opportunity to provide information to interested citizens via the World Wide Web. Their web pages flourish, providing biographical information, position papers, invitations to join E-mail and regular mail lists, and so forth. It remains to be seen how much the use of these will spread beyond what is likely a very small segment of hard-core (and computer literate) political activists.

Uncontrolled Media. Uncontrolled media are equally if not more important and mainly include coverage by the news media. Such coverage can provide greater reach across voters and bestow greater credibility to a candidacy—and the coverage is virtually "free" to the candidate. However, the campaign has no direct control over what messages end up on the air or in print.

Virtually all types of campaigns actively solicit news coverage of their "product," whether it be soap or safe driving or a presidential candidate. Political campaigns employ "media relations" specialists to provide broadcast and print news reporters with reams of press releases, position papers, and other documentation supporting the virtues of the candidate. Campaign events are often timed to coincide with the schedules of evening network television programs and morning newspapers. Journalists are accorded preferential treatment in the campaign entourage and are privy to behind-the-scenes comings and goings and the occasional "exclusive" interview with a candidate.

The pace of news coverage has quickened considerably over the past decade, with the coming of around-the-clock news coverage on CNN and

---

Box 12.2   The "Willie Horton" Attack Ad

One of the most notorious—and allegedly successful—attack ads in recent years was aired in September 1988 at the beginning of the George Bush versus Michael Dukakis presidential race. Vice President Bush and Dukakis, then governor of Massachusetts, were running fairly even in the national polls early in the campaign, and crime was emerging as a high agenda item in the campaign. Bush favored the death penalty; Dukakis did not. The Bush campaign began airing a series of television spots suggesting that Dukakis had been soft on crime as governor and, specifically, that Massachusetts prisons were a "revolving door" for dangerous criminals, freeing them soon after they were sentenced.

The most graphic spot in the series featured a black man convicted of first-degree murder—Willie Horton. Horton had been allowed a weekend furlough from a Massachusetts prison, during which he kidnapped and raped a white woman. The spot arguably highlighted the racial angle to the crime and clearly exaggerated the risks associated with the long-running furlough program. The ad also suggested that Dukakis had implemented the program, which had been in place prior to his governorship. The spot was memorable and controversial enough to be replayed in televised news reports. Although in many cases these replays included criticism of its content, they served to increase public exposure to the spot, and to the issue. Bush almost immediately began pulling ahead of Dukakis in the national polls, never to slip back. To be sure, miscues in Dukakis's own campaign appeared to contribute to Bush's advance, but "the spot" was widely credited with getting the momentum going.

---

its competitors, instantaneous satellite transmission to local broadcast stations and newspapers, and continuous news coverage in great detail on the Internet. This has led to even greater public access to candidates, though also perhaps to a greater tendency of reporters to get the news out quickly to beat the competition. Inaccuracies can and do occur; one notable example is the overwillingness of some television networks to jump the gun on predicting election winners before valid samplings of returns are in. News coverage varies considerably with the nature of the campaign. A candidate for alderman in a small city might revel at getting one interview in the daily newspaper over the whole course of a campaign, whereas major gubernatorial or presidential contenders may blanch at what they see as wholesale surrender of their private lives to the news media on a daily basis.

The most important drawback of press coverage is that no matter how hard the candidate tries to impress journalists, what ultimately gets reported is out of the campaign's direct control. The press chooses the content to be reported, the context in which it will appear, and often interprets the information from the point of view of other candidates or offers the media's own news judgments. An ongoing matching of wits often follows for the duration of a campaign, with politicians recognizing their own need for press coverage and trying to get the most positive spin possible along with it. Journalists, working from a different vantage point, generally recognize their own obligation to inform the public about candidates' pros and cons but need to rely on candidates to supply crucial information.

Somewhat hybrid and interactive campaign events ranging from candidate debates to talk show appearances to Internet chat lines are probably best described as a mix of both controlled and uncontrolled media: Candidates certainly have control over what they say and reach their audience directly with it, but the give-and-take of live interviewing of any sort can quickly move the locus of perceived control from interviewee to interviewer, or inquisitor.

Ideally, there should be tension between media controlled by the campaigners and the uncontrolled media, represented mainly by the press in its various forms. This tension can work to bring public interests and concerns more into the media mix—to assure that questions the public wants answered are put to the candidates. However, as noted previously, there is a risk that the press may have its own agendas to follow—and more elitist ones at that—lessening the opportunity for public influence on choosing and shaping campaign issues. In a study of news depictions of the 1991 Philadelphia mayoral campaign, for example, June Rhee found that some print stories framed the campaign more in campaign strategy terms, while others framed them more in issue terms. Using an experimental manipulation, Rhee also found that readers tended to interpret the campaign more in terms of the frames they read. Readers more exposed to strategy stories described the campaign more as a strategy process, while those reading stories framed around issues concentrated more on those.[18]

Kim Fridkin Kahn offers a telling account of press coverage of female candidates and possible impact upon voters. In an analysis of gubernatorial and senatorial campaigns, Fridkin Kahn found that press coverage of campaigns of female candidates focused less on issue positions than did coverage of male candidates. Personal or image attributes of women received more attention. Moreover, the press appeared to follow the lead of male candidates in covering the content emphasized by their campaigns more often than it did for female candidates. Fridkin Kahn argues that media stereotypes of women in campaigns can hinder their getting their messages over to voters, although in some contexts the stereotypes may work in favor of female candidates.[19]

Impact of Campaigns on Public Opinion and Voting

How do election campaign strategies and tactics actually affect voters? We will now examine what we know about what voters learn from such campaigns, how the campaigns influence vote decisions, and how campaigns might impact other political orientations of voters.

Learning from Campaigns

Voters may learn a considerable amount from news coverage of candidates. Both newspaper and television news play significant roles in informing the public about campaign issues and usually about candidate positions on them.[20] Many earlier studies suggested that newspapers did a far better job than television in informing voters.[21] Nevertheless, extent of learning from each medium can vary by the kinds of people being examined, the type of campaign, and other factors as well. A national study by political scientists Craig Brians and Martin Wattenberg of the 1992 Bush-Clinton contest showed very low levels of learning about the candidates' positions from either newspaper or television news.[22] Whether this came about from peculiarities of citizen response to the candidates, from press coverage during that particular campaign, or from other reasons is puzzling. Brians and Wattenberg suggest that a possible diminishing of coverage of substantive issues in both newspapers and television may have played a role.

As for differences in citizen response, politically interested people may learn more about candidates from newspapers than from television, but television and newspapers appear about even in informing the less involved.[23] Television has often been assumed to do a better job of giving voters "image" impressions of candidate personality attributes, but the evidence on this is less clear.[24] Thomas Patterson found television's image impact pertinent only in the early-impression formation stages of a campaign.[25]

Well-publicized events such as debates provide a wellspring for issue learning and impression formation[26] and may be especially effective in informing citizens not as attuned to other aspects of the campaign.[27] Some individuals may also learn from the much-maligned television commercials. Patterson and Robert McClure were the first to suggest that the ubiquitous spot ads contained enough nuggets of basic information—and were repeated often enough—to enlighten viewers as to candidates' basic policy stances.[28] The less politically involved and less news attentive who thrive more on entertainment television may find commercials to be their primary window and information source.

However, there was little research support to back up this controversial claim until the 1992 presidential election, when Brians and Wattenberg found that watching campaign spots was highly associated with learning more about candidates' issue positions—and clearly more predictive of learning than either newspaper or television news use (see Table 12.1). This could be particularly true for such situations as Republican presidential candidate Steve Forbes's multimillion-dollar television advertising blitz in the

TABLE 12.1   Predicting Issue Knowledge and Issue-Based Candidate Evaluation by Media Sources[a]

	Knowledge of Candidates' Positions	Candidate Evaluation Issue Salience
Political ad recall	.247[c]	.363[d]
	(.084)	(.101)
Newspaper index	.010[b]	.003
	(.005)	(.006)
TV news index	.011[b]	.004
	(.005)	(.006)
Education	.268[d]	.024
	(.028)	(.034)
Sex (female)	−.079	−.004
	(.082)	(.098)
Age in years	−.016[d]	−.018[d]
	(.002)	(.003)
Campaign interest	.183[d]	.260[d]
	(.033)	(.039)
General political knowledge	.449[d]	.291[d]
	(.030)	(.036)
Interview date	−.088	.028
	(.080)	(.096)
Constant	1.410[d]	.978[d]
	(.183)	(.219)
Adjusted R^2	.39	.16
Standard error	1.64	1.96
Number of cases	1,809	1,809

NOTE: Figures are unstandardized OLS regression coefficients: standard errors are in parentheses.

[a] Variables defined and missing data cases explained in the appendix in Brians and Wattenberg.

[b] $p < .05$.

[c] $p < .01$.

[d] $p < .001$.

SOURCE: From Craig L. Brians, and Martin P. Wattenberg, "Campaign Issue Knowledge and Salience: Comparing Reception from TV Commericals, TV News, and Newspapers," *American Journal of Political Science*, 40 (1) (February 1996), table 2, p. 181. Data derived from 1992 American National Election Study. Reprinted by permission of University of Wisconsin Press.

early 1996 primaries. Although many of Forbes's spots attacked other candidates, voters also arguably learned of Forbes's "flat" income tax plan from them. Brians and Wattenberg found that viewing negative campaign ads— those that attack or bash the opponent's positions or personal characteristics— was also associated with knowing more about issues. This finding is partially backed up in a series of studies of the 1992 presidential campaign and of a number of California state and local campaigns by Steven An-solabehere and Shanto Iyengar, who also note that the strength of the effect differs across a wide range of candidates and voters.[29] One argument goes that the negative ads attract more attention and whatever issue information is contained in them may be better remembered.

Whether citizens learn more about candidates from newspapers, debates, televised news, or televised ads is likely to depend on the type of campaign, what voters already know about the candidates, and how well news media and campaign media managers carry out their jobs. A recent integration of how people learn about candidates and issues over six different campaigns found television news to generally be the main source, but televised ads sur-passed news in one Senate campaign in which both candidates spent huge sums on airing the spots.[30]

How Persuasive Are Campaigns?

Election campaigns work their influences on public opinion in several ways, much in keeping with what we would expect from the previous chapter. "Strong" effects on the order of campaigns causing dramatic changes in voter moods or preferences are unlikely, but "weaker" influences on citizen perceptions and opinions are probable, given the relatively intensive stimuli campaigns bring to bear on politically charged preelection environments.

One main impact that campaigns are often assumed to have that is actu-ally the least likely to occur is convincing voters to switch from one candi-date to another.[31] A quite small percentage of voters—usually in the low single digits—in any election campaign end up doing this, and the propor-tion of those who do who may be swayed by the campaign is typically too negligible to calculate. We need to keep in mind, however, that although the number of voters influenced by the campaign to change candidates is low, such vote switching may be decisive in close races. Many major elections are decided by a fraction of a percentage point, and relatively few voters shifting here or there can make all the difference. (Social scientists doing studies of campaigns sometimes rightfully dismiss very small differences in voting behavior as "statistically insignificant"; yet candidates can and do win or lose elections by handfuls of votes.)

A persuasive influence election campaigns are more likely to have is to keep already decided supporters of a candidate on track, reinforcing their decisions and motivating them to go to the polls. As long as "my" candi-dates keep feeding me reasons that I should vote for them, it is unlikely, short of a major blunder or scandal on the candidate's part, that I would be attracted by the arguments of other contestants to whom I had started out opposed. But faced with a rash of messages from opposing politicians and little or no communication from my initial choices, I could begin to at least waver in my decision. Although I might not switch sides, I could simply not bother to vote. A second persuasive influence involves pulling in the undecided voters, who form an increasingly large pool in our more volatile electoral environment. A more difficult task is to reach out to uncommitted and less involved citizens—another increasing cohort—most of whom will end up not bothering to vote at all.

The relative persuasive influences of controlled versus uncontrolled campaign media on the public are unclear. The problem is in separating the possible influences of commercials from those of speeches or debates and those of news coverage and other avenues. Recalling where we heard overlapping bits of information is difficult enough for most of us, let alone recalling who out of a heady mix of sources may have affected or influenced us. News events, commercials, key speeches, debates, and other stimuli likely reach different voters in different ways at different times.

The increased volatility exhibited by the voting public from 1975 through the 1990s has focused more attention on both the kinds of citizens and the kinds of election situations that may lead to greater or lesser campaign effects. People are clearly less consistent in voting by party labels and more apt to choose a candidate later in the campaign or to opt out of voting altogether. Voters who pick a candidate closer to election day are more likely to be influenced by the campaign and to base their choice on issues or candidate characteristics emphasized in the campaign.[32]

An individual's level of *involvement* in a particular election is likely an important indicator of how the person's decision will be reached and of the kinds of information that will be more influential in that choice. Recall the discussion in Chapter 4 on level of involvement in terms of its impact on how people process information and how much of an impact that information is likely to have. Studies have found that people with higher involvement in a problem or issue—or an election—will make decisions more "logically," carefully processing information and looking for cues more *central* to the problem at hand.[33] In choosing a candidate, for example, the more involved voter may make a close inspection of contenders' issue positions, voting records, administrative abilities, and the like, comparing and contrasting them.

People with lower involvement, however, make decisions less logically and systematically and base them on more *peripheral* cues or on ones more available but less central to the decision per se. Not being interested enough in the election, such voters are less willing to go through the difficulty of actively processing information about issues or character. They take the easier way, settling for a set of cues that will justify their decision to themselves. In election decisions, these people might be more swayed by perhaps the looks of a candidate, the offhand advice of a friend, a celebrity endorsement, or by the cleverness of a political ad.

Citizens vary a great deal in how willing they are to be involved in election decisions—if at all. Some of us may spend weeks agonizing over a presidential or Senate race choice but may cast a ballot on the same election day for a city council person based on whose name is first on the ballot. Involvement is in part a personal attribute, in that some people are less politically interested overall, and a situational one, in that some elections simply generate low attention levels. Campaigners recognize this, particularly in their efforts to reach the less concerned citizens who may be marginally likely to vote. Television commercials that may seem senseless and repetitive to a politically astute voter could conceivably be the only salient message that happens to cross the mind of a far less interested person on election day. Ansolabehere and Iyengar, in their previously mentioned 1992 California studies, found television ads were far more reinforcing of existing partisan sentiments among voters than manipulative or causing changes in candidate predispositions.[34] Party-unaffiliated citizens appeared the least persuaded—perhaps because they paid less attention to the ads. As for attack ads, for whatever reasons, the California study found Republican attack ads more reinforcing for Republicans, whereas Democrats were more reinforced by positive ads.

Building Citizen Interest

Campaigns build citizen interest in the election, in a sense alerting potential voters that an event of consequence is coming up. Even the most politically disenfranchised and disinterested people find major campaigns hard to avoid, especially given their play on television. Skipping the news is easy, but commercials on popular programs are difficult to avoid, even when they are spiritedly disliked. In presidential campaigns, television appears to heighten early interest among citizens during the primaries, with subsequent spikes of attentiveness during the nominating conventions and candidate debates (see Table 12.2).[35]

Newspapers may stimulate interest more gradually over the period, being less intrusive: Newspaper readers can choose what to read, following their own interests; television may be more able to spark new interest among the initially less motivated because of the "unavoidability" of political content slipped into unrelated programming. Television's penchant for the more visually dramatic probably contributes here as well. The visual spectacles of the conventions and debates can draw in more of the less curious, of course giving candidates an opportunity to impress themselves upon the only marginally politically interested.

Campaigns also can build the morale of committed campaign workers. Rallies, stump speeches, and blitzes of attractive media ads can add luster and meaning to the otherwise drab and hard work of preparing mailings

TABLE 12.2   Election Interest at Various Times During the Campaign, 1976 (in percent)

Level of Interest and Location	February	April	June	August	October
Erie					
Strong interest	22	28	26	33	32
Some interest	28	30	34	33	34
No interest	50	42	40	34	34
Total	100	100	100	100	100
Los Angeles					
Strong interest	19	27	32	37	29
Some interest	26	28	33	32	33
No interest	55	45	35	31	38
Total	100	100	100	100	100

SOURCE: Thomas E. Patterson, *The Mass Media Election: How Americans Choose Their President* (New York: Praeger, 1980), table 7.1, p. 68.

and canvassing by phone, keeping energy levels and work quality high. Election campaigns can also contribute to the public spiritedness of the citizenry overall, perhaps reinforcing the legitimacy of the political system.

However, if citizens are exposed to heavy doses of negative advertising across campaigns, one risk is that people will believe all candidates to have salient weaknesses, resulting in less enthusiasm for supporting any of them. Negative advertising may also increase political cynicism and decrease willingness to vote or participate in other ways.[36] Ansolabehere and Iyengar found citizen exposure to attack ads partially related to lower voter turnout in their 1992 California study, especially among independent, less-partisan potential voters.[37] And the authors make the case that these ads appear to have stimulated greater partisanship and polarization among those who did vote.

This is not unlike the argument made for the "videomalaise" syndrome purportedly brought on by negative television news. Although some interesting evidence supports such ill effects of attack ads on the public under some circumstances, it is hardly clear how widespread the influence may be or in what kinds of campaign contexts it might operate. Should "attack" ads that accurately portray genuinely negative characteristics of an arguably poor, or even dangerous, candidate be disallowed?

Preelection polling results have also recently gotten something of a drubbing from some observers. Although there is little evidence that such poll results sway voters from one candidate to another, poll findings may dull interest in a contest in which one candidate or the other appears impossibly ahead, and this might possibly lessen voter turnout.[38]

What We Do Not Know About
Election Campaign Influences

We do not know that much about how political campaigns *as campaigns*—
in the sense of the term defined at the beginning of this chapter—affect voting decisions. One reason for this is that we have not done a very good job
of studying how political campaigns work. That may sound strange, given
the wealth of curiosity about presidential races, especially, and the seemingly endless supply of articles, books, and documentaries analyzing election outcomes. Although such analyses may offer reasoned and sometimes
accurate speculation about voting behavior, they lack an adequate view of
the multitude of factors that impinge on why citizens vote as they do.

Much of the problem lies in separating the impact of the candidate per se
and dramatic events beyond the candidate's control from the campaign operation itself. Many have acclaimed Richard Nixon's 1968 television-based
campaign tactics over Hubert Humphrey as pioneering and masterful, yet
many polls showed Humphrey gaining significantly on Nixon over the final
weeks of the contest. The point is that it is exceptionally difficult to separate out either the campaign plan overall or specific elements of it and point
to any one factor as decisive in winning an election. And perhaps fortunately, much of what happens during and around election campaign periods is out of the hands of the planners and strategists. "Real life" goes on,
with war, scandal, economic ups and downs, disasters, and similar events
being quite out of the control of the candidates, yet often dramatically affecting how voters respond to them.

To get a more complete picture of what kinds of campaign strategies and
tactics have what kinds of impact on which voters, we need a far more
holistic view of the contest than past analyses have provided. We need to
examine carefully the approaches of competing campaigns, the central message themes, the media strategies. We then need to tie those to extensive observations on voters—through surveys and other methods—before, during,
and after the campaign. Finally, we need to have some way of in effect
"controlling" for the type of candidate in each campaign, the issues raised,
and the events unrelated to the campaign that took place during it. This is a
tall order and is impractical for many, if not most, campaign research situations. Perhaps the best we can realistically aim for is to tease out which factors are more apt to be important in what kinds of campaigns to what
kinds of voters and focus on those.

To get back to key points raised at the beginning of this chapter: If the
candidate (or "product") is a dud, even the most technically perfect campaign operation is unlikely to save that person if the opponent has more
going politically.

Also, most previous analyses have dealt with presidential races—the most significant in some ways but also the most closely attended to by the public. We know far less about the role of campaign operations and media use in more localized races, where they could have a greater impact. Media in particular have much more of a chance of establishing a persona for candidates who are normally less in the public eye, about whom voters may know very little, if anything.

As noted above, candidates have turned more to "alternative" media, such as televised talk shows, MTV, and cable offerings more generally. These give candidates more leeway in presenting their own views in an extended format, at least as compared to traditional news programming. Although such audiences are smaller, they tend to be more segmented and may include individuals less involved in politics—or attuned to traditional media formats. There is little evidence so far that viewers who watch them learn much from these appearances, but as they grow in frequency with greater channel diversification, that could change.[39]

How Well Is the Public Served by Campaign Press Coverage?

Criticism of such campaign techniques as attack messages is as old as democracy and the arts of persuasion and propaganda. Very thin lines exist between trying to put the best possible perspective or spin on a person or event and outright misrepresentation. Equally open to criticism—at least over the past two centuries—has been the way the press reports campaigns. As we saw in the last chapter, very seldom can journalists be seen as objective or disinterested observers of political events, and the coverage of campaigns is certainly no exception.

In recent years, more criticism of press campaign coverage has focused on a charge that newspapers and television news show more concern with the "horse race" aspects of campaigns and with negative depictions of candidates' personal attributes. Critics argue that the news media report more on the campaign as a phenomenon, as opposed to reporting on the substance of the issues of the day, how candidates respond to those, and the candidates' competence to hold office (see Figure 12.6).[40]

Such coverage includes the "horse race" or "hoopla" issues of campaign strategy and tactics, who is ahead and who is behind in the polls, fallout from attack ads and other negative techniques, and making the most of candidate idiosyncrasies and blunders. Competitive aspects of the campaign can make for easier and more exciting day-to-day deadline coverage reporting, whereas reporting the "deeper" aspects of issue positions requires more

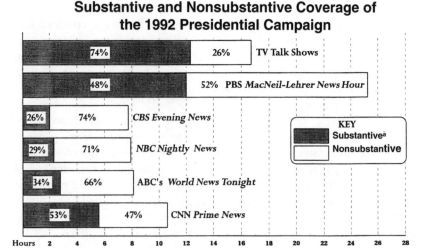

Substantive and Nonsubstantive Coverage of the 1992 Presidential Campaign

74%	26% TV Talk Shows
48%	52% PBS *MacNeil-Lehrer News Hour*
26%	74% *CBS Evening News*
29%	71% *NBC Nightly News*
34%	66% ABC's *World News Tonight*
53%	47% CNN *Prime News*

KEY
Substantive[a]
Nonsubstantive

Hours 2 4 6 8 10 12 14 16 18 20 22 24 26 28

[a]Substance category includes stories primarily about the candidates' qualifications and policy issues.

FIGURE 12.6 Substantive and Nonsubstantive Coverage of the 1992 Presidential Campaign. SOURCE: S. R. Lichter and R. E. Noyes, *Good Intentions Make Bad News: Why Americans Hate Campaign Journalism* (Lanham, MD: Rowman and Littlefield, 1995), p. 247.

difficult and skillful explanation to make it appealing to citizens-at-large. The emphasis on reporting who is ahead in the early polls of presidential and other primaries can also have substantial consequences for candidate fund-raising: Donors are obviously attracted much more easily and quickly to candidates whom they think can win, and donors pegged as early supporters of a successful candidate gain in luster and perceived influence. Critics charge that candidate performance on the stump may not translate into effective coalition building, thoughtful policy planning, or leadership in time of crisis. Journalists often respond to these charges by saying that public interest in such matters runs high and that how well candidates manage their run for office can be a telling indicator of administrative ability and style.

The press has also been accused of capitalizing on and magnifying personal flaws of candidates, and indeed of public persons overall, to the point where some otherwise viable public servants may shy away from the fray because they do not want so much of their personal background and that of their families open to scrutiny. The response of the press is typically an argument that citizens need to be made aware of the character of officeholders and that one relinquishes the private persona by becoming a public person. Critics retort that much of such coverage is simply titillating *National Enquirer*–type reporting to attract a bigger audience and that it is often blown out of proportion.

More recent, and perhaps less important, controversies have grown over such issues as the amount of live television coverage given the national party nominating conventions and that accorded to debates between presidential candidates. Many journalists would argue that these are simply news judgments: If something of public interest is expected to happen at such an event, it will be covered. The political viewpoint is that there is an obligation of the press to cover major national events, even if the outcomes are easily predictable and nothing "new" is anticipated to happen. As political scientist Thomas Patterson notes, the press is "fundamentally ill-suited to fulfilling its inherited role as an election mediator. . . . The problem is that the press is not a political institution. Its business is news, and the values of news are not those of politics.x"[41]

Resolution of these conflicts is highly unlikely, but much can be gained by greater public awareness of the contrasts among (1) the realities of the political environment, (2) the image of the environment that campaigns present, and (3) the image of that environment that the press presents. In sum, the call is for public awareness that the media in their varied shapes and forms provide varied "pictures in our heads" of an environment we do not directly experience, as Lippmann put it so well.[42]

Notes

1. Everett M. Rogers and J. Douglas Storey, "Communication Campaigns," in Charles R. Berger and Steven H. Chaffee, eds., *Handbook of Communication Science* (Newbury Park, CA: Sage Publications, 1987), p. 821.

2. Philip Kotler and Eduardo L. Roberto, *Social Marketing: Strategies for Changing Public Behavior* (New York: Free Press, 1989).

3. June A. Flora, Nathan Maccoby, and John W. Farquhar, "Communication Campaigns to Prevent Cardiovascular Disease: The Stanford Community Studies," in Ronald Rice and Charles Atkin, eds., *Public Communication Campaigns*, 2d ed. (Newbury Park, CA: Sage Publications, 1989), pp. 233–252.

4. Rogers and Storey, "Communication Campaigns"; Garrett J. O'Keefe and Kathaleen Reid, "The Uses and Effects of Public Service Advertising," James Grunig and Larissa Grunig, eds., *Public Relations Research Annual*, vol. 2 (Hillsdale, NJ: Lawrence Erlbaum, 1990), pp. 67–94.

5. Jean Baudrillard, "Consumer Society," in *Jean Baudrillard, Selected Writings* (Stanford, CA: Stanford University Press, 1988), pp. 29–56.

6. Leo Bogart, *Commercial Culture: The Media System and the Public Interest* (New York: Oxford University Press, 1995).

7. Charles T. Salmon, "Campaigns and Social 'Improvement': An Overview of Values, Rationales, and Impacts," in Charles T. Salmon, ed., *Information Campaigns: Balancing Social Values and Social Change* (Newbury Park, CA: Sage Publications, 1989), pp. 19–53.

8. David Paletz, Roberta Pearson, and David Willis, *Politics in Public Service Advertising on Television* (New York: Springer, 1977).

9. Lana F. Rakow, "Information and Power: Toward a Critical Theory of Information Campaigns," in Salmon, ed., *Information Campaigns,* pp. 164–184.

10. Shirley A. White, with K. Sadanandan Nair and Joseph Ascroft, eds., *Participatory Communication* (Thousand Oaks, CA: Sage Publications, 1994).

11. Richard W. Pollay, "Campaigns, Change and Culture: On the Polluting Potential of Persuasion," in Salmon, ed., *Information Campaigns,* pp. 185–198.

12. Stephen J. Salmore and Barbara G. Salmore, *Candidates, Parties, and Campaigns: Electoral Politics in America* (Washington, DC: CQ Press, 1985).

13. Lawrence R. Jacobs and Robert Y. Shapiro, "The Rise of Presidential Polling: The Nixon White House in Historical Perspective," *Public Opinion Quarterly* 59 (1995):163–195.

14. Larry J. Sabato, *The Rise of Political Consultants: New Ways of Winning Elections* (New York: Basic Books, 1981).

15. Salmore and Salmore, *Candidates, Parties, and Campaigns.*

16. Margaret M. Conway, "ACs, the New Politics, and Congressional Campaigns," in Alan J. Cigler and Burdett A. Loomis, eds., *Interest Group Politics* (Washington, DC: CQ Press, 1983), pp. 126–144.

17. For an extensive historical overview, see Edward Diamond and Steven Bates, *The Spot: The Rise of Political Advertising on Television* (Cambridge: MIT Press, 1984).

18. June Woong Rhee, "Strategy and Issue Frames in Election Campaign Coverage: A Social Cognitive Account of Framing Effects," *Journal of Communication* 47, 3 (Summer, 1997):26–48.

19. Kim Fridkin Kahn, *The Political Consequences of Being a Woman* (New York: Columbia University Press, 1996).

20. Steven H. Chaffee, Xinsho Zhao, and Glenn Leshner, "Political Knowledge and the Campaign Media of 1992," *Communication Research* 21 (1994):305–324.

21. John P. Robinson and Dennis K. Davis, "Television News and the Informed Public: An Information-Processing Approach," *Journal of Communication* 40 (1990):106–119.

22. Craig Leonard Brians and Martin P. Wattenberg, "Campaign Issue Knowledge and Salience: Comparing Reception from TV Commercials, TV News, and Newspapers," *American Journal of Political Science* 40 (1996):172–193.

23. Thomas E. Patterson, *The Mass Media Election: How Americans Choose Their President* (New York: Praeger, 1980).

24. C. Richard Hofsteter, Cliff Zukin, and Terry F. Buss, "Political Imagery and Information in an Age of Television," *Journalism Quarterly* 55 (1978):562–569.

25. Patterson, *Mass Media Election.*

26. Stanley Kraus, *The Great Debates: Carter vs. Ford* (Bloomington: Indiana University Press, 1979).

27. Kathleen Hall Jamieson and David S. Birdsell, *Presidential Debates: The Challenge of Creating an Informed Electorate* (New York: Oxford University Press, 1988).

28. Thomas E. Patterson and Robert D. McClure, *The Unseeing Eye: The Myth of Television Power in National Politics* (New York: G. P. Putnam's Sons, 1976).

29. Steven Ansolabehere and Shanto Iyengar, *Going Negative: How Attack Ads Shrink and Polarize the Electorate* (New York: Free Press, 1995).

30. Xinshu Zhao and Steven H. Chaffee, "Campaign Advertisements Versus Television News as Sources of Political Information," *Public Opinion Quarterly* 59 (1995):41–65.

31. See, for example, Diana C. Mutz, Paul Sniderman, and Richard Brody, eds., *Political Persuasion and Attitude Change* (Ann Arbor: University of Michigan Press, 1996).

32. Steven H. Chaffee and Sun Yuel Choe, "Time of Decision and Media Use During the Ford-Carter Campaign," *Public Opinion Quarterly* 44 (1980):53–69.

33. Richard E. Petty and John T. Cacioppo, *Communication and Persuasion: Central and Peripheral Routes to Attitude Change* (New York: Springer, 1986).

34. Ansolabehere and Iyengar, *Going Negative*.

35. Patterson, *Mass Media Election*.

36. Kathleen Hall Jamieson, *Dirty Politics: Deception, Distraction, and Democracy* (New York: Oxford University Press, 1992); Ansolabehere and Iyengar, *Going Negative*.

37. Ansolabehere and Iyengar, *Going Negative*.

38. Everett C. Ladd, "The Election Polls: An American Waterloo," *Chronicle of Higher Education* November 22, 1996, p. A52.

39. David Weaver and Dan Drew, "Voter Learning in the 1992 Presidential Election: Did the 'Nontraditional' Media and Debates Matter?" *Journalism Quarterly* 72 (1995):7–17.

40. Larry Sabato, *Feeding Frenzy: How Attack Journalism Has Transformed American Politics* (New York: Free Press, 1993); Twentieth Century Fund. *The Report of the Twentieth Century Fund Task Force on Television and the Campaign of 1992: 1-800-PRESIDENT* (New York: Twentieth Century Fund Press, 1993); S. Robert Lichter and Richard E. Noyes, *Good Intentions Make Bad News: Why Americans Hate Campaign Journalism* (Lanham, MD: Rowman and Littlefield Publishers, 1995).

41. Thomas E. Patterson, *Out of Order* (New York: Knopf, 1993), p. 25.

42. Walter Lippmann, *Public Opinion* (New York: Macmillan Co., 1922).

Chapter Thirteen

Looking Ahead

We have covered enormous ground in this text because public opinion is such an interesting and complex phenomenon. This complexity makes the field of public opinion research very broad and multidisciplinary. Since there is so much varied research in the area, it is difficult to wrap things up, to come to a clean and decisive halt in our analysis of public opinion. Early on in this book, we argued that the meaning of "public opinion" is always shifting: How we think about the concept depends upon historical circumstance as well as upon our research hypotheses and the technologies we have on hand to assess public opinion. At this point in American politics, it seems as though our techniques for opinion expression and measurement are very sophisticated, but there will always be new developments because candidates for office, elected officials, interest group spokesmen, journalists, party leaders, and citizens will always have an interest in the effective evaluation of the popular mood. We must remember, too, that market researchers have contributed greatly to the development of public opinion measurement techniques and that political actors will continue to look to the commercial world for ideas about persuasion and assessment of public opinion.

From a scholarly perspective, one thing about public opinion is clear: It must be studied from an interdisciplinary viewpoint. As you saw in this book, public opinion is a psychological, sociological, and political phenomenon all at the same time. Public opinion formation takes place constantly as people react to the world around them. We are bombarded with persuasive communications daily, from the mass media, from local political leaders, from our friends and our families. This flood of incoming information—often symbolic in nature—has a tremendous effect on the way we think about particular political events, actors, and policy. We have studied the way individuals' opinions are shaped, but we have also looked at those who do the shaping, the mass media in particular. And we have spent some time on the relationship between public opinion and the nature of American government and social policy. All of these linkages—between people and media, among people, and between people and their leaders—are critical to understanding the role of public opinion in American democracy. It is a challenge to think about the nature of public opinion and how it changes, but it is also one of the most exciting phenomena in democratic theory. We can only improve our democracy by paying attention to public opinion, since the voice of the people is the foundation for self-rule.

It may be clear where scholarship is headed, and we can detect that an increasingly large community of researchers across fields and across academic and commercial lines are interested in studying public opinion. Yet what about public opinion itself? How will citizen expression change in the future? This is an impossible question to address with any confidence, since it involves looking into a crystal ball and speculating on the future. What public opinion becomes, what the channels for expression will be, and how much attention will be paid to it are all highly dependent upon general social trends and the development of our political institutions. For example, if the American political parties decline in strength, will interest groups become more central to the articulation of public opinion? Or will the parties experience a resurgence as strong players on the political scene, becoming more ideological and different from each other? If this were to happen, parties might develop different means of understanding and articulating public opinion.

As we have seen in this book, technologies for public opinion expression matter very much in any historical period. For the last thirty years, television has dominated the scene as the shaper of public attitudes. Before television, there was radio, and before that, the heyday of newspapers. But what next? The Internet is undoubtedly becoming a crucial site for discussion of political affairs, a site for persuasion, and a source for a tremendous amount of news and information. We are just beginning to look to the Internet as a place to express opinions and collect the opinions of our fellow citizens. And politicians are still exploring ways to keep in touch with constituents and persuade them through this new medium. Possibilities for public opinion expression and evaluation over the Internet are astounding at this early stage, so we can only imagine how diffusion of Internet access will affect citizens. But it is important to keep in mind that technology is ultimately controlled by people: Political culture will always determine how and when the Internet is used for the expression or manipulation of public opinion since technologies do not act—people do. It is likely that many of the theories and research findings in this book that deal with public opinion change may be replicated in computer-mediated environments. A persuasive speech may be persuasive in the same ways, whether it is received in person at a town meeting, in one's living room via television, or over the Internet. Some theories will receive support across media environments, but we will also have to develop new ideas about public opinion that are tied specifically to new technologies like the Internet. Perhaps interpersonal communication looks very different over the Internet than it does in face-to-face interactions, as so many communication scholars have argued. If this is the case, an entirely new sort of political conversation style has developed and we must figure out how best to study such dialogue among citizens and their leaders.

When we think about the future, we must always think about the past. A historical perspective is crucial if we are to consider the shape of public opinion—and indeed democracy—in the next few decades. Our older theories and ideas are of enormous value since they give us guidance, telling us what to look for and what might be important as we describe and analyze the political world. It is a certainty that as long as we live in democracy, public opinion will be the focus of great efforts. People will always want to express their opinions and politicians will always want to hear those opinions, whether to serve citizens better, to manipulate them more effectively, or perhaps just to stay in office.

Perhaps it is best not to end on a cynical note, but on a hopeful and historical one. Abraham Lincoln, one of the most impressive democratic leaders of all time, was also—not surprisingly—very attentive to public opinion. He was attentive to it and thoughtful about it. In many ways, Lincoln anticipated the problems of mass democracy and how difficult it would be for American presidents to hear all the citizens all the time. But Lincoln did his best, creating forums for public expression and listening as hard as he could, given the pressures of his office. Lincoln's writings on public opinion and his thoughtfulness about the concept are inspiring for us. A look back to the nineteenth century, to the words of one of our greatest presidents, should give us all pause as we think about the often troubled but crucial relationship between the public and its leaders. As the Civil War raged in 1863, Lincoln explained to a journalist why he had common citizens visit him at the White House:

> I feel—though the tax on my time is heavy—that no hours of my day are better employed than those which thus bring me again within the direct contact and atmosphere of the average of our whole people. Men moving only in an official circle are apt to become merely official—not to say arbitrary—in their ideas, and are apter and apter, with each passing day, to forget that they only hold power in a representative capacity. Now this is all wrong. I go into these promiscuous receptions of all who claim to have business with me twice a week, and every applicant for audience has to take his turn, as if waiting to be shaved in a barber's shop. Many of the matters brought to my notice are utterly frivolous, but others are of more or less importance, and all serve to renew in me a clearer and more vivid image of that great popular assemblage out of which I sprung, and to which at the end of two years I must return. I tell you . . . that I call these receptions my *"public opinion baths,"* for I have but

little time to read the papers and gather public opinion that way; and though they may not be pleasant in all their particulars, the effect, as a whole, is renovating and invigorating to my perceptions of responsibility and duty. (emphasis in original)[1]

Do our own leaders do as well as Lincoln in taking public opinion so seriously? No matter how times change, we can only hope that our highest elected officials listen to the voice of the people.

Notes

1. Introduction to "My 'Public Opinion Baths,'" in Mario Cuomo and Harold Holzer, eds., *Lincoln and Democracy* (New York: HarperCollins, 1990), pp. 284–285.

Index